'Lew Aron's and Libby Henik's previous two volumes in the *Answering a Question with a Question* series have provided a vital set of materials linking psychoanalysis and Jewish thought. In this new collection, dedicated to Aron and including a self-reflective chapter by him, debates produced by this linkage are advanced in a gripping and fertile way. Structured across three areas – clinical presentation, biblical commentary, and historical content – the book is an essential contribution to the literature on religion and psychoanalysis, with a profound Jewish twist: interpretation is never-ending and our deepest concerns can always be made the topic of a new set of questions.'

Stephen Frosh, *Professor of Psychology in the Department of Psychosocial Studies at Birkbeck, University of London*

'This is a beautiful, rich, and theoretically complex book. Dedicated to the memory of Lew Aron, the contributors explore the links between Jewish and psychoanalytic thought. Its contributors, many world-renowned scholars, address a multiplicity of overlapping issues organized around the threads of Judaism and psychoanalysis.'

Joyce Slochower, *NYU Postdoctoral Program*

'The third volume in this important series continues to illustrate the mutuality of influence between Judaism and psychoanalysis – how they encounter, inform and transform each other.'

Seth Aronson, Psy.D., *Director of Training, Training and Supervising Analyst, William Alanson White Institute; Faculty, Yeshivat Chovevei Torah*

'In this third volume of the series, traditions dedicated to upsetting facile representations of the human condition, Judaism and Psychoanalysis, are once again creatively and unabashedly brought together. From this conversation emerges an abundance of riches for the reader – with deep implications on our ethical, clinical, historical, political and theoretical approaches and ideas. The authors should be applauded for bringing us such powerful and dimensional ways of formulating ourselves drawing from the wealth of these traditions.'

David Goodman, *Boston College*

'My encounter with Libby Henik's new book – the next volume in a series that she co-wrote and edited with my late friend and colleague Lew Aron – has been a beautiful discovery for me. Each of the chapters has a tantalizing frame in which one gets the feeling of "just let me read a little more..." But it was my reading of Libby Henik's own introduction that left me thinking, "Oh my God I have to take a closer look at this." Outwardly about the fundamental similarities of psychoanalytic and Jewish modes of thought, the introduction is itself an example of thinking about the creation and elaboration of our own minds, within ourselves and within relationships, in a way that is extraordinarily profound, beautifully expressed, and anchored in self-evident experience.'

Jonathan H. Slavin, Ph.D., *Clinical Instructor, Department of Psychiatry, Harvard Medical School: Adjunct Clinical Professor, Postdoctoral Program in Psychotherapy and Psychoanalysis, New York University; Former President, Division of Psychoanalysis (39), American Psychological Association; Founding President, Massachusetts Institute for Psychoanalysis*

CONTEMPORARY PSYCHOANALYSIS AND JEWISH THOUGHT

Demonstrating the connections between contemporary psychoanalysis, Jewish thought and Jewish history, this volume is a significant contribution to the traditions of dialogue, debate and change-within-continuity that epitomize these disciplines.

The authors of this volume explore the cross-disciplinary connections between psychoanalysis and Jewish thought, while seeking out the resonance of new meanings, to exemplify the uncanny similarities that exist between ancient Rabbinic methods of interpretation and contemporary psychoanalytic theory and methodology, particularly the centrality of the question and the deconstruction of narrative. In doing so, this collaboration addresses the bi-directional influence between, and the relevance of, the Jewish interpretive tradition and psychoanalysis to provide readers with renewed insight into key topics such as Biblical text and midrash, religious traditions, trauma, gender, history, clinical work and the legacies of the Holocaust on psychoanalytic theory.

Creating an intimate environment for interdisciplinary dialogue, this is an essential book for students, scholars and clinicians alike, who seek to understand the continued significance of the multiple connections between psychoanalysis and Jewish thought.

Libby Henik is a graduate of the Wurzweiler School of Social Work (Yeshiva University) and the American Institute for Psychoanalysis (Karen Horney Psychoanalytic Center).

Lewis Aron was director of the NYU Postdoctoral Program in Psychotherapy and Psychoanalysis and served as president of the Division of Psychoanalysis (39) of the American Psychological Association.

Psyche and Soul: Psychoanalysis, Spirituality and Religion in Dialogue Book Series

Series Editors: Jill Salberg and Melanie Suchet

The *Psyche and Soul: Psychoanalysis, Spirituality and Religion in Dialogue* series explores the intersection of psychoanalysis, spirituality and religion. By promoting dialogue, this series provides a platform for the vast and expanding interconnections, mutual influences and points of divergence amongst these disciplines. Extending beyond western religions of Judaism, Christianity and Islam, the series includes Eastern religions, contemplative studies, mysticism and philosophy. By bridging gaps, opening the vistas and responding to increasing societal yearnings for more spirituality in psychoanalysis, *Psyche and Soul* aims to cross these disciplines, fostering a more fluid interpenetration of ideas.

For a full list of titles in this series, please visit the Routledge website: https://www.routledge.com/Psyche-and-Soul/book-series/PSYSOUL

CONTEMPORARY PSYCHOANALYSIS AND JEWISH THOUGHT

Answering a Question with More Questions

Edited by Libby Henik and Lewis Aron

Routledge
Taylor & Francis Group

LONDON AND NEW YORK

Designed cover image: Designed by Moshe Halevi Spero

First published 2024
by Routledge
4 Park Square, Milton Park, Abingdon, Oxon OX14 4RN

and by Routledge
605 Third Avenue, New York, NY 10158

Routledge is an imprint of the Taylor & Francis Group, an informa business

British Library Cataloguing-in-Publication Data
A catalogue record for this book is available from the British Library

Library of Congress Cataloguing-in-Publication Data
Names: Henik, Libby, editor. | Aron, Lewis, editor.
Title: Contemporary psychoanalysis and Jewish thought : answering a question with more questions / Libby Henik, LCSW and Lewis Aron, Ph.D.
Description: Abingdon, Oxon ; New York, NY : Routledge, 2024. |
Series: Psyche and soul | Includes bibliographical references and index. |
Identifiers: LCCN 2023019055 (print) | LCCN 2023019056 (ebook) | ISBN 9781032210704 (hardback) | ISBN 9781032210711 (paperback) | ISBN 9781003266600 (ebook)
Subjects: LCSH: Psychoanalysis and culture. | Psychoanalysis and religion. | Jewish philosophy.
Classification: LCC BF175.4.C84 C65 2024 (print) | LCC BF175.4.C84 (ebook) | DDC 296.3/71--dc23/eng/20230519
LC record available at https://lccn.loc.gov/2023019055
LC ebook record available at https://lccn.loc.gov/2023019056

ISBN: 978-1-032-21070-4 (hbk)
ISBN: 978-1-032-21071-1 (pbk)
ISBN: 978-1-003-26660-0 (ebk)

DOI: 10.4324/9781003266600

Typeset in Times New Roman
by MPS Limited, Dehradun

Dedication to Lew Aron

הוא היה אומר לא עליך המלאכה לגמור ולא אתה בן חורין להבטל ממנה

[Rabbi Tarfon] would say, "It is not up to you to finish the work, yet you are not free to avoid it."

Pirkei Avot:2:16

IN MEMORY OF LEW ARON

Too Late

I wanted to put this book
In your hands
And thank you
But I am
Too late

I imagined your smile
Secret priestly blessing
Your head titled
Receiving well earned tithe
But I am
Too late

I needed
Your critique
And your embrace
Words above all true
But you are gone
Too soon

This poem was composed by Dr. Alan Flashman in memory of his dear friend, Professor Chaim Cohen. It touched me deeply, and I thank him for allowing me to dedicate it in this book to the memory of Lew Aron and his love of, and devotion to, the book series we published together. Dr. Flashman is a child psychiatrist living and working in Israel's Negev.

CONTENTS

ACKNOWLEDGEMENTS

Many thanks to the authors who have contributed to this book, not only for their chapters, but for the enthusiasm and encouragement they expressed regarding the importance of this project. Their dedication supported me during a very difficult time.

At this first venture at editing a book on my own, my deep gratitude goes to Jill Salberg and Melanie Suchet, co-editors of *Psyche and Soul: Psychoanalysis, Spirituality and Religion in Dialogue* at Routledge/Taylor&Francis Group, for their patience, advice, direction and support in navigating the multi-faceted aspects of this editorial task.

Thank you to all my family and friends who have "lived" this project with me and helped me in advancing it to its conclusion.

It was a special joy to work with my daughter Erika on this project. A talented and capable woman in many spheres, whose editorial experience guided me through unfamiliar territory in the editorial process, Erika has been a marvelous resource in the publication of all three books of this series and an unrelenting support in this important work.

My thanks to Georgina Clutterbuck, Editorial Assistant at Routledge, and Annabel Flude, Permissions Administrator, for assisting me in the permissions process and the many technological wrong turns, blips and bumps I ran into. In particular, thank you to Kate Hawes, Senior Publisher, and Georgina Clutterbuck for approving the original book cover design. Thank you also to Julia Schroeder of the APA, Publishers of Penguin Random House, and LAP LAMBERT Academic Publishing for permissions to republish.

I wish to give special mention to my colleague and friend, Dr. Moshe Halevi Spero, who from the beginning was a devoted contributor to the book series and remained a sustaining force, both to Lew as he became ill and to me as this work progressed. Dr. Spero fashioned the cover to this book, and I thank him for capturing the content and meaning of this volume.

INTRODUCTION AND CHAPTER SUMMARIES

In October 2019, I attended a psychoanalytic conference in London. It was eight months since Lew Aron had passed away, and only a month since his memorial service. How could one go to London without visiting Freud's home and museum? How could I not be in the presence of the man who started it all, and whom Lew Aron loved and argued with every day?

I studied with Lew for over 20 years in one of his reading groups and, during that time, we worked together on his vision of a book series that would provide a forum for articles exploring the multiple connections between psychoanalysis and Jewish thought. Together we co-edited *Answering a Question with a Question: Contemporary Psychoanalysis and Jewish Thought* and *Answering a Question with a Question: A Tradition of Inquiry, Vol. II.* Lew (2009) held that "there has always been a link between psychoanalysis and Jewish thought, going back to Freud and the earliest origins and precursors of psychoanalysis"[1] (p. 16).

From the beginning, Lew and I decided to cast a wide net for articles, opening the content to a wide variety of psychoanalytic and Jewish subjects. Our aim was to provide a *home* for writers interested in addressing the bi-directional influence of, and connection between, the Jewish interpretive tradition and the theoretical world of psychoanalysis, as well as the relevance of psychoanalytic orientations regarding the intrapsychic and the inter-personal to Jewish thought. It was to be a *space* that facilitated multiple perspectives, questioning and debate. The writers who contributed to our first two volumes and to this current book – many of whom knew Lew well and were his friends, some who have been with us throughout this entire journey – felt the importance of the continuity of this project and this *space* and the need to have a *home* for addressing the interface of Jewish thought and contemporary psychoanalysis.

DOI: 10.4324/9781003266600-1

Our objective here, and in all our collections, was to continue the tradition of seeking the multiple connections between Jewish thought and contemporary psychoanalysis based on the Midrashic method of *hidush*, i.e., seeking connections between new meanings while holding onto the bonds of tradition. *Midrash* actually expresses the theme of all our books from the time of their origination, namely, the transmission of traditions of inquiry both Jewish and psychoanalytic. Lew and I felt strongly about addressing that transmission.

What follows are thoughts I have had that situate what Lew and I envisioned. In some ways, these thoughts could have formed their own chapter, but this introduction also serves for me as a tribute to Lew's lasting influence on me and on the fields of psychoanalysis and Jewish thought.

Lew did not hide his interest in Biblical study, *midrash* or the influence of his religion on his chosen field of psychoanalysis.[2] In fact, he felt it enhanced his thinking and brought another level of depth and meaning to his work and life: "Today we have reached a point where psychoanalysts can examine their personal perspectives and subjectivities, including their religious beliefs and backgrounds, and examine how this effects their clinical work and theoretical formulations. This shift creates the environment for interdisciplinary dialogue between religious studies, Jewish thought and modern psychoanalysis"[3] (Aron, L. 2009, p. 20).

The objective of this third edition, with the help of our current contributors – some new, some returning – is to continue the work of our first two books in exploring the intersection between Jewish thought and psychoanalysis, a link/connection going back to Freud and his early circle of analysts, the majority of whom were Jewish. "From the moment that Freud identified interpretation as his method of creating meaning, psychoanalysis became inextricably linked to, and some may say, a continuation of Jewish thought."[4]

Origins of Scriptural Interpretation

Following the national and religious trauma of the destruction of the second temple (70 CE) and the end of the priestly sacrificial rituals, prophecy and, finally, exile, the Rabbis searched for a new method of understanding an invisible God and His Covenant. The Rabbis centered religious life around the study of Torah, and interpretation became the method by which to understand the multiple, latent meanings they believed were embedded in the language and narrative of Torah text. Jewish tradition holds that an Oral Law was given to Moses together with the Written Law, which endowed them both with equal divine authority and holiness and which were passed down from Moses to Joshua (Pirkei Avot (Ethics of Our Fathers) 1:1) to the elders and then through the generations.

Biblical Hebrew is very concise and the syntax condensed with a very compressed narrative style, with verbs often dominating the narrative. The

Oral Law interprets and expands this enigmatic language. New and different meanings were believed to be embedded in the slips, anomalies and gaps, the repetition of words and phrases, and the absence of linear thinking of the text. Time is fluid, with past and present informing and illuminating each other. Textual inconsistencies are considered indicative of subtext and psychological complexity. Without interpretation, the Biblical text would be incomprehensible. The Rabbis in Pirkei Avot (5:22) instructed, "Turn it and turn it, for everything is in it," requiring a study method of ongoing interpretation.

The Hebrew Biblical word for search, inquiry or investigation of text is *drash* (דרש), and from this comes the word *midrash*, which has come to mean "interpretation." *Midrash* is a searching out, a finding of a new/different meaning by studying every minute detail of the Torah. "The search for *Drash*, for the 'meaning other,' is carried out by questioning. Only an 'interrogative thought' makes ... the dynamism of meaning ... possible"[5] (Ouaknin, M. & Brown, L., 1998, p. 205). *Hidush*, in Hebrew, means something absolutely new or different. In Torah and Talmud study, *hidush* is a teaching that encourages an interpretive act of creation of meaning and, consequently, "interpretation cannot be repetition"[6] (Ouaknin, M., & Brown, L., 1998, p. 171). Rabbi Nachman of Braslav would say: "It is forbidden to be old"[7] (*Sichot Haran* 51). "*Hidush* seeks neither factual truth nor a better understanding, but rather, understanding differently, a permanent renewal of meaning. *Hidush* refuses wisdom in favor of asking a question that it cannot answer, a refusal to settle for an answer that would no longer call the question into question"[8] (Ouaknin, M. & Brown, L., 1998, p. 171). "Confronted with the text, man *(Adam)* does not say: 'I think, therefore I am,' but 'I question, therefore I am'"[9] (Ouaknin, M & Brown, L., 1998, p. 205). The late, renowned Israeli author Amos Oz would say: "Fundamentalists live life with an exclamation point. I prefer to live my life with a question mark"[10] (Sasso, S.E., 2007).

In examining Biblical text from these perspectives, we find that preserved in the narrative are other narratives, a subtext of other meanings and stories. If all this sounds similar to the interpretive method of psychoanalysis, then we should recall Harold Bloom's (1987) statement that "Freud's most profound Jewishness, voluntarily and involuntarily, was his consuming passion for interpretation."[11] Despite all Freud's protestations and efforts, psychoanalysis could not escape "feeling" Jewish[12]. Psychoanalysis, Jewish thought and Hebrew Biblical exegesis share a hermeneutic/interpretive tradition of revealing unconscious content embedded in narrative. As Susan Handelman (1981, p. 207) points out: "Freud absorbed the Midrashic hermeneutic approach to accessing the latent/unconscious/hidden meanings of narrative through interpretation ... Freud, the master of interpretation, did not arise in a vacuum. The Talmudic mode of thought became the ingrained model of the Jewish psyche, the intimacy and identity which Freud so keenly felt ... For both Freud and the Rabbis, interpretation was the preeminent mode of knowing, applicable in every context and to every idea."[13]

Whereas subtexts of other meanings and stories are called *midrash* in Biblical exegesis, in psychoanalysis, they are called the unconscious. Biblical and psychological interpretation have many principles in common. To name just a few: the concept of *nachtraglichkeit*, the concept of non-linear time (אין מוקדם ומאוחר בתורה: there is no earlier or later in the Torah – i.e., the Torah does not proceed in chronological order (Pes. 6b)), intertextuality, the juxtaposition of texts (סמיכות פרשיות, adjoining chapters), attention to slips, gaps and inconsistencies in narrative, the co-creation of meaning, the *pshat* (the literal, manifest, conscious, content of narrative or text) and the *drash* (the latent, unconscious content).

Moses and Rabbi Akiva: A Midrash

The Rabbinic attitude toward the non-linearity of time is most prevalent in understanding a famous and much-loved *midrash* about Moses and Rabbi Akiva where Moses travels back and forth through generations of time. This *midrash* came to mind as I wandered through the Freud Museum, thinking of Lew and Freud. Following the death of his good friend Stephen Mitchell, Lew often mused about the day when he would "join" Steve and Freud, debating the fine points of psychoanalytic practice and theory over a glass of bourbon. This was Lew's *chavruta* (a word derived from the Hebrew *chaver*, or "friend"). A *chavruta* is a study partner or small study group that originated in the early Rabbinic Talmudic study halls and continues until today, where, rather than agreement, what is encouraged is the inclusion of differing opinions/understandings that would be challenged and debated. And into this *chavruta*, I think Lew secretly imagined pulling in God Himself to debate Biblical text, *midrash* and interpretation.

I bring you an abbreviated version of the *midrash*. The Babylonian Talmud (*M'nachot* 29b) records that: "When Moses climbs Mount Sinai to receive the Torah, he sees God affixing 'crowns' [the scribal ornaments that adorn Torah script to this day] on the letters of the Torah. Moses questions God as to the necessity of the crowns: Moses asks: 'Master of the Universe, who is preventing You from giving the Torah without these additions?' Rather than an explanation, God says to him, 'There is a man who is destined to be born after several generations, and Akiva ben Yosef is his name; he is destined to derive (interpret) from each and every crown many laws. It is for his sake that the crowns must be added to the letters of the Torah.' Moses replies, 'Master of the Universe, show him to me.' God says to him, 'Return behind you (turn behind).'" Moses is magically transported to the future, to the end of the eighth row in Rabbi Akiva's *beit midrash* (study hall), and he does not understand what they are saying; he does not understand the modern discussion of the law. Moses' strength wanes as he thinks his Torah knowledge is deficient. When Rabbi Akiva arrives at the discussion of one matter, his students ask him, "My teacher, from where do you derive this?" Rabbi Akiva says to them, "It is a *halakha* (law) transmitted to Moses from Sinai (הלכה למשה מסיני – *halacha l'Moshe mi-Sinai*)." When Moses hears this, his mind is put at ease, as this, too, is part of the Torah that he is to receive. This will be the legacy of Akiva.[14] Akiva's method of interpretation, uncovering and revealing the sources within the Biblical Oral and Written text, did not abandon the principles given at Sinai or the chain of transmission that began with Moses. By the end of the midrash, Moses comes to understand that his work had not disappeared by the time of Akiva – in fact, it had been enhanced and will be made more relevant as each generation builds on the accomplishments of the previous one. This is what God explains to Moses.

The reader of this *midrash* is not in disbelief, but is enchanted by the "fairy tale" quality of the imagery of time travel that carries along with it the meaning, or *drash*. This *midrash* encapsulates the essence of the Rabbinic interpretive practice: that in the process of continuous encounters with the text, the interpretation of the Oral and Written Law remains rooted in the tradition given at Sinai, while at the same time, the transgenerational transmission of meaning is continuously changing. This approach to Torah, God explains to Moses, will be the legacy of Akiva (Kahn, A., 2020).[15]

We see here the seeming contradiction between absolute origin and authority, and adaptation and change through interpretation. Similarly, Freud's theories contain concepts of absolute origins: complexes, primal crimes, desires and traumas, yet today's many divergent theoretical orientations and praxis will find a chain of transmission traced back to Freud.

Another principle of Biblical hermeneutics evident in the *midrash* is that there is no temporal distance separating the interpreter from the text (Ouaknin, A. & Brown, L., 1998). Biblical interpretation, as well as psychoanalytic interpretation, invites interpreters from multiple generations and texts to "meet and shed light on each other so that the interpreter, in order to reveal the text in its entirety, must grasp it in one of its particular aspects, and conversely, a particular aspect of the text must await the interpreter capable of perceiving it"[16] (Ouaknin, A. & Brown, L., 1998, pp. 173–174). Biblical text, similar to the unconscious, is awaiting an "other," a reader/analyst with whom to make new meanings.

New Findings, or a New *Chavruta*

Edgar Levenson, in his 2001 article "Freud's Dilemma: On Writing Greek and Thinking Jewish," discovers that: "I'd been practicing *midrash* without knowing it. Like Freud … I either never knew, or unconsciously denied, any familiarity with this tradition. Freud, one might say, wrote Greek and thought Jewish"[17] (p. 378). Levenson has had a long interest in the detailed inquiry. "I used the inquiry deconstructively, to 'unpack' the text"[18] (p. 380). In discovering Rabbinic *midrash* with its emphasis on "the infinity of meaning and plurality of interpretation,"[19] Levenson experiences his personal psychoanalytic exodus from Egypt (the Hebrew name for Egypt is *Mitzraim*, meaning "straits or strictures"). "The movement of Rabbinic interpretation is not from one opposing sphere to another, from the sensible to the non-sensible, but rather 'from sense to sense,' a movement into the text"[20] (Handelman, S., 1982, p. 21). "It is taken as a given that by questioning, the therapist is inevitably participating – no matter how unstructured the inquiry might be. Transference and counter-transference emerge seamlessly from the inquiry"[21] (p. 379). Playfully, Levinson calls out: "*Mirabile dictu* [amazing to say], the detailed inquiry becomes *midrash*"[22] (p. 379).

Levenson describes a printed page of Talmud text: "The text is followed by a conversation in the *Gemarah*. Both the *Mishnah* and the *Gemarah* evolved orally over hundreds of years, yet even in a few lines of text, Rabbis who lived generations apart participate and give the appearance ... of speaking directly to each other. In addition, there is the commentary of Rashi, who lived in the Middle Ages, and then his descendants and students commenting on his work. There are also cross-references to other commentators of different periods in history."[23] And Levenson doesn't leave out of this mix the "student himself, who participates in a conversation that began over two thousand years ago"[24] (p. 383).

Levenson wonders about Freud's connection to *midrash*: "Free-association is not exclusively a tapping into an intrapsychic reservoir, but also a relationship with another person, one who tries to listen without agenda or purpose. The extraordinary singularity of this event creates an interpersonal space, a vacuum that the patient fills, moving into it, with the therapist slightly behind the process, following it. Rather than dragging the patient through analysis, the therapist rides the process. Isn't this why Freud's earliest clinical cases seem so fresh? When Freud did not know what he was looking for, the entire enterprise seemed livelier"[25] (p. 384). Levenson sees in midrashic interpretation this liveliness that he recognizes in the "early" Freud in contrast to the Aristotelian system. "What does the rabbinical method supply? A creative force of multiple explanations, unclarity, open-ended inquiry"[26] (p. 386).

Quoting Handelman[27] (1982, p. 75), Levenson (p. 388) learns that "there is never any one single interpretation to which all understandings of the text aims, but a continuous production of multiple meanings ... conflicting interpretations are set side by side with no concern for reconciling them. There is no hierarchical scheme in *Midrash*; no interpretation has more authority than any other."[28] To Levenson's understanding, "Freud bifurcated metapsychology and praxis, in a manner totally consistent with his own dichotomized cultural tradition. His metapsychology was literary, classic Greek, Apollonian – reason in control of impulses. His praxis was pure *midrash*, talmudic. In other words, Freud simultaneously developed a meta-theory of neurosis *and* a perspective on the *praxis*, the act of therapy – what actually takes place in the interactional field of patient and therapist[29] (p. 382)." "It may turn out that the praxis of psychoanalysis – not its theory of therapy – lies closer to the Rabbinic or hypertext model than we have suspected"[30] (p. 388).

Tom Ogden (2016), in the final chapter of his book *Reclaiming Unlived Life: Experiences in Psychoanalysis*, presents a conversation with San Francisco psychoanalyst Dr. Luca Di Donna in which he talks about himself, his psychoanalytic orientation and his writing. In this chapter, I hear echoes of the *midrash* of Rabbi Akiva and Moses, and reverberations of midrashic thinking, principles and language, perhaps unknown, or perhaps unconscious, to Ogden himself, of the co-creation of meaning and mind, and of the non-linear, bi-directionality of influence. In talking about "going to great writers" [both psychoanalytic and literary], whom Ogden calls his "psychoanalytic ancestors" (p. 172), I give you Ogden in his own words: "To conceive of ancestry in this way is to reject the notion of strictly chronological time. The movement of influence and time is not only from past to present to future. Movement of influence and time is also from future to present to past. We who are the present readers of Freud, Isaacs, and Winnicott alter the past (transform their work as they understood it) in our present act of transforming (reinventing) what they wrote. Most important, in making their work our own, we are coming into being as thinkers in our own right, whose ideas others in the future will make use of in the process of creating themselves in ways that are unimaginable to us now" (p. 174). "I have, without ever putting it in this way to myself, created my own psychoanalytic family tree … In writing about these authors, I have in a sense rewritten their work in a way that is my own and in another sense they have rewritten me by means of their influence on me" (p. 172). "They have seen me in a way that I have not yet seen myself and I read them in a way that they have not yet been seen. It is in this sense that I create my own ancestors who create me as I read their work" (pp. 173–174). "Thinking together is the other essential feature of psychoanalysis that I have in mind … It takes two or more people to think"[31] (p. 175).

I interrupt Ogden's narrative and bring in the midrashic voice: *Midrash* is a relational experience. The text and the reader. Two making one mind. Similar to Levenson, Ogden is speaking/practicing *midrash*, as well. Meaning, in Jewish tradition, is co-created within the context of the intersubjective field of a meeting of minds.[32]

Ogden offers a quote by William James, whom he defines as the most undervalued psychologist in the analytic literature, who in 1900, concurrent with *The Interpretation of Dreams,* "insisted that we should use verbs, adverbs, prepositions and conjunctions, not nouns and adjectives, in describing all psychic events ... we ought to have words for feelings of *but,* and feelings of *and,* and feelings of *of.* I [Ogden] would put it in slightly different terms: We don't have memories, we remember sadly, dimly, hauntingly, and so on, and these ways of remembering transform us as we transform them, drown in them, and come back together in a form that is different from whom we had been and is still in the process of changing. Change is the one constant in psychological states"[33] (p. 168). James finds that verbs, adverbs, prepositions and conjunctions are indicators of psychic events.

James and Ogden would make a great *chavruta* with Robert Alter, the noted translator of the Hebrew Bible. Alter (1981) raises an interesting question: "How is it that, from the compressed narrative style of Biblical text, where few indicators of individuality (in the way of motive, feelings, attitudes and intention) are offered, have such 'indelibly vivid individuals' [become etched] in the imagination of a hundred generations?"[34] (p. 114). For Alter, the resolution of this paradox lies in the dominant role of the verb in Biblical text: "Verbs tend to dominate this biblical narration of the essential, and ... sudden dense concentrations or unbroken chains of verbs, usually attached to a single subject ... indicate some particular intensity, rapidity, or single-minded purposefulness of activity"[35] (Alter, R., 1981, p. 80). "According to the principles of Biblical hermeneutics, the complexity of the individual is to be gleaned from the verb ... Repetition of verbs and phrases, whether appearing in one story or in different stories, is intended to create connection and association of motivation"[36] (Henik, L., 2009).

Alter (1981) also gives examples of how Biblical writers used parataxis, such as "and" to convey expressiveness of emotion, action and causal relation (pp. 28–29) and bemoans that translators have removed these conjunctions in the process of "modernizing" Biblical language in translation, with the "grave consequence of obscuring much of the literary artistry of the Bible, especially in the narrative prose"[37] (p. 28). Roy Schafer's (1976, 1993) new language of action, with its emphasis on verbs, is particularly suited to a psychoanalytic understanding of Biblical narrative that almost exclusively uses action and sparse dialogue to suggest the internal struggles and psychological complexities of its main characters. Schafer insisted that verbs were the descriptors of conscious and unconscious human activity.[38,39]

Musings

I've wondered whether, just as Moses felt lost in the school of Rabbi Akiva, would Freud not understand the *beit midrash* of contemporary psychoanalysis? What would Freud understand in the *beit midrash* of Lew Aron? Would Freud recognize his psychoanalysis were he to engage with Lew in psychoanalytic theory or sit in on a class of most of the psychoanalytic disciplines of today? What would he understand of the discussion and debate about the analyst's subjectivity, of mutuality, enactment, the use of countertransference, the evolution of object relations, the concept of a mind as co-created, Bion's "alphabet," or Stern's "unformulated experience?" Would Freud recognize Lew and his contemporaries and our authors as today's Akiva? Yet, all would agree that Freud is the originator of psychoanalytic thought, theory and methodology. Lew would often dig deep to midrashically find a relational intimation/bent at the "navel" of Freud's writings.

Conclusion

Lew and I began collecting articles together for this, our third book. Even though Lew was experiencing a recurrence of his illness, he found sustenance in our project. Sadly, he could not complete the project. Our objective was to continue the tradition of seeking the multiple connections between Jewish thought and contemporary psychoanalysis based on the midrashic method of seeking *hidush*: connections between new meanings while holding onto the bonds of tradition both in Jewish thought and psychoanalysis. We were encouraged by our supportive group of contributors, scholars in their fields, from the United States and Israel, who continue to be interested in, and want to write about, the connective tissue of interpretation between psychoanalysis and Jewish thought.

From the beginning of our collaboration, Lew and I hoped that the articles presented would stimulate the scrutiny of successive readers, raising new questions and interpretations, formulating ever-changing meanings and arriving at different understandings, keeping open the connection, and some may say, the genetic link between psychoanalysis and Jewish thought.

This collection is grouped into three categories: clinical presentation, biblical commentary, and historical content. Categorization was difficult because some of the articles bridge more than one category due to the wide range of scholarly knowledge and professional experience of the authors. In addition, the authors explore subjects of our universal, personal, subjective experience, whether in the biblical, clinical or historical category. As Avivah Zornberg (1996) pointed out regarding reading the Torah: "[In detecting] the intimations of disorder within order ... we are assured to find ourselves, with our most radical dilemmas, reflected in these ancient texts" (p. xv),[40] and I take the liberty to add, and in psychoanalysis.

1. Clinical Presentation

Mitchel Becker – "You Are Requested to Raise Your Eyes and See": The Reconstruction of Religious and Psychoanalytic Belief during the Analytic Encounter. In this chapter, Mitchel Becker describes how the transformation of his religious world led to a double effect: a shedding of undesired dogma, and paradoxically, a creation of a new impetus to break down dissociations and create a synthesis between his religious and psychoanalytic worlds. He contends that a unique personal synthesis can sometimes create a space for the de- and re-construction of myth, dream life and fantasy as they take place in the therapeutic relation and interact with a true other. He presents a clinical case in which the true other is needed in a time of peril to supplement the true self.

Sue Grand – God at an Impasse: Devotion, Social Justice and the Psychoanalytic Subject. Grand explores what happens when a patient has a collectivized self and no individual psychology. Her chapter uses a clinical impasse to study the philosophical premises and cultural biases that inform the foundations of psychoanalytic theory. She also questions the impact on the analyst when a patient's Christian worldview is radically disjunctive with the Jewish ethos of psychoanalysis,

Moshe Halevi Spero – This Bread Is *Not* My Body: Biblical Manna as a Psychoanalytic Paradigm. The author is particularly interested in the metaphor of the biblical *man* or *manna* (the fabulous "bread from heaven" [Exodus 16:1–36] that sustained the Children of Israel throughout their 40-year wanderings in the desert) that was brought up by an analysand at several points during his therapy. The author thinks the story or myth of *manna* harbors great potential as a paradigm for crucial dimensions of the psychoanalytic process, especially as a latent component of the analytic frame.

Lewis Aron – God's Influence on My Psychoanalytic Vision and Values. Contemporary psychoanalysis has come to view all aspects of the analyst's subjectivity as potentially exerting an influence on the analysis. The analyst's personal experience is now generally taken for granted as relevant analytic data. Nevertheless, the analyst's religious background and beliefs about God have not been investigated for their influence. Aron's theoretical and clinical contributions have centered on the themes of mutuality and asymmetry in the analytic relationship. It is not accidental, therefore, that his religious imagination also rests on these dimensions of the relationship between God and the individual. In this article, Aron uses his own experience as an example of the subtle ways in which religious ideas may influence psychoanalytic theorizing and practice. He also examines one very specific aspect of his own religious background, the nature of his relationship to and dialogue with God, to illustrate the role it has played in his psychoanalytic vision and how it has influenced his ideas of mutuality.

2. Biblical Commentary

Libby Henik – In the Beginning There Was … Envy. Henik argues that Freud's theories of oedipal aggression, which have shaped psychoanalytic interpretation of Hebrew Biblical narratives of the relationship between God and mankind, and attitudes born of Greco-Western thought, which have influenced theories of female sexuality and sin, are not reflective of Biblical (Torah) narrative or interpretation. She presents Melanie Klein's theories on the psychogenesis of the self and her conceptualization of desire, aggression, hate and envy, together with Rabbinic and contemporary Biblical commentary, which she feels more closely reflect Jewish thought and open another way to understand the Garden of Eden story, its cryptic Tree of Knowledge and the emergence of the agentic self.

Aton Holzer – The Unthinkable Satanic: A Psychoanalytic Insight into the Shofar as Symptom. In this article, Holzer argues that the Shofar is intended to accomplish a deconstruction of the ego-ideal, as explained by Jacques Lacan. In Rabbinic thought, the expression of the inchoate mental state comes to full expression via Shofar blasts, particularly as set against the highly organized Rosh HaShana prayer service. Commentaries on a cryptic Talmudic passage take the matter to a depth compatible with certain psychoanalytic ideas of regression followed by a reformation of the ego in a manner that enables a more refined entry into the Symbolic order and a more sober recognition of what cannot be altered by human struggle.

Avivah Zornberg – Abraham Bound and Unbound: The *Akedah.* This article explores the *Akedah* episode (the Binding of Isaac) as more than simply a test of obedience, but rather Abraham's profound engagement with his own psychic history. Zornberg cites a radical *midrash* that recounts a filicidal attack by Abraham's own father that results in the death of Haran, Abraham's brother. The impact of this repressed traumatic memory gives the *Akedah* test its primal force. Zornberg argues that God's command requires Abraham to bring to consciousness and "work through" his own unthought experience that centers on sacrifice and fatherhood and haunts his inner world.

3. Historical Content

Jill Salberg – Trauma, Gender and the Stories of Jewish Women: The Other Within. Salberg draws on stories of women in Jewish literature (Beruriah and Yentl), psychoanalytic theories of gender and the intergenerational transmission of trauma to unpack how women carry vulnerability and helplessness. Salberg believes that gender performance and "passing" highlight how gender becomes enlisted as a mode of traumatic transmission and possibly one type of internal psychic reparative resolution to complex traumatic experiences.

Ilene Philipson – Fearing the Theoretical Other: The Legacy of Kohut's Erasure of the Analyst's Trauma. Philipson examines how Heinz Kohut's struggle with his own Holocaust trauma may have influenced and continues to influence self psychology. This article is in keeping with other recent work that has begun to chart new territory in understanding the ways the Holocaust has impacted psychoanalytic theory construction since World War II.

Klara Naszkowska – Give Me Permission to Remember: Judith S. Kestenberg and the Memory of the Holocaust. At least 86 first- and second-generation female psychoanalysts emigrated to the United States as Nazism came to dominate Europe. However, their contributions are at risk of being marginalized or falling into oblivion. In this chapter, Naszkowska revives and reconstructs the biography of Judith S. Kestenberg, a psychoanalyst who emigrated to the United States during the rise of Nazism and who opened up an entirely new field of psychoanalytically-oriented work with "child survivors" - those who experienced Nazi persecution at a very young age.

Pamela Cooper-White – Freud's Moses, Schoenberg's Moses: Two Expressions of Trauma. Cooper-White examines Sigmund Freud's and Arnold Schoenberg's obsessive fascination with the figure of Moses and their two major creative works about Moses, *Moses and Monotheism* and "Moses und Aron," respectively, produced nearly simultaneously. Cooper-White argues that both men were deeply impacted by the trauma of the Holocaust and the racialization of anti-semitism that preceded it for over a decade.

Notes

1 Aron, L. 2009. *Answering a Question with a Question, Contemporary Psychoanalysis and Jewish Thought*, eds. L. Aron, L. Henik. Academic Studies Press, Brighton Mass.
2 Aron, L. 2004. "God's influence on my psychoanalytic vision and values." *Psychoanalytic Psychology*, 21(3): 442–451.
3 Aron, L. 2009. *Answering a Question with a Question, Contemporary Psychoanalysis and Jewish Thought*, eds. L. Aron, L. Henik. Academic Studies Press, Brighton, Mass.
4 Ibid.
5 Ouaknin, M. & Brown, L. 1998. *The Burnt Book: Reading The Talmud*. Princeton University Press, Princeton, NJ.
6 Ibid.
7 Kramer, R. January, 16 2022. It's Forbidden to Be Old!, Parshat Yitro, Breslov.org.
8 Ouaknin, M. & Brown, L. 1998. *The Burnt Book: Reading The Talmud*. Princeton University Press, Princeton, NJ.
9 Ibid.
10 Sasso, S. E. 2007. *God's Echo: Exploring Scripture With Midrash*. Paraclete Press, Brewster, Mass.
11 Bloom, H. 1987. *The Strong Light of the Canonical*. The City College Papers, 20: 1–77. New York.
12 Handelman, S. A. 1981. "Interpretation as Devotion: Freud's Relation to Rabbinic Hermeneutics," *Psychoanalytic Rev.* Summer; 68(2):201–8.
13 Ibid.
14 Kahn, A. 2020. *The Crowns on the Letters: Essays on Aggada and the Lives of the Sages*. OU Press/Ktav Publishing House, Brooklyn, NY.
15 Ouaknin, M. & Brown, L. 1998. *The Burnt Book: Reading the Talmud*. Princeton University Press, Princeton, NJ.
16 Ibid.

17 Levenson, E. A. 2001. "Freud's Dilemma: On Writing Greek and Thinking Jewish." *Contemporary Psychoanalysis*, 37:375–390.
18 Ibid.
19 Ibid.
20 Handelman, S.A. 1982. *The Slayers of Moses: The Emergence of Rabbinic Interpretation in Modern Literary Theory*. State University of New York Press, Albany, NY.
21 Levenson, E. A. 2001. "Freud's Dilemma: On Writing Greek and Thinking Jewish." *Contemporary Psychoanalysis*, 37:375–390.
22 Ibid.
23 Ibid.
24 Ibid.
25 Ibid.
26 Ibid.
27 Handelman, S.A. 1982. *The Slayers of Moses: The Emergence of Rabbinic Interpretation in Modern Literary Theory*. State University of New York Press, Albany, NY.
28 Levenson, E. A. 2001. "Freud's Dilemma: On Writing Greek and Thinking Jewish." *Contemporary Psychoanalysis*, 37:375–390
29 Ibid.
30 Ibid.
31 Ogden, T. H. 2016. *Reclaiming Unlived Life: Experiences in Psychoanalysis*. Routledge, New York, NY.
32 Aron, L. 1996. *A Meeting of Minds*. The Analytic Press, Hillsdale, NJ.
33 Ogden, T. H. 2016. *Reclaiming Unlived Life: Experiences in Psychoanalysis*. Routledge, New York, NY.
34 Alter, R. 1981. *The Art of Biblical Narrative*. Basic Books, New York, NY.
35 Ibid.
36 Henik, L. 2009. "Rebecca's Veil: A Weave of Conflict and Agency" (pp. 264–285). *Answering a Question with a Question, Contemporary Psychoanalysis and Jewish Thought*, eds. L. Aron & L. Henik. Academic Studies Press, Brighton, Mass.
37 Alter, R. 1981. *The Art of Biblical Narrative*. Basic Books, New York, NY.
38 Schafer, R. 1976. *New Language for Psychoanalysis*. Yale University Press, New Haven, CT.
39 Schafer, R. 1993. *The Analytic Attitude*, H. Karnac (Books) Ltd., London.
40 Zornberg, A. 1996. *The Beginning of Desire: Reflections on Genesis*. Image Books, Doubleday, New York, NY.

References

Alter, R. 1981. *The Art of Biblical Narrative*. Basic Books, New York, NY.
Aron, L. 1996. *A Meeting of Minds*. The Analytic Press, Hillsdale, NJ.
Aron, L. 2004. "God's influence on my psychoanalytic vision and values." *Psychoanalytic Psychology*, 21(3): 442–451.
Aron, L. 2009. *Answering A Question With A Question, Contemporary Psychoanalysis and Jewish Thought*, eds.L. Aron, & L. Henik. Academic Studies Press, Brighton Mass.
Bloom, H. 1987.*The Strong Light of the Canonical. The City College Papers*, 20:1–77. New York.
Handelman, S. A. 1981. "Interpretation as Devotion: Freud's Relation to Rabbinic Hermeneutics,"*Psychoanalytic Rev. Summer*, 68(2):201–208.

Handelman, S.A. 1982. *The Slayers of Moses: The Emergence of Rabbinic Interpretation in Modern Literary Theory*. State University of New York Press, Albany, NY.

Henik, L. 2009. "Rebecca's Veil: A Weave of Conflict and Agency" (pp. 264–285). *Answering A Question With A Question, Contemporary Psychoanalysis and Jewish Thought*, eds. L. Aron & L. Henik. Academic Studies Press, Brighton, Mass.

Kahn, A. 2020. *The Crowns on the Letters: Essays on Aggada and the Lives of the Sages*. OUPress/Ktav Publishing House, Brooklyn, NY

Kramer, R. January, 16 2022. It's Forbidden to Be Old!, Parshat Yitro, Breslov.org.

Levenson, E.A. 2001. "Freud's Dilemma: On Writing Greek and Thinking Jewish." *Contemporary Psychoanalysis*, 37: 375–3907.

Ogden, T.H. 2016. *Reclaiming Unlived Life: Experiences in Psychoanalysis*. Routledge, New York, NY.

Ouaknin, M. & Brown, L. 1998. *The Burnt Book: Reading The Talmud*. Princeton University Press, Princeton, NJ.

Sasso, S.E. 2007. *God's Echo: Exploring Scripture With Midrash*. Paraclete Press, Brewster, Mass.

Schafer, R. 1976. *New Language for Psychoanalysis*. Yale University Press, New Haven, CT.

Schafer, R. 1993. *The Analytic Attitude*, H. Karnac (Books) Ltd., London.

Zornberg, A. 1996. *The Beginning of Desire: Reflections on Genesis*. Image Books, Doubleday, New York, NY.

PART 1
Clinical Presentation

1

"YOU ARE REQUESTED TO RAISE YOUR EYES AND SEE"

The Reconstruction of Religious and Psychoanalytic Belief During the Analytic Encounter

Mitchel Becker

There are many psychological truths contained in the Book of Genesis. As a young psychologist these were for me innocent truths that belonged to the realm of myth and legend; for Freud, an obsessional neurotic illusion and for me a sweet illusion. These simple truths coexisted in a state dissociated from the other areas of my maturing psychoanalytic sense of reality. The science of psychic change seemed to me to be a pragmatic analytic task, whereas the spiritual was a closed-off inner chamber, its expression confined to religious practice and seemingly in harmony with Eros, Thanatos, love and hate.

In Freud's (1927) paper "The Future of an Illusion," he lays out his eloquent argument with a protagonist that is his god, Logox, the god of logic. Freud is rational man par excellence who sees scientific reasoning as the only road to understanding our reality. Belief in God is, at its worst, a coercion of civilization that prohibits questioning and doubt. At its best, religion can repress our fears of death and destruction, and assuage our sense of helplessness by believing in a father who forgives our own wish to kill him.

Ironically, though being an orthodox Jew, as a young psychologist I felt a real comfort in Freud's words. The sweet illusion of religion was comfortably dissociated from the scientific analytic work. Passion was part of being human but not an analytic stance. Today, it seems that the young man who chose to dissociate these worlds made a wise choice. The experience of integrated worlds would have been far too complex for him – as it still is today. I'd like to explore the process and meaning of the dissociation's breakdown. And en route to perhaps begin to re-conceptualize the meaning of truth in the relation between self and other.

DOI: 10.4324/9781003266600-3

Dissociation and Its Breakdown

My emigration 25 years ago from the United States to Israel marked, and, in retrospect, *seems* to have evoked, a subtle though deep transformation of my Jewish faith and its relation to, or integration with, my psychoanalytic world. My 12 years of grade school education was in the United States in a Jewish day school in which the secular and religious studies were clearly demarcated. This was true of my yeshiva university education as well. This demarcation was a wall creating departments. Separation of church and state. This was and still remains a basic principle of a moral society.

At the age of 20, trauma hit my life. A close friend was murdered in New York City in an anti-semitic incident. The event had great impact on me – with clear influence on moving to Israel and becoming a psychologist. Israel and psychology were associated with hope and reparation, while destruction was left dissociated. As a young psychologist, Melanie Klein's (1946) theory of the paranoid schizoid stage seemed to be utterly morbid. Similarly, for many years destruction was seen by me as out of God's realm. It took me many more years to grapple with why God and humans destroy. The expansion of truth to include evil, malice and cruelty was indeed an unavoidable conception born in the encounter between psychoanalysis, religion and living in Israel.

During my years in Israel, belief and faith became significant dilemmas, and new questions entered into and ignited fresh dynamics in a realm that was amorphous and ineffable. The gradual maturation of my religious world led to a double effect; a shedding of undesired dogma and, paradoxically, the creation of a new impetus to break down the dissociation that had previously held sway between my religious and psychoanalytic worldviews. Having so stated, I wish to make it clear that I am quite aware that heightened religious practice can be a significant aspect of maturity just as lessened religious practice may sometimes be. My feeling though is that a concrete rituality that veers too close to what Hanna Segal (1957) referred to as "symbolic equation," often has become an immature idolatry. Thus, for me this shedding of dogma at times served to enhance and intensify both my religious and psychoanalytic practice in a far more symbolic manner than I had known before.

As I came to understand my experience, this shedding of imperative dogma occurred in both worlds. Certain "rules" of my classic psychoanalytic training, such as anonymity, rigid use of setting and tight interpretive styles, seemed to be no longer appropriate for me. Similarly, some of the "laws" of Jewish practice began to feel idolatrous in their concrete anthropomorphic content. A more profound look at what was happening made me aware that I was not abandoning the essence of these rules and laws, but rather I had transformed them from the rigid space of imperative into a new place of living, a place of inquiry involving questioning, exercising choice, taking responsibility and ultimately surrendering to new spiritual realms. These changes in my experience and practice of my religious and psychoanalytic worlds have a direct connection to my experience of living in Israel, a country that seems to constantly invite and even provoke confrontation between sameness and difference, internality and externality, individual and collective identity.

My wife and I "made aliyah" (עליה) (a term meaning "to ascend" and symbolically "to transcend") to Israel on the week that in synagogues all over the world the Sabbath torah reading is "lech lecha" (לך לך) (Gen.12:1), literally meaning "go unto you."

In this reading, God tells Abraham, "lech lecha" – to leave his land of birth and home and move to Israel. Begin an adventure of the spirit by creating a crisis of the spirit entailing destruction and loss. The only other time God will say "lech lecha" (go unto you) was the akedah (עקידה) when Abraham is asked to sacrifice his son (Gen. 22, 1–19). And on that occasion, and only on that occasion, Abraham answers: "*heneni*" (הנני) – "I am here with all my soul." Being well defended and seemingly adjusted, I knew not what I was doing. The loss and destruction were rationally assessed and accepted as the price for one's identity. I had not begun to understand the meaning of true surrender that is encapsulated in God's requests of *lech lecha* and Abraham's response "*heneni.*" I had yet to read Kierkegaard's (1843) portrait of Abraham, "the first to feel and to bear witness to that prodigious passion that disdains the terrifying battle with the raging elements and the forces of creation in order to contend with God, you who were the first to know that supreme passion, the holy, pure and humble expression for the divine madness that was admired by the pagans" (p. 23). I was as yet unaware emotionally of my fear of the passion described by Kierkegaard.

My experience of Israel is an experience of encountering unknown truths, which are indeed complex, integrating and fragmenting, seeking and destructive, creative and un-digestible. I would like to begin with a simple discovery I met after some ten years of living in Israel while reading the torah. I came across the sentence "and God regretted creating the human" (וינחם ה' כי עשה את האדם) (Gen. 6:6) and decides to destroy with a flood the creatures he created. I was familiar with the word being here used as "regret" (וינחם) in a better-known use, meaning "to console" (נחמה). What a strange combination of meanings! I had read this passage tens of times, but now the Hebrew was beginning to come alive. So, regret and consolation were identical though opposite twins. I then remembered Freud (1900) discussing ancient languages as speaking the language of the unconscious – where the negative and the positive are contained as one theme or category. The ancient language of Hebrew has many words that can convey opposite meanings depending on the context of the sentence or situation. I then searched for other narratives in which the verb *regret/console* appeared in the torah (תורה). I found it in two fascinating places. When Isaac is comforted by the loss of his mother by being matched with Rebecca. "And Isaac brought her into his mother Sara's tent, and took Rebekah, and she became his wife; and he loved her, and Isaac was comforted for his mother" (Gen. 24:67). The aggadah[1] tells that Sarah was told that Abraham took Isaac to the akedah and Sarah died of a broken heart. The theme of destruction and creation are at one. The second time this verb appears is when Joseph consoles his brothers saying that he intends no revenge but rather intends to protect them even though they engineered his kidnapping. "And he comforted them and spoke to their hearts" (Genesis 50:21). And so, the Book of Genesis begins with God's regretting creating and ends with a human gesture of transcending the human being to becoming related to an Other.

These ideas were born to me while I was becoming acquainted with Bion. I remember the first time I came across Bion's (1970) "O." Bion defines O as "that which is the ultimate reality, absolute truth, the godhead, the infinite, the thing in itself" (p. 26). I wondered if he had begun to lose hold of reality and go the way of many genius thinkers who seemed to lose a sense of ground. Today, Bion's way of thinking is for me a *Guide to the Perplexed*[2]. Bion's pursuit of truth is harsh, dreadful and vital. I will speak more of truth, but first a clinical story.

A Clinical Story

This clinical narrative touches upon my attempt to grasp the complexity of our truths beyond a binary-like dogma and to confront the most poignant element of the therapeutic encounter via the relation.

There was once a little girl who taught me about split-off worlds and how to love them once again. She was small and ferociously brave, fragile as the tears of her sea. She lived in a huge very sick body whose terrors I knew only a bit, which will leave me haunted to the end of my days.

Sophie accompanied her friend, who was herself a terrified battered woman who brought her son to therapy. From the waiting room, Sophie heard laughter, and her heart demanded that she meet me some day. And so, Sophie managed to begin play therapy. Sophie was 40. Her previous therapist told her she was a borderline and needed to learn how to create borders. Sophie was an ultra-orthodox woman, and she knew that these borders were also her culture's borders. Yet, the touch of a hand is what the brazen and trampled little girl needed. Of course, she remembered her mother calling her a tramp and a prostitute, but that is a long story.

Sophie had six children and eight miscarriages. Her body was interminably attacked by cancerous tumors, and she had been through 20 surgeries. She was a corporeal time bomb of diabetes, heart congestion and renal failure. And all she wanted was a hand. Is that too much to ask for? She plopped herself from the seat onto the rug – stretched out her hand and I saw Ein-sophie (אֵין-סוֹפִי). (The word *sophie* (סוֹפִי) in Hebrew means "finite or final." The prefix "ein" (אֵין) means "none or not." Together the words *ein-soph* in Hebrew form the word for "infinity" and "noteworthy," one of the many names for G-d). Ein-sophie was a redheaded little girl with fiery green eyes. My grandmother was the same. Grandma Eve loved life and maybe most important loved the little boy that was me. I thought grandmother was a witch – a magically good witch who can mend all hurt. This was my first sign that I was about to meet truths that I had never successfully confronted before. I looked into Ein-sophie's eyes and I saw not a borderline Sophie but the fearless hope to mend hearts. My grandmother represented for me that fearlessness to see life as it was and to enlist one's passion to confront one's fears. This was a truth born of the intersubjective moment that could not have been fathomed by either of us alone.

I took her hand and thanked G-d that I was not in a prison of rigid rules, and then prayed to G-d that I wasn't in Ferenczi's "wild psychoanalysis."[3] I didn't understand that this was my first unconscious I–thou dialogue that I had with G-d while being a psychotherapist, that my very thanking G-d and praying to G-d were suddenly vibrant and vital and that this passion was missing in my relations with people and with my G-d. I didn't know then that what was being foreshadowed was the breakdown of my own dissociative modes of being.

Sophie took little time to explain to me how very complex and rich was my decision to take her hand. Sophie worked for years in her previous therapy on the repeated sexual violations that her father performed against the precious alive little girl. What she had then been less aware of, was the utter nameless dread that was her mother. The horrific sexual abuse by her father became true "child's play" when attempting to confront the unfathomable physical abuse that her mother performed. Her sick body was wrapped in scars by cigarettes, irons and boiling water. All perverse attempts of the mother to drive away the vital and erotic from Ein-sophie.

Sophie would grab the pillows and blankets in the corner of the therapy room – fiercely hug them and begin to abreact. We knew when it would come, and I would sit on the rug and try to hold her. My physiologic response was to feel my eyes rise to the top of my eyelids as if I too was dissociated. How was I to remain intact? Should I remain intact? Or should my soul split into bits of screams. I was in her nursery of the incomprehensible. With a disdain for anything tangible that was associated with ever-present cruelty and with a wish to tear the little princess from her wicked parents. There was something almost of royalty about her desire to see her truth. The father in me imagined holding all pain, all aggression, all hate and finding some solace. And yet in the here and now Ein-sophie is experiencing herself being abused by the foundations of her broken basic trust, mother and father.

And where am I? An involved parent, an innocent bystander, a freedom fighter, a revenging enraged angel? How does one simultaneously survive, contain and take the Levinas (1974) responsibility – *Heneni* (הנני). Yes, I sensed the 1000 years between G-d's asking Cain, "Why do I hear the blood of your brother scream from the ground?" (Genesis 4,10) and 1000 years later G-d seeking Abraham and Abraham answering Heneni (Gen. 22:1). These 1000 years were the time needed to create an I–You relationship in which a subject sees an Other.

I can, of course, go on and on to the world of the akedah (עקידה), to the world of the flood and to the brotherly relations throughout the Book of Genesis. I cite these because they are deep complexities of a desire to be and a desire to destroy. But for now, I need to go back to why my soul began to synthesize. What did Sophie and Ein-sophie bring that contributed to ending a long period of almost 20 years in which parallel worlds of psychoanalysis and religion lived side by side without love or hate for each other?

I think there were many lines of development that somehow came to a meeting place; Bion and truth, O (Grotstein, 2004), Ein-sophie's belief in the capacity of a relation to heal seemingly unsoothable pain, my feeling finally at home in Israel, and my personal return and transformation as a religious Jew. I must share with the reader that I need to attempt at addressing these issues further in an almost free associative stream of conscious. I hope to keep the reader with me in mind while I search not only emotionally but also spiritually.

My Struggle and Searching

The prison of dogma or of rules is clearly subjective. My prison was apparently the derailment of free choice. It gradually became clear to me that this core issue was indeed quite similar in both the religious and psychoanalytic realm. The issue of choice is extremely complex. Where does choice interact with a leap of faith. As if there was a call, in which I say to myself: "Know that your choice, your will, your surrender to belief is all that matters. Seek, with all your heart, might and soul(Eigen 1981)." How does one negotiate between the sense of choosing from a place of peaceful surrender, versus coercive submission (Ghent, 1990)? In the Jewish literature this was a dialectic between "lishma," meaning "in the name of heaven" versus not in the name of heaven – a place of self-interest. As I became acquainted with the thinking of relational analysts, they seemed to me to speak this very same language of the dialectic. I began to sense that the conceptualization of the dialectic opened up a capacity to see continuums of our being. Destruction and creation, surrender and submission, conscious and unconscious, attachment and independence were all dialectics in which each aspect was creating, destroying and ultimately shaping the other. The dialectic insists

that not only is "X" not "Y" but that "X" cannot be defined without "Y".
Man without woman, right without left, autonomy without surrender, container without contained, and for me psychoanalysis without religion.

Each clinical choice meant another choice was not taken. The analyst's choice of not speaking or not doing is an action. My deliberation to take Sophie's hand was in the dialectic of disruption and repair in which every choice must realize that it belongs to a dialectic.

And for me, beyond the imperative to hold all the dialectics of being, there was a clear voice saying: "Mitchel, declare. Declare who you are." This declaration could no longer be a function of a specific "self" of the multiple selves. Somehow the dissociation of multiplicity could not work. Ein-sophie's plea for help demanded all of my heart, might and soul. The container of a specific "therapist" self would not be sufficient. As my eyes lifted, my soul instinctively searched everywhere, and "everywhere" was something beyond all of my selves. I suddenly saw the words of the torah: "And he lifted his eyes and he saw" (וישא עיניו וירא) (Gen. 22:4,22.:18).

This phrase is not a very frequent phrase, but I knew it from the akedah. That night I returned to my torah and researched the occurrence of the phrase "lift your eyes and see" (וישא עיניו וירא). It appeared about 12 times, almost all in the Book of Genesis.[4] Each time the phrase appears in the torah it indicates a stormy spiritual event in which the hero metamorphosizes. In only two places does the phrase appear twice in the same story. One of those is the akedah (Genesis 22:1–19). Did I think of akedah and then raise my eyes? Or did my raising my eyes remind me of the akedah? Regardless, this reverie was transformational.

While Sophie needed for me to know and contain her boundless pain, there was a finite limit to both how much Sophie could handle and how much my subject could contain. My search upward was for the infinite and the meeting place of psychoanalysis and religion.

The word *la'sait* (לשאת) has many meanings. It is the word used in the phrase I referred to "and he raised his eye, and he saw." The word *la'sait* means "to lift," but also "to bear, to hold, to transport, to receive, to contain, to suffer, to forgive and to marry." Now that's a container! a therapist! This was one of many short adventures in the Hebrew Bible, which could only really be learned through experience. And experience was living in Israel. Living the language of the bible. This "living" was gradually linking to the dissociated.

The very first reference in the bible to bearing, as in "la'sait" is with Cain. Before he reacts with murderous rage the bible has God say, "if you can try to make something good (out of the envy and rage you feel) then it can be contained." (הלוא אם תיטיב שאת) (Gen. 4:7). What a beautiful illustration of how opposites reside in the same word of an ancient language.

And so, I lifted my eyes and saw the walls of sensibility crumble. And what was left was the torment of Ein-sophie's abandonment in the dark nursery.

And she was being refused the most basic touch. I could not fathom how Ein-sophie created any sense of hope or meaning. In her community, her family was seen as a significant symbol of righteousness, charity and meaningful religious values. The monstrous was concealed in an image of the sacred. The hallow was indeed hollow. But Sophie was told that she was "crazy," "retarded" and "perverse." Any hint in my eyes of the slightest disbelief or even incomprehension led Sophie to feel absolutely vilified, and I felt I was dropping her into an abyss. Reality was such a tenuous place – there was no place to stand, to withstand, the pull of the abyss – no reality, no sanity, no voice of good-enough good. How can belief be born in such a nursery? How can belief survive such parents? Why did I suddenly search for the infinite when confronted by such a Shoah (שואה- the Hebrew word for "holocaust") – Sophie's description of her childhood? In retrospect, I think in the past I managed in a very economical, efficient and adoptive way to dissociate the spiritual from the self. My self was driven, aware of need, and aware of an other. Yet, my self was far too efficient and far too logical. And in parallel, my spiritual side was not only dissociated from the psychological but was also too rational. Today I sense that something was lost in my rational style. What was lost was a sense of a capacity to contain the complete truth of our lives in an integrated manner. My issues concerning my Judaism saw destruction, the Shoah and anti-semitism as a foreign, unwanted, dissociated element of a sickly world. As loss and despair touched my personal and clinical life, I was struck by my lack of true insight into evil, abuse and cruelty. Sophie allowed my soul to enter realms never looked at.

Abuse, Destruction and the True Other

Destruction is at the heart of creation. "And G-d regretted creating man and sought to destroy him" (Gen. 6:5–7). If we look at the literature of Western civilization there are many examples of this as well. Mary Shelley's *Frankenstein* bespeaks of the creator's wish to undo the creation, to destroy the baby. And Cronos swallowed his babies for fear that they would seek to kill him. And Laius heard from the oracle that his son Oedipus would kill him, so he sends him to the desert to be killed. And Abraham sent his son Yishmael to die in the desert (Gen.21:9–21). And Abraham sent his hand to cut the throat of Isaac. And I brought myself to the land of Israel knowing I endangered my future offspring. It is of course an even more threatening development when one begins to uncover one's own personal evil and destructiveness.

Why do we destroy? The reasons are infinite. There is a most basic tension between creator and created. And it seems to me that the essence of truth and O is a chaotic chaos inherent in every creation. Today, Bion's O rings for me true. O is the infinite, the ultimate, the godhead, the mystic, the preconception that was always there to be sensed. This truth is not synonymous with the objective or the scientific proof. It is not reason or logic. Bion (1970) writes, "Reason is emotion's slave and exists to rationalize emotional experience" (p. 1). Both Bion (1965)(1970) and Winnicott (1971) realized that mental health requires much more than solid reality testing. They spoke of dream and play as the core of emotional experience, and they sought a truth that was beyond the objective. In their works I found the birth of the mutuality of becoming. This mutuality is about creator and created. Ferenczi wrote (1932) that every parent must amend his unilateral decision to bring the child into this world. He must bear the child's wish to not live and ultimately seduce him to live. Be this primary maternal preoccupation or containment of the projective identification of the unbearable, only a parent's mature capacity to sense, contain and survive these toxic emotions of living enables the child's psyche to thrive.

The lessons we learn as parents and as analysts are also potentially infinite. Yet my thoughts return again and again to the wish to destroy. The Oedipal complex in the mutuality perspective as previously elaborated also involves a murderous parent. And in the Benjamin (2004) perspective, it is the parent's responsibility "to go first" in containing such urges. Bion seems to see the meaning of the paranoid schizoid phase as essentially attempting to digest O. He writes (Bion, 1970),

> The impact of the evolving O domain on the domain of the thinker is signalized by persecutory feelings of the paranoid–schizoid position. Whether the thoughts are entertained or not is of significance to the thinker but not to the truth. If entertained, they are conducive to mental health; if not they initiate disturbance. The lie depends on the thinker and gains significance through him. It is the link between host and parasite in the parasitic relationship. (p. 103)

Bion claims, as is beautifully elaborated by Grotstein (2000), that O is there whether we choose to entertain it or not. If not in a hospitality mode (Levinas, 1961), then in a form of cancer. This endless challenge with the O of life is played out ever more sublimely in the parent–child relation. The creator is naturally overwhelmed with the responsibility inherent in the newly found role. While theories of envy, projective identification and the in-capacity to create a sense of a separateness (a separate subject, or in Winnicott's terms, "use" of the other; 1969) may serve to explain the phenomenon of abuse, I would like to offer an additional perspective.

I will start with Grotstein's (2000) description of the parent's role in protecting the child's innocence – this includes protecting the child from preconceptions and O that may prematurely attack the child's psyche. Grotstein states,

I believe that one of the fundamental dynamics of child abuse and of abuse generally involves parental envy of the child's innocence because of the parent's belief that they have lost their own sense of innocence. (p. 248–9)

He goes on to describe a process of projective identification leading to children being sent to roles of heroes, messiahs, scapegoats and pariahs. In my opinion we can expand our view of abuse through the lens of O and envy. Abuse is an attack on linking to an O that is the dread that the parent cannot face, and thus the parent forces the abused child to submit and swallow the undigested.

What Grotstein calls envy of innocence may also be an envy of the child's capacity to contain O, be it in the child's way. Thus, innocence is not a passive not-knowing but an active containing of the infinite, the incomprehensible. The word for "innocence" in the torah is *temimut* (תמימות). But this word, *temimut,* has three biblical meanings; innocence, uprightness and wholeness. As a child, Jacob is called an innocent tent dweller. It seems the uprightness and wholeness can only come with maturity. The initial innocent containment of the holy is not whole, but it is an ultimate reality. The role of the parent and analyst is trying to hold the whole chaotic mess of destruction and creation. This holding of the un-integrated, (Winnicott, 1945) and the undigested of the other is the sacrifice inherent to the parental role. This role entails being a loyal servant to the O that becomes actualized in the birth of the other. This is one of the meanings of Bion's servant (Grotstein 2004) and Ghent's (1990) surrender. Bion (1970) writes that a lie needs a speaker, while truth never needs a speaker. Here I think Bion speaks of egoism, of interests, desire and memory. Truth must be entertained, and in my conception, this entertaining is an inter-subjective quest. The true self needs a true other in the pursuit of truth, in the pursuit of O. We surrender in a link to the true other, the non-self-interested other. Sophie's capacity to sense truth terrorized her parents, and thus Sophie learned that her truth is toxic.

Levinas' primordial mission born before birth of the "self" is an inner commandment to see the face of the other. In Levinas' (1974) words

The responsibility for the other cannot have begun in my commitment, in my decision. The unlimited responsibility in which I find myself comes from the hither side of my freedom, from a prior to every memory prior to or beyond essence. (p.10)

Levinas struggled desperately with his experiences during the Shoah. He felt that the human has a most basic innate drive to see the other, and this drive captures us as if we were a hostage to the inevitable need to say Heneni to the pain of an other. The child is born with a capacity to sense truth but needs a parent to learn to contain their truth.

What is happening in a session when the cry of one soul is in contact with an other? There is an unsaid dilemma that may appear as a counter-transference, in which the therapist puts aside his true self for the patient's need. The empathic, containing authority "who goes first" role, is the mature caretaker role. While this is indeed true, it is not all of the truth. This formulation is lacking the awareness of a basic a priori role, task, or essence, which I am calling the true other.

The true other is needed in times of peril in which the true self is incapable of holding by himself or containing alone the hate, destructive, annihilating dread or the infinite. The other brings their difference and their will and capacity to link to truth. This truth belongs to the analytic couple in which the other is an other, taking a role that cannot be done by the patient's true self. This is not the work of the therapist's true self but rather his true other. In mother–infant terms, the mother and infant play many roles: holding and held, containing and contained, two subjects playing, and the bond of peril in which self and other see the mutual truth in an asymmetrical relation of self and other. The joint encounter with O or raw ultimate reality requires a true other to say "*Heneni*" – here am I for you in my capacity to bear the infinite in ways that you cannot (Orange, 2009). We are different, separate and I am surrendered to your need to see the uncontainable. This surrender is to the child's or patient's need to face what and when he chooses to face, or surrender himself to face, a preconceived truth actualized in the here and now. In retrospect, while Sophie and I interpreted her mother's envy of Ein-Sophie, this envy was seen as an envy of her smile and affection, of her innocent eroticism and vitality. Today I can see a far deeper experience of O, a real genuine unrefined sense of the vital and erotic. A sense of Ein-sophie seeing her mother's face and saying "*Heneni*" and her mother viciously attempting to destroy her daughter's recognition of her mother's truth. And Ein-sophie also looked into her therapist's face and said "*Heneni*". And I, as therapist, responded by declaring that I am here to not only be but also to take responsibility for the other. And the other pines to see the face and enliven the other. A truth that neither of Sophie's parents could fathom.

The Place of Truth and Transformation

The first time the word *truth* (אמת) is spoken in the torah, it is from the heart of Abraham's servant (Genesis 24:27). This wondrous ego-less and self-other linked servant actually speaks of truth three times, the first, an almost incomprehensible O, then a subjective truth and then an intersubjective truth (Ogden, 1994). The seeking of truth is a servant's surrender to the thing in itself. Of course, this must undergo transformation (Bion, 1965) to be comprehensible and only then communicated. But before this transformation happens there must be a true other that bears the truth. This role of truth bearer is a mission that may seem as deceptively simple as the saying, "just say the truth!" But we all know that nothing can be more complex and full of dread. Perhaps the created, the child and the analysand all possess truths, O, and the no-thing,[5] all of which frighten the creator, the parent and analyst. As we pursue this drama of destruction, we gradually become aware of the interconnectedness of this mission to bear, contain and face the truth of O. The mutuality of the contained and of the containing strains our consciousness to sort out the question, "whose O is it?" Truth needs no speaker, and O belongs to he who seeks to link.

Concluding Remarks: Discovering Co-constructed Beliefs

My beliefs are co-constructions involving my subjective experience with the religious and psychoanalytic worlds. The real corpus of literature of these two worlds can only truly meet within fantasy in an ever-evolving process continuously seeking, creating and destroying ultimate truths and ultimately creating a novel third (Aron 2006, Ogden 1994).

Freud's perception of belief is one of submission and coercion – a coercion forced upon us by civilization to contain the helplessness that people feel when encountering the cruel nature of nature. Freud is outraged by religion's tendency to forbid the process of curiosity and inquiry. And rightly so. Religion too frequently demands submission. For Freud, religion was saying "You are requested to close the eyes." While I know that as a young psychologist I deeply identified with Freud's (1927) scientific passion for truth:

> Scientific work is the only road which can lead us to a knowledge of reality outside ourselves. It is once again merely an illusion to expect anything from intuition and introspection. (p.13)

I gradually sensed that Freud missed out on how the aesthetic (Bollas, 1987) transcends the need for sublimation. Monet's lily ponds singing, dancing, inviting and engaging meant to me a beyond being. Abuse is at times the beyond that has been distorted and perverted. As Ghent taught us, this beyond is a place that is not submission or coercion and yet it is not a voluntary surrender or totally conscious choice. It is a transitional experiencing of space, time and the I-you. The place between coercion and choice can be described as such: I can choose (to go to surrender) to let go, but not to become. This becoming stems from the encounter between I and other, in which true self meets true other and the storm of O is created and regretted, constructed and deconstructed. This potential space is both a playground and battleground in which myth, dream-life and fantasy are the truths enlivened by the meeting of a true self with a true other.

As a result of the transformation described above, certain basic beliefs have evolved in my psyche. These beliefs are as follows:

1 We are born in a relational matrix and born to a basic aloneness (the myth of the creation of man).
2 All creations are destined to disappoint and thus provoke a need to destroy (the flood).
3 Containing disappointment is a lifelong goal (Cain).
4 Only a psychic link can assuage the pain (Joseph and brothers).
5 Moments of transformation, expressed as a symbolic mode of "lifting of one's eyes and seeing" (throughout Genesis), occur in the transitional space in which we live.
6 Truth, or "O," is experienced by the "servant," who by his servitude can surrender to truth without personal agenda (one of the Hebrew words for "servant" is אמה, which is closely similar to the Hebrew word for "truth," אמת (Abraham's servant in his spiritual journey to find Isaac a wife, Rebecca [Gen: 24:1–67]).
7 The time between the question "where are you?" (איכה – Gen. 3:9) and the response "here I am!" (he'ne'ni) can be interminable (Gen. 4:10) and (Gen. 22:1, 11).

I end with a lesson learned from my son on the struggle to contain truth. I once told my six-year-old an Aggadah, or myth, which goes as follows: Before each baby is born, an angel teaches him all of the torahs, written and oral. Upon completion of the lesson, the angel gently touches between lip and nose and causes the yet-to-be-born baby to forget all that he learned.

Upon completion of my story, I asked my son why the angel would go through all of the teaching to then erase it.

Edo then answered: "Abba (dad), it's like this. In the beginning, the baby doesn't know anything, so the angel teaches the baby all the torah. Only one problem, the baby knows all the torah, but still doesn't believe in God. So, the angel touches the baby, and all the torah leaves his head and goes to his heart. So, the baby doesn't know the torah, but then he believes in God."

Afterword

I wrote this article ten years ago. Some five years ago I found myself telling my rabbi that my love for G-d has always been bounded and limited by my unsuccessful love relationship with my wife. Transcendence was lacking in both relationships. As I reread my article, I re-experienced the holes in my soul. This paper was for me the true beginning of an unravelling of a relational dissociation. And in my quest for wholeness, there was a divorce and regrettably its inherent destructiveness. My search in this paper for a meeting of selves ultimately brought me endless love and joy. And simultaneously my love of G-d found a genuine dialogue with psychoanalysis. In essence, all that I wrote in this article was a prelude to the events I did not know were to be.

The truth, O, was patiently waiting to be known. My first step toward an encounter of an unmet synthesis was with the audience who listened to my presenting of this paper at an IARPP conference in Madrid 2011. A small audience came to hear, and I heard some listeners crying. They were there as true others containing the O that I did not yet know.

And I desire a very brief word about Lew. I loved Lew's love of paradox, learning, braiding the strands and re-questioning. He was for me the quintessential Talmudist. And I dream of him saying, "if you hug the contradictions, and hug even tighter the seekers of knowledge who brought them, you will begin to sense how each of them are rich vitalities of our existence and there will your path be seen."

Notes

1 Aggaddah is the collection of legend and folklore of biblical heroes written in ancient midrash and Talmud.
2 The Guide to the perplexed is the name of Maimonides well known philosophical text on Jewish theology.
3 Ferenczi was criticized as engaging in "wild psychoanalysis" in which therapist and patient interminably switched roles and thus abandoned basic psychoanalytic structure. Ferenczi's reputation has been redeemed in a vast literature rediscovering his work in a very positive light.
4 Gen. 13:10, Gen. 18:2, Gen. 22:4, Gen. 22:13, Gen. 24:63, Gen. 33:1, Gen. 33:5, Gen. 43:29.
5 The No-thing is a concept of Bion (1970), which encompasses the realm of things either in actuality not being or of an infinite potential for creation out of the nothingness.

References

Aron, L. (2006). Analytic impasse and the third: Clinical implications of intersubjectivity theory. *Int. J. Psycho-Anal*, 87:349–368.

Benjamin, J. (2004). Beyond doer and done to: An intersubjective view of thirdness. *Psychoanal. Q.*, 73:5–46.

Bion, W.R. (1965). *Transformations: Change from Learning to Growth*. New York: Basic.

Bion, W.R. (1970). *Attention and Interpretation*. London: Tavistock.

Bollas, C.J. (1987). *The shadow of the object*. New York: Columbia Univ. Press.

Eigen, M. (1981). The area of faith in Winnicott, Lacan and Bion. *Int J. Psycho-Anal.*, 62:413–433.

Ferenczi, S. (1932). *The Clinical Diary of Sandor Ferenczi*, Ed.J. Dupont (trans. M. Balint & N.Z. Jackson). Cambridge, MA: Harvard University Press, 1988.

Freud, S. (1900) The interpretation of dreams. *S.E.*, 4–5.

Freud, S. (1927) The Future of an Illusion. *S.E.*, 21:3–56.

Ghent, E. (1990). Masochism, submission, surrender –masochism as a perversion of surrender. *Contemp. Psychoanal.*, 26:108–136.

Grotstein, J.S. (2000). *Who is the Dreamer Who Dreams the Dream: A Study of Psychic Presences*. Hillsdale NJ: Analytic Press.

Grotstein, J.S. (2004). The seventh servant. *Int. J. Psycho-Anal.*, 85:1081–1102.

Kierkegaard, S. (1843). *Fear and Trembling*. Ed.& Trans. Howard V. Hong and Edna H. Hong. Princeton, NJ: Princeton University Press.

Klein, M. (1946) Notes on some schizoid mechanisms. In: *The Writings of Melanie Klein, Vol. 3*. Hogarth Press, pp.1–24.

Levinas, E. (1961). *Totality and Infinity: An Essay on Exteriority*. Trans. Alphonso Lingis. Pittsburgh, PA: Duquesne Press, 1969.

Levinas, E. (1974). *Otherwise than Being or Beyond Essence*. Trans. Alphonso Lingis. Pittsburgh, PA: Duquesne Univ. Press, 1981.

Ogden, T.H. (1994). *Subjects of Analysis*. Northvale, NJ: Aronson.

Orange, D.M. (2009). *Thinking for Clinicians: Philosophical Resources for Contemporary Psychoanalysis and the Humanistic Psychotherapies*. New York, Routledge Press.

Segal, H. (1957) Notes on symbol formation. *Int. J. Psycho-Anal.*, 38:391–397.

Winnicott, D.W. (1945). Primitive Emotional Development. In *Through Paediatrics to Psycho-Analysis* (pp. 145–156). New York: Basic Books 1975.

Winnicott, D.W. (1969). The use of an object. *Int. J. Pscho-Anal.*, 50:711–716.

Winnicott, D.W. (1971). *Playing and Reality*. New York: Basic Books.

2

GOD AT AN IMPASSE

Devotion, Social Justice and the Psychoanalytic Subject[1]

Sue Grand

I cannot give this patient a false name, and I cannot use his real name. What he wants is to be recognized, identified and identifiable. But he needs to persist as no one. He is an identical twin in a family of 11 children. Sent to work, called to dinner, these were two boys in tandem. Always fused, always fungible, always referred to as "the twins." Inseparable, indistinguishable to his own parents, my patient's own mother never called him by his name. Invisible, uncertain of his own specificity and existence, he would open the family Bible. There, on the front page, he was listed with the other children. He would read the names and appear. But the reassuring inscription would turn upon itself. His family was Christian fundamentalist. They preached hellfire. The Bible burned with the prospect of his damnation. Named, the devil could locate him; he would be a "sinner in the hands of an angry God." He closed the family Bible, and disappeared.

While he was avoiding Hell in the afterlife, he was living in Hell on this earth. The ninth of 11 children, he was born to White evangelical farm laborers. His parents were depleted by poverty but prohibited from birth control. They had no love for their offspring. Children were hired out as day laborers. At home and at work, children were beaten; they went hungry; their bones broke from harsh labor; they collapsed from dehydration. Sometimes infants died, and sometimes they didn't. Toiling in the fields, small hands bled from picking cotton. Looking up from his work, my patient saw gnarled

1 We thank Taylor & Francis Ltd. for permission to publish the article by Sue Grand Ph.D. (2013), "God at an Impasse: Devotion, Social Justice, and the Psychoanalytic Subject," *Psychoanalytic Dialogues*, 23:4, 449–463, DOI: 10.1080/10481885.2013.810503.

DOI: 10.4324/9781003266600-4

limbs, bent backs, an infinite series of hands, reaching. If he worked, he got to eat. When the harvest was over, there was nothing to eat. They moved, and moved again and again. For years, they were homeless.

If any comfort existed, it was not from his parents. Comforting had to occur in secret, in stolen moments, between the siblings. They nursed each other's wounds. They carried each other's burdens. They shared food, and took beatings for each other. These children met other children, gathering the harvests. All of them dehumanized and reduced, and still, they seemed to recognize one another. As Orange (in press) described such children, they transmitted trauma, but they also consolidated their own resourcefulness and resilience. Sometimes, they even laughed. In other families, there were parental gestures of warmth and protection. With my patient's parents, there was only grimness, brutality and neglect. And there was no such thing as God's love. Suffering was sanctified by religious rhetoric. Satan was purged by hard labor, by hunger and by the fist.

In this anonymous world of migrant labor, no one was as fungible as my patient. He had been born, unexpectedly, about 20 minutes after his twin brother. His mother thought that childbirth was over. His twin was normal, but my patient had trouble taking his first breath. He knew his mother had wished for his death. No amount of future labor would ever compensate her for having to feed *two* infants at the same time. She had failed to recognize the humanity of her other children. But her refusal of him was spectacular: until a few years prior to her death, she never called him by name. Like the twin treated by Rappoport, he was the "unwelcome other" and was non-existent in any maternal reverie (Rappoport, 2012, p. 376). My patient was no one; he was "the twins," and he was *any one of many*. This predicament was written into his psyche-soma. He could never know, or name, himself.

In many ways, he never came into self-being. But he was a miracle of resourcefulness and resilience. When he arrived in my office, he was a doctor, in his late 50s. He had a house in the suburbs, investments, a faculty appointment and a nuclear family. He was married. Both of his children were in graduate school. He had fulfilled the American Dream. His achievements were stunning, but he was modest, self-effacing and depressed. He came because his marriage was ending. For many years, he had merely cohabited with his wife; they led alienated lives. Now, she was moving out. He felt raw and anxious and pre-occupied and lost. He had read up on the talking cure. He knew he was suffering from separation anxiety. He had tolerated a distant, but stable, marriage because he had lacked a maternal bond. Brilliant and self-educated, he had prepared himself to be a good patient. By the second session, he was free-associating. He welcomed interpretations. He explored dreams, genetic material and inter-personal dynamisms, and he knew about transference. This engagement was real: affectively resonant, thoughtful and reflective. But he didn't seem to know *whose* interior was the subject of this reflection.

Nameless to his mother, he was nameless to himself. At home and at work, he was in unending service. As a physician, he took meticulous care of other bodies. But he never took care of himself. He was immune deficient, asthmatic, allergic, arthritic, riddled with heart disease, bad lungs, vertigo, kidney stones, neuropathies and an unending series of infections. He had already had a triple bypass. With his patients, he advocated wellness, but he ate at McDonald's. His life was a rhythm of disease and survival. But he was always there to serve, to help the other, even when the other was not really in need of his help, even when overcommitments might result in breakdowns in his health. He ejected his needy self onto the other, and then he rescued the other, without ever encountering that other as himself (see also Grand, 2010). If he is not disabled by his own illness, he works 15-hour days six to seven days a week. He is always accessible, infinitely providing, until hospitalization finally stops him from offering any kind of provision.

His own illness existed in dissociative disregard. He arrived late for a session. He had slipped on the ice, fallen and lain there until someone came. The next session, his secretary calls, and cancels: he is in the hospital with pneumonia. When he returns, pneumonia isn't mentioned. This "talking cure" is a *psychic* excavation: a treatment in which his body will be left out. He lies on my couch and lets his mind wander. I am distracted from listening. He is shaky and obese. It is no surprise that he fell on the ice. Rising from my couch, he stumbles and clutches the wall. When sessions end, I have no real memory of what he's been saying. My back is braced, and my arms are in readiness. My hands are reaching out to steady him. And yet, my muscles feel weak. I anticipate him falling. I anticipate broken bones, my smallness inadequate to his ungainly fragility. Both of us crashing to the ground: him needing to be saved, and me failing to save him. In my mind's eye, we are entangled human detritus, bruised, shaken and embarrassed, on the floor of my office.

Body Talk: Conjuring Analytic Attachment

Sitting in my chair, I start to scan the environment for obstacles to his egress. Before he arrives, I move chairs, ottomans and pillows. I worry about hard wood floors, slick weather, his leather-soled shoes; about him stepping up to my entrance, stepping down on wet leaves, snow, mud, ice. I am relieved at protracted dry spells in the weather. I want him to stop talking about his dreams. He wants to be a "good" patient. I want an *intact* patient. We can talk about dreams later. I want to talk about where he can purchase some warm, waterproof boots, with solid grips on the bottom. He's free-associating, and I interrupt: has he looked at the snowboots in the camping goods store on Route 17? And while he's buying boots, what about buying a down coat? He pauses and says, "Is there something wrong with my shoes?"

He's a little offended, but mostly, startled. I say, "They are nice loafers, but those are indoor shoes. For the ice you need snow boots. So you won't fall again." He's lying on the couch, and I'm sitting behind him, but I can feel his eyebrows raise. I visualize the thought bubble over his head. "And this is relevant to psychoanalysis … how?" So I add, "That's how you got pneumonia." "Oh." Silence. Then: "There are snowboots?" I'm wondering if he can see the thought bubble over *my* head: "Does he really not know this?" "Yes, they sell great ones on Route 17." He doesn't have a rulebook for this intervention. I can tell he's puzzled. But he's a good guy, he's a quick study, and he spends his life accommodating to others. And then, too, I am the authority on this psychoanalysis stuff. If being a "good" patient means going to the camping store, he'll do it. If purchasing snow boots will purchase him a mother, he'll get the boots. Intervening like this, I feel at one with the humanity of every good analyst; the patient's safety and self-care come first. After all, the talking cure won't work if the patient is deceased. Shyly, he asks, "After that, do we talk about dreams?"

I don't know if he *wants* to talk about dreams, or if he's trying to follow a changing set of instructions. But I am taken by the tone in his voice. He is polite, and quiet and droll. "I haven't seen anything about outdoor clothing in Freud and Klein. Maybe you can suggest some references?" It's a pointed and gentle kind of ridicule, which I am particularly fond of. It gives me hope that we can find out who he is. I laugh, and he laughs with me. Now, his analysis is beginning. I know I'm being directive, and I wonder: is this wiping out his subjectivity, or constructing it for the first time? Maybe both. I ask him what he's feeling about me talking about his fall. He's forgotten the fall. He's confused. He's embarrassed. He's touched by my concern. He never had a mother. He has read up on maternal transferences; he knows he has always longed for a mother. I say, "Coming to analysis, you knew you would talk about your wish for a mother. Now, it looks like you've got yourself a Jewish one." He's lived on the East Coast for 20 years, and he knows what a Jewish mother is. I analyze this encounter, but I also want him to know what it feels like to receive warmth, and humane protection. Teasing him, I think: maybe this child can even learn how to play. If I can keep him alive, I can heal his attachment disorder.

For a year and a half, it seems possible that we can know and name him. He needs to be held by an idealized, idealizing mother. He wants to be born anew, to be particular to my heart, to hear me speak his name. Much of the time, he lives in what Kohut would call a mirroring transference, or what Slochower (1996) and Winnicott refer to as a "holding environment." He feels comforted and frightened. He feels enlivened in his sessions, but he also feels damaged and damaging. Attachment is broken up by persecutory fragments, by primal phantasies and ancient terrors. He feels like a bad and destructive infant, a hungry, needy child. He is afraid that he will poison me with his badness, that he will consume and exhaust his depleted mother, and that there will be no mother left. Slowly, he internalizes object constancy, and integrates old affect with current somatic experience. This seems to have an effect. He is treating himself better. He's making better decisions about his health, and he's forming more mutual relationships. He is adapting to his divorce, and his dread is diminishing.

Clinical Impasse: Testing Our Models of Attachment

Of course, his health was at risk, and his self-endangerment continued. Still, I thought treatment was going well. My patient had a variety of self-states, and we had a variety of corresponding relationships. In all of them, he was my child, and I called him by his name. Sometimes, we were a maternal dyad. An abusive father would appear, and trauma was placed into a malignant oedipal triangle. We spent many sessions on his cold, authoritarian, brutal father. This father commanded submission and was infinitely replicated: in the overseers, in God the Father, and in the subsequent arrogance of male doctors. In all this work, his history was assimilated to the "maternal" language of psychoanalysis. This was the language of attachment, attunement, empathy, rupture and repair; trauma, mentalization, self states and dissociation. I hoped that our evolving bond would birth him as a subject. He would come to know, and name, himself. Gradually, his dissociation did start to lift, and his narrative began to shift. But that shift turned into a dangerous clinical impasse. He risked his life, and I failed in everything I tried. Attachment didn't hold him, and I realized that our attachment theory couldn't know, or name, him. This crisis illuminated the culture trouble embedded in our theories. We pay too much attention to the psychic nuclear family. And we pay *too little* attention to *spirit, ethics and political resistance* (see also Layton, 2006).

Rituals of Loss: Impasse and Mystification

Recently, he has been linking his affects to bodily states and disturbances during his sessions. Now, when he arrives in my office, he states the date, year, time: Thursday, 7/12, 2006, 4:50 p.m. He is quiet; he senses pain in his abdomen. Then, he associates his pain to the colon cancer of his mother and sister; to the burst appendix of his secretary's cousin. All of this occurred on 7/12, in another time: 1998, 1984, 1976. Death at 2:15, in the afternoon. Death at 3:45 a.m. Every session, he makes these links: the date, the body sensation, the mortal illness of someone else who came before. Every death was recorded with numerical precision. These figures carried a strange equivalence of grief. He seemed to collect any kind of death. Intimate, anonymous, casual, remote; those he had lived with, and those he had never even known. He had no sense of relational parameters and distances, no sense of who belonged to whom, which loss was his and which belonged to someone else. He always knew exactly how and when and where these people had died. He was in almost daily attendance at wakes, shivahs, funerals – of those he knew, and those he barely knew. His calendar was crowded with memorial detail. The year became a repetitive cycle in which each date was already written up by tragedy and by loss.

At first, I shared a resonance with this grief. I understood that we were mourning a dead self, born to a "dead mother" (Green, 1986). But this mourning seemed excessive, rigid, codified and preordained in arithmetic patterns. The deceased began to appear in duplicate and triplicate: there was the Mary who was a sister, who died of kidney cancer, at 3 p.m. on December 11. There was the Mary who was his friend's cousin, who recently died of suicide. Each December 11 was freighted with their deaths. I felt overcome by dates, times, numbers, diagnoses, by the infinite strangers for whom we were in "mourning." I felt challenged to remember their names and found it impossible to sustain this memory.

Prior to this turn, I had been hopeful. Now, he was placing his health at risk to attend all these funerals: his 15-hour workdays turned into 20 hours. He got no sleep. He was attending the bereft; he had no time for self-care. He gave money and free medical care to the widows and children. He visited them, again and again. Everyone knew he had a big heart. Sometimes these people knew him, and sometimes they didn't. Every abandoned soul introduced him to another. His devotion was melancholic and tender. But he had already had a triple bypass; he was exhausted and was heading toward another heart attack. Antibiotics failed, and one infection flowed into the next. For several months, he barely came to treatment.

Everything was unraveling: our attachment, and his health. In phone sessions, I analyzed anything I could think of: his survivor guilt and grief; his penance and acts of reparation; his addiction to depriving objects, the savagery of his internalized father; the brutal commands of God the Father; his Christ complex, his dread of life, his love affair with death. I wondered if his prior relationship to me had been one of falseness and compliance. I told him how sad I was about his decline. I told him I was attached to him and didn't want to lose him. I teased him, I scolded him, I analyzed him in every way I could think of. Each intervention seemed to take, and then, it didn't. Our attachment didn't hold him. Every time his symptoms abated, he attended funerals, not sessions. He was sick for months. When he returned to therapy after a long winter break of illness, I told him that I wanted him to live, but that I was afraid that we would be unable to keep him alive. He has read about Thanatos, and masochism, trauma, and the repetition compulsion; he had words for his death drive. He has insight and affective resonance with all my interpretations, but I have learned that this process is futile. Without this dialogue, we fell silent. He was quiet, and the room filled with his melancholy and my despair. Then, he replied, "I am fused with the entire universe of suffering bodies."

Rituals of Duplication: Beyond Maternal Dyads

I have always thought of fusion as a one-body-for-two referent to primal oneness with mother (McDougall, 1989). But I realize that he is not referring to this type of fusion. I had forgotten he was anyone and no one. Suddenly, I heard his referent to fusion in a different register. For the first time, I recall that he was "the twins." Throughout the analysis of his maternal transference, I forgot about the twin-ship, even though he talked about it as a formative experience. I had bonded to him readily, but in the mode in which he longed to be attached: in singular relationship to mother, unique and identifiable. Now, I began to think again, about twins as "doubles" and as "fractions," and as "halves." The way they replicate one another and are always both more, and less, than one. I thought about his daily calendar, the way it replicated and multiplied itself each year, and then, the way it would be divided into fractions: 6 months from this death anniversary, 4 months from that one. I reflected on the way he had measured names and bodies in their final illnesses: the two Marys, the two Lorraines, the three Michaels. There was all that confusion that would arise, for me, which one is which, which one is linked to which story. Every story overlaid with another story; each history separated out into its specificity, and then returned to doubling and conflation. All this linked to life and death.

I remembered this: from birth, his brother's half was life, and his was near-death. This was only one of many ways that the brothers measured, and divided, human existence. My patient was ill; he overworked; he sacrificed himself for others, and was prohibited from pleasure, and from all considerations of the self. His twin was well; he had little loyalty, and no empathic capacity; he was irresponsible, rootless, deceitful, and he spent his life in the casual pursuit of his own pleasures. My patient was fused with his brother, and he grew troubled by his brother. Identical in appearance, they conjured a split moral universe. Sacrifice was nobility and compassion; self-concern was greedy and bad. In his near-death practices, my patient was becoming ever more "good" as his brother became more "selfish" and "bad." In analysis, I was trying to help my patient resolve this moral split. I had placed hope in my model of attachment, in the pursuit of depressive integration (see Ogden, 1990). But in the transference, his half was death, and my half was life. The more I clamored for the self, and for life, the more he pursued his sacrificial destiny.

This dyadic splitting would keep emerging between us. In this treatment, splitting is a Trickster. It fades away, and it shape-shifts; it heals in one dynamism, and reappears in another. Belatedly, I would catch one dynamism, but I never caught hold of the Trickster, himself. But what I now knew was this: in the area of the twin-ship, I kept reducing his communication to that *fraction of human experience* that conforms to my individualist construct of human subjectivity. In speaking to him as if he was as unique, identified and identifiable, I had begun to register him in the book of life. But in refusing to know him as a twin, I was yet another mother who refused to speak his real name. And so, he signaled his *half* of the human condition. He presented me with fusion, duplication, replication, multiplications and divisions. In the transference, he co-created himself as half, as a fragment, an infinitely subtracted subject.

Rituals of Multiplication: Beyond the Psychoanalytic Family

But with these realizations about twinning (see also Lewin, 2004), I became open to the significance of his anniversary calculations. Psychoanalysis has always privileged language. For months, his numeric recitations had evoked my impatience and my absence. I attributed this boredom to him. I saw his calculus as an obsessional, "autistic-contiguous" defense (see Ogden, 1990); or as a form of chuntering that was projectively *undoing* my capacity for mentalization. I had ignored his numbers and focused on his words. I never thought I had any trouble "mentalizing" (Fonagy & Target, 1998) him. I kept him in my mind when he wasn't there. But after I realized I wasn't listening to the twins, I also realized that I had actually failed to mentalize his mind. For the psychoanalyst, his mind had an alien shape. It did not exist in a singular relationship to mother. My patient's psyche-soma is a registry for twins. But it is also a registry for *any one of many.* My patient is not simply functioning in the domain of doubling and halves and subtractions. He has been operating, as well, in the zone of multiplication and division. His calendar inscribes both individual, and mass, death: It registers wars, genocide, earthquakes, hurricanes. In this way, his life was a transcript for what Holt (2006) called "math murder." When I stopped privileging language, I understood this: my patient *does* have a self. But his is a form of self-being that psychoanalysis has failed to recognize: it was not shaped by parent–child dyads and triangles. His physiognomy doesn't inscribe McDougall's "one body for two" – and it doesn't inscribe father in relationship to mother in relationship to son. My patient's physiognomy is *any one of many. To name his subjectivity, we must meet his collectivized abjection, in a world where the nuclear family does not exist.*[1]

In the psychoanalytic situation, we have no language for this form of subjectivity. Our numeric universe has always been an intimate one. We are entered into existence in relations of one, two, three. This is the bedrock of attachment theory, and of diverse psychoanalytic theories. Baby, parental coupling, mother–infant dyad and oedipal triangle. My patient never lived in a universe of one, two, three. As I think past the two-ness of dyads, past the three-ness of oedipal triangles, and even past twin-ships, my mind engages a large group of children. I begin to visualize what Davoine and Gaudilliere (2004) called the "plural body" of such collectively traumatized children. Now meaning can be restored to his funeral devotion and his anniversary recitations. He weeps. He must keep faith with the children, but he can never memorialize all their wounds. In childhood he tried to memorize them all: faces, ages, dates, times, places. Now, he is attending their losses. Their pain is inscribed on his body. *"And what about attending to your own wounds,"* I ask. He answers, *"Mine will be last. Afterwards. When I meet God the Father, I will feel his embrace."* He has never spoken this before. As anyone and as no one, my patient has been a shape-shifter. To be bonded in psychoanalysis, he has only shown his agnostic self-states. Now he is subverting the very bedrock on which I stand. And in speaking these words, he has also startled himself. In childhood, he felt terrorized, and abandoned, by God. In his adult life, he was a nonbeliever, like me. He has repudiated the harsh, authoritarianism of his evangelical roots. But suddenly we discover this: inside his "masochistic compulsion" there is a dissociated area of faith. In this place, he *has* no individual psychology, and he *doesn't* share my existential premises. Am I going to lose him *and* my own faith in psychoanalysis?

Clinical Impasse: Near Death and the Sacred

If psychoanalysis has trouble naming collectivized poverty and abjection, we have even more trouble answering his spiritual concerns. My patient can find love only in the afterlife. Of course he is undaunted by death. How can I answer him? Psychoanalysis is a Godless encounter (see Gay, 1987). At best, we leave our patient's religious beliefs *out*. At worst, as Aron (2004) noted, we subject them to reductive interpretation (see Fenichel, 1939; Freud, 1927, 1928; Gay, 1987). Prior to this moment, my patient had only spoken of the cruelty, and terror, of his religious indoctrination. In his childhood, religious fundamentalism sanctified suffering, and prohibited birth control. Christianity produced submission, silence and labor. This confirmed my own Marxist perspective: that religion is the opiate of the people. I thought he agreed with this perspective. I know that fundamentalist beliefs can have a tenacious hold on our "social unconscious" (Layton, 2005). When I had tried to analyze his unconscious Christ complex, we had focused on his internalized oppression. But I didn't know that he had written back on this subjugating text (see Bhaba, 1985; Raboteau, 2004). He had conflated his old oppression with a liberating idiom: the idiom of Christ's compassion for the poor. In this process, he seeks the ecstasy, and grace, of his own of "transcendent goodness" (Grand, 2012). This is a "non-self-centered subjectivity"(see Rubin, 2003) that we do not adequately recognize in psychoanalysis (Grand, 2011)[2] even though we admire it in Ghandi, Martin Luther King, Nelson Mandela and Sophie Scholl.

Rituals of the Spirit: Psychoanalysis and the Problem of Salvation

My patient has been irreligious, agnostic; he repudiates his fundamentalist roots. But his manic body practices of risk and reparation have always signified a self of purity and compassion. Crucifying himself to attend another soul, he seems assured of resurrection. As the uncared-for-caregiver, he does not need to be named by his own mother. He will be named, and found, by a better Father than his own father: a Father who can embrace the suffering of *all of his migrant children,*

> I am the Good Shepherd. *I know my own and my own know me, just as the Father knows me and I know the Father* [emphasis added]. And I lay down my life for the Sheep. … For this reason, the Father loves me, because I lay down my life to take it up again.
>
> (*St. John, 10:14–17*)

In his childhood, Christianity was persecutory and savage; it was bereft of all compassion. Now, his near-death practices anticipate God's love in the hereafter. My patient has constructed a brilliant, and risky, solution. He reenacts the savagery and exploitation of his childhood. He toils in the fields and is enslaved to internalized bad objects. But he also vanquishes the Devil, finds Christ's compassion and bonds to a good object that cannot die or leave him. He refuses the "bestial transformation" (see Grand, 2000) that he witnessed in his own parents. His life is a traumatic transcript. But it is also a heroic (see Grand, 2009) form of *ethical and spiritual resistance,* which counters the ethical bankruptcy of child labor. Liberation theology is written into his body. With other children, he once searched for the I–Thou relation (see Buber, 1923). Now, his life is a perverse restoration of the I–Thou relation, in which a sacrificial, and collectivized, "I" will be embraced by God's love. There is a promise of self-transcendence, in which the absence of self-differentiation embodies a "non-pathological expanded sense of self" (see Rubin, 2003, p. 83). But to attain this state, he must be "obedient unto death, even death on a cross" (Epistle to the Philippians, 2:7–8). There are many psychoanalytic ways to think about my patient's masochism. But none of them can disrupt this compulsive dance with death. We cannot offer a gateway into God's embrace (see also Stein, 2002). We are Godless, and we have more death anxiety than my patient. My patient rewrote death, and he didn't need to survive, in this world. If he wasn't afraid of death, he could push back against "The Man." He could receive God's love *and* act as the Prophet, God has thrust a burden upon his soul, and he is bowed and stunned at man's fierce greed. Frightful is the agony of man; … Prophecy is the voice that God has lent to the silent agony, a voice to the plundered poor, to the profaned riches of the world." (Heschl, 1955, p. 5)

I'm a Jew and an atheist and a psychoanalyst. My patient is inspired by sacrifice, by devotion, by the selflessness of goodness. I can only talk of compulsive masochism. Why come to sessions? He knows that I can't accept, or understand, his quest. Realizing this, I think I've lost him. He is lying on my couch. My tears must be audible. I say, "*I want you to be well, here, on this earth. Why can't you feel my embrace?*" He answers me: "*Your embrace isn't enough. You would have to hold all of us, and you can't.*" Well, there it is. It's true; a psychoanalytic mother *can't*. God the Father can hold *all of his sheep.* The psychoanalytic mother only exists in a psychic universe of one, two, three: she extrudes politics, and culture, and religion, and class, and ethical and spiritual crises. She doesn't think twins. She only "mentalizes" (Fonagy & Target, 1998) *one* child at a time, in a nuclear family; she can't even think her children in relationship to each other.

As Mitchell (2003) noted, the psychoanalytic family is grounded in a patriarchal, bourgeois heterosexuality.[3] In this construction, the self comes into being in hierarchical relationships infused with parental authority and power: one child in relation to mother and father. The psychoanalytic family omits the lateral peer relations that form the bedrock of social justice. Ultimately, it is the sibling bond that can empower us to collectively resist arbitrary authority and social injustice. Fraught with competition and with rivalry, sibling relations are also the wellspring for solidarity with our human brothers and sisters. Sibling bonds offer us our first exit from domination and received truth; they are an important corrective to hierarchical deference, submission and obeisance. When this peer bonding is eclipsed, power hierarchies are consolidated, and social activism will be diminished. In psychoanalysis we keep contributing to this problem. We are committed to transformation, but we situate transformation *exclusively* in *hierarchical* relations. We don't know about children comforting other children; or about the way that children "give care from empty hands" (Orange, p. 9). When we do, that experience is readily marginalized or forgotten (see A. Freud & Dann, 1951; Ornstein, 2011). In this treatment, I, too, have forgotten. But my patient's psyche-soma is insistent: it only exists as the "twins" and as any one of many children. But while I am confounded, and he is struggling, he is also constructing another model of transformation: collectivized children, known to one another, are known by God's empathic embrace. Our impasse is a critique of psychoanalysis; it gives voice to his ethical, cultural and spiritual trouble. Once, he was an outsider in the United States. *Now he is an outsider to our practice; he is not a psychoanalytic subject. Until we rewrite psychoanalysis, we cannot name, or know, him. And we will not be empowered in the pursuit of social justice.*

Rituals of Transcendence: Spirit and Ethics in Psychoanalysis

There are more things in heaven and earth, Horatio, than are dreamt of in your philosophy (*Hamlet*, Act I, Scene 5).

I have been quiet, reflecting on my patient's last words: "You can't hold all of us." At first, I just thought, he's right, psychoanalysis can't. Then, I start thinking *Maybe he knows Someone who can.* Alone, my patient could not have saved himself. Alone, as an analyst, I cannot save my patient. And psychoanalysis, alone, cannot heal him. But now, in this reverie, my empathy starts to cross disciplines; it embraces mystery; and it is fortified by the wisdom of others, speaking throughout the ages. I have always thought about politics and ethics and culture. But now, I am also thinking spirit. As citizens, and as psychoanalysis, we all need to embrace the cultural, political, ethical, and spiritual markers that shape human subjectivity. As analysts, are closing the gap between clinical and applied psychoanalysis. We are familiar with research on mirror neurons, empathy, embodied simulation and social identification (see Gallese, 2009). We see pathology as socially constructed, and we are conversing more about siblings. We have written about Good and Evil (Grand, 2000, 2009). We know trauma. We are converging on forms of I–Thou relatedness *constructed by a multitude of children, in abjection.* We have begun to converse about spirituality (Aron, 2004; Gargiulo & Spezzano, 2003; J. Guss, personal communication, 2010; Rubin, 2003; Sorenson, 2003). Now, near-death has arrived for me, as a great teacher. I am being called toward a new integration. Once, my patient thought psychoanalysis was a treatment in which his *body* would be left out. Now, he is telling me that I have left *spirit* out. I have never attended to questions of the spirit. I have no religious training, but Jewish ethics and philosophy are bred into my bones. I can resonate with the words of the Prophet, and with Christ's compassion. But I *cannot* comprehend Christ's death upon the Cross. Or at least I think I can't. I am repudiating my patient's savior complex, but what analyst is without one? I am suffering to save his life, as he is suffering to save the other. As a woman, and as an analyst, I have been well tutored in sacrifice and self-effacement. Why can't I recognize myself? I peer into this mirror, and still, I can't praise this death upon the Cross. I don't see suffering as sacred. In Proverbs it is written that, "He that oppresses the poor blasphemes His maker, but he who is gracious unto the needy honors Him." But in Jewish theology, we must stay alive to honor Him: "See I have set before thee this daily life and good, death and evil ... choose life" (Deuteronomy 30:15–19).[4] Perhaps, the problem in this psychoanalysis is not *just* my disavowal of religion. I have always been inspired by acts of *transcendent goodness*, but how would my patient know this? I have disqualified his devotional practices. We have never talked about the "radical amazement" (Heschl, 1955) of his goodness. Psychoanalysts focus on I–Thou relatedness, and the emergence of the self, but we never talk about an ecstatic Self, awakening through devotion *to the other.*[5]

I am trying to see through my patient's eyes, but our worldviews still seem to have foundational differences. I am an inheritor of intertwined traditions:

an Eastern European, leftist, Jewish secularism; a post–World War II distrust of submission to authority; and a psychoanalytic preference for Eros over Thanatos. For me, transcendent goodness is located in mankind's deeds, in *this* life. For him, good deeds promise him transcendence in the afterlife. Neither of us seems to believe in the joyful immanence of God, present in the pedestrian realities of life on this earth. To attain the afterlife, my patient mortifies the flesh to save his soul. I think his flesh *is* part of the soul that needs saving. To psychoanalysts, self-preservation is essential to the Good, and I find this affirmed by Rabbi Akiba, in the Talmud. I can recognize my patient's devotional spirit, but I don't have much reverence for his afterlife. And I cannot share his passion for self-negation and submission. If liberation theology is written into his cells, "question authority" has been written into mine. My consciousness was shaped by the contagion of Nazism, by the civil rights movement, and by the 1960s protests of the Vietnam War. I distrust all ecstatic surrender to "higher" authority. I suspect deification. Like the doubting Thomas of the New Testament, I can see my Christ-patient suffering, but I do not believe in his resurrection. Unlike Thomas, I do not reach out to touch his God.[6] I do not want to surrender to faith as Thomas did, as Thomas instructs his fellow disciples, "Let us all go that we may die with him" (JN: 11:16). I can honor the philosophy of St. Paul, but I can only address these words to my earthly brothers and sisters, "You are in our hearts, to die together and to live together" (Corinthian, II, 7:3).

Our therapeutic impasse has destabilized my worldview, but only so far. Psychoanalysis is Godless, but it is infused with Jewish ethics as Aron (2004) suggested. No wonder we cannot answer my patient's trouble. I can *almost* grasp my patient's Christian search for Grace, but I cannot relinquish attachment to *this* life. I will share my patient with God's embrace, as long as God's love inspires him to live. This I'm not giving up. I'm reading up about Christ's compassion, and I think we could use more of it, across the globe. Maybe my patient and I can meet in a new attitude toward sacrifice and devotion – that "the self may be turned into a friend of the spirit if one is capable of developing a persistent perception of the non-self, of the anxiety and dignity, of fellow beings" (Heschl, 1955, p. 399). My therapeutic practice; his Christian theology; his embodiment of collectivized abjection; his construct of the "plural body" (Davoine & Gaudilliere, 2004); my Jewish ethics and philosophy; our shared awe for humanity's acts of transcendent goodness – perhaps together we can formulate a new subject for psychoanalysis.

I am rethinking politics, culture, ethics and spirit, while my patient traces the Stations of the Cross. I have seen the limits of my attachment theory, and now, I'm seeing the limits of reason. I am still wary of deification. As my patient knows all too well, there are grave risks to mystical authority, ecstatic submission and surrender. But I have stopped denying my own religious inquiry. I am still a Godless Jewish psychoanalyst, but somehow I have a benign vision of the God I don't believe in. This God would take offense at migrant labor, and He would advocate for social justice. If He would just step up and protect the innocent, I would become a believer. I am waiting for the answer to Abraham's question, "Shall not the judge of all the earth deal justly?" (Genesis 18:22). I receive no answer; I can only see an "eclipse of God" (Buber, 1957). So, if there *is* a God, this "creator spoiled reality so that mortals might set it right" (Soloveitchik, 2002, p. 93). I'm placing my faith in mortals, although we are not doing such a good job either. I don't read the Talmud, but my life seems infused with its questions.

As Aron (2004) suggested, even atheists have a vision of the God whom they have chosen to reject. How strange all of this is: that an atheist imagines a benign, here-and-now God of Justice; that a believer's God requires a sacrifice unto death. I hope my patient and I can find our way to this: that "The Lord is good to all, and His compassion is over all that He has made" (Psalms 145:10). I return to my patient's image of beatific arms, holding all of the children. I suggest to my patient that God already knows my patient's compassion, and that God's embrace may already be there. Perhaps God is immanent in the snow boots my patient wears now in icy weather. Perhaps my patient can be held by God the Father *and* by my embrace. Love in the hereafter *and* love here on this earthly plane.

As I offer this, I am still persuading him to stay alive. I can almost grasp collectivity, spirit, body and political resistance. But I start to collapse back into psychoanalytic reduction: placing my child into a nuclear, parental triangle. Returning him to one, two, three. Psychoanalytic Mother, God the Father and Christ the Son. The Son is nested and held in those hierarchical forms of attachment that have actually eclipsed the sibling of social justice. In many ways, Judeo-Christian religion reifies the nuclear family phantasm from which my patient has been excluded. In Judeo-Christian religion, as in psychoanalysis, transformation only occurs in benign relation to authority: parent, analyst, God. As I slip back into this hierarchical model, my patient conjures, and disrupts, it once again. He longs for God's embrace, but he is always fused with migrant children. To name him, we must invent a new model of transformation and subjectivity.

Rituals of Birth: Body, Collectivity and Imagination

I have offered to hold him with God. I didn't really know what this meant. My meaning is "unformulated" (Stern, 1997). My patient always sees my confusion, even when I don't reveal it. He says, "But, all of the other children." I say, "Maybe *we can hold YOU holding them*." I don't really know what this would look like, for him or for me. I'm hoping God will open his arms to the migrant children, but I'm not counting on it, either. Then, my patient's body speaks to us again. A sonogram reveals an enormous mass in his kidney. He is afraid that he has the kidney cancer that his sister died from on December 11, 1988. But it is a giant kidney stone that needs to come out. In telling me, he is relieved, and his tone conveys pride at having produced something so impressive. He is never proud of himself, even though he has so much to be proud of. We haven't played together for six months. Somehow joy and play have returned. I say, "Oh! You've created something enormous!" He laughs, he is surprised and pleased, and there is a moment of lightness. And he tells me he has benign, competent doctors, this time. The stone will be pulverized in the hospital, and then its particles will pass out through the urine. He says, "It feels like a birth." I ask, "Who will be born?" One by one, he names all ten siblings. Part of the whole, part of the family, coming through the birth canal of his urethra, healthy, received, beloved. Secure from rape, from beatings, from disease, homelessness and starvation. Allowed to play with the other children. His anxiety melts away in anticipation of his procedure. He becomes quiet and calm, and his breathing is slow and steady. Finally, I ask, "And what of little you? Can he be born?" "Yes," he says, "I can be born, at the very end." "And can you live and breathe this time?" I ask. "Yes," he says, "this time, I can breathe." He says, *"I will be birthed into the arms of God."*

He is peaceful, and he is ready. He imagines white light, and anticipates this meeting. I am afraid that this encounter will be lethal. At last, he will find his death upon the Cross. But he has created himself as a new heroic form: he feels phallic and anal and vaginal, a whole-body birth canal. In possession of both penis and vagina, he is no longer half of the human condition. He can contain death, and he can claim life. His body is holding other children, in their wholeness. In the hospital, his self-preservation is no longer the antagonist of his goodness. Their flesh is *his flesh.* The will to goodness became linked to the will to survive. He is infused with Christ's compassion. The stone dissolves, and children pass through the birth canal. He names them as human. He has named himself *as more than one, and he has named a new subject* for psychoanalysis.

Coda

Throughout the history of psychoanalysis, we have negotiated the intersection between psyche, ethics, politics, spirit and culture. This negotiation has largely existed as the "un-thought known" (Bollas, 1995) that we have tended to eject, or deny. Historically, we have bifurcated our discipline: reserving analysis as the domain of "pure" psychic processes, we deposited politics and culture in applied psychoanalysis. Ethics and spirituality were extruded into philosophy and theology. Recently, in relational psychoanalysis, we are querying these categories. In dark times, social responsibility is infusing our work. In this, we owe a debt to our Inter-personal, Self-psychological and Freudian colleagues. Increasingly, psychoanalysis becomes an instrument of social change. We cannot do this fast enough. All over the globe, children are suffering.

My patient will always be one with these children. He briefly awakened to life on this earth. In that period, I wrote up our process, much as it appears here. He read it and approved its publication. He made forays into life. He started dating. He began a practice of meditation and a nutritional regimen. He continued his devotion to the suffering other, but he did it with more lightness and self-attention. He continued to be a very sick man. About a year after this breakthrough, he had another heart attack. He died suddenly. Would he have been saved by a different therapeutic approach? Perhaps, but I doubt it. Illness was written into his cells from the moment of his birth. He died of the residual effects of migrant labor: chronic starvation and malnutrition. Overwork. Disease. Crop-dusting and bad lungs. Parasites and insecticide in the drinking water. Skin burned in the sun. Battering. No sleep and no medical care. No template for self-care. Most of his siblings had already died of cancer. It was a miracle that he actually lived for so long. He was a miracle of compassion – and resilience. On the anniversary of his death, I mourn him. I mark the day, date, year. I remember the hour of his last session. I wonder about the hour of his death. I think about all of the other children. I wonder where he is now. I hope he has been released from his Earthly body, and found the state of Grace that he longed for. As the day ends, I meditate on this: "At the end of days, evil will be conquered by the One; in historic times, evil must be conquered one by one" (Heschl, 1955, p. 377).

Notes

1 For a discussion of the collective self, see Rozmarin (2009, 2011).
2 For an exception, see Kohut (1985).
3 See also Gilman (1993).
4 As Aron (2004) noted, this ethos infuses psychoanalysis.
5 For an exception, see Rubin (2003).
6 For these interesting reflections, I would like to thank Allyn Marie Dunne (personal communication, April 3, 2012).

References

Aron, L. (2004) God's influence on my psychoanalytic vision and values. *Psychoanalytic Psychology* 21: 442–451.

Bhabha, H.K. (1985) Signs taken for wonders: Questions of ambivalence and authority under a tree outside Delhi. *Critical Inquiry* 12(1): 114–165 May 1817.

Bollas, C. (1995) The structure of evil. In, *Cracking up: The work of unconscious experience* ed., New York, NY: Hill and wang 180–221.

Buber, M. (1923/1970) I and Thou. Translator: Walter Kaufman. Charles Scribner Sons: New York.

Buber, M. (1957) *Eclipse of God: Studies in the relation between religion and philosophy* ed., New York, NY: Harper Books.

Buber, M. (1970) *I and thou* ed., New York, NY: Scribner.

Davoine, F., Gaudilliere, J.M. (2004) *History beyond trauma: Whereof one cannot speak, thereof one cannot stay silent* ed., New York, NY: Other Press.

Fenichel, O. (1939) Problems of psychoanalytic technique. *Psychoanalytic Quarterly* 8: 438–470.

Fonagy, P., Target, M. (1998) Mentalization and the changing aims of child psychoanalysis. *Psychoanalytic Dialogues* 8(1): 87–114.

Freud, A., Dann, S. (1951) An experiment in group upbringing. *Psychoanalytic Study of the Child* 6: 127–168.

Freud, S. (1927) The future of an illusion. *Standard Edition* 21: 1–56.

Freud, S. (1928) A religious experience. *Standard Edition* 21: 167–172.

Gallese, V. (2009) Mirror neurons, embodied simulation and the neural basis of social identification. *Psychoanalytic Dialogues* 19: 519–537.

Gargiulo, G., Spezzano, C. (2003) Introduction. In C. Spezzano & G. Gargiulo (Eds.) *Soul on the couch: Spirituality, religion and morality in contemporary psychoanalysis* ed., Hillsdale, NJ: The Analytic Press, 31–43.

Gay, P. (1987) *A godless Jew: Freud, atheism and the making of psychoanalysis* ed., New Haven, CT: Yale University Press.

Gilman, S.L. (1993) *Freud, race and gender* ed., Princeton, NJ: Princeton University Press.

Grand, S. (2000) *The reproduction of evil: A clinical and cultural perspective* ed., Hillsdale, NJ: The Analytic Press.

Grand, S. (2009) *The hero in the mirror: From fear to fortitude* ed., New York, NY: Routledge.

Grand, S. (2011) Celebrations of courage: A discussion of 'counter-transference and the heart of the heroic' by Gladys Foxe. *Psychoanalytic Perspectives* 8(1): 46–52.

Grand, S. (2012) Devotion and the self: Comment on Freeman. *Journal of Theoretical and Philosophical Psychology*.

Green, A. (1986) *The dead mother. On private madness* ed., London: Hogarth Press, 142–173.

Heschl, A.J. (1955) *God in search of man* ed., New York, NY: Farrar, Straus and Giroux.

Holt, J. (2006) Math murders. *The New York Times Magazine* 3/12: 11–12.

Kohut, H. (1985) *On courage. Self psychology and the humanities: Reflections on a new psychoanalytic approach* ed. Strozier, C., New York, NY: Norton, 5–50 (Original work published 1972).

Layton, L. (2005) *From culture to couch: Investigating a social UCS* ed., New York: Paper presented at the meeting of Division 30 of the American Psychoanalytic Association.

Layton, L. (2006) Attacks on linking: The UCS pull to dissociate individuals from their social context. *Psychoanalysis, class and politics: Encounters in the clinical setting* ed., New York, NY: Routledge, 107–118.

Lewin, V. (2004) *The twin in the transference* ed., London: Whurr.

McDougall, J. (1989) *Theatres of the body: A psychoanalytic approach to psychosomatic illness* ed., New York, NY: Norton.

Mitchell, J. (2003) *Siblings* ed., Cambridge: Polity Press.

Ogden, T. (1990) *The matrix of the mind* ed., Northvale, NJ: Aronson.

Orange, D. (in press) *Out of time: Siblings as trauma transmitters, protectors, sources of courage* ed. Psychoanalytic Inquiry.

Ornstein, A. (2011) *Childhood losses, adult memories*. Paper delivered to the Margaret Mahler Symposium ed., Philadelphia, PA.

Raboteau, A.J. (2004) *Slave religion: The invisible institution of the Antebellum South* ed., New York, NY: Oxford: University Press.

Rappoport, E. (2012) Creating the umbilical cord: Relational knowing and the somatic third. *Psychoanalytic Dialogues* 22: 375–388.

Rozmarin, E. (2009) I am yourself: Subjectivity and the collective. *Psychoanalytic Dialogues* 19: 604–617.

Rozmarin, E. (2011) To be is to betray: On the place of collective history and freedom in psychoanalysis. *Psychoanalytic Dialogues* 21: 320–346.

Rubin, J.B. (2003) Psychoanalysis is self-centered. *Soul on the couch: Spirituality, religion and morality in contemporary psychoanalysis* ed. Spezzano, C., Gargiulo, G. Hillsdale, NJ: The Analytic Press, 87–102.

Shakespeare, W. (1917) *Hamlet* ed., New Haven, CT: Yale University Press.

Slochower, J. (1996) *Holding and psychoanalysis* ed., Northvale, NJ: The Analytic Press.

Soloveitchik, J.B. (2002) *Worship of the heart* ed., New York, NY: Ktav Publishing.

Sorenson, R.L. (2003) Transcendence and intersubjectivity: The patient's experience of the analyst's spirituality. *Soul on the couch: Spirituality, religion and morality in contemporary psychoanalysis* ed. Spezzano, C., Gargiulo, G. Hillsdale, NJ: The Analytic Press, 43–62.

Stein, R. (2002) Evil as love and liberation: The mind of a suicidal terrorist. *Psychoanalytic Dialogues* 12: 393–420.

Stern, D.B. (1997) *Unformulated experience: From dissociation to imagination in psychoanalysis* ed., Hillsdale, NJ: The Analytic Press.

3

THIS BREAD IS *NOT* MY BODY

Biblical *Manna* as a Psychoanalytic Paradigm

Moshe Halevi Spero

I would like to begin my contribution with two epigrams, whose significance will unfold both metaphorically and perhaps even concretely, or practically, as our examination progresses:

> Even though his guest's story was such *empty stuff*, every word of it rained down upon his heart like manna from heaven.

> No one should expect that an interpretation of his dreams will fall into his lap like manna from the sky.

The first comment belongs to Fyodor Dostoyevsky (1846, p. 145), speaking of "*manna*" poetically, metaphorically, alluding to some kind of unexpected sustenance or materiale that might fill a gaping existential void. In context, his allusion to the biblical term "*manna*" can be judged as nonspecific. The second citation is from Sigmund Freud (1900, p. 522)[1], and though he, too, evokes "*manna*" for the literary likeness he seeks to conjure – and in its context, the metaphor might also be judged as nonspecific – Freud is also alluding, wittingly or unwittingly, to an analogy that I believe is of great theoretical and clinical (i.e., practical) significance.

Each psychoanalytic therapy is defined by a variety of existential struggles and transformations, unfolding on shifting sands and illusory planes, with tumultuous phases of adoration and devaluation, confusion and clarity, skepticism and faith, taking in and spitting out, and ever-changing proportions of concrete and symbolic, literal and virtual dimensions of experience. It is quite apt to say that analysis is an odyssey, a journey through intense conflict and even bondage in an intransigent spatiotemporal zone of constricted dimensions, through a wilderness, across an edge, toward virgin territory and

DOI: 10.4324/9781003266600-5

tractable, even transcendent spatiotemporal dimensions. At some point in all analyses, however, the "journey" metaphor must be precisely tailored to the individual patient and his or her manner of narration if it is to effectively identify microscopic symbolic pathways in the specific process (Freedman, *et al,* 2011). Over time, as we know, a host of such symbols has been identified in the psychoanalytic literature; others are completely idiosyncratic.

I wish here to take up the biblical term *man* or *manna* (*màn, màn·na*)[2] – the fabulous "bread from heaven" (Exodus 16:1–36) that sustained the Children of Israel throughout their 40-year wanderings in the desert. The well-known pericope of Exodus 16 offers a condensed narrative portraying a state of extreme existential threat or need, an outburst of anxiety, the sudden appearance of an unfamiliar and unidentified form of purportedly perfect nourishment, characterized by an atypically detailed set of aesthetic qualities, a gift of plenty that nevertheless must be gathered in a specific amount and used in a specific way, eventually evoking dissatisfaction and unease. From a traditional psychoanalytic perspective, such an amalgam of factors would immediately be considered base notes of an archaic oral-anal fantasy at the heart of the conflict between dependence and autonomy, a stage of development that would be classified as pre-oedipal, pre-Sinai and – intentionally alluding to Jacques Lacan – pre-Law.

But here we must confront a perennial epistemological question: Can contemporary psychoanalytic assumptions about human nature legitimately elucidate ancient texts, behaviors and motives? Strong arguments in support of this possibility have been taken up elsewhere.[3] Similarly persuaded, the ideas I share here stem from a synthesis of biblical texts, rabbinic-midrashic (10–135 CENT), talmudic (70–640 CENT), medieval and later commentaries and elaborations that reveal an infra-text rich in recurring psychological elements that offer strong parallels to contemporary psychoanalytic thought. Naturally, theoretical literature is only one spring-board for new thought. In addition, an analysand of mine referred to *manna* at several points throughout his 7-year-long analysis, an unprecedented (or, at least, unreported) event that occurred frequently enough within this one analysis as to be convincingly nonrandom, revealing at each stage significant advances from concretism to mature metaphor. In fact, I believe that the meaning of the *manna* myth and metaphor is not limited to persons familiar with Old Testament culture and might be a broader paradigm for crucial dimensions of the psychoanalytic process, a unique name for a significant latent component of the analytic frame.

The Concrete Entity Known as *Manna*

One can readily review the complete details of the debut of *manna* recorded in Exodus 16 (*esp.* 16:8–16), summarized rhetorically by Moses in his final addresses to the Israelites poised to enter the Promised Land (Deuteronomy 8:2–5).[4] On the surface, the story seems clear enough: the Hebrews, about one month into their freedom from Egypt, parched for water and bereft of food rations, cry out in despair, and God provides a miraculous kind of food substance from heaven, with a few attendant regulations. This "bread" or *manna* nourishes the Hebrews for the next 40 years until they are at the edge of the Land, though we also learn at some later point that the Israelites became intensely dissatisfied with this gift (Numbers 11:5–9). Compared, the three main biblical texts reveal numerous inconsistencies and complexities, often further complicated by the numerous conflicting ancient rabbinic interpretations. Does this unevenness simply portray varied authorship and editing, textual erosion and stylistic embellishment, or does it perhaps express an inherently *dynamic* dimension of a gradual psychic process from primitive consumption (ingestion) to internalization and mature symbolization?

A large previous literature has carefully investigated various aspects of *manna*: philological (to what language does the term *man* belong, and what does it mean?), chemical-botanical (was *manna*, in natural terms, true bread, a lichen, a psychedelic residue?),[5] metrological (was the prescribed daily measure, one *o'mer*, adequate?),[6] anthropological (is *manna* related to the oceanic-animistic concept of "mana"),[7] and, of course, theological. Surprisingly and ironically, the dedicated psychoanalytic literature, despite its affection for myth and symbolism, contains but a single discussion by Edmond Bergler (1934, 1941) regarding oral passivity, during which he coins the terms *Mannatypus*[8] and *Mannaträume*, "*manna* dreams." Taking the concrete biblical story at face value (*manna* = food), Bergler asserts that *manna* dreams, for which he offers no examples, symbolize a wish to be independent of the mother's, and later the father's, overwhelming role as the sole source of food and sustenance.[9] While space prohibits review, my assessment of this scant literature frees me to explicate *manna* in a unique manner, as illuminated by clinical psychoanalytic experience.

I am well aware of the cross-testamental literature dealing with the way in which *manna* is viewed in the Qur'ān (2:57, 7:160, 20:80) and Ḥa'dīth literature – as a divinely provided natural substance[10] – and the way it is totally transformed or, more correctly, transubstantiated (*metousiosis*) through Jesus's equation of his own body with the broken "bread" (Gospel According to John, 6:30–33, 34–40, 51–58; 1 Corinthians 11:23–24; cf. Revelations 2:17).[11] While Jewish theology has no direct need to interpret the challenging quasi-symbolic Eucharistic concept (cf. Macy, 1999; O'Connor, 2014), the mechanics of transubstantiation certainly highlight *some* kind of representational process – ranging from pathologically regressive to creative – which we will later observe in the evolution of my analysand's experience of *manna*.

The Psychoanalytic Perspective

It is not a novel idea to maintain that Mosaic *manna* was explicitly intended to wean the desert tribes (or, to speak generally, humankind) from a sense of dependency upon bread, representative of all forms of material aliment and nourishment, so as to create instead a wider, trusting, faithful relationship with God and the internalization of the divine *Logos* or word (Deuteronomy 8:3; see esp. Philo [20 BCE-50 CE], 1993). It is also a given that food; the mouth; and the so-called natural processes of ingestion, digestion, assimilation, metabolism and excretion are always steeped in, and their psychological impact and meaning affected by cultural norms and values, including sacred or profane, ritual or mundane, healthy or unhealthy, natural or artificial (Johnson, *et al,* 2011; Rizq, 2017). Thus, our appetite for and relationship to any aliment can potentially serve as a metaphor for speech, knowledge – divine or earthly – and self- and group-identity.

The psychoanalytic view sharpens the above by stating that all somatic-biological activities, such as ingestion, elimination, sleeping, dreaming and the protective functions of the skin, must develop *psychic correlates that express the archaic functions in narrative-symbolic terms* – fantasies or "proto-beliefs" (Wollheim, 1982, p. 62) – that will eventually become mature object representations. This primal step is crucial in order to enable bodily functions to aspire to and express *desirability* and creative flexibility in their new form as *mental expressions* – such as the relationship between the primitive neuro-auditory "capping" or envelopment function and the more advanced capacity for emotional containment; elementary reflux and vomiting and the psychological mechanism of projection; or early hallucinatory imagery accompanying nursing that eventually matures into the capacity for productive, symbolical dreaming, "filmed" upon the screen-like psychic representation of the breast (Lewin, 1946, 1953; Matte-Blanco, 1941; Ogden, 1997). These mutations all begin with inchoate, enigmatic impressions collated by the budding "ego" and gradually evolve into fully advanced representational states and fantasies (Laplanche, 1995, 1997; Snelling, 2000), enabling these advanced functions to enter the dimension of *mind* and *mindedness.* Absent this, the otherwise smooth, autonomous function of the mind becomes exhaustingly entangled with various unclear psychosomatic messages and disorders, whose functioning has remained too concrete, such as occurs in certain skin conditions, compulsive cutting, eating disorders and so forth (Charles, 2021). My idea is that the *manna* myth houses the story of such transition, from the concrete ingestion of bread toward tolerance of the ambivalent experience of inwardness, and ultimately, the mature symbolization of internalization; a *fantasy correlate* of crucial psycho-somatic struggles on the path toward integration and – from a psychic as well as theological point of view – faith.

The importance of the *manna* story, then, is not simply that it is another cultural legend about "faith being the true food." Somewhat as in Christian belief, *manna* touches upon an uncanny transubstantiation, though not one that results in a permanent mathematical isomorphism between any body and any particular substance.[12] Perhaps it is most useful to state that *manna* is *infrasubstantial* in the sense that it describes a psychic process that takes place *beneath and prior to* the surface of the object world, be that world substantial or illusory. And the structure of the myth itself is required, as we shall further explain, in order to sustain the constant dynamic struggle between the concrete and the symbolic. In fact, several transformations are packed within the lexical envelope of the *manna* narrative that can always deploy to create or deal with conflicts that percolate afresh every time a material brain begins to "starve," "ingest," "digest," "metabolize," and "excrete" in the process of developing a psyche, every time creative regression is required by aesthetic challenges, and every time the overall mental structure is stimulated by something like psychoanalysis.

Myth as an Analytic Tool

No matter what dynamic axes of treatment one views as making psycho-analysis effective, from attunement to transference to empathy, at some point there must take place at the micro-psychic level an *articulation of these dynamics* in the form of words, eventually a story, a narratable fantasy, a myth, often reiterated and refurbished at significant junctures in the analytic processes (Hamburger, 2015; Oliner, 2013; Weisel-Barth, 2021).[13] In many instances, analyst and analysand, wittingly or not, bring in cultural myths and memes that permeate their culture, though they will enlist these materials in accordance with their own psychic needs as well as the contours of the transference-countertransference. The importance of myth is that it already contains key psychic experiences expressed in terms of a "lexical event," a literary capsule (text, dream, art) *that contains within its architecture* – within the interactions between the myth's characters, mise-en-scène and events – pertinent *inner psychological* transformations that have crystalized over time.

Of even greater significance are special myths – Oedipus comes immediately to mind – whose structure is built into the analytic frame, bringing their unique dynamic, and *the way they contain* their dynamic, into the analytic processes. To a certain degree, one goal of psychoanalysis is that the analysand's resident mythic structures engage the mythic interior of the analytic frame, where the two sets may coalesce "quietly" or explode in disharmony. Hence, the unique importance of what we might call *frame myths:* configurations of crucial psychic operations that pertain to the analysand's conflicts, especially the uncanny dreads that take form around variations or disturbances of the analytic setting. Such disturbances would go without notice were it not for the fact that the "material" setting – in and of itself just a mélange of "things" (couch, lighting, tissues, clock, door) – derives its potential significances by virtue of being a simulacrum of certain ultra-structures (Bleger, 1967a,b; Wallon, 1945) embedded within the protective "walls" of the analytic frame.[14] For example, the analyst's or analysand's clock, present or absent, is an expression of the myths of Chronos; the doorway evokes the myths of Hermes, the god of boundaries and thresholds; and so forth. I believe that *manna*, too, is among these primary background "pre-ego safety" firewalls that enable the analytic frame to operate and contain smoothly[15] – it is, I shall show, a very accurate story about the consumption of nourishment, ambivalence toward all "otherness" that enters or exists the body, and the eventual metabolization of aliment, be the latter in the form of words or faith.

Until such time as the human mind can negotiate all the immediate data of experience, our experience must be condensed and synthesized in symbolic form within myth. All myths – whatever their apparent theme – are simultaneously stories about the *incompleteness* of our perception! "It is solely by the agency [of myth] that anything real can become an object of intellectual apprehension, and as such is made visible to the mind" (Cassirer, 1946, p. 8; Neumann, 1954, p. 13). Cassirer argues that logical thought is free to roam, to seek generalization and conceptualization. In contrast, the structure of myth is not free in this sense. Myth strikes us *as such,* for it embodies the phenomenological immediacy and purity of a given wondrous, unfamiliar or uncanny experience, filling our consciousness, overcoming the mind with its immediacy (Cassirer, 1925, 1946, pp. 27–28, 32–35, 70–80).[16] Concurring, Lévi-Strauss (1955, 1984) argued that aside from the *theme* of any myth, one must pay attention to the relationship among the myth's "mythemes," that is, the minimum units or structural building blocks that tend to reappear in all variations of the myth through time, pointing to the invariant human or environmental elements, internal and external, that the myth conveys.[17] And it is precisely for this reason that psychoanalyst Wilfred Bion strenuously advocated the harvesting of myths through which to better understand the therapeutic process (Bion, 1962, 1990).

The Peculiarities of *Manna*

I will now unpack the *manna* myth by highlighting the main textual peculiarities detected by midrashic commentators and how they chose to resolve these oddities, accompanied by brief commentary of my own. There is no special significance to the order of these items. Afterward I will unify these elements to determine just what kind of object is *manna*.

1 God and then Moses identify the freshly fallen *manna* as *le'ḥem* (Exodus 16:4, 8, 12, 16), although *le'ḥem* in Hebrew is not defined solely as "bread," connoting all forms of nourishment or sustenance (cf. Leviticus 3:1, Jeremiah 11:19; see Ibn Ezra, *ad* loc). Later references to *manna* as "wheat [*de'gan*] from heaven; bread of angels [*le'ḥem a'bi'rim*] ... provender He sent them" (Psalms 78:24–25) are purely metaphoric. Indeed, note that the Israelites *did* have something to eat throughout their travels (cf. Exodus

12:38, Numbers 31:1–4), suggesting that their complaint was largely based on anxiety, *dreading* loss while expressing the wish *to lack for nothing*. *Manna* refers, then, to any necessary nourishment, even symbolic; a psychological "gift," like the analyst's "milk," that provides a unique sense of time and space, sustained empathy, the containment of barrages of projection, the willingness to tolerate and explore countertransference.

2 In his final address to the tribes of Israel, Moses emphasizes that *manna* was a singular phenomenon, "which you knew not, neither did your fathers know" (Deuteronomy 8:3). Yet, the commentators noted a pleonasm: if the Israelites knew not of this creation, certainly their fathers did not! The Talmud replies that the "cakes of *ma'ẓah* [bread]" which the liberated Hebrews hurriedly prepared as they left Egypt (Exodus 12:39) already had the taste of *manna* (T., *Kiddushin* 38a). The idea is augmented in T. *Pir'kei A'vot* (5:6), where *manna* is listed among the ten mysterious entities "created just before the first Sabbath" as part of the original cosmic frame, somewhat like Platonic forms. However ingenious this solution, we can sense the intuition that *manna* might be a nonsemantic preconcept (Bion, 1957, 1959, 1962), always exerting transitional dispositions that straddle primitive perceptual experience and higher mentation. Bion's domain of preconcepts includes many elements he viewed as *a priori* components of the analytic frame. Neither Bion nor I imply that the literary stories of Oedipus and Exodus 16 *as such* are prewired deep within the mind; rather, their latent schematic or algorithm are inherent, unconscious psychic constituents, vibrating rhymically and silently within the transitional zone contained by myth and by the analytic frame, unless evoked. Such evocations, however, are the lifeblood of the therapeutic process!

3 *Manna* bore several distinct aesthetic qualities: preceded by a gossamer layer of dew (*shikh'vat tal*), then covered by an additional layer, so that the *manna* lay protected within this envelope or packet (*ha'fi'sah;* in Greek: *deluskema* [Rashi based on T. *Yoma* 75b]). Once the upper layer evaporated, a "fine, flake-like substance (*dak m'ḥus'pas*)"[18] was exposed, "as fine as the hoarfrost on the ground ... like coriander seed, [and] white" (Exodus 16:14, 31), "like wafers made with honey" (Exodus 16:31). Later (Numbers 11:8), *manna* is described as having the color of bdellium, flavored of "fresh [moist, fatty] oil [*le'shad ha-sha'men*]." The text even troubles to record that *manna*, though needing no preparation before consumption, could be "ground in mills, or beat in a mortar, and baked in pans, and made cakes of it" (Numbers 10:8). Why this exceptional aesthetic descriptiveness?

4 We noted that *manna* tasted of "fresh [moist, fatty] oil." The Hebrew term לְשַׁד *le'shad* (or *le'shed* לְשֶׁד) contains the two-letter root word *shad* שַׁד or "breast." This homophony evoked perhaps the most important embellishment to this myth (T. *Yoma* 75a): "Rabbi A'ba'hu taught – as the

breast enables the infant to taste the foods that the mother eats, so, too, was the case with *man.* Other [rabbis] taught – *le'shad* refers to the breast itself; as the breast conforms to many textures [*ge'va'nim*], so, too, did the *man* conform to many textures." Another midrashic source (*Tosefta, Sotah* 4:1; *Sifri, Numbers* 11:8) attributes four elements (my paraphrase): "As the breast … *manna* was essential and everything else secondary; as the breast … even if one consumed *manna* all day, the *manna* was unchanged; as the breast … though *manna* [itself] was a single entity, it took the form of any entity the People desired; as the breast … when the People were [eventually] weaned from *manna*, they experienced pain." Another midrashic writer elaborated upon *manna's* versatility: "The Writ [refers to *manna* with] the words 'bread,' 'oil,' and 'honey.' Rabbi Yosi ben Ḥa'nina taught – the youth tasted bread; the elderly, oil; infants, honey. [Another sage took up this passage and asked] Elsewhere the Writ [uses] the words 'bread,' 'cakes,' and 'grounded.' Why different words? [To teach]: the righteous tasted bread [needing no preparation]; the average person, cakes [needing some preparation]; the wicked, [as] grounded [requiring lengthy preparation]" (T. *Yoma* 75a to Exodus 16:4). Finally, the rabbis (T. *Yoma* 75a) opined that *manna* fell at the doorway of the tents of the righteous (Numbers 11:9), farther out in the field for the average person (Exodus 16:4) and at an even farther distance for the wicked (Numbers 11:8). Unequivocally, then, the midrash portrays *manna* as a breast-like object, enabling variable illusory experiences, tightly linked to varying kinds of thresholds, yet not always an "all good" breast.

5 The rabbis addressed several digestive aspects of *manna.* Overall, declared Rabbi Neḥemiah, *manna's* taste conformed to the wishes of the consumer, requiring only that the desired taste *be named* (Mid. *Tehilim Rabba* 23), but Rabbi Aba argued that it was sufficient to *imagine* the desired taste (Mid. *Shemot Rabba* 25:3). Some rabbis held that *manna* would in general adopt the *form* of the desired food, while others argued that the *manna* did not change form, rendering only the *haptic* experience of the desired food (*Emek ha-Neẓiv* to Numbers, chap. 28 citing *Maharsha*). If the consumer imagined no taste, then the *manna* yielded default tastes per age (described above). However, based on the Israelites' disgruntled longing for foods they remembered eating in Egypt (Numbers 11:5; *Sifri*), some rabbis deduced that *manna* would *not* taste of watermelon, onion, squash (or cucumber [Rashi]), garlic and fish since these substances are difficult to digest and untoward for nursing mothers. Other rabbis held that even these tastes could be achieved if so desired, *but* the *manna* would not change its physical form to *become* these foods, the physical form being the cause of untoward effects! Finally, while most exegetes agreed that *manna* did not require preparation, others stated that preparation was necessary because preparation of food is a natural need (*Mekhilta d'Rabi*

Yishmael to Exodus 16:16 [*ish le'fi okh'lo*, "… each man according to his way of eating"]). In sum, imagination and intention were central to a full appreciation of *manna,* in tandem with a powerful projective process. The projection screen would be the breast-*manna.*

Thus, while the concrete myth tells us that *manna* must be consumed, the deeper psychic truth is that nourishment must be internalized and symbolified in order to enable thought. We remain with a question: What is the significance of additional "molding" of the *manna* beyond its super-adequate heavenly form (cf. Warttig-Mattfeld y de la Torre, 2003)? Would it be correct to sense here a precursor of anal sublimation, akin to shaping and sculpting, material or psychic?

6 *Manna* was accompanied by various instructions, including when to collect the fallen bread, what quantity, and how to dispose of it. And no matter how much *manna* one gathered in the field, one would arrive home and find a single *o'mer* in one's basket. Unused *manna* was not to be saved but left outside to evaporate. Yet, it seems contradictory to describe *manna* as a paragon of bounty and kindness (*ḥe'sed*) (Abravanel, *ad loc*) alongside strict limits on the measure and use of *manna.*

7 *Manna* eventually evoked dichotomous tendencies. From the outset, it was characterized as a "test" (Exodus 16:5), and when Moses addresses the People at the edge of the Wilderness (Deuteronomy 8:3), he explicitly emphasizes an element of "affliction" (עינוי *e'nuy*) or intense humbling (ענבה *a'na'vah*) that is intrinsic to the miracle of *manna* – "He humbled you [alt.: He afflicted you], *causing you to hunger,* and fed you with *man* [ויענך וירעבך *va-ya'an'kha va-yar'e've'kha va-ya'a'khil'kha et ha-man*]." Textually, the obvious source of affliction or anxiety was the ordinance that left-over *manna* was to be put outside of the house and not saved (Ibn Ezra, Exodus 16:19). Those who disregarded this rule learned quickly that the *manna* they hoarded rotted, attracted worms and stank. The Talmud records another test of faith: *manna* did not actually fall daily, such that every day generated a renewed sense of crisis (T. *Yoma* 74b, Rashi s.v. *eyn*). Other rabbis traced the "affliction" to the fact that despite *manna's* rainbow of tastes, the substance their eyes beheld did not change appearance (*op cit.*, Rashi s.v. *ey'no*). Indeed, Rabbi Yishmael [var., Reish La'kish] upheld the tradition that, as "perfect" nutriment, *manna* was digested immediately, completely metabolized into the body, and yielded no waste product, but causing many people to consider *manna* both weirdly insubstantial and toxic, bound to result in physical explosion (Rashi).[19] Hence, the murmurers referred to *manna* as "this disgusting bread [*le'ḥem ha-klo'kel*]"[20] (Numbers 21:5; Numbers *Rabba* 21:5; Psalms *Rabba*, 78:4). Neḥamah Leibowitz's (1976, pp. 263–72) summary seems most accurate: daily dependence upon unnatural, unpredictable, super-regulated bread is an affliction. I would redefine this as the painful

but natural developmental tension of establishing object constancy and consistency, overcoming splitting ("all-good" *vs.* "all-bad"), leading toward the more mature capacity to contain ambivalence. But this requires the capacity to embrace the losses that enable symbolization.

8 *Manna* was round "like a coriander seed" (Exodus 16:31), *ke-ze'ra gad.* The midrashic writers flexed the noun *gad* into the infinitive *le-ha'ged* – "to tell" and "to testify" – linking it to the word *ha'ga'dah* (var., *a'ga'dah*): stories, narrations and books. Rabbi Eliezer ha-Moda'i taught, "*Manna* is akin to words of *ha'ga'dah* in that [both] evoke emotion [*mo'she'kh libo shel adam*]" (*Mekhilta*, T. *Yoma* 75a). Rabbi Yishmael, in his *Mekhilta*, expounds upon this theme: "Just as the prophet tells [*ma'gid*] secrets and hidden things, so, too, [could] the *manna*. How so? Say that someone sold a slave to his friend. The latter claimed, 'I bought,' while the former claimed, 'I never sold.' They inquired of Moses. In the morning, if [the slave's] portion of *man* was found in the home of his original master, clearly the slave had been stolen; if the *man* was found in the second claimant's home, clearly the slave had been sold." Following several similar illustrations in this *Mekhilta*, we see again that the archaic, concrete food-mouth-digestion triad is intimately connected with the functions of differentiation, discernment, narration and even trust. The measured portions of "bread" are now clearly revealed to be the metered cadences and structures of speech, even the word of God, but not merely by virtue of some theological jump, *but because ingestion, ambivalence, assimilation, loss and symbolization are in fact the primary stages of language formation and mentation.* This interpretation places the *manna* myth squarely within the integument of the analytic frame.

9 At what point did the *manna* cease to fall? The Bible states (Exodus 16:35) that the miracle of *manna* lasted 40 years, but defines the terminus in apparently contradictory terms: "… until they reached *inhabited* land [*e'reẓ no'sha'vet*], the *manna* they did eat; until they came to the border of Canaan [i.e., the *deserts* of Moab]." Rashi accepts the plain meaning (based on T. *Kiddushin* 38a) – the *manna* indeed ceased when Moses died at the border of Canaan *and* the Israelites stored sufficient reserves to last them until after the first Passover in the inhabited territory of Gilgal. Alternatively, suggests Rabbi Joshua, *manna* continued for another 40 days after crossing the Jordan River, as per Joshua 5:12, and Rabbi Eliezer ha-Moda'i offers a calculation to prove that *manna* continued to fall for 70 days. A final group of rabbis insisted that *manna* continued to be available throughout the entire 14 years of conquest and division of the Land (*Mekhilta* and Mid. *ha-Ga'dol*, Exodus 16:35). Even this view is further qualified to mean that while *manna* was available for those who still required it, most food was now derived through natural agricultural processes. Technicalities aside, it is conspicuous that this debate centers

upon the exit–entry point, against a background of several loses and stages of mourning; the *threshold* of what ought to be a transitional zone between two important time periods, locales, and levels of identity, each laden with its own anxieties. Evidently, the transition was not smooth: for some, *manna* was a quasi-literal "linking object" (Volkan, 1981), inhibiting mourning; for others, a transitional object; for still others, a fully symbolized internal representation.

10 Moses instructed Aaron to place a single *o'mer* of *manna* into an urn (צנצנת [*ẓinẓen'et*]), possibly earthenware or copper but mostly likely glass (from *ẓaẓ* = something that sparkles [*Mekhilta* Exodus 16]), to be stored alongside the Holy Ark as a "memorial throughout the generations" – buttressed by a special commandment (*miẓ'vah*) that the miracle of *manna* be remembered (Exodus 16:33; Rambam, M.T., *Hil. Beit ha-Beḥirah*, 4:1). This act is another aspect of the ideal mourning process, since whatever one contends is contained *within* the mythemes of the *manna* myth, now it is the *manna* itself that is contained, representationally transparent, capable of memorialization.

11 The final quandary in my list might well have been the first, but it will serve to summarize all of the preceding points. Why is the "bread" from heaven referred to as *man* (*manna*) and not simply as *le'ḥem*, as specifically forecast (Exodus 16:12)? Two biblical texts are important here: "And when the Children of Israel saw it, they said to one another 'What is it?' מן הוא [*man who*], for they knew not what it was [*ki lo yad'e'u mah who*]" (Exodus 16:15). Moses responds that this substance *is* the bread that the Lord had promised to provide. As noted above, the intention was not to equate *manna* with material *le'ḥem*. Yet, in Exodus 16:31, after the first Shabbat experience with the double portion of *manna* that had fallen on Friday, we read, "And the House of Israel called the name of it *man*," even though the substance had been named earlier. The varied solutions (see Kasher, 1959, pp. 208–209) depend upon how one interprets the inquiry *man who*, "What is it?" Some hold that the word *man* denotes "to assign a measure," "to apportion" (see Jonah 2:1 and Daniel 1:5 using the verb *va-yi'man*), akin to the Hebrew *ma'ta'nah*, a generic gift (cf. Leviticus 5:29; I Samuel 1:5). In this light, the assembly was reacting to the sudden sight of an alien substance by naming it eponymously, or metonymically, "gift" or "measure" (*Be'khor Shor* to Exodus 16:15; see Haupt, 1922). Another view is that the Israelites surmised that what had fallen was some sort of elementary ingredient, some basic "thing" *from which* they would then need to make bread (Rashi). Alternatively, they misrecognized the substance as a medicinal food known to all desert travelers as *manna*, but *also* as ephemeral, accidental, insufficient. If so, the text would need to be read as follows: "… and they said to one another 'This *looks* like *manna* but *is* it; is that *all* it is?! *Is that* all *there is?!*'" Moses strives to correct this

misunderstanding by saying, "No, this *manna*, if you wish to call it that, is a *complete* portion of nourishment in itself, on all levels; it is *not* the *manna* you recognize from elsewhere" (see Kasher, 1959, p. 109, n. 90; Rabbenu Beḥaya to Exodus 16:15; cf. Ibn Ezra).

Most investigators, however, accept that the word *man* that appears in the Exodus 15:16 fragment ("*man who … ki lo ya'de'u mah who*") is equivalent to the Hebrew interrogative *mah*, "what," indicating wonderment, a total lack of recognition. The Israelites were fundamentally shocked, reacting to a mystery, sputtering "What is it?!" Once these words left their mouths, the cross-over between familiar cognate terms led them to transform their perplexity into sound, simply as *mah* or *man*, "what," *it-food, what-food* or *what-the-hell-is-it-food. Manna as such was* utterly *other.* The abject emptiness, and perhaps despair, crying out through this bewildered nomination is amplified by Barukh Halevi Epstein's observation that the Hebrew interrogative *mah* generally signifies diminution, exclusion, or void (*Tosefot Brakhah*, Deuteronomy 10:12).[21] Only later, after the Israelites' first Shabbat, some of their anxieties quelled, did they formally adopt *man* as a proper noun, symbolizing the intrinsic movement from *what*-ness to a more deeply internalized sense of nourishment.

Manna as Mental Digestion

We see that at least one significance of the *manna* myth derives from its functional and thematic parallels to "mental digestion."

The link between early oral ingestion, identification and the thinking process as a whole was already implicit in Freud's earliest writings. Later, Freud (1895, 1905, 1925, p. 237) understood from infant observation and the study of primitive cultures that objects are "taken into" the mind, especially when the latter is still a "body-ego," by "cannibalizing," "swallowing," or "incorporating" them, where these stimuli then push toward enhanced object-representations and subjective relationships. Freud did not further delineate this process, but Karl Abraham (1927) hypothesized a process of "psychological metabolism" or "psychosexual metabolism" to explain how perceptual input must be repeatedly broken down and transmuted (transubstantiated?) into truly psychic quality. Waelder explained (1933, p. 214; cf. Matte-Blanco, 1941, p. 26), "The whole process is perhaps best compared to the rumination of certain animals. The morsel is too large to be digested at one time and the undigested meal remains in the stomach. It must be chewed again if it is to be digested [...] The pressure of the undigested meal is, so to speak, the passive, id component, and digestion, by the act of chewing the cud, the ego component of the process." The inevitable loss of some raw content is outweighed by the enhanced flexibility and reach of new representations and, eventually, concepts (Compton, 1985).

Later, Alice Bálint described identification as a kind of "mental digestion" that turns previously repellent entities into assimilable ones (1931[1943], p. 98). Bálint then asked, "What happens when this process of 'mental digestion' encounters difficulties?" Her answer is consistent: to the degree that primitive (i.e., non-symbolized) incorporation remains the main way of taking the world in, one could expect to stumble upon a psychic horizon of painful "mental swallowing without digestion" (Perls, 1947), populated by so-called "bizarre objects."

Wilfred Bion also accepted that "The mental component – love, security, anxiety – as distinct from the somatic, requires a process analogous to digestion" (1962, p. 35, 1956, 1990, p. 42; Da Silva, 1990, 1998, p. 199, 2017; Edelman, 1992; Meltzer, 1984, p. 42).[22] Bion added to our developmental theory and clinical interventions by conceiving the process of psychic digestion as one in which what he termed *alpha function* – the capacity to dissolve, configure, imagine and symbolize – assimilates raw sensory, pre-mental experience, referred to as *beta* or *beta elements*, enabling the latter to be dislodged from the realm of the somatic and the chaotic, and be transformed into a psychically malleable form, now known as *alpha elements*. Only *alpha* elements are amenable to further digestion and enrichment through reverie, dreams, myth and art. The *alpha* tendency toward knowability, creative mystic experience and faith – and the capacity to contend with the unthinkable and unknown – should operate continuously both at the conscious and unconscious level, unless pathology impedes the process (López-Corvo, 2003). When it is not possible for *beta* elements to be digested and made into symbols they are experienced as uncanny somatic sensations, atemporal thing-representations, or poorly differentiated hallucinatory apperceptions, or, worse, a pervasive sense of "nameless dread" (Bion, 1962). The immature or regressed mind, with its concrete tendencies, will tend to relieve pain via biological modes, expelling bizarre elements through massive projective identification. Most important clinically, the figures of speech that characterize *alpha*-deprived persons tend to be flatly *nonmetaphorical* (Brown, 2005, 2012), easily split-off into extreme idealizations of "all-bad"/"all-good" variety.

It should now be abundantly clear that the digestive model of mental interiorization, assimilation and excretion (output) is more than a metaphor, though our limited minds require a metaphor, myth, or narrative that can contain these elements, which eventually enables "digestion" to be configured into the deep integument of the analytic frame. I know of no myth of similar complexity and applicability to this task than *manna*.

Interim Integration

These varied but interrelated dimensions support the view that *manna* is a *summum genus*, one of the oldest and mysterious of semi-organized elements of psychic development[23] that cannot be known by the mind initially *since this organization coalesces as the mind is taking form* against the "desert" conditions of unconsciousness, atemporality, boundarylessssness, undifferentiated symmetry and atextuality. There *is* some moment when pre-ego states give way to awareness, though the exact transition tends to be inaccessible to the ego. Only later can such states be representationalized by the mind. *Manna* straddles both poles in the transition, as the rabbinic midrash depicts clearly. The "hyperactivity" of the rabbinic literature reflects the fluid nature of *manna* itself, or changing perceptions at different stages of relationship with *manna,* as well as the changing perspectives of the analytic couple regarding the historicity of events, the "psychological reality" of fantasies, the multiple layers of causality, the progression of symbolization, and the meanings of dreams.

As I noted above, *manna* was never the *sole* food of the Israelites, nor was it intended to last for 40 years, just as the journey from Egypt to the Holy Land was not intended originally to take that long, for reasons that are not germane here. Once extended wanderings became their fate, however, the psychological task was to modulate the preemptory impact of brute hunger, undifferentiated needs and free-floating anxiety with more sophisticated sublimations and greater appreciation of the insatiability of desire, clear but negotiable thresholds, acceptance of the inevitable losses inherent in symbolization, and more resilient forms of internal psychic internalization. Centuries later, the analytic pair endeavor to work with whatever prevents the silent operation of the *manna* process that is already deeply internalized in the walls of the analytic ark. In crisis, the analytic frame beckons: "It is not *bread* [or other entities] that you really need, because you do not lack this. Yet you feel loss; and lost. Perhaps, then, reconsider *manna* – that uncanny 'what,' 'it,' or 'other' substance that supports this very working setting – whose proper digestion can create transitional space where a sheer hole or sense of empty loss once was."

Clinical Material

"Ben," born to an Israeli couple that escaped Europe just before WW II, raised on a nonreligious kibbutz, undertook psychoanalysis with me for about 7 years, conducted in Hebrew, three times a week, reclining. When previous clinical interventions proved unsatisfactory, Ben sought psychoanalysis to cope with a variety of carefully hidden neurotic eating and toilet habits that interfered with his high-tech and very public jet-set lifestyle. While he was neither conspicuously bulimic nor anorectic, he tolerated only three to four kinds of food, mostly nuts and berries, generally uncooked, and necessary vitamins. He loathed any form of bread or milk. He ate whatever came to hand, but was obsessed with the color, odor, and consistency of his bowel movements, striving for absolute constancy, and considered these qualities the basic indicators of his physical and mental health. Despite several accomplishments, Ben felt full of holes, "voided" (*ḥa'lul*) and empty (*reyk*).

At the time that Ben sought analysis, his superiors at work felt that his creative ideas were becoming stale and sparse. He found technical dialogue increasingly boring. At the same time, Ben had become exhausted by, and was exhausting others with nagging, largely unproductive speculations about his elementary level of religious education and faith. He preferred mathematical order and law, not customs, mannerisms, or traditional ideas that he viewed as mere convention, amorphous, "un-filling."

Growing up on his kibbutz was difficult: children lived in a group nursery, with what seemed like "good enough" caring; mothers visited but were encouraged to not offer the breast. His family did not share the ideological passion of the community, so a certain blandness marked family table-talk. He hated the way animal husbandry and agriculture were idealized ("stinking like chickens was a badge of courage!"), food was skimpy and flat, and commodities tightly apportioned, except for members who had "pull." Ben felt that his parents never strived for more, except when it came to pressuring him to excel. He portrayed himself as a form of "kaki" (feces, shit), preferring and even enjoying the childhood term, and revealed a tendency toward intensely embarrassing shame reactions over his own and others' gaffs and errors. Ben often returned to kaki-related topics and self-images, and squirmed on the couch as he spoke, aware but seemingly unable to control this, as if trying to pass a bowel movement or experiencing some rectum-related pain. For the first 3 years of work, Ben related this movement to his being kaki or a rectum.

On several occasions during different phases of the analysis, Ben referred to the Old Testament biblical story of *manna*. What proved most significant was that the manner – or the *measure* – of Ben's appeal to *manna* changed qualitatively over the course of our work in tandem with key internal analytic transformations, particularly his relationship to the setting.

During the first 15 months of meetings, Ben was greatly relieved by his sessions and idealized the worthwhileness of the analysis and the rhythm of my interventions. He commented positively about the qualities of my consulting room, especially the warm lighting, the plentiful books and art, and the garden that he espied through the glass door behind me as he entered the room. Each session began with fresh material; previous sessions seemed not to have occurred. During one of the sessions during the sixth month, Ben entered, sniffing the cooking aromas circulating in the hallway to my clinic, sat silently for a long while, and murmured quietly, "*Manna* from heaven" (*man min ha-sha'ma'yim*). *Manna,* Ben explained, was supposed to be an ideal, safe food. His associations were simple and unreflective, "Every school kid has heard this phrase, no? Something minimal to tide you over, something that smells good, doesn't fill you up too much, *because it doesn't last long!*"

The idealization of my office jarred with his description of his own arid, spartan way of living, aside from business-related equipment and multi-functional gadgets. He considered all other furnishings artificial "excess," though he never criticized my office that way, as he well might have. Over time, it became clear that terms like "excess," "leftovers," and "stuffed," were important leitmotifs, yet his descriptions came across as thing-like and totalistic, as opposed to proper adjectives. I soon found myself atypically unable to imagine the states he described, other than feeling both he and I were being bloated out of the room by his concrete wordiness.

As transference themes began to emerge, Ben became preoccupied with my physical thinness. He wondered whether am I ever "full" after a meal, and soon began to hint that my office might be a bit "too cluttered" (*a'moos*), all of which gradually brought him closer to underlying memories having to do with his parents' furtive eating habits, messy bathroom habits, shameful public showering, and never-ending work schedules bereft of any sort of compliment. He recalled his parents' tendency to save old food and to fret over left-overs – "Why couldn't I enjoy the luxury of throwing out garbage? The house was always too full, where was it all supposed to go?!" Ben said with disgust, "And the bread they saved stank after a while, so, in my mind, we were eating 'kaki.'"

I could no longer ignore the primacy of the themes of the *manna* myth. I interpreted this dimension to Ben, without directly referring to the Bible story, emphasizing his growing awareness that a mature sense of completeness implied "throwing stuff out," some kind of effacement for the sake of increasing psychic space. Ben let out a loud groan, as if he was concretely relieved, and became freer to explore the topics of containment and waste more deeply (new themes having to do with sexual victimization arose at this time, but this direction is not pertinent to my illustration).

Ben soon began coming to sessions just as he was finishing some food morsel, performing a conspicuous mouth-wiping or swallowing ritual while still in the doorway. As Ben reclined and spoke, the sounds of munching and swallowing accompanied his narrative. I had my own silent hypotheses about the enactment of a noisy, conspicuous, and perhaps shameful mode of lusty breast feeding, but I decided to first highlight Ben's need to have a mouthful of food when crossing the threshold to our workplace, somehow framing the experience. We learned that the doorway, and other thresholds such as gradations of light or edges of carpets, were anxiety-provoking for him; growing up, every turn of a corner meant exposure, vulnerability, and shame. Ben gradually understood that eating while betwixt the threshold was like having food in his stomach: food that had already passed into the mouth – the first great anxiety – but was not yet in his intestines where it would become "kaki" and need to be expelled – the second anxiety.

At this juncture, to my surprise, Ben mentioned *manna* again. He remembered hearing from some "overzealous" nursery teacher that the Children of Israel complained about *manna* because it was such an absolutely efficient food – he likened it to astronaut paste or freeze-dried campers' cakes – that it yielded no "kaki," and so they feared they would burst. Ben had always found this idea frightening and could not budge from interpreting it literally since, he reasoned, that is the kind of eating he remembered on the kibbutz. "In their need to have us trained as soon as possible, they would feed us on these wooden highchairs that had a hole on the seat with a potty underneath. These Socialists must have thought this was so damn clever. Disgusting! I remember it; I can *feel* it; I can always feel it. For many of us, the chair did not encourage us to 'do' anything; it made me seal up, because for me this whole process felt as if I was either eating 'kaki' or excreting uneaten food!" Ben squirmed violently as he continued, "The seats were yet another threshold, a signal that it was time to swallow a 'portion' [of food; he used the single word '*ma'nah*'] and turn it magically into a piece of 'kaki.'"

I now felt I could offer more to Ben. I regarded my own surprise at his mention of *manna* as an introjected echo of the Israelites' own surprise and wonderment upon first gazing at the *manna*. I wondered to myself: did they experience the sudden appearance of this unidentified substance as a gift, as something good, a kindness (*he'sed*), or as an intrusive breast, an uncanny meal, not unlike Ben's "overzealous" mother and nursery teacher, obsessed with survival but unable to name their dreads, consuming but unable to express satisfaction in a natural way? At some point I added, "It seems like you felt almost irrelevant to the process of eating and digestion, as if you were some sort of tube, sitting at the edge of a great height, over an abyss, through which food passed unchanged. You gain nothing from it, and so you cramp down tightly on whatever you can."

Ben was visibly moved and took up the interpretation. His squirming ceased, and he soon brought a dream:

> I am somewhere, holding a large burlap or camel-skin bag full of bird seed mixed with bread, and soon I am walking into a large, deserted field, half sand, and half grassy knoll, such as exists now near my home located at the edge of my village. It appeared that I am feeding bits of bread to a flock of pigeons, happily, carefree, but as I reached the end of my supply, the pigeons began to attack me violently.

Among his associations, Ben now felt certain that he had revived elements of the *manna* story: the sand was the desert; the knoll, an oasis; the burlap bag, "some kind of travel bag (*sak*) or container (*mei'khal*) that someone crossing the desert would carry"; the seeds and bread, *manna*. Ben emphasized that in this unidentified wasteland, near a boundary (the edge of his village), his anxiety reached a crescendo, *not primarily for lack of food, but because thresholds are uncanny.* Ben remarked that he must have crushed up a loaf of bread (*ki'kar le'ḥem*)²⁴ in order to provide crumbs. I underscored the interesting term *ki'kar le'ḥem,* and Ben replied "Well, it reminds me of army slang, *ki'kar*, a loaf of stool. This *was* me. This is what bread had come to feel like to me. So, I negated bread and milk" – "Your mother's breast and body," I interjected – "*Quite!* So, when the pigeons saw me as the source of food, like a child sees a mother, maybe they equated me with food, and wanted to eat *me.*"

The next months were difficult. Ben now felt I had rendered him vulnerable by explaining to him what his imaginings meant. Until now, as concrete-like entities or concepts, he could safely control his obsessions, and solve problems mathematically, by measuring amounts of food, "kaki," or other forms of input and output, rather than through creative reverie. He now felt my office was a "mess," a bewildering array of colors, carpets and "bits of paper," "far too more things for me to have to think about, and not the simple tastes that I prefer … also, the [couch] pillow seems each time to need to be molded to my head, so that it would hold *me*, not anyone else. These days I feel I must ignore your tastes and replace these in my mind with my own fantasies of how I would design this room or like it to feel." I pointed out that Ben was indirectly referencing *manna* – he quickly acknowledged that he had *manna* in mind – capable of many tastes but requiring the hard work of imagination to become something desirable, more sumptuous than "astronaut paste." I then pointed out that "molding the pillow" seemed like an anal and breast realization, the depiction of relaxing into something more malleable than his previous experience of food and relationships, and the ability to express a bit of possessiveness and envy in that context. At the doorway leaving, Ben said, "I wonder if anyone ever *played* with *manna?*"

Ben occasionally feared that I would punish him for his anger, for being ungrateful, for getting his "kaki" all over the place, but increasingly these expressions were becoming metaphoric. Now the volume of my room became a theme. In one session, Ben moved his hands in a fulsome gesture of taking in the entire room, as if it could be both an ample breast and one that was too large to handle at once. He commented, "If the *manna* was a breast idea, then it at least allowed for a kind of consensual control, taking in as much as one wants and not having to consume the rest." At some point, I mentioned the notion that the mother must enable her child to experience violent feelings but also to "survive" them, to become an effective container (i.e., Winnicott, 1955, 1965, 1969, 1986). A symbolizing container could sustain the tiny but significant gap between the concrete mouth and lips, *manna,* and the mythic representation of *manna,* generating trust. Toward the beginning of the fourth year of work, Ben shared, "I have begun to feel as if I can 'eat' with my mind and not only by placing something into an opening or relying on my sense of touch or my gut. No food is perfect, no clinical room or container is perfect, but keeping my 'kaki' inside me is also not perfection. My 'kaki' is not me."

Gradually, the *manna* theme became less focal. It was as if "it" had receded into the autonomous zones of the frame. Toward the date of termination, I wondered to myself if Ben would refer to *manna* once more, poised as we were at the cusp of a profound border. He did not. At the same time, in one of the last sessions Ben said, "All of our work has been filling. I will never forget this room; all that it has *and all that it doesn't have.* I am leaving lighter, with *ample supplies* for the long road ahead." For the last phrase, Ben used the expression *zey'dah la-de'rekh,* a metaphor for travel provisions, usually well-wrapped to sustain road conditions. The root verb *zay'id,* "to hunt, to capture," implies goal-directed preparation.[25] Ben was able to transform the dreads and ambivalences that *manna* subsumes – the "kaki" that his one-dimensional version of the myth could not contain, and the imaginative freedom its use required – into a trustworthy form of metaphor, generalizable and suitable as long-term, well-enveloped psychic aliment.

Discussion: "What"-Bread versus Non-Bread?

The combination of ancient text, rabbinic elaboration, and case material convinces me that *manna* reflects the genetic itinerary of the psychotherapeutic process in general, containing a deeper formula than the familiar and certainly crucial nursing-milk-breast-container or skin-oral matrix. I have argued that the myth beautifully figurates the internal schematic known as the "analytic digestive process," from archaic psychic ingestion and metabolization to imaginative presentation to symbolic representation, as well as its effects upon the global quality of mind–body synthesis (Bion, 1962; see Da Silva, 1990; Edwards, 2015). Thus, *manna* is not merely a story about an "alimentary predicament" (Zwart, 2015); it is a story about the "thinking predicament."

I insist that the primary significance of *manna* inheres in what it *is not,* its unnameability, its enigmatic, elusive nature, its temporal vicissitudes, and its hard-to-win transitional qualities. Whether appearing in dream content, literary metaphor, artistic media, or as an explicit or implicit theme during psychotherapy, *manna* highlights the threshold of pre- or proto-verbal development, the enigmas of the primary needs and desires of the oral stage at its overlap with the anal phase, and the symbolizing functions of the formative ego. Gradually, as available myths coalesced in Freud's unconscious as he began to imagine the uniquely psychoanalytic process, *manna* became part of the insulation of the analytic frame. As such, *manna*-work ensconces questions such as to what degree and how the analytic frame satisfies; what aspects of the clinical support system can be presumed and depended upon symbolically; how much ambivalence can it contain; must the analysis satisfy all needs completely or can residual, excess, and even waste be tolerated during the process; how do we identify otherness; must the work be articulated in terms of demands, prompts, questions and answers or can imagination and playful conjecture be enjoyed?

This "bread" urges us to accept that the coordinates where it is presumed to be located – in the body, outside of, or extimate to it – are largely illusional, extensions of imagination. *Manna* seeks to preserve the "it"-quality of thought and language, by reiterating the existential question *man* or *mah who*, "What is it?!," while simultaneously resisting the superficiality of functional or conventional definitions. Ultimately *manna* connotes an uncanny "It," an *x*-factor, *Ça, Das Es* – *ha-stam* (הַסְתָּם) in Hebrew – the domain of the nameless, symmetrical id and unrestrained *jouissance.* As such, *manna* is a "floating signifier," as Lévi-Strauss (1950, pp. 63–64; Mehlman, 1972) famously proposed – an ambiguous term or sign that points to no actual object and has no agreed-upon meaning, *yet which by that very zero-status enables symbolic thought to operate despite the contradictions inherent in all transubstantiations.* In each individual history of ego development, the infant must eventually accept the paradox: "And they called it *man,* for they knew not what it is."

In her profound exposition on the Book of Numbers, Bible scholar Aviva Gottleib Zornberg (2015, pp. xvi–x) appreciates that *manna* is both bread and not-bread, its epistemological status lying somewhere between a thing and a word. This point can be sharpened. More than it is any kind of substance, *manna* is essentially a unit, a measure, an *o'mer*, of uncanniness, enigmatic otherness, that can only be somewhat fathomed by developing imagination, signification and symbolization. Hence, the importance of the biblical "rules" attending the use of *manna.* Following Freud (1919), *manna* is an object that is at once familiar and attractive as well as unfamiliar and ill-fated, but requires some kind of frame in order to benefit from it. *Manna*, and the analytic frame that subsumes it, addresses a *gap or void* that can eventually become *representational space.*

This perspective was anticipated years ago by Rabbi Yehudah Aryeh Leib Alter (1847–1905) of Góra-Kalwaria, Poland. In his commentary to Exodus (*Se'fat Emet*, nos. 662–663), Alter reiterates the Israelites' question (Exodus 16:15), "'What is it?', for they did not know what it is," adding presciently: "[T]he purpose of this 'knowledge' was that we should *not know* [*ki taḥlit ha-ye'de'ah she'lo ney'da*]." Alter, like most religious commentators, goes on to emphasize the importance of implicit faith, but I hear an intuition that the true identity of this uncanny aliment is precisely its *je ne sais quoi,* enigmatic, atemporal, displaceable status. As a floating marker, *manna* creates space for the transition between tasks that are essentially pre-ego in nature, their gradual representation in the form of a myth, and, last but never finally, the potential for loss of the concrete, broadening of lexical-metaphoric boundaries, and enhanced creativity.

The task of *what*-bread or *no*-bread – like the breast – is to be "willing" at the proper time to benevolently absent itself, enabling the conceptualization of the breast- or *manna*-function to replace of the concrete thing (Bion, 1962). Without this, the mind is left with *non*-breast, *non-manna*, which is a sheer hole. In a sense, this requirement was built into the daily appearance and dissipation of *manna*. Once *no*-bread has been internalized, it is no longer a concrete lack, negation, or hole but useable psychic webbing. Thinking is no longer the equivalent of consuming the breast-mother or simply eating *from* the breast. Ingestion and excretion have transcended toward material-free thought and imagination.

What Kind of Object Is *Manna?*

We can readily imagine the initial sighting of *manna* as an encounter with a *"bizarre object,"* a foreign entity (Darling, 2009; Williams, 1997), whose ingestion, at least at first, might have been an exercise in literally controlling the object even as it wreaked havoc inside the infant's body-ego, as opposed to a matter of desire or appetite. Such incorporation cannot salve the inner psychic dilemma, and so repetition sets in, leaving the individual, like my analysand Ben, feeling "too full; dirty inside," stuffed with *le'ḥem ha-klo'kel,* like those Israelites who continued to "belly-ache" over the undigested psychic events taking place around them (Da Silva, 1990). It is no surprise that the unassimilable *beta* bits that the murmuring People ejected – like the bits of bread in Ben's dream – challenged Moses's and God's breast-containing function (see further Numbers 11:11–15; Spero, 2010).

We can also portray *manna* as an *aesthetic object*, as theorized by Donald Meltzer (Harris Williams, 2018; Meltzer & Harris Williams, 1988). The biblical narrative elaborated the aesthetic details of *manna* in order to emphasize this special unconscious dimension of the early skin-mouth-stomach-mind experience, as the newborn attempts to regulate and understand the dazzling, all-inclusive, and even overwhelming experience of mother and breast. The initial encounter with the mother's breast, with the *"shad"*-*manna*, represents the interminable beauty of the world, and puts the newborn in a conflictual situation: the emotions arising from the impact of this beauty also overwhelm and appall him. The first experience of milk, unexpected, soothing and intrusive, is both beautiful and alarming.[26] The essence of what Meltzer called the "aesthetic conflict" is that *there exists no impact of beauty without conflict.* A conflict occurs between beauty that can be perceived and an interior that is not observable, unknown, enigmatic. The existential riddle that the myth of *manna* contains is that the capacity to provoke passion, awe and desire that certain objects possess is matched by the capacity of that very same object to generate alarm, doubt, uncertainty and mistrust. The *manna* myth and the analytic frame ask – *"What is it?!"* "Is the inside of the thing as beautiful as the outside? What is the nature of the Source of this *manna*?" Both myth and frame respond: *"Man who?!"* – despite the rules and limits of the setting, there ultimately is no full answer; *mindedness* requires the capacity to tolerate the question and the questioning.

We can now resolve the apparently paradoxical affliction-kindness dimension of *manna*. First, all the dawns and awakenings that we have described here ultimately aspire to an acceptance of loss and mourning as the condition of mature symbolization. This perforce evokes pain. Struggling with aesthetic conflict is additionally painful. The very struggle with the limits of language and loss that enable meaning is also painful (Ragland, 1995, p. 92). Protomental impressions and later memories of the initial shock of feeling filled by the breast, taking in milk, grieving over its delay or absence and anticipating its return, cause a third kind of pain. With increasing maturation, we learn to search only for replacements of the "lost objects" of early experience, *manna* instead of the specific but limited foods of Egypt. The aboriginal *jouissance* can never to be totally rediscovered because language itself has forever closed off the road back to the original archaic impressions. All we can search for is loss itself, clarify what we really desire, and representationalize aesthetically and verbally the uncanny gaps that remain.

I would also argue that the Israelites – and my patient Ben centuries later – needed to accept that *manna* is what Jacques Lacan conceived of as an object (*a*), or *object petit a* (Glowinski, Mark & Murphy, 2001; Lacan, 1964, 1966). In Lacan's terminology, the (*a*) stands for the French *autre* or "other," and later came to also stand for the Greek concept of "*agalma*," that tantalizing "something," some dazzling "it" that is intended to capture the mind, treasured despite dubious worth, seducing us to feel that this "other" thing or person is actually the true object of our needs and the satisfaction for our desires. As such, object(*a*) signifies a part- or incomplete-object, masked by semblance, something we idolize because it appears to hold the promise of returning to the original *jouissance* lost with the advent of language (Ragland, 1995, pp. 154–55). It signifies the fact that all representations contain a modicum of otherness within them, rendering them alien as well as familiar, even though they manage to create within us the feeling that the other's enjoyment might be an enjoyment that *we* could have if we were to identify with the other, even when this means sacrificing much of our own subjectivity. Relating to the analytic setting, Lacan proposed that the *(a)* or "agalma" is the treasure sought after in analysis, the unconscious "truth" we wish to know and believe to be residing within the analyst. The fact that *manna* was viewed by God and Moses as an object-of-desire – sparkling in the morning dew, protected by various regulations, so easy to grasp, yet so ephemeral to retain and amass – must have made the People desire this mysterious substance, but also caused them to envy it, disparage it and displace their desire from substance to substance. The divine intent was that the use of *manna* be restricted, understood to be a temporary illusion of surplus. Ben, as well, had long lived with the conflict of having to experience himself as a self-sufficient yet disgusting substitute for the very "bread" he both hated and desired, and gradually changed his experience as he brought his *manna*-transference into the analytic room, transubstantiating his concrete "kaki"-bodyself into a fantasy and symbol of what he himself desired and could achieve through symbols.

On a final clinical note, it is clear that my and Ben's mutual "play" with *manna* transformed it into an *analytic object* (Ogden, 1994, 1997), that unique constituent of the "third" intrapsychic and intersubjective dimension, unique to the analytic relationship between myself and this analysand. As Ben began to "mold" the pillow of the couch, as we turned "kaki" into something more akin to clay, he assumed more of his own agency, and was thereby able to create more distance between himself and the overly exciting but overly enslaving concrete *manna* (see March, 2019). Transitional objects must be created by the child. Psychoanalysis by definition strives to create the lacking mental containers, through the struggle with transference, that create enhanced psychic space and *enable* true transitionality at the edge of new domains. Slowly, Ben and I began to transform our own inner dimensions, to risk loss, and to sculpt old/new *manna*. Following that, the *manna* myth could slip quietly back into its dormant place within the frame – the glass urn resting in sacred space – awaiting the next analytic sojourner.

Notes

1 James Strachey's translation is a perfectly sensible embellishment of Freud's own words, "Es wird niemand erwarten dürfen, daß ihm die Deutung seiner Träume mühelos in den Schoß falle" (G. W., vol. 2, p. 526). The words "…mühelos in den Schoß falle" translate simply as "easily fall into one's lap," and make no direct reference to the biblical metaphor. Earlier however, in a letter dated August 2, 1873 to his close friend Eduard Silberstein (Freud, 1871–1881, p. 28), Freud appeals to the *manna* metaphor by name.
2 The biblical term *manna* is often mistaken for an English transliteration. In fact, the only term we encounter throughout the biblical texts (Ex. 16:15; Deut. 8:16) is מָן, *man*, a single-syllable word, pronounced *màn*, the "a" sounding like the "o" in the word "ouch" or the "a" in "father." *Man* was translated into Syrian-Aramaic by both classical *targumim*, Onkelos (35–120 CE) and Yonatan ben Uziel of the Talmudic period as מַנָּה, *manna*, pronounced *màn·na*, /ˈmànə/ in the Masoretic vowel system (and in Greek, μάννα) (see *Anchor Yale Bible, Exodus,* 1964; Ben Yehuda, 1955, p. 3075; Brown, Driver & Briggs, 1906, p. 577).
3 The relationship between psychoanalytic, midrashic and talmudic modes of hermeneutics, and their parallel "traditions of inquiry," has a profound and intricate history, reconsidered not long ago by the late Aron Lewis (2007) and in the numerous essays collected by Lewis and Henik (2010, 2015).
4 The *manna* is also mentioned in Psalms 78:24 and Neḥemiah 9:20 (*u-man'kha,* "… and your *manna*").
5 To ensure that my ideas were not anticipated by other researchers, I studied Black & Rowley (1962, pp. 244–245); Bodenheimer (1947, 1956, pp. 297–302); Hecker (2005); Knapp (1995); Malina (1968); Merkur (2000); Ron (2010); Wotton (2010) and many others (a complete survey is available from the author). All attempts to identify *manna* as a specific natural substance are obliged to match all the characteristics in the biblical text (light as snow, melting in the sun and disappearing by sundown, falling ["raining"] each day, etc.), and this has yet to be achieved.

For example, McKenna (1993) identifies *manna* as the *psilocybe cubensis* mushroom, disregarding the fact that very few mushrooms grow in arid desert areas. Bodenheimer (1947), Donkin (1980) and others believed that *manna* is *lecanora esculenta*, a lichen that does appear in large quantities during rainy years in central Asia, blown by the winds to the Asian steppes, yet such a phenomenon has not been recorded in the region of the Sinai, and there is no similarity between this brand of lichen and the biblical descriptions of *manna*.

6 The ancient biblical measurement of one *o'mer* (עומר) is a unit of volume for grains and dry commodities (Exodus 16:36). In traditional Jewish standards of measurement, 1 *o'mer* has the weight of 43.2 eggs, the equivalent of 1.560 kg. to 1.770 kg., 3.3 to 3.7 pounds. The text evidently considered this amount sufficient for each individual per day (see Danby, 1977, Appendix II, p. 798).

7 Despite the seductive phonetic homonymy, biblical *manna* must not be confused with the similar sounding word "mana," common in anthropological research (Kolshus, 2016; Meylan, 2017). "Mana" is a Polynesian, Melanesian and Austronesian term that refers to a wide variety of spiritual energies or forces pertaining to the cosmic and individual creative endowments of all things – power, authority, ownership, prestige, status, influence, dignity, respect derived from the gods or nature – that can be earned, lost and transmitted. The term was adopted in 1891 in order to describe the "minimum base of religious experience and ritual," a bedrock mental attitude, pre-animistic, deeper than any specific beliefs in specific spiritual beings (see Blust, 2007, 2016). Cassirer (1925, pp. 76–78) and Lévi-Strauss (1950) strove to disconnect "mana" from any spiritual context, viewing it as indicating nothing more than a natural reaction to any startling, uncanny, amazing, wonderous, unexplained phenomenon. As well, Carl Gustav Jung's notion of the "mana personality" (Jung, 1953; Sorge, 2020) – a gifted, charismatic, potentially narcissistic psychological expression of deeper archetypes – draws from this oceanic concept and not the biblical one.

8 Bergler writes (1934, p. 347 [my translation – MHS]). "[I have in mind] people who have a very loose relationship with food and who acknowledge any disappointment [in life] with loss of appetite, which they often use aggressively against the environment; or types who answer the withdrawal of the mother's breast with an eternal, always unsuccessful search for it ... In dreams of orally fixated or re-gressed patients, one often finds the so-called 'Manna type.'"

9 In a fascinating analysis of an orthodox rabbi's wife, Lubin (1958) writes at one point: "[The analyst] was treated with a blind faith; each statement was regarded as manna from Heaven. [The patient] would exclaim, 'You read my mind!' and 'How do you do it!'" Allusions such as this, made by the analyst, do not advance our knowledge.

10 Islamic tradition accepted the miraculous character of *manna* while at the same time identifying the substance among earthly constituents (Abdul Wadud, 2009). By comparison, no ancient or classical-medieval Judaic commentator ever pursued the exact identity of *manna*, likely in view of Deuteronomy 8:3. Shemesh (2021) explicates the acrimonious debate between the Spanish Jewish linguist and com-mentator Abraham Ibn Ezra (1090–1164) and Persian Bible critic Ḥiwi al-Balkhi (*ca* 9th CENT) who insisted that biblical *manna* is the Persian *taranjebin* (*tar-anjabin*; "wet honey" or "honeydew") in the effort to prove that this nourishment was not miraculous. As Ibn Ezra demurs, *taranjabin* fails to meet most of the "criteria" of the biblical description.

11 Also consider the expression in the fourth petition of the Lord's Prayer, "Give us this day our daily bread" (Matthew 6:11; Luke 11:3), which is a clear hint to *manna*, though the word is not explicitly used. The Latin translation refers simply to "bread," *Panem nostrum quotidianum*, though the earlier Greek allows for a

broader translation, "our daily needs." In the Vulgate, St Jerome translates *panem* directly into the earlier Greek ἐπιούσιον (*epiousion*), "supersubstantial" bread, emphasizing its dual identity, rooted in the biblical *manna* and perpetuated by the Eucharist.

12 For example, the psychologist as well as the theologian would need to query whether a change of the kind referred to by Jesus (*manna* into body) is intended to be understood as a literal *consubstantiation* (i.e., two entities coexisting in a single [apparent] space and time – or a *signification*, in which case the two entities may *overlap*, though not be mathematically identical. And if an immediate consubstantiation cannot be upheld, is this theologically problematic for some interpreters? One could adopt the position that the bread = body transformation *is* a metaphor, yet a very *special kind of metaphor*, one that, in a *non*-psychotic world, gives reality, force, depth and timelessness to the equation implied (see Macy, 1999; Need, 2002). On the other hand, if one holds that – however mysteriously – the bread of the Host takes the form of Jesus's body within the body of the individual at one and the same time, the epistemological task is much more difficult.

13 Even in very disturbed personalities, various nonsemantic and proto-conceptual strains borrow from mature propositional and conceptual elements such as myth and "hang on" to them, as it were, thereby attaining expressability (Gunther, 2003, Matte-Blanco, 1975, pp. 244–50; Stern, 1997).

14 It is for this reason that the "narrative envelope" (Mandler, 1983; Stern, 1993) that contains the kernel of the myth, and the changing qualities of the envelope, are of great significance during the analytic process.

15 See Grotstein's (1980, 1991) important contribution regarding the "background presences of primary identification," which I believe are part and parcel of the analytic frame, but cannot be used by patients who have developmental conflicts, flaws or depletions in this domain. *Manna* is one of the representations that contribute to this background presence, including the *symbolized* ambivalences that are inherent in the *manna* myth.

16 Thus, while many authors identify *manna* with a variety of psychedelic substances (McKenna, 1993; Merkur, 2000) that might have provided some of the disposition to sustain, or imagine, the numerous phantasmagorical stories of the Bible, they overlook the capacity of mythic astonishment alone to generate altered states of consciousness.

17 Lévi-Strauss stated explicitly (1955, pp. 216–217) that a myth includes all its major variations, for these variants represent the impact of the core myth upon whoever felt the need to modify it, and they are no less authentic. Myths grow, to be sure, but in tune with a much less continuous inner structure, until such time as the psychological or cultural dilemma or riddle the myth was intended to address ceases to emit energy or impulse. See also Poole (1986).

18 The word *me'ḥus'pas* מחוספס is a hapex legomenon and has exercised Hebrew linguists. The word bears an antithetical meaning, always significant from the standpoint of psychoanalysis (Freud, 1910) – the rare quadrilateral root of the word spans the definitions "covered," "uncovered," "open like a satchel" [Rashi], "to wrap," "to reveal" (see Cassuto, 1967, pp. 187–199). Such duality would add to the uncanny quality of the *manna*-envelope.

19 As stated, the assumption behind the textual complaint and the classic interpretations of it is that it is abnormal ("not good") to not be able to experience normal bodily motion from ingestion to elimination. I will interpret this in my own way in this essay. On a private occasion (May 26, 2022), I discussed this aspect of my essay with Rabbi Joseph Polak, a child survivor of Bergen-Belsen, scholar and author of *After the Holocaust the Bell Still Rings* (2015). Polak associated to Terrence Des Pres's (1976, pp. 51–80) awful yet crucial notion of "excremental

assault," referring to the systematic mechanism by which inmates of the concentration camp were very quickly immobilized, primitivized and ultimately – with few exceptions – sapped of any basic semblance of humanity. Specifically, De Pres underscores the Nazi mode of disallowing normal exercise of bowel functions, hygiene and modesty, to the degree that the camps were, around the clock, at work and at rest, a hellish swamp of toxic sewage and excrement, resulting in chronic variations of diarrhea, dysentery and typhus, and constant filthiness. Ultimately, this excremental existence assaulted the entire sensory apparatus and the mind itself. One of the few ways to counter this draconian debasement, if one could, was to maintain some ritual of cleanliness, no matter how minimal, pitiful (using one's own soup bowl as a toilet and one's single piece of clothing as wiping paper) and Sisyphean. Polak then reconsidered the midrashic commentary in light of the fact that if one contemplates an enormous group of people living in relatively close quarters needing to contend with hygienic disposal in a desert – sometimes encamped for long periods and sometimes for days – then perhaps the absolute digestibility of the *manna* was indeed a benevolent ergonomic quality. The complainers obviously saw things otherwise. In their favor, I would add that the only thing that the body is able to totally absorb is sugar, which is turned into energy or stored as fat. But eating pure sugar, unless one conscientiously maintained a very rigorous regimen, would result in chronic diarrhea; as well, the eliminative system must rid the body of bacteria and dead cells. Thus, a total excremental hiatus would easily be alarming, not to say life-threatening, in more senses than one. However, I wish to return to my approach, which treats the mytheme of zero-eliminative behavior as symbolizing an immature wish for total retention.

20 The key Hebrew term *klo'kel* קְלוֹקֵל has been translated differently by translators and rabbinic commentaries, including: "horrible," "dry," "contemptible," "worthless," "wretched," "miserable," and "light" (Malbim, from the word *kal*) or "insubstantial."

21 E.g., Genesis 23:15, 37:10; Exodus 16:7; Psalms 30:10; 1 Kings 9:13; Ecclesiastes 1:3.

22 The earliest modern reference to "the unconscious processes of digestion and assimilation" is the work of the great German metaphysician and philosopher, Eduard von Hartmann (1868 [1931]). His text was a classic by the time Freud was beginning to do his own psychoanalytic thinking, yet although Freud refers to von Hartmann's work in the Dream book, he does not refer to van Hartmann's digestion model.

23 True or complete organization would require more advanced symbolization and integration, cognitively and affectively, so I use the preface "semi" to keep my description modest.

24 The root *k'k'r* כִּכַּר, Akkadian in source, means "round," and can refer to loaves of bread (Exodus 29:23, Judges 8:5, 1 Samuel 10:3, Jeremiah 37:21), a wheel, wild dancing (*le-kar'ker*), or a round block of territory (Genesis 13:11–12, Exodus 36:24).

25 Genesis 27:3, 42:25, 45:21; Joshua 1:11, 9:11; Proverbs 12:27. Most supportive of this crossover is Psalms 78:25 that states poetically, "The bread of angels [*le'ḥem abi'rim a'khal*], you did eat; provisions he sent them for their satisfaction [*ẕey'dah sha'laḥh la'hem la-so'va*]." The "bread of angels" alludes explicitly to *manna*.

26 Van de Vijver, Bazan and Detandt (2017, pp. 27–28) offer a keen description of this combination of joy and shock during sucking. Importantly, they note: "Again, what drives the child to act and repeat its actions is not the possibility of relief alone; it is the attempt to grasp what initially escaped, namely the surprising event. And in this grasping attempt, the other, as a speaking being, is once more an ineliminable factor."

References

Abdul Wadud, P.K., Subhaktha, J.P., Saketh Ram, T., & Narayana, A. (2009). Manna: A holistic substance and a drug. *Journal of Indian Medicine Heritage*, 39:153–170.

Abraham, K. (1927). A short study of the development of the libido. In *Selected Papers of Karl Abraham, M.D.* ed. E. Jones, trans. D. Bryan & A. Strachey. London: Hogarth/The Institute of Psychoanalysis/Routledge, 1979, pp. 418–480.

Anchor Yale Bible (1964). ed.D.N. Freedman. New Haven: CT: Yale University Press, 2008.

Aron, L. (2007) "Black fire on white fire, resting on the knee of the Holy and Blessed One:" Discussion of Philip Cushman's "A burning world, an absent God: Midrash, hermeneutics, and relational psychoanalysis. *Contemporary Psychoanalysis*, 43:89–111.

Bálint, A. (1931 [1943]). Identification. In *A Gyermekszoba Pszichologiája* [*The Psychology of the Nursery*], chap. IV. Republished in the *International Journal of Psycho-Analysis*, 24:97–107.

Ben Yehuda, E. (1955). *The Complete Dictionary and Thesaurus of Ancient and Modern Hebrew*. London: Yoseloff.

Bergler, E. (1934). Zur problematik des 'oralen' pessimisten: Demonstriert an Christian Dietrich Grabbe. *Imago*, 20:330–376.

Bergler, E. (1941). A new approach to the therapy of erythrophobia. *Psychoanalytic Quarterly*, 13:43–59.

Bevins, J. (2008). Some comparative notes on proto-Oceanic mana: Inside and outside the Austronesian family. *Oceanic Linguistics*, 47:253–274.

Bion W.R. (1957). Differentiation of the psychotic from the non-psychotic personalities. In: *Second Thoughts: Selected Papers on Psychoanalysis*. London: Heinemann, 1967, pp. 43–64.

Bion, W.R. (1959). Attacks on linking, In *Melanie Klein Today: Developments in Theory and Practice. Volume 1: Mainly Theory*. ed. E. Bott Spillius. London: Routledge, 1988, pp.87–101.

Bion, W.R. (1962). *Learning from Experience*. London: Tavistock/Maresfield.

Bion, W.R. (1990). *Cogitations*. ed. F. Bion. London: Karnac.

Black, M. & Rowley, H.H., eds. (1962). *Peake's Commentary on the Bible*. London: T. Nelson.

Bleger, J. (1967a). *Symbiosis and Ambiguity: A Psychoanalytic Study*. eds. J. Churcher & L. Bleger. London: Routledge, 2013.

Bleger, J. (1967b). Psycho-analysis of the psycho-analytic frame. *International Journal of Psychoanalysis* 48:511–519.

Blust, R.A. (2007). Proto-Oceanic 'mana' revisited. *Oceanic Linguistics*, 46:404–423.

Blust, R.A. (2016). *History of the Austronesian Languages*. Manoa: University of Hawaii.

Bodenheimer, F.S. (1956). *ha-Ḥai be-Arẓot ha-Mikra*, Vol. 2. Jerusalem: Publisher, pp. 297–302.

Bodenheimer, F.S. (1947). The manna of Sinai. *Biblical Archeologist*, 10:1–6. Reprinted in eds. Wright, G. E. & Freedman, D. N. *The Biblical Archaeologist Reader*. Chicago: Quadrangle, 1961, pp. 52–65.

Brown, F., & Driver, S.R. & Briggs, C.A. (1906). *The Brown-Driver-Briggs Hebrew and English Lexicon*. Boston: Houghton-Mifflin, 1960.

Brown, L.J. (2005). The cognitive effects of trauma: Reversal of alpha function and the formation of a beta screen. *Psychoanalytic Quarterly*, 74:397–420.

Brown, L.J. (2012). Bion's discovery of alpha function: Thinking under fire on the battlefield and in the consulting room. *International Journal of Psychoanalysis*, 93:1191–1214.

Cassirer, E. (1925). *The Philosophy of Symbolic Forms. Vol. 3. Mythical Thought.* trans. R. Manheim. Yale: Yale University Press, 1955.

Cassirer, E. (1946). *Language and Myth.* trans. S. Langer. New York: Dover, 1953.

Cassuto, U. (1967). *A Commentary on the Book of Exodus,* trans. I. Abrahams. Jerusalem: Magnes.

Charles, M. (2021). Meaning, metaphor, and metabolization: The case of eating disorders. *American Journal of Psychoanalysis*, 81:444–466.

Compton, A. (1985). The concept of identification in the work of Freud, Ferenczi and Abraham: A review and comment. *Psychoanalytic Quarterly*, 54: 200–233.

Da Silva, G. (1990). Borborygmi as markers of psychic work during the analytic session: A contribution to Freud's 'Experience of satisfaction' and to Bion's idea about the digestive model for the thinking apparatus. *International Journal of Psychoanalysis*, 71:641–659.

Da Silva, G. (1998). The emergence of thinking: Bion as a link between Freud and the neurosciences. In *Psychoanalysis and the Zest for Living*, ed. M. Grignon. Bingham, NY: ESF Publications, pp. 195–210.

Da Silva, D.L. (2017). Bion, Britton, and the neo-Kleinian model of the mind: A dialectical critique. *Canadian Journal of Psychoanalysis*, 25:158–171.

Danby, H. ed. (1977). *The Mishnah.* Oxford: Oxford University Press.

Darling, L. (2009). A case of body image and eating difficulty. *Psychoanalytic Psychotherapy*, 23:61–77.

Des Pres, T. (1976). *The Survivor: An Anatomy of Life in the Death Camps.* New York: Oxford University Press.

Donkin, R.A. (1980). *Manna: A Historical Geography.* Dordrecht: Springer.

Dostoyevsky, F. (1846). *The Double: Two Versions.* trans. E. Hardin. New York: Ardis, 2004.

Edwards, J. (2015). Teaching, learning and Bion's model of digestion. *British Journal of Psychotherapy*, 31:376–389.

Edelman, G. N. (1992). *Bright Air, Brilliant Fire: On the Matter of Mind.* New York: Basic.

Freedman, N., Geller, J.D., Hoffenberg, J., Hurvich, M. & Ward, R. (2011). *Another Kind of Evidence: Studies on Internalization, Annihilation Anxiety, and Progressive Symbolization in the Psychoanalytic Process.* London: Routledge.

Freud, S. (1871-1881). *The Letters of Sigmund Freud to Eduard Silberstein 1871–1881.* ed.W. Boehlich, trans. A. Pomerans. Cambridge, Mass: Belknap/Harvard University Press, 1990.

Freud. (1895 [1950]). Project for a scientific psychology. In *S. E.*, IV:281–397.

Freud, S. (1900). *The Interpretation of Dreams.* In *S. E.*, Vol V:339-751.

Freud, S. (1905). *Three Essays on Sexuality.* In *S. E.*, VII:123–244.

Freud, S. (1910). On the antithetical meaning of primal words. In *S. E.*, XI:155–161.

Freud, S. (1911). Formulations on the two principles of mental functioning. In *S. E.*, XII:215–226.

Freud, S. (1913 [1912–1913]). *Totem and Taboo: Some Points of Agreement Between the Mental Lives of Savages and Neurotics.* In *S. E.*, XIII:vii–162.

Freud, S. (1919). The 'Uncanny.' In *S. E.*, XVII:217–256.

Freud, S. (1923). *The Ego and the Id.* In *S. E.*, XIX:1–64.

Freud, S. (1925). Negation. In *S. E.*, XIX, 235–242.

Freud, S. (1936). A disturbance of memory on the acropolis. In *S. E.*, XII:237–248.

Glowinski, H., Marks, Z., & Murphy, S. eds. (2001). *A Compendium of Lacanian Terms.* London: Free Association Press.

Grotstein, J.S. (1980). A proposed revision of the psychoanalytic concept of primitive mental states – Part I. Introduction to a newer psychoanalytic metapsychology. *Contemporary Psychoanalysis*, 16:479–546.

Grotstein, J.S. (1991). Nothingness, meaninglessness, chaos, and the "black hole" III – Self- and interactional regulation and the background presence of primary identification. *Contemporary Psychoanalysis*, 27:1–33.

Gunther, Y. (ed) (2003). *Essays on Nonconceptual Content.* Cambridge, MA: MIT Press.

Hamburger, A. (2015). Refracted attunement, affective resonance: Scenic-narrative microanalysis of entangled presence in a Holocaust survivor's testimony. *Contemporary Psychoanalysis*, 51:239–257.

Harris Williams, M. ed. (2018). *Aesthetic Conflict and its Clinical Relevance.* London: Karnac.

Hartmann, K. R. E. von. (1868 [1931]). *Philosophy of the Unconscious.* trans. W.C. Coupland. London: Routledge, 2014.

Haupt, P. (1922). Manna, nectar and ambrosia. *Proceedings of the American Philosophical Society*, 61:227–236.

Hecker, J. (2005). *Mystical Bodies, Mystical Meals: Eating and Embodiment in Medieval Kabbalah.* Detroit, MI: Wayne State University Press.

Johnson, K., White, A., Boyd, B., & Cohen, A. (2011). Matzah, meat, milk, and mana: Psychological influences on religio-cultural food practices. *Journal of Cross-cultural Psychology*, 42:1421–1436.

JPS Torah Commentary: Numbers. (1990). ed. J. Milgrom, Philadelphia: Jewish Publication Society.

Jung, C.G. (1953). Two essays on analytical psychology: The relations between the ego and the unconscious – the mana personality. In: *Collected Works of Carl Gustav Jung.* Vol. VII, Princeton: Princeton University Press, 1967, pp. 227–244.

Kasher, M.M. (1959). *Ḥu'mash To'rah She'lei'mah*, Vol. 14. Jerusalem: Bet Torah Sheleimah, 1991.

Knapp, B. (1995). *Manna & Mystery: A Jungian Approach to Hebrew Myth and Legend.* Asherville, NC: Chiron.

Kolshus, T. (2016). Mana on the move: Why empirical anchorage trumps philosophical Drift. In eds. M. Tomlinson, M. & P. K., *New Mana: Transformations of a Classic Concept in Pacific Languages and Cultures.* Canberra: Australian National University Press, pp. 155–182.

Lacan, J. (1964). *Seminar XI: The Four Fundamental Concepts of Psychoanalysis.* trans. A. Sheridan. London: Norton, 1979.

Lacan, J. (1966). *Écrits.* trans. B. Fink, H. Fink & R. Grigg. New York: W.W. Norton, 2006.

Laplanche, J. (1995). Seduction, persecution, revelation. *International Journal of Psychoanalysis*, 76:663–682.

Laplanche, J. (1997). The theory of seduction and the problem of the other. *International Journal of Psychoanalysis*, 78:653–666.

Leibowitz, N. (1976). *Studies in Shemot: Part I: Shemot-Yitro.* trans. A. Newman. Jerusalem: World Zionist Organization.

Lévi-Strauss, C. (1950). *Introduction to the Work of Marcel Mauss.* trans. F. Baker. London: Routledge, 2007.

Lévi-Strauss, C. (1955). The structural study of myth, In *Structural Anthropology*, trans. C. Jacobson & B. Grundfest-Schoepf. Middlesex: Penguin, 1963, pp. 206–231.

Lévi-Strauss, C. (1984). *Anthropology and Myth.* trans. R. Willis. Oxford: Blackwell, 1987.

Lewin, B.D. (1946). Sleep, the mouth, and the dream screen. *Psychoanalytic Quarterly*, 15:419–434.

Lewin, B.D. (1953). Reconsideration of the dream screen. *Psychoanalytic Quarterly*, 22:174–199.

Lewis, A. & Henik, L. eds. (2010). *Answering a Question with a Question: Contemporary Psychoanalysis and Jewish Thought.* Vol. I. Boston: Academic Studies Press.

Lewis, A. & Henik, L. eds. (2015). *Answering a Question with a Question: Contemporary Psychoanalysis and Jewish Thought.* Vol. II. *A Tradition of Inquiry.* Boston: Academic Studies Press.

López-Corvo, E.R. (2003). *The Dictionary of the Work of Wilfred R. Bion.* London: Karnac.

Lubin, A.J. (1958). A feminine Moses: A bridge between childhood identifications and adult identity. *International Journal of Psychoanalysis*, 39:535–546.

Macy, G. (1999). The dogma of transubstantiation in the Middle Ages. In: *Treasures from the Medieval Storeroom: Medieval Religion and the Eucharist.* ed. G. Macy. Collegeville, MN: Liturgical Press, pp. 81–120.

Malina, B.J. (1968). *The Palestinian Manna Tradition: The Manna Tradition in the Palestinian Targums and its Relationship to the New Testament Writings.* Leiden: Brill,

Mandler, J.M. (1983). Representation in cognitive development, In: *Handbook of Child Psychology, Vol. 3: Cognitive Development.* eds. J.H. Flavell & E. Markman. New York: Academic Press, pp. 420–494.

March, P.L. (2019). Playing with clay and the uncertainty of agency: A Material Engagement Theory perspective. *Phenomenology and the Cognitive Sciences*, 18:133–151.

Matte-Blanco, I. (1941). On introjection and the processes of psychic metabolism. *International Journal of Psychoanalysis*, 22:17–36.

Matte-Blanco, I. (1975). *The Unconscious as Infinite Sets: An Essay in Bi-Logic.* London: Maresfield.

McKenna, T. (1993). *Food of the Gods: The Search for the Original Tree of Knowledge, A Radical History of Plants, Drugs, and Human Evolution.* New York: Bantam.

Mehlman, J. (1972). The "floating signifier": From Lévi-Strauss to Lacan. *Yale French Studies*, 48:10–37.

Meltzer, D. (1984). *Dream Life: A Re-Examination of Psychoanalytic Theory and Technique.* Perthshire, Clunie Press.

Meltzer, D. & Harris Williams, M. (1988). *The Apprehension of Beauty: The Role of Aesthetic Conflict in Development, Art and Violence.* London: Karnac.

Merkur, D. (2000). *The Mystery of Manna: The Psychedelic Sacrament of the Bible.* Rochester, NY: Park Street Press.

Meylan, N. (2017). *Mana: A History of a Western Concept.* London: Brill.

Need, S.W. (2002). Jesus the bread of God: The Eucharist as metaphor in John 6. *Theology*, 105:194–200.

Neumann, E. (1954). *The Origins and History of Consciousness*. trans. R.F.C. Hull. Princeton: Princeton University Press, 1995.

O'Connor, J.T. (2014). *The Hidden Manna: The Theology of the Eucharist*. San Francisco: Ignatius Press.

Ogden, T.H. (1994). The analytic third: Working with intersubjective clinical facts. *International Journal of Psychoanalysis*, 75:3–19.

Ogden, T.H. (1997). Reverie and interpretation. *Psychoanalytic Quarterly*, 66:567–595.

Oliner, M.M. (2013). "Non-represented" mental states. In *Unrepresented States and the Construction of Meaning: Clinical and Theoretical Contributions*. eds. Levine, H.E., Reed, G.S. & Scarfone, D. London: Routledge, pp. 152–172.

Perls, F.S. (1947). *Ego Hunger and Aggression: A Revision of Freud's Theory and Method*. London: Allen & Unwin/The Gestalt Institute, 1992.

Philo, J. (1993). *The Works of Philo: Complete and Unabridged*. trans. C.D. Younge. Peabody, MA: Hendrickson.

Polak, J. (2015). *After the Holocaust the Bell Still Rings*. Jerusalem: Urim.

Poole, F.J.P. (1986). Metaphors and maps: Towards comparison in the anthropology of religion. *Journal of the American Academy of Religion*, 54:411–457.

Ragland, E. (1995). *Essays on the Pleasures of Death: From Freud to Lacan*. London: Routledge.

Rizq, R. (2017). On food, faith, and psychoanalysis: Isak Dinesen's *Babette's Feast*. *British Journal of Psychotherapy*, 33:537–554.

Ron, Z. (2010). "What is it?" *Mānn who?* Interpreting Exodus 15:16. *Jewish Bible Quarterly*, 38:230–236.

Shemesh, A.O. (2021). "He said that the manna is that called *taranjebin*": Ibn Ezra against Hiwi al-Balkhi's interpretation of the biblical story of the manna. *HTS Teologiese Studies/Theological Studies*, 77:1–8.

Snelling, D. (2000). Subject, object, world: Some reflections on the Kleinian origins of the mind. In: *Analytic Freud: Philosophy and Psychoanalysis*. M.E. Levine, ed. London: Routledge, pp. 101–118.

Sorge, G.V. (2020). The construct of the 'mana personality' in Jung's works: An historic-hermeneutic perspective. *Journal of Analytic Psychology*, 65:366–388.

Spero, M.H. (2010). Moses Lactans: Evidence in support of the latent mythic value of Freud's 1914 "Moses of Michelangelo". *American Imago*, 67:183–242.

Stern, D.B. (1997). *Unformulated Experience: From Dissociation to Imagination in Psychoanalysis*. Hillsdale, NJ: Analytic Press.

Stern, D.N. (1993). The pre-narrative envelope. *Journal of Child Analysis*, 14:13–65.

Van de Vijver, G., Bazan, A., & Detandt, S. (2017). The mark, the thing, and the object: On what commands repetition in Freud and Lacan. *Frontiers in Psychology: Psychoanalysis and Neuropsychoanalysis*, 8:22–44.

Volkan, V. (1981). *Linking Objects and Linking Phenomena: A Study of the Forms, Symptoms, Metapsychology, and Therapy of Complicated Mourning*. Madison, NY: International Universities Press.

Waelder, R. (1933). The psychoanalytic theory of play. *Psychoanalytic Quarterly*, 2:208–224.

Wallon, H. (1945). *Les Origins de la Pensée chez l'Enfants. II: Les Tâches Intellectuelles*. Paris: Presses Universitaires de France, 1963.

Warttig-Mattfeld y de la Torre, W.R. (2003). The *manna* of the Sinai wilderness and the solving of the 3000-year-old mystery as to why it was ground, beaten, boiled and baked into cakes (including analysis by F. Bodenheimer). www.bibleorigins. net/mannasinaibodenheimer.html.

Weisel-Barth, Y. (2021). *Theoretical and Clinical Perspectives on Narrative in Psychoanalysis: The Creation of Intimate Fiction*. London: Routledge.

Williams, G. (1997) *Internal Landscapes and Foreign Bodies*. London: Duckworth.

Wilson, E. (2004). *Psychosomatic: Feminism and the Neurological Body*. London: Duke University Press.

Winnicott, D.W. (1955). Withdrawal and regression. In *Through Paediatrics to Psychoanalysis: Collected Papers*. Hogarth Press & The Institute of Psycho-Analysis, 1975, pp. 255–277.

Winnicott, D.W. (1965). *The Maturational Processes and the Facilitating Environment: Studies in the Theory of Emotional Development*. New York, NY: International Universities Press.

Winnicott, D.W. (1969). The use of an object. *International Journal of Psychoanalysis*, 50:711–716.

Winnicott, D.W. (1986). *Holding and Interpretation: Fragments of an Analysis*. London: Hogarth.

Wollheim, R. (1982). The bodily ego. In: *Philosophical Essays on Freud*. eds. Wollheim & J. Hopkins Cambridge: Cambridge University Press, pp. 124–138.

Wotton, R.S. (2010). What is manna? *Opticon1826*, 9:1–9.

Zornberg, A.G. (2015). *Bewilderments: Reflections on the Book of Numbers*. New York: Schocken.

Zwart, H. (2015). Tainted food and the Icarus complex: Psychoanalyzing consumer discontent from oyster middens to oryx and crake. *Journal of Agriculture and Environmental Ethics*, 28: 255–275.

4

GOD'S INFLUENCE ON MY PSYCHOANALYTIC VISION AND VALUES[1]

Lewis Aron

Freud asserted that psychoanalysis did not necessitate any values other than those of science, which it embraced. Hartmann (1960) recognized that psychoanalysis endorsed "health values." Under the influence of feminism, constructivism and postmodernism, analysts have become more willing to acknowledge the role of individual and societal values in analytic theory and practice. Despite this relatively recent recognition of the institutional values of psychoanalysis, there has been little talk about the influence of God. Speaking of values is still safer than speaking of religion directly.

The effort to talk openly and directly about religious differences and the implications for psychoanalysis is enormously complicated and filled with a variety of dangers. Years ago, a book about psychoanalysis and money was titled The Last Taboo (Krueger, 1986). I think it is more accurate to say that religion generally, and God in particular, have remained taboo among analysts. And feelings about God run strong. Some people, upon hearing of this symposium, have directly confronted me with their outrage. "Why are you bringing God into a professional meeting? If I want to hear about God I can go to my church or synagogue; why bring God into a psychoanalytic forum?"

1 We thank The American Psychological Association for permission to publish the article by Aron, L. (2004), "God's Influence on My Psychoanalytic Vision and Values," *Psychoanalytic Psychology*, 21(3), 442–451. https://doi.org/10.1037/0736-9735.21.3.442. Copyright © 2004 by American Psychological Association. Reproduced and adapted with permission. The official citation that should be used in referencing this material is Aron, L. (2004), "God's Influence on My Psychoanalytic Vision and Values," *Psychoanalytic Psychology*, 21(3), 442–451. No further reproduction or distribution is permitted without written permission from the American Psychological Association.

DOI: 10.4324/9781003266600-6

Religious conflict, repression and deep fears about religion pervade the history of psychoanalysis. Freud was concerned, even preoccupied, with the "danger" involved in the psychoanalytic movement "becoming a Jewish national affair" (Klein, 1985, p. xviii). Although Peter Gay (1989) may be correct that in many respects Freud was "A Godless Jew," Philip Reiff makes the stronger point that "despite his irreligion," Freud's cultural Jewishness "was more binding than religious orthodoxy" (Gilman, 1993, p. 7). It was Freud's worry that psychoanalysis would be seen as a "Jewish science" that led him to choose a non-Jew, Jung, to lead the movement as his successor. Ironically, Jung would later publicly stress the differences between a Jewish and an Aryan psychology and would privately disparage the "essentially corrosive nature" of Freud and Adler's "Jewish gospel" (Gilman, 1993, p. 223). Can four analysts of different religious traditions or persuasions come together to discuss the impact of God on their psychoanalytic thinking without the discussion degenerating into religious reductionism and hostility?

But religious belief is taboo among psychoanalysts not only because of the psychology of religious, ethnic and racial differences and its role in psycho-analytic history. It has also resulted from Freud's view of religion as an illusion—I am tempted to say the mother of all illusions, but to stay con-sistent with Freud's imagery it would be better to say the father of all illu-sions. Here is a single but poignant illustration: Listen to Otto Fenichel, from his 1939 classic "Problems of Psychoanalytic Technique," a text that influ-enced the theory and practice of psychoanalysis for decades, even to our own day:

> It has been said that religious people in analysis remain uninfluenced in their religious philosophies since analysis itself is supposed to be philo-sophically neutral. I consider this not to be correct. Repeatedly I have seen that with the analysis of the sexual anxieties and with maturing of the personality, the attachment to religion has ended. (p. 89)

Is it really any wonder that it would have taken until now for analysts to gather together to discuss the impact of their religious backgrounds and to acknowledge the influence of God on their psychoanalytic vision and values? To examine the place of their own "God representations," to use Ana-Mar-'a Rizzuto's (1979) term, as influences in their psychoanalytic thinking and practice?

Freud's Enlightenment ideal of science saw it as liberating the individual from the illusion of religion. Psychoanalysis offered Truth as replacement for regressive fantasy. Religious belief was "a lost cause," a "childhood neurosis" (Freud, 1927/1961, p. 53), and Freud paid homage only to "Our god Logos—Reason" (p. 54).

But as modern psychoanalytic thinkers and philosophers of science have pointed out, "a more contemporary and nuanced view of science challenges any strict dichotomy between natural science and all other fields, including psychoanalysis and religion" (Jones, quoted in Spezzano & Gargiulo, 1997, p. x). Freud's worship of the god Reason is ironically not supported by the contemporary empirical sciences, which challenge a unitary conception of rationality. Both science and rationality, on the one hand, and religion and spirituality, on the other, are more complex and multidimensional than Freud envisioned (Spezzano & Gargiulo, 1997).

Stephen Mitchell's (1993) presentation of relational psychoanalysis offered a strong critique of the dichotomizations of fantasy and reality, illusion and rationality, religion and science. For him, "What is inspiring about psycho-analysis today is not the renunciation of illusion in the hope of joining a common, progressively realistic knowledge and control, but rather the hope of fashioning a personal reality that feels authentic and enriching" (Mitchell, 1993, p. 21). With its goal as the enhancement and revitalization of human experience, and in its primary concern with felt meaning, significance, pur-pose, and value, the sharp division between religion and psychoanalysis diminishes.

In accord with this shift in our view of science and rationality, our con-temporary epistemology gives greater recognition to the subjectivity of the scientist and of the psychoanalyst. Freud was intent to eliminate "the sub-jective factor" (letter of January 4, 1928, cited in Grubrich-Simitis, 1986, p. 271), as he called it. For psychoanalysis to be an objective science the uniqueness of the individual analyst was not to matter. In its most extreme form this became the doctrine of the interchangeability of the analyst—as long as the analyst was well trained and well analyzed, it shouldn't matter who the analyst is as a person. Sander Gilman (1993) has persuasively demonstrated that Freud's goal was to universalize racist characterizations of Jews such that the scientist–analyst was to observe with a neutral, universal gaze and not with a unique, idiosyncratic and Jewish one. Medical ideology in Vienna especially stressed the central role of the physician as objective sci-entist and the neutral role of the scientist–diagnostician.

As we pay greater attention to the subjectivity of the analyst, and to the patient's experience of the analyst's subjectivity, we now expect analysts to attend to their countertransference and to report on their own responsiveness in presenting case material (Aron, 1996). The analyst's personal experience is now generally taken for granted as relevant analytic data. Our clinical sen-sibility, across most schools of psychoanalysis, leaves much more room for the analyst as an observing participant (Hirsch & Aron, 1991).

In this chapter, I examine one very specific aspect of my own religious background to illustrate the role that it has played in my own psychoanalytic vision. I discuss only one dimension of my religious experience, but an important one, namely, the nature of my own relationship to and dialogue with God.

Let me emphasize some of what I am not doing. I am not suggesting that analysts should or must believe in God, nor am I promoting any particular religious view or claiming that one religious perspective is more closely tied to psychoanalysis. I am simply demonstrating the way in which my relation to God has affected my own values and how these have become a part of my psychoanalytic identity. I assume that other analysts have been shaped and influenced by their own experience with God, and I am suggesting that an examination and comparison of these influences would be productive. And, yes, like Rizzuto (1979), I do assume that all of us form some God representations, whether or not we believe in God. If we are atheists, then there is some particular God or gods that we have chosen to reject. Who this God is that we do not believe in may be just as significant an influence on our values as a God that we choose to worship.

There are many aspects of my Jewish heritage – aside from God – that have influenced my psychoanalytic approach. Many of these have been discussed by others who have examined various aspects of Judaism and psychoanalysis, but these have generally not taken up in any direct way the analyst's personal relation to God. They have focused on a wide range of other topics, such as Freud's Jewish background and identity, the Jewish origins of the psychoanalytic movement, Freud's identification with Moses, Freud's relation to the B'nai Brith, Freud's dream theories and parallels from the Talmud, the psychoanalytic meanings of Jewish rituals, Freud and rabbinic hermeneutics, psychoanalytic interpretation of stories from the Hebrew Bible, psychoanalytic memory and forgetting and Jewish memory and forgetting, Freud as an embodiment of Jewish Viennese emancipatory thinking, Freud as reacting to his father's Haskalah (Jewish Enlightenment) vision, Freud and the Jewish mystical tradition, or Freud's Jewish anxieties. This literature is vast, and I mention these topics just to give a glimpse of the range of subject matters covered. Two recent examples of excellent scholarship are Daniel Rothenberg's (1997) study of psychic space and time in the underlying structure of Judaism and psychoanalysis and Stephen Friedlander's (1997) examination of language and death in these two discourses. But of all of these and many, many more, I would certainly single out, along with Harold Bloom, the subject of psychoanalysis and interpretation. As Bloom (1987) wrote, "Freud's most profound Jewishness, voluntary and involuntary, was his consuming passion for interpretation" (p. 52). As Bakan (1958) persuasively argued, Freud applied to the study of individual behavior the traditional Jewish methodological principle of interpretation in which every letter of the Torah was assumed to be meaningful and subject to multiple understandings. The role of interpretation in Judaism and psychoanalysis can be explored endlessly, and I hope to contribute to this topic at a later date. But in this article my area of exploration will have to be more limited. I'm only going to focus on God.

In my own psychoanalytic research, I have given a great deal of attention to an examination of the dimensions of mutuality and symmetry. My book *A Meeting of Minds* (Aron, 1996) is organized around the theme of the different aspects of mutuality that can be conceptualized between patient and analyst. I explore mutual recognition, mutual regulation, mutual resistances, mutual generation of data, mutual empathy, mutual regression, mutual participation and enactment, mutual construction of interpretation and so on. Mutuality implies reciprocation, sharing together, community and unity through inter-change. I differentiate mutuality, which emphasizes what patient and analyst have in common or between them, from symmetry, which implies correspondence in form or arrangement. Symmetry implies a degree of similarity and equality. I argue throughout the book that psychoanalysis is best viewed in many respects as mutual but asymmetrical because of the significant differences between patient and analyst in role, function, and responsibility. This contrast between mutuality and asymmetry was not original, but I like to think that my contribution was to sustain a detailed examination of these concepts as they have shaped contemporary psychoanalytic thinking and practice.

During the time that I worked on these ideas for my book, I was not attending to their reverberation with my religious beliefs, background, or values, although I did give considerable attention to Martin Buber's (1923/1970) relational philosophy of I–Thou. What I would like to do is to review some of the ideas about God with which I grew up and that continue to speak to me spiritually. I am interested in examining the influence of my "God representations" on my own psychoanalytic conceptualization. I present themes and images that have been meaningful to me personally. I recognize that others, even others who have been raised within the same Jewish tradition, have different visions and relate to God differently than I do. In particular, I recognize that women's experiences within the tradition may have been quite different from my own. It should be added that just as my religious background has affected my psychoanalytic vision, so, too, my psycho-analytic experience has influenced my spiritual values and ideals. Consider the centrality of the theme of mutuality and asymmetry in the following reflections on Jewish belief.

The Jewish tradition, as I understand it, is radically relational in its assumption of a mutual and intersubjective relationship between God and humanity. The Brit, or covenant, between God and Israel is the core foundation of the Jewish faith. A covenantal relationship requires mutuality, not symmetry or equality, for it is clearly hierarchical, but nevertheless it must be a two-way street, a reciprocal agreement. Revelation necessitates give-and-take, a creative tension between the giving of Torah, God's teaching or law, and the receiving of Torah; the Brit (the covenant) implies Judaism's foundations in this mutual relation. Rabbi Joseph Soloveitchik (known simply as "The Rav," a leading figure of modern Jewish philosophy) described the covenant as resting on "free negotiation, mutual assumption of duties and full recognition of the equal rights of both parties concerned" (1992, p. 29). Chancellor Ismar Schorsch of the Jewish Theological Seminary writes, "Reciprocity holds the key to eternity for each of us," citing as a proof-text, "If my light will be in your hand, your light will be in My hand" (Shemot Rabbah 36:3). Elsewhere he quotes Leviticus: "You shall not profane My holy name, that I may be sanctified in the midst of the Israelite people—I the Lord who sanctify you" (22:32). The verse depicts a reciprocal relationship between God and Israel in which sanctification operates bidirectionally. The nation has an obligation to bring credit to God even as God sanctifies it. Holiness is a reciprocal relationship. According to the Talmud, if we strive to hallow our lives here on earth, we will be bathed with a burst of holiness from above.

Jewish daily liturgy expresses an ongoing theme of reciprocal love and a mutual and dynamic relationship between God and humanity. Our prayer "With abounding love you have loved us" is reciprocated with "and you shall love your God." Jews wear ritual bindings, tefillin, encasing the pronouncement, "Here O' Israel, the Lord our God, the Lord alone," and reciprocally, in the rabbinic imagination, the Talmud asserts that God dons tefillin proclaiming "who is like thy people Israel, one people on earth."

Rabbi Louis Finkelstein, who was Chancellor of the Jewish Theological Seminary from 1934 to 1972, used to say that when he prayed, he talked to God, but when he studied, God talked to him. The tradition in which I grew up led me to imagine an ongoing internal experience of conversing with God. Praising, beseeching, thanking, complaining, questioning, challenging and even arguing with God is simply expected. Prayer presupposes an intimate personal experience with God. As young children we repeatedly hear the bible story of Abraham audaciously arguing with God over Sodom, even going so far as to challenge God's morality: "Shall not the judge of all the earth deal justly?" (Genesis 18:22). The very name Israel means "one who struggles with God" and was given to Jacob after he wrestled with a divine being (Genesis 32:29). Jews are taught to grapple with God, to question and confront God and to maintain an ongoing dialogue with God.

What does it mean, what could it possibly mean, to think of a human being as having an intersubjective relationship with God? Is God a subject to be engaged? An interpersonal relationship with God? But certainly God is not a person, and isn't it sacrilegious to attribute to God such personal attributes? In what sense can we think of ourselves as God's partners, God's lovers? Rabbi Neil Gillman (1992) elegantly reviews the Jewish literature that so pervasively, in spite of philosophical objections, portrays a personal God. Our tradition does indeed affirm an intersubjective relationship, an I–Thou relationship, between God and humanity, between God and Israel, and even between God and the individual. God does seem dependent on our recognition, subject to our affirmation. This is not the God of the rationalist philosophers; the God of the Rambam (Maimonidees), following Aristotle, is abstract, transcendent, unmoved and certainly beyond the need of anyone, but his is only one of many authentically Jewish conceptions of the Divinity, and important as it is, according to Gillman, the rationalistic view needs to be held in tension with a more personal view of God. It should also be noted that Maimonidees himself paradoxically preaches a moral ideal of continuous fellowship with God (Soloveitchik, 2002, p. 93).

In the Western philosophical tradition, dependency is considered a weakness, a sign of inadequacy, incompleteness, femininity and neediness, and so to think of God as reliant on people is to reveal God's limitation and hence to deny God's omnipotence. For the rationalists, an all-powerful God must be depicted as abstract, autonomous, independent, above it all and alone. But if we value relation and engagement and view it as an ideal state to be connected and attached, then we may challenge the conventional assessment and instead regard God's need for humanity as one aspect of omnipotence rather than as a limitation or deficit.

Throughout the Jewish tradition, God is portrayed as caring about all human beings. The Creator of the Universe is also, paradoxically, Kel Malei Rachamim, the Lord Full of Compassion. The Torah repeatedly uses metaphors of God and Israel as husband and wife, parent and child, even depicting the relationship as between lovers and soul mates. Song of Songs is interpreted by the rabbis allegorically as an erotic love song between God and the people. The relationship between the lovers in Songs is egalitarian anti-patriarchal, and the mutuality of their desire is the recurrent theme. What could more poetically characterize mutuality than "Ani ledodi ve'dodi li"—I am for my beloved and my beloved for me? Ilana Pardes (1992) argues that "for once the relationship of God and His bride relies on mutual courting, mutual attraction, and mutual admiration" (p. 127). Pardes then cites a Midrash that celebrates Song in which

> their hymn to God is answered by a hymn to them. Thus God praises Israel, saying [Songs I: 15]: 'Behold thou art fair, my love; behold thou art fair'; and Israel responds with a paean to Him: 'Behold, Thou art fair, my Beloved, yea, pleasant.'
>
> (Pardes, 1992, p. 127)

In our literature, God is moved, feels emotions, negotiates, becomes enraged, shows compassion, appears vulnerable and ambivalent. Often frustrated are God's dreams for humanity and for the world that God created. Abraham Heschel (1959) designated "the divine pathos" (p. 116) as the key to the Jewish worldview. For Heschel, God cares and reaches out, yet is frustrated and vulnerable. God even laughs and cries with us. Our rabbis portray

God weeping after the destruction of the temple, and by contrast, in Psalms, in an image that some find disturbing, God laughs at the destruction of our enemies. The Talmud (Baba Meziah) famously depicts God laughing with joy at the rabbis' triumph as they overrule celestial authority in the interpretation of law, for "the Torah is not in heaven!" When the people crossed the sea escaping the Egyptians, they sang the Song of the Sea. The Baal Shem Tov, the founder of Chasidism, taught that when Israel sang, this caused God to join in and sing the song with the people.

Reciprocity may be seen in the Bible's naming of the holiday of Passover. The designation of the holiday as Passover reflects a human point of view, in which we celebrate God's passing over the Israelites during the tenth plague. God, on the other hand, refers to the holiday as the Feast of Unleavened Bread, a name that reflects God's recognition of Israel's haste and sacrifice in following God into the uncharted wilderness.

The theme of mutuality between God and the Jewish people is most fully developed in the literature of Jewish mysticism and particularly in 16th-century Lurianic Kabbalah. In the Kabbalistic myth, at the center of creation is humankind, who, through proper acts and devotion, the fulfillment of both ritual and social–ethical commandments, can repair the world, tikkun olam. In the theosophy of the Kabbalah, God creates the world through tzim'tzum; God contracts or withdraws himself to make room for creation. Homiletically, tzim'tzum, the self-limitation of God, is understood by many Kabbalists as the foundation of free will, as if God's self-contraction is necessary to make room for human freedom. With the Shevirat ha-Kelim ("breaking of the vessels") there is a failure of the divine emanation to be contained, resulting in the descent of divine sparks, which need to be rescued and returned to their source. Through the performance of commandments with the proper intention (kavanah), we gather the divine sparks and hence contribute to cosmic restoration and reintegration. Restating this insight, Rabbi Soloveitchik (1984) said that it is as if "the creator spoiled reality so that mortals might set it right" (p. 148). God does not unilaterally liberate Israel from Egypt, but rather in Kabbalistic thought, it is as if the liberation is mutually necessary because God, as well as the world and humanity, needs to be mended, repaired, liberated and redeemed. The central image here is that of two partners sharing in the task of repairing the world, tikkun olam. We are partners with God in creation, revelation and redemption.

The medieval sage Nachmanides asked why the Ten Commandments begin with God's proclamation "I am the Lord your God who took you out of the Land of Egypt" instead of asserting "I am the One who created heaven and earth." Levi Yitzchak of Berditchev, who was one of the most beloved figures of the Hasidim, answered this question in the following way: To say that God created the universe is abstract and philosophical. Such an assertion places God as the first of all firsts, the prime mover, abstract and distant; it speaks of

God as an idea, a principle—God as transcendent. By beginning with the declaration that God took us out of Egypt, God is revealed as showing love, intimacy and involvement—God as immanent in our lives and our history. God's commandments are in fact part of a deal. Like the Hittite vassal treaties on which the structure of the Decalogue may be modeled, the Brit enacts a mutual understanding, a bilateral agreement with reciprocal responsibilities. I did this for you, and so you do these commandments for me. I am with you so you be with me; "You must be holy, for I, the Lord your God, am holy." Because we are to imitate God's holy ways, there are implications regarding mutuality for our human interpersonal relations as well. To mention a single instance, perhaps if we imagine God as reliant on us for support and reparation, we might feel less shame about our own vulnerability and dependence on others.

Following the existential tradition of Martin Buber, who emphasized the primacy of the I–Thou relationship, others have highlighted that in all relationships there are moments of intimacy and moments of withdrawal. Irving Greenberg emphasizes the alternating movements of presence and absence, faith and denial. "Faith, then, is never a permanent acquisition but rather a momentary achievement, all too easily dispelled. Atheism is a legitimate stage in the dynamic of faith" (Greenberg, cited in Gillman, 2000, p. 453). In our relationship with God, along with the gift of human freedom, we must endure the vicissitudes of all relationships and live in an unpredictable and sometimes cruel and pernicious world. We all undoubtedly recall moments when it seems as if God's face has been hidden from us or, as Martin Buber (1957) referred to it, moments where there seems to be an "eclipse of God." At these times we remember that God too is waiting to resume our partnership. As it is written, "Turn back to me—said the Lord of Hosts—and I will turn back to you" (Zechariah 1:3).

We have seen that in the Jewish tradition, God turns with us, waits with us, sings, prays and rejoices with us, laughs, cries and mourns with us. All too often in Jewish history, it seems that God must be crying with us. Perhaps even through our suffering, we may experience God's seeming absence and abandonment, our confrontation with nothingness, as a summons from God in the form of a catastrophic revelation, a "call out of the whirlwind" (Soloveitchik, 2003). Our souls cry out in longing for God, but in Heschel's (1976) classic phrase, likewise, God is "in search of man." Mutuality and intersubjectivity can take place only between two subjects who count on one another, seek each other, recognize each other, let each other down, negate each other, and repair and mend the inevitable disruptions of the alliance. The feeling that God is absent is no less a legitimate religious experience than the sense of divine presence. Relationships are by their nature conflicted, mercurial and inconsistent; the presence of the other is subject to ebb and flow. There are moments of faith and moments of doubt or outright disbelief, but both faith and doubt participate in one's ongoing internal dialogue. In my conversation with God I can say, "I don't believe in you. You don't exist, you can't exist, you make no sense, you are absurd, my rational mind denies you." Still, my conversation with God goes on. I would think of this relationship with God in terms of ongoing regulation, disruption and repair, and heightened affective moments (Beebe & Lachmann, 2002).

For the purposes of this essay, I have emphasized mutuality and taken asymmetry for granted, but of course mutuality is only one side of a complex dialectic process. If the story of Abraham standing up to God in regard to Sodom illustrates the mutuality of their relationship, then the Akeda, the binding of Isaac, depicting Abraham's silent submission to God's will, is perhaps the quintessential exemplar of asymmetry. The asymmetry is inherent in our transience and nothingness in relation to the Creator; the mutuality derives from our dignity as human beings who are created in the image of the divine, allowing us to commune with God. In the words of Rabbi Soloveitchik (2003),

> In God, man finds both affirmation of himself as a great being, and a ruthless, inconsiderate negation of himself as nothing. This is the main, the dominant theme of Judaism. ... Finding God is, on the one hand, the greatest victory which man may obtain and, on the other hand, the most humiliating, tormenting defeat which the human being experiences. ... In a word, the dialectical movement of surging forward and falling back is the way of life ordained by God for the Jew. (p. 108)

And here I want to add a brief tribute to the memory of Mannie Ghent, who, among his many other contributions, did so much to champion a legitimate place for spirituality in psychoanalysis. Although Mannie took his influence for what he called "surrender" from the eastern Buddhist traditions, there is a striking, almost uncanny similarity to the Rav's dialectic approach as seen in his emphasis on the total surrender of body and soul, the need to maintain dignity in defeat, the universal alternation between surging forward and conquering versus withdrawal and defeat, opposing suffering and yet accepting mortality. Ghent (2002) concluded his most recent article,

> Every day in our practice we pay homage to, and stand back in awe of, the marvels of the human mind caught up in the struggle to heal and transcend itself, while holding back in fear, jousting with itself in dread of walking through the valley of the shadow of death. (p. 804)

Judaism places great emphasis on the value of life. God proclaims in Deuteronomy (30:19), "I have put before you life and death, blessing and curse. Choose life" (Hebrew-English Tanach, Philadelphia, 1999). This utterance embodies two cardinal values (choice and life) that are also fundamental to psychoanalysis. An existential dimension of psychoanalysis champions agency that is developed through making choices, exercising our will, our authorship of our own lives (see my discussion of rank, will and agency in Aron, 1996). The ultimate value of psychoanalysis is for the analysand to choose life, to choose vitality, meaning and authenticity (see Ogden, 1995). Freud was right in spirit in his recognition that psychoanalysis sides with the life over the death instincts. As psychoanalysts, we should recognize that some of our cherished ideals are central to religious traditions and that in analyzing forms of aliveness and deadness, and thus in helping our patients to choose life, we are performing a sacred task.

The relational emphases on mutuality and asymmetry have structural parallels in Jewish theological formulations with which I live. I present these to you simply as an illustration of the influence of one select aspect of the analyst's subjectivity on psychoanalytic values and ideals. I do want to end with one final point. Analysts have too often played God. We have acted as if we were omnipotent and all knowing, aloof and above it all. I hope that I have in some way indicated my belief that being deeply engaged with God, imitating God's ways, may paradoxically help keep us from playing God. Michael Eigen (1998), drawing on his own study of Judaism and Kabbalah, described psychoanalysis as a form of prayer. Indeed, psychoanalysis may be envisioned as a religious practice, a form of worship, in which contact is made with the Almighty through immersion in the richness and depth of the inner life and in communion with the Other.

References

Aron, L. (1996). *A meeting of minds*. Hillsdale, NJ: Analytic Press.

Bakan, D. (1958). *Sigmund Freud and the Jewish mystical tradition*. Princeton, NJ: Van Nostrand.

Beebe, B., & Lachmann, F. (2002). *Infant research and adult treatment*. Hillsdale, NJ: Analytic Press.

Bloom, H. (1987). *Kafka, Freud, Scholem: Three essays*. Boston: Beacon Press.

Buber, M. (1957). *Eclipse of God: Studies in the relation between religion and philosophy*. New York: Harper Books.

Buber, M. (1970). *I and thou* (W. Kaufman, Trans.). New York: Charles Scribner's Sons. (Original work published 1923)

Eigen, M. (1998) *The psychoanalytic mystic*. Binghamton, NY: ESF Publishers.

Fenichel, O. (1939). Problems of psychoanalytic technique. *Psychoanal. Q.*, 8, 438–470.

Freud, S. (1961). The future of an illusion. In J. Strachey (Ed. & Trans.), *The standard edition of the complete psychological works of Sigmund Freud* (Vol. 21, pp. 1–56). London: Hogarth Press. (Original work published 1927)

Friedlander, D.J. (1997). The confluence of psychoanalysis and religion: A personal view. In C. Spezzano & G.J. Gargiulo (Eds.), *Soul on the couch* (pp. 147–162). Hillsdale, NJ: Analytic Press.

Gay, P. (1989). *A godless Jew*. New Haven, CT: Yale University Press.

Ghent, E. (2002). Wish, need, drive: Motive in the light of dynamic systems theory and Edelman's selectionist theory. *Psychoanal. Dial.*, 12, 763–808.

Gillman, N. (1992). *Sacred fragments*. Philadelphia: Jewish Publication Society.

Gillman, N. (2000). Contemporary Jewish theology. In J. Neusner & A.J. Avery-Peck (Eds.), *The Blackwell companion to Judaism* (pp. 441–460). Malden, MA: Blackwell Publishing.

Gilman, S.L. (1993). *Freud, race and gender*. Princeton, NJ: Princeton University Press.

Grubrich-Simitis, I. (1986). Six letters of Sigmund Freud and Sandoʹr Ferenczi on the interrelationship of psychoanalytic theory and technique. *Int. Rev. Psycho-Anal.*, 13, 259–277.

Hartmann, H. (1960). *Psychoanalysis and moral values*. New York: International Universities Press.

Heschel, A.J. (1959). *Between God and man*. New York: Free Press.

Heschel, A.J. (1976). *God in search of man*. New York: Farrar, Straus & Giroux.

Hirsch, I., & Aron, L. (1991). Participant-observation, perspectivism and counter-transference. In H. Siegel, L. Barbanel, I. Hirsch, J. Lasky, H. Silverman, S. Warshaw, et al. (Eds.), *Psychoanalytic reflections on current issues* (pp. 78–95). New York: New York University Press.

Klein, D.B. (1985). *Jewish origins of the psychoanalytic movement*. Chicago: University of Chicago Press.

Krueger, D.W. (1986). *The last taboo*. New York: Brunner/Mazel Publishers.

Mitchell, S.A. (1993). *Hope and dread in psychoanalysis*. New York: Basic Books.

Ogden, T.H. (1995). Analysing forms of aliveness and deadness of the transference-countertransference. *Int. J. Psycho-Anal.*, 76, 695–709.

Pardes, I. (1992). *Countertraditions in the Bible: A feminist approach*. Cambridge, MA: Harvard University Press.

Rizzuto, A.-M. (1979). *The birth of the living God*. Chicago: University of Chicago Press.

Rothenberg, D.J. (1997). Formulation, psychic space, and time: New dimensions in psychoanalysis and Jewish spirituality. In C. Spezzano & G.J. Gargiulo (Eds.), *Soul on the couch* (pp. 57–78). Hillsdale, NJ: Analytic Press.

Soloveitchik, J.B. (1984). *Halakhic man*. Philadelphia: Jewish Publication Society.

Soloveitchik, J.B. (1992). *The lonely man of faith*. New York: Doubleday.

Soloveitchik, J.B. (2002). *Worship of the heart*. New York: Ktav Publishing.

Soloveitchik, J.B. (2003). *Out of the whirlwind*. New York: Ktav Publishing.

Spezzano, C., & Gargiulo, G.J. (Eds.). (1997). *Soul on the couch*. Hillsdale, NJ: Analytic Press.

PART 2

Biblical Commentary

5

IN THE BEGINNING, THERE WAS … ENVY

Libby Henik

In Genesis, the first book of the Hebrew Bible, we read: "And God planted a garden outward, in Eden and there He put the human/earthling [Adam, אדם from the Hebrew word *adama*, אדמה – earth] whom He had formed … . And God commanded the earthling saying: 'From every tree of the garden thou mayest freely eat, but of the tree of the knowledge of good and bad thou shall not eat of it'" (Genesis 2:8). Commenting on this cryptic name, "the tree of knowledge of good and bad," Ramban (a 13th c. commentator on the Bible) identified good and bad as love and hate, respectively. Seven centuries later, Melanie Klein made love and hate and envy the cornerstone of her psychoanalytic theory.

It is remarkable that Klein, building on a secular, enlightenment tradition, favoring reason and scientific objectivity over affective, less empirical experience in her theoretical development of the nature of psychic life, pulled away from the rational to the very beginnings, to the most primitive experiences of being. Her description of the world of the infant, replete with love, hate and envy, is evocative of ancient Jewish tradition found in the earliest, most archaic of Torah narratives, the biblical description of early human life as related in Genesis 1–4.

In this paper, I present Kleinian theory as a "midrashic" reading of the Garden of Eden story, a story whose early Hebrew motifs have been muted by the phallo-centric emphasis of classical psychoanalysis, by Greco-Western emphasis on reason and logic, and by Christian concepts of sin. I suggest that applying the tradition of Midrashic interpretation together with Kleinian Object Relations Theory to the Garden of Eden story will reveal a different reading of the narrative, one that I propose is closer to the Jewish intent of the text.

DOI: 10.4324/9781003266600-8

My intent here is not a thorough exposition of Kleinian theory, but rather to give selective emphasis to aspects of her theory and its expansion and re-conceptualization, particularly by Thomas Ogden and Wilfred Bion, into a theory of mind being a construction of object relations (i.e., "self" as a construct of relationship with the early internalized representations of relationships with m(other)), in the hope that, together with Rabbinic biblical interpretation, a Kleinian return to "the beginnings" of life will cast previous understandings and influences of the biblical story of the Garden of Eden and its first inhabitants differently and in a new light. I hope to show how love, hate and envy, the building blocks of the Kleinian drama of man's emergent psychic reality, can offer a different perspective of biblical narrative and illuminate another dimension, or storyline, of the Garden of Eden text, one that more closely reflects Jewish-Rabbinic thought about the psycho-genesis of man and the unfolding of humankind-in-relation.

I am proposing a reading of Melanie Klein's psychoanalytic theories of the dialectic tension between the paranoid-schizoid and depressive positions and her concepts of splitting, love, hate and envy as a *midrash*, a method of biblical interpretation that encourages different understandings of biblical narrative and the dialogue of multiple meanings.

The earliest Jewish thoughts about man and God are found in Rabbinic interpretations of the biblical text. And although Rabbinic interpretations do not use psychoanalytic terminology (e.g., we will not find them pondering "the psychogenesis of the self"), we do find that the Rabbis exhaustively contemplated and debated the realities of human nature and the ubiquity of conflictual emotions and desires that impact psychic life and relationships. We also find abundant discussion about sex and the nature of impulses. Rabbinic understanding of biblical text and its understanding of the human experience is all of one piece: The Torah – not nature, science or Greco-Western reason/*logos* – offers the blueprint for all aspects of life and understanding[1] (Kass, L., 2003).

Freud: A Theory of Conflict: For Freud, the History of the World Started with Rebellion

Interestingly, the concept of "self" as we have come to think of it today did not occupy Freud's thinking. The concept of "self" was not considered a separate line of development, but rather an end-result, a byproduct, of working through developmental conflict, particularly the oedipal conflict. The central human struggle for Freud was the conflict between gratification of the sexual, aggressive drives and the defenses against them. Focusing on the male child of age 5 or 6, Freud turned to the Greek myth of Oedipus in developing his theory of innate sexual and aggressive impulses against the father: the wish to murder the father and possess the mother. For Freud, the aim of the impulse was discharge. The object, i.e., the receiver of the discharge, was accidentally discovered. Freud's "drives are objectless, directionless packets of energy. The objects are only accidentally discovered and are only used to eliminate the libidinal tension of the drive"[2] (Greenberg, J.R. & Mitchell, S.A., 1983).

Through the interpretive method of psychoanalysis, Freud's goal was to make the unconscious sexual and aggressive desires conscious, thereby enabling the individual to move developmentally and sequentially from stages of oedipal embeddedness/merger to autonomy. For Freud, autonomy and independence, not "self," were man's ultimate achievement. Man's only salvation was to be found in science, i.e., intellect/*logos*[3] (Rieff, P., 1959, p.267). Freud valued movement away from embeddedness with oedipal objects, a movement from dependence to autonomy, from passivity to activity.

Freud believed that there is an unconscious longing to return to symbiosis/merger with the mother and to give up the struggle to become an autonomous individual. He equated this loss of individuality-through-merger to death. He determined that all instincts fall into one of two major classes: the life instincts or the death instincts[4] (Freud, 1920). The death drive opposes the drive for life, the tendency toward survival, propagation, sex and other creative, life-producing drives. Oedipal aggression toward the father influenced Freud's psychoanalytic understanding of religion and interpretation of biblical/Torah text. Freud's linear psychosexual theory of development (moving sequentially from stages of oedipal embeddedness to autonomy) and, in particular, his theory of oedipal aggression against the father/God, shaped 20th-century psychoanalytic interpretation of the Jewish biblical canon. His reading of biblical text through the lens of oedipal conflict produced a narrative of primal crime, repetition and guilt that muted Hebrew biblical motifs.

In *Moses and Monotheism* (1939), Freud reframed the biblical story of Moses, putting forth a history of patricide: rebellion and murder of the leader/father. The murder of the primal father/God aroused guilt that is expiated through religious ritual, injunctions and devotion. Freud viewed religion as a regression to the childish illusion of safety, dependence on and reunion with, an all-powerful/sustaining father figure. Freud equated religion with passivity, femininity, submission and dependence. Religion ritualized the illusion and strengthened the child-like wishes that safety through union with the all-powerful father-figure will assuage God's retribution. Jewish religious law was seen by Freud as a reaction-formation to guilt resulting from the murder of Moses, who represented the primal father. I suggest that this is a theory borne of Greco-Western thought, a product of the ideal man of Enlightenment, and is not reflective of biblical narrative or interpretation.

It should be noted that relationships replete with fratricidal envy and aggression, not patricide and oedipal competition, dominate biblical relationships, particularly in Genesis. It should also be noted that early Hebrew

Judaism inveighed against the emphasis in Hellenistic culture on cognitive mastery, the deterministic/fatalistic repetition of the death cycle of nature inherent in pagan cultures, and the fatalistic character of tragedy (there is no Hebrew word for "nature or tragedy" in the Torah). In Hebrew thought, the unseen God must not be identified with nature, nor is nature, or any of its forms, a source of ultimate reality[5] (Kass, L., 2003).

In addition, William Kolbrener brings out that Rabbinic Judaism

> strongly resists Freud's definition of the concept of unity, certainly as Freud defined it as a ... return to an 'infantile dimension.' The command, following the biblical vocative, 'Hear O Israel!' 'You shall love the Lord your God with all your heart, with all your soul, and with all your might,' may require ... a service of integrated mind and body, [but] it is not ... a command to mystical union, [but rather] an injunction to study, to know the Law in all its multiplicity. Love of God is achieved through cleaving to 'these words,' not to an abstract conception of the mystical divine (Sifre, 1986). In the rabbinic model, what Freud calls secondary process differentiation takes precedence and is the paradoxical means by which unity is achieved through multiplicity and difference pursued, affirmed, and maintained. The rabbinic sensibility embraces contradiction in Judaism's most highly articulated secondary process languages, Talmudic argument.[6]
>
> (Kolbrener, W., 2010)

However, it is around the subject of sexuality that a huge divide exists between Jewish and Greek/Christian thought. While sexual themes are prevalent in biblical narrative, and desire creates a good deal of mayhem (to put it mildly), the ancient Hebrews understood sex to be part of mankind's innate constitution and never considered, or referred to, sex as a sin, not even in God's rebuke to Adam and Eve following the transgression ("In Judaism, in biblical Hebrew, there are about twenty words for sin. Rabbis rarely talk of sin in the abstract, but focus on specific sins"[7] (Ashwin, M. 2007)). Equating sex with evil or sin is inconsistent with the Jewish attitude toward sex. Sexuality/procreation is the first commandment given to the first human couple (Genesis 1:21). The biblical word for sexual relations is *yadah* (ידע) – to know. Hence, the English expression "to know someone in the biblical sense." However, y'd'h is also the root derivative of the Hebrew word *da'at* (דעת) – knowledge. In biblical Hebrew, the tree of knowledge is *Etz Ha-Da'at* (עץ הדעת). In biblical thought, knowledge/*da'at* is closely linked to intimacy. Unlike the Greek concept of knowledge as impersonal, observable, scientific, the ancient Hebrew concept of *da'at* is personal, an intimate proximity of subjectivities. Biblical knowing, *da'at*, lies at the core of the relationship of self with "other." When the Torah says, "And God knew," Rashi (the foremost commentator on the Torah, 1040–1105) explains, "And God was moved."

Rabbinic interpretation understands from the language of the text and the tense of the verb that Adam and Eve had sexual relations prior to their transgression and expulsion from Eden. According to Rashi, following the expulsion, the text (Genesis 4:1) says: והאדם ידע (*yadah* – Hebrew past tense), "And the man KNEW" his wife – i.e., Adam and his woman had had sexual relations already, before the transgression and expulsion. Had the text said וידע אדם (*va-yeh'dah* – Hebrew present tense), it would have implied that sexual relations occurred for the first time after the couple was driven out of Eden and that children were born to him then (Genesis Rabbah 22:2). The story of the transgression does not hold the central place in Hebrew biblical canon that it does in Christian belief, and its characters are not mentioned again. The Garden of Eden text is "brought to establish the centrality of emergence, not finality. Beginnings not endings"[8] (Kass, L., 2003).

Melanie Klein: The History of the World Started with Love, Hate and Object Relatedness

Unlike Freud, Melanie Klein is not a household name outside of psychoanalytic circles. Her theory and ideas of the earliest stages of life are difficult and often unsettling, and go straight for the primitive and archaic. Yet, while her imagery can be approached metaphorically, rather than literally, we should take Melanie Klein seriously[9] (Alford, C.F., 1989).

Like some other psychoanalytic theorists of her time who followed Freud, Melanie Klein began to be interested in the psychogenesis of the "self." These theorists came to understand mind as a construct of relationship with the early internalized representations of relationships with others/m(other). As these theories evolved, influenced one another and diverged from one another, what emerged was a concept of "self" as a relational construct, a sense of oneself shaped by the context and meaning of a relationship with others, real and imagined, internal and external, and this sense of "self" is not static, but constantly changing, evolving, conflicted and shifting. Object Relations Theory, as Klein's theories came to be known, account for the origin of love and hate and the centrality of these emotions in the organization and content of one's experience toward "self" and others/objects. Rather than sexual conflict, "self" came to be understood as fashioned from the working through of relational conflict.

My intent here is to briefly and selectively highlight one aspect of Melanie Klein's theory of mind, the paranoid-schizoid position, as it relates to the biblical Garden of Eden story. Melanie Klein focused on the newly born infant, and she was interested in the earliest primitive stages of infant mental life that form the human mind. As soon as Klein understood mind as object-related from the start, the basic building blocks of mind shifted from sexual drives to relationships of love and hate and to a different view of the underlying dramas of mental life. She situated the infant "in the beginning" in a dyadic relationship with the m(other) and proposed an organization of experience of both external and inner reality.

Klein's perception of the infant is not one of innocence or passivity. Klein's infant is born with innate destructive impulses and oral-sadistic phantasies, and Klein argued that the super-ego emerges earlier than Freud suggested[10] (Klein, M., 1946). Klein understood that, from the very beginning of life, and ongoing throughout life, one is torn between love and hate toward oneself and one's internal and external objects. These conflicted experiences, which are the cause of anxiety, are dealt with in different core feelings and nuclear affective structures, which imply differences in states of ego integration[11] (Stein, R., 1990). Klein termed these affective structures as either the paranoid-schizoid (hate/aggression) position or the depressive (love/reparation) position. From birth, the infant's earliest reality is a wholly internal, phantastic (which she spelled with a "ph" to distinguish it from daydreaming and imaginings) living, filled with the anxiety stirred by the conflict between love, the life instinct, and destruction, the death instinct. She conceptualized the infant's experience as struggling between these two positions, with both external and inner reality. The object world of the Kleinian infant is "a continuous, unconscious phantasy, a little 24-hour theatre in the mind"[12] (Alford, C.F., 1989, p. 51).

Although she retained Freud's terminology, Klein moved away from Freud's theory of psycho-sexual development. For Klein, the first major discovery of the human mind is "otherness," not sexuality. She replaced Freud's concept of drive regulation with a web of relations with "others," real and imagined. Although she started out as a drive theorist, Klein came to understand that drives are not about sex and aggression, but about envy, greed, competition and destruction. Unlike Freud, Kleinian drives are about desire – with the object of desire implicit in the experience of desire itself[13] (Greenberg, J.R & Mitchell, S.A., 1983). It is in the object-seeking nature of desire that one becomes capable of experiencing the "other" in its separateness: "Desire is the individuated, unmediated, unexplicated experience of otherness"[14] (Ahlskog, G., 1990). Desire is always for something, images of the outside world that are sought for gratification, in either love or destruction, independent of real others in the external world. From the very beginning, the infant has an unconscious awareness of the existence of the mother and structures a world of meaning around its mother's body, and all the good things for the infant belong to the mother's breast[15] (Greenberg, J.R., & Mitchell, S.A., 1983). "This reformulation of the properties of drives as knowledge of, and the seeking of, objects ... represents a fundamental shift in the vision concerning human motivation and mental processes ... and places object relationships at the center of emotional life"[16] (Greenberg, J.R. & Mitchell, S.A., 1983, p.137–8).

The child at the breast can feel loved and nourished, at a state of "one-ness," and feels love in return. The breast is "good" and idealized. But sometimes the child at the breast can experience the m(other)/breast as a subjectivity outside of its self-enclosed needs. This leads to frustration and to the terrifying experience of separation between self and (m)other. This separation is experienced with envy and sadism towards the "good" (satisfying) breast and the wish to destroy its contents. The breast is now experienced as "bad," persecutory and withholding, and the infant becomes filled with destructive, retaliatory fantasies towards this "bad" breast. In order to cope with the conflict of love and hate and the anxiety that arises from it, the infant engages in omnipotent phantasies of "splitting" the breast into two separate objects, not belonging to the same mother, creating an idealized, loving and loved "good breast" that is now protected by the "split" from a "bad breast," which is hated, attacked and devoured. A perpetual cycle of projection and introjection of both good and bad objects ensues. This "split" world of good and bad breast occurs long before the infant is capable of any sort of reality-testing.

As a consequence of the projection of hateful feelings, the infant becomes filled with paranoid fears of retaliation and persecution created by its own destructive phantasies. The split of the object is in actuality a defensive strategy, a psychological refuge for the infant to negate its early awareness of mother's separate subjectivity. "Splitting" creates a lack of ego boundaries or a sense of "I" and maintains the experience of fusion. The infant is in a continual psychic process of introjecting and projecting these good and bad objects. These are the infant's first, rudimentary relationships. But because differentiation caused by the mother's subjectivity is negated by the split, the internal, introjected objects of "good" and "bad" are experienced as extensions of one's "self" as good or bad. Klein termed this early experience of splitting, projection, idealization and omnipotence the "paranoid-schizoid position." The paranoid-schizoid position is a prerequisite to begin thinking and is the underlying basis for a sense of "self," "for identifying a consciousness of oneself in relation to others"[17] (Greenberg, J.R. & Mitchell, S.A., 1983, p. 93). The gradual dawning of experience of oneself as separate physically and psychically from m(other) begins the emergence of the subjective, an experience of self and mind in relation to another self and mind, a relationship of different, sometimes clashing desires and boundaries. According to Tom Ogden, the paranoid-schizoid and the later-developed depressive/reparative position are not developmental stages, but are in constant dialectic tension throughout life, where each position creates, negates and preserves the other. The intolerable conflict between love and hate towards oneself and toward both internal and external objects is unconsciously managed and titrated in dialectic tension throughout life[18] (Ogden, T. 1992).

In Biblical Thought, the History of the World Started with Separation

With all of the above in mind, let us turn to the story of creation and the Garden of Eden, two narratives that reverberate with Melanie Klein's themes of separation, love, hate and envy. In Jewish thought, Biblical narrative is the story of psychological-relational beginnings, not sexual beginnings. I start with Bereisheet (בראשית – beginning/Genesis), which is where Klein begins, as she states in her article *On the Development of Mental Functioning* (Klein, M., 1975): "From the beginning of life …"[19] And I start with perhaps the most famous opening line in narrative/literature/writing: "In the beginning, God created heaven and earth" (Genesis 1:1).

The Torah describes creation as occurring over a period of six days. In the creation story of Genesis 1, the principles of separation and differentiation are crucial to the entire account of creation. The world before distinction was chaotic, fused. Each day's creations are brought into existence by God's Word. The verb b'd'l (בדל), meaning "to separate/differentiate," occurs five times, emphasizing spatial, temporal and phylogenetic separation. In biblical text, repetition is a stylistic form indicative of emphasis. and the idea is suggested ten more times in the expression "after its kind," implying a separation of plants and animals by species. Distinction/differentiation implies otherness. From the beginning, there is a relationship of a subjectivity external to oneself, an "other"/differentiated self in which the desire to create meaning can be only mediated through language. In fact, the Hebrew word *kadosh* (קדש), which in English is most often translated as "holy," in its biblical Hebrew origin means something that is separated, set apart[20] (Kass, L., 2003, p. 52), so that when God "hallowed" the seventh day, God separated it from the other days and thereby made it distinct. After each creation by differentiation, the Torah states "And God saw that it was good." The concepts of separateness, differentiation and distinction of the cosmic and living world – not union – are the themes of Genesis 1 and continue in Genesis 2 and 3 to extend to human life. "The origin of the object world and psychic structure begins with the imposition of limitation and differentiation"[21] (Lutzky, H., 1989).

There is also another aspect to the creation story that is germane to our understanding of the Garden of Eden story. By creating, separating, differentiating, biblical text is intent on demonstrating the non-divinity of the celestial creations and that nature is morally neutral and intellectually vacant. The creation narrative is not a text of evolution, but rather comes to teach that the cosmos, which was worshiped by other cultures, has nothing to teach us about relationships, righteousness and ethics[22] (Kass, L., 2003, p.45). Contrary to Greek thought, "guidance in life is not found by reason, intellect, nor is it rooted in nature"[23] (Kass, L., 2003, p.58).

On the sixth day, God decides to fashion a creation from earth, hence the name Adam (from the Hebrew *adama*, אדמה, meaning "earth"). God gives the earthling/Adam dominion over all living creatures and vegetation for the purpose of sustenance. The Adam, we are told, is created male and female. God blesses the creation and commands it to multiply and to rule over creation. The earthling is initially presented as an undifferentiated, embedded, fused creation. A self-reflective ego/a mind, has to emerge from this primitive embeddedness, this dreamlike state, through a process of differentiation. This idea is expressed in the Midrashic recognition of the omission of the phrase "and God saw that it was good" that appears after each act of creation in Genesis 1 except that of the Adam. The description "good" (טוב), *tov*, as it relates to creation, has no moral valence. The meaning of "good" indicates "complete, perfect, fully formed, clear and distinct, and fully what it is meant to be"[24] (Kass, L., 2003, p.39). The Rabbis noted that in an archaic, primitive state, the Adam was not complete. As Roiphe (1968) states: "With physical birth the infant has not yet attained those attributes of the uniquely human psychic life: namely, self-awareness and consciousness."[25] This process takes place once the Adam is placed in the Garden of Eden.

In Genesis 2, the narrative language changes. Instead of *barah* (ברא), "create," we have the verb y'tz'r (יצר – form) to describe this act of creation (Genesis 2:7). Here, creation is fashioned. God breathes life into this creation, and the Adam/earthling becomes a living being. The Rabbis noted an anomaly in the narrative, in the spelling of the verb *va'yyetzer* (וייצר – "to form"): "And God formed the human" (Genesis 2:7). Instead of one *yud*, the verb is spelled with two *yud*s. One is extra. The Rabbis sought meaning. The Hebrew word *create* has the same root as the noun *yetzer* (יצר), an impulse/inclination. The Rabbis understood that this unusual spelling and its similarity to the noun *yetzer* (יצר) – "impulse" – indicated subtext and gave the Rabbis the interpretive opportunity to determine that man struggles throughout life with two competing impulses: the good/creative impulse (*yetzer ha-tov* – יצר הטוב) and the transgressive/destructive impulse (*yetzer ha-ra* – יצר הרע). I want to emphasize that these impulses are not drives in the Freudian/Kleinian use of the term, but reflect the early Rabbinic understanding, similar to Klein's, that the meaning attributed to one's self experience is determined by the quality of relatedness with "other." From the beginning, Rabbinic thought recognized the dialectic tension between good and transgressive impulses. The transgressive *yetzer* was perceived by some as an internal aggressor threatening the infant with persecutory fantasies, which, in Kleinian theoretical construction, creates paranoid anxiety. Envy was also recognized as an expression of the transgressive *yetzer*. Early rabbinic thought, like Klein, saw envy as the impulse to destroy the "good" that one cannot possess. However, the transgressive *yetzer* has little in common with the principal of evil in theology. Passion and desire are necessary for acts of creativity. Klein and Ogden recognized in the paranoid-schizoid position the source of creativity and a vitalizing influence on the depressive position, in that without the "de-integrative pressure of the paranoid-schizoid pole," the depressive position "would reach closure, stagnation and arrogance"[26] (Ogden, T.,1992, p.616).

We find that early Rabbinic thought expressed the attitude that the transgressive impulse is not entirely negative. Having been created by God, it has its good and creative purpose. The Rabbinic conclusion is recorded in the Talmud (b. Sukkot): "Were it not for the transgressive *yetzer*, a man could neither build a house, nor marry a wife, nor beget children, nor engage in commerce." In this midrashic interpretation of the second *yud*, the Rabbis understood something about human nature – that man is split from the beginning between competing forces within the self between love and hate, life and death, and the pull towards, and the trauma of, subjectivity, envy and reparation. These parts of the self are given and always present to be struggled with, but one can never fully be rid of them[27] (Schofer, J., 2003).

This is the story of the original human. This is the psychoanalytic subtext of the Garden of Eden narrative – not a story of sin, but of struggle and emergence, the stuff of everyday life. "The beginning of Genesis shows us not so much what happened as what always happens"[28] (Kass, L., 2003).

In Genesis 3, the story of the dawning of subjectivity through experiences of differentiation between self and "other" begins – at first slowly, and then with the full thrust of destruction and envy that, according to Klein, is innate to the birth of psychic life. For Klein, psychic life begins with the destruction of the object, the source of nurturance.

Klein's description of the world of the infant is evocative of the biblical description of early human life. Initially, the child exists in a state of primitive embeddedness, an omnipotent world where all wants are provided. There is no experience of frustration. The distinction between subject and object/ "other" is blurred. The Adam does not converse with God. In fact, he seems as unaware of God as he is of himself. The Adam is still in an undifferentiated, solipsistic state. Satisfaction of his needs is experienced as resulting from his own omnipotence.

One of Klein's most innovative, as well as controversial, concepts, was projective identification. Genesis 2:18 conveys perhaps the earliest description of Bion's (1959)[29] extension of Klein's concept of projective identification as an unconscious means of affective communication between infant and m(other). "In this sense – projective identification, which is the experience of another's emotion *as if* it were one's own … provides the possibility for empathic engagement in which one can sympathetically feel the suffering (or joy) of the other person as if it were one's own"[30] (Robbins, B.D., 2005, p. 526).

The Adam appears devoid of any sense of interiority, no interpretation of experience. Like the good m(other) containing the infant's primitive anxieties, God feels the Adam's affective state and identifies it as loneliness. "And God said: 'It is not good for man to be alone. I will make a fitting helper for him'"

(Genesis 2:19). Upon the first mention of "not good" in the creation narrative, the Rabbis wondered: "What is not good about loneliness?" With psychological intuitiveness, Rashi comments that if man were alone, he would think he was God-like. Loneliness, the absence of the "other," creates the presumption, the phantasy, of omnipotence[31] (Zornberg, A., 2009, p. 9).

But, first, God brings before the Adam all the animals for naming (Genesis 2:19). This is the first step in the separation of inner and outer, body and mind, self and other. The dawning of subjectivity begins with language. This is the beginning of an awareness of difference. In such a primal state, the Adam, in naming the animals, displays some intelligence and rudimentary experience of distinction between himself and the world around him, but there is no subjectivity involved; rather, there is simply registration of sensation with an absence of a feeling of "I-ness." Initially, Adam experiences himself as indistinguishable from the world around him. It is a state of archaic consciousness ruled by instincts and biological drives. In the act of naming the animals, i.e., a process of differentiation through verbal representation, language, Adam begins to distinguish his inner experience from that of the external world. It is the dawn of subjectivity, still primitive. Consciousness as a self-reflective ego begins in an undifferentiated state and evolves through various experiences/stages of differentiation.

At this point, God returns Adam to his dreamlike state and creates a female "other" from a part of the Adam's body. This "other" is initially not fully realized by the Adam as a separate "other," but rather as an extension of self. The Adam remarks: "This one at last is bone of my bones and flesh of my flesh. This one shall be called woman (*ish'shah*, in Hebrew) because from man (*ish*) was she taken" (Genesis 2:23). Adam gives her a name that does not reflect her as a fully differentiated status from himself. She is named woman/*ish'shah* because she is an extraction/extension of man/*ish*.

This concept of the early life of the infant, undifferentiated, helps to explain what I consider one of the most psychologically misunderstood verses of the story: "And the two of them were naked, the Adam and his woman, and they were not ashamed" (Genesis 2:25). Again, it is an "other" – in this case, the narrator – who is aware of the Adam and the *ish'shah*. They, as yet, have no self-awareness.

In her book, *The Murmuring Deep* (2009)[32], Avivah Zornberg, one of the leading biblical commentators of our time, presents the Ramban's understanding that, before the Tree of Knowledge transgression, the Adam and Eve act "with unchanging and unemotional purpose, like the stars in their courses" (p.13), in what Zornberg describes as "unselfconscious sexuality" (p.9). Zornberg quotes the Ramban: "The experience of love and hate, one of the most powerful modes in which we recognize ourselves, are absent" (p. 14). She goes on to say: "The fruit of the Tree of Knowledge engenders wish and desire, which the Torah never calls 'sin' ... . What they ingest is a new intentionality. A sense of each having his/her own mind" (pp. 13–14). In addition, Zornberg brings a remarkable discussion from Ha'amek Davar (19th c.) focusing on the word "shame" (ולא יתבוששו – *ve-lo yitboshashu* – they were not ashamed [Genesis 2:25]). Ha'amek Davar derives a meaning of this word from a different root, בושש (*boshesh*), meaning "late, delayed" (see Exodus 32:1), borrowing the meaning from Moses' delay in coming down the mountain (בושש לבוא, he tarried, or was late). "Prior to their transgression, the primal experience of Adam and Eve was without time lag ... a spontaneous and uninhibited mode of desire: hence the 'shameless' quality" (p. 15). From a psychological point of view, *va-yitboshashu* is not about sexuality, but, in their undifferentiated state, a state of indistinction between self and other; they experience each other as extensions of self and, as such, an unselfconscious sexuality. This verse is not purported to teach a moral lesson of chastity, but rather to reflect on their undifferentiated state.

When Adam and Eve are placed in the Garden of Eden, they are boundaried by the subjectivity of an "other," their provider, God, "breast." They are not to eat from the Tree of Knowledge of Good and Bad. This is the first time they encounter a "no": "It is God who sets in motion the events that trigger desire, by banning the tree. He creates the conditions for desire. By choosing the root of desire, God effectively brings to an end ... the fantasy of fusion and oneness, the repudiation of mythic union ... Adam and Eve become fully human only when a primal single-mindedness ... gives way to the separate minds, the separate desires, of man, woman and God"[33] (Zornberg, 2009, pp. 12–13).

The *Ish'shah* – The Woman

There are significant threads of thought linking Klein's paranoid-schizoid position and the biblical narrative of the conversation between the *ish'shah* and the serpent in the Garden of Eden. I suggest that we consider this conversation as an example of the infant's internal struggle with the split between the good and bad breast and with the bad, depriving, persecutory object being projected outward and represented by the serpent. The tree, split into good and bad, is the symbolization of the limitations effected by the subjectivity of the "other" – God. In the Kleinian paranoid-schizoid position, the distinction between metaphorical and literal conceptualization and communication collapses, and the subject treats the metaphorical as literal. "Although any two objects are similar in some respects, while being different in others, in the paranoid-schizoid position, individuals are frequently induced to repress either similarity or difference in order to alleviate painful effects of anxiety and depression"[34] (Carveth, D.I., 1984). In contrast, in discussing the use of metaphor in biblical narrative, Handelman (1982) points out that "a central characteristic of metaphorical truth is that it preserves the conflict and tension between identity, the 'is not' within the 'is,' in any given concept ... . Metaphor juxtaposes but does not fuse ... . There is similarity within difference, each retaining its own independent identity"[35] (Handelman, S. 1982, pp. 23–24). Rabbinic thought values differentiation, metaphorical multiplicity, multiple meaning, and highlighting the similarity in dissimilarity[36] (Handelman, S., 1982, p. 33).

Bion (1957) suggests that the omnipotent aspect of the self is so outraged by emerging reality that it assaults its own mental functions. This assault erases the capacities needed for symbol formation and abstraction, entrapping one in the world of literal conceptualization. The split of the object is in actuality a defense, a way for the infant to deny early awareness of mother's separate subjectivity and thus maintain the experience of fusion. Splitting prevents thinking and obliterates the ego-boundaries necessary for a sense of "I," a subjective interpreter of experience (Bion, W.R., 1957).[37]

In discussing the Garden of Eden, Zornberg (2009) emphasizes that prior to any human act is desire. Without desire, it is impossible to do anything. Desire moves things forward. Paradoxically, however, desire is generated by obstacles. "God sets in place obstacles to sharpen that desire ... to keep the fires stoked. The obstacle is there for the sake of desire"[38] (p.10). The obstacle in the Garden of Eden is the prohibition, the limitation by the subjectivity of the "other," God, symbolically represented by the cryptically named Tree of Knowledge of Good and Bad. Rather than infantile sexuality, the primary principle of development in Kleinian theory is destructive infantile omnipotence defensively employed in the paranoid-schizoid position to withstand/confront the terrifying and annihilating feelings of separation, hate and envy when confronted by the subjectivity of the m(other). As Zornberg frames it: "the abrasive priority of the other"[39] (p. 13).

As mentioned earlier, embedded in the language of the Genesis 1 story of creation is the proposition that nature is not divine or magical. "Thus, trees don't impart knowledge and serpents don't speak"[40] (Kass, L., 2003). Therefore, we need to search for the latent, or metaphorical, meaning of the story. I suggest that this latent subtext reflects Kleinian themes of love, hate and envy as the psychic bedrock of the human mind. I propose analyzing the *ish'shah*'s conversation with the serpent not as a story of sexual awakening or sin (a word absent from the entire episode, even God's rebuke), but as an example of the Kleinian paranoid-schizoid position, where the equilibrium of the infant is disturbed owing to "[de]privations of internal and external sources"[41] (Klein, M., 1975). This disturbance of equilibrium incites an intrapsychic defensive maneuver of projection and introjection of split good and bad objects. "Thus, the picture of the object, external and internalized, is distorted in the infant's mind by his phantasies, which are bound up with the projection of his [own] impulses onto the object"[42] (Klein, M., 1975).

Dialogue is very condensed in biblical narration, and in biblical Hebrew, emotions and thoughts are usually expressed through verbs. Since this is the *ish'shah*'s first conversation, her dialogue with the serpent requires close attention. The cunning/shrewd serpent is the representation of the woman's primordial, innate, disquieting desire for unlimited, immediate and everlasting gratification. In the paranoid-schizoid position, feelings, rather than being repressed, are experienced as extremely painful and dangerous, and tend to be expelled, split off and projected to objects. These objects become figments of the child's mind and turn into persecutory villains. The *ish'shah*'s own destructive, envious impulses incited by the boundary placed on her omnipotence and omniscience by the tree begin with the serpent's devastating attack on the abundance and nurturance of the good object, i.e., God, by inflating the limitation to ALL of the trees/ALL the sources of goodness, thus inflaming the persecutory anxiety of a withholding breast/other: "And the serpent said to the woman: Did God really say: You shall not eat of **any** tree of the garden? (Genesis 3:1)." From the onset, the paranoid aggression attacks the abundance of the good breast by conjuring up negation: "you shall not." The serpent extends the persecutory power of negation to all the trees, all the sources of goodness. However, according to Klein (1975): "Even during the earliest stage … persecutory anxiety is to some extent counteracted [in fleeting experiences] by the infant's relation to the good breast [and] help to counteract persecutory anxiety."[43] The *ish'shah*, struggling to hold onto the good, struggling to stay more cohesive, idealizes the good breast. In her attempts to prevent fragmentation, she repeats God's generosity: "We may eat of the fruit of the other trees of the garden" (Genesis 3:2). But her "splitting" is exposed when she augments God's injunction to include a prohibition against touching the tree. "And the woman replied to the serpent: 'It is only about the fruit of the tree in the middle of the garden that God said "you shall not eat of it or **touch it,** lest you die".'" (Genesis 3:3). From the beginning, the infant has been prepared for the disappearing satisfying breast by the harassing presence of annihilatory anxiety. In the paranoid-schizoid position, destructive impulses and persecutory anxiety are at their height. In order to account for the serpent's next response – "And the serpent said to the woman, 'You are not going to die'" (Genesis 3:4) – the Midrash fills in the textual lacuna by telling us that the serpent pushed her against the tree, and she sees that she does not die. With what appears now as an empty threat from God, and an arbitrary limitation, the *ish'shah*'s persecutory anxiety is transformed into envy.

Envy

The concept of envy represents a major evolution in Kleinian theory. "I arrived at the conclusion that envy is a most potent factor in undermining feelings of love and gratitude at their root, since it affects the earliest relation of all, that to the mother ... . An element of frustration by the breast is bound to enter into the infant's earliest relation to it, because even a happy feeding situation cannot altogether replace the pre-natal unity with the mother"[44] (Klein, M., 1975). Envy is distinguished in that its aim is the destruction and spoiling of the good – here, the good breast. Envy is "a spoiling hostility at the realization that the source of life and goodness lies outside the self"[45] (Segal, H., 1983, p.270). In envy, paranoid phantasy experiences the breast as hoarding the good for itself. "The first object of envy is the feeding breast ... it possesses everything [that is desired] and it has an unlimited flow of milk, and love, which the breast keeps for its own gratification. This feeling adds to [the] sense of grievance and hate"[46] (Klein, M., 1975). Envy undoes the splitting that protects the good breast. Metaphor becomes literal, concretized. The *ish'shah*'s envy undergoes paranoid ideation, with the good breast/God becoming the 'envious other,' the denier, the withholder. Now, not only is sustenance being withheld, but all omnipotent and omniscient experience. Klein highlights that, in addition to spoiling, in order to bolster the illusion of omnipotence, devaluation of the object is inherent in envy[47] (Klein, M., 1975). The ideation of a devalued object forms the serpent's response, together with omnipotent grandiosity, as he casts suspicion on God's motivation: "And the serpent said unto the woman: 'You are not going to die; but G-d knows that as soon as you eat of it, your eyes shall be opened, and ye shall be like G-d, knowing good and bad'" (Genesis 3:5). God here is cast as an envious and hoarding persecutor. The rush of the *ish'shah*'s reactions carries the affective quality of a manic triumph, an enactment heightened by a hatred of the crushing reality of the subjective 'other' and thus one's own limitations and separateness. Segal understands envy as a derivative of the death instinct in that it attacks life and the sources of life[48] (Shoshani, et al., 2012). The *ish'shah* is willing to destroy all. In the pre-symbolic state, where omnipotence shapes experience, the realization that the source of life and goodness lies outside the self is defended against vehemently through envious attacks. Eating and biting are orally sadistic internalizations of the breast, destroying all distinction between herself and "other." All subjectivity is erased. In the infant's mind, the breast now becomes entirely its possession and under its control. All the good that the *ish'shah* attributes to it will be her own. "And when the woman saw that the tree was good for eating and a delight to the eyes, and that the tree was desirable as a source of wisdom, she took of its fruit and ate" (Genesis 3:6). Rather than biblical metaphor, where there is a separation between signified and signifier, in the paranoid-schizoid position, the metaphor becomes substantialized. "[The *ish'shah*] becomes tightly imprisoned in the realm of fantasy objects as things in themselves ... psychological dialectic of reality and fantasy has collapsed in the direction of fantasy ... feelings are facts to be acted upon and not emotional responses to be understood"[49] (Ogden, T., 1985, pp.133–134).

Meaning now is connected to nature, to the Tree. The visual and oral are the determinants/sources of wisdom. There is no interpreting subject of experience. The capacity to have perspective on ideas and feeling is erased. "Thoughts become plans; feelings become impending actions ... . Understanding the meaning of one's experience is possible only when one thing can stand for another without being the other"[50] (Ogden, 1985, pp.133–134).

Conclusion

Recontextualizing the *ish'shah*/serpent story through the lens of Kleinian paranoid-schizoid dynamics, the creation narrative, together with the Garden of Eden story, place separation, love, hate and envy – not oedipal aggression, sexual awakening or sin – at the beginning of human unfoldment. "It is with melancholy that the child is given psychological birth"[51] (Robbins, B.D., 2005). Metaphor and the multiplicity of meaning, central to Biblical thought, collapse under the weight of paranoid-schizoid ideation and become literalized so as to defend against the reality of a subjective "other" and the dialectic tension between love and hate aroused by "being finite creatures and the desire to stretch beyond the here and now"[52] (Borodowski, A., Skirball Institute, 2013). "Experience is unconsciously shaped by metaphor, which, when literalized, assumes the status of myths"[53] (Carveth, D.L., 1984).

Notes

1 Kass, L. R., 2003. *The Beginning of Wisdom: Reading Genesis.* University of Chicago Press, Chicago, Ill.
2 Greenberg, J. R. & Mitchell, S. A., 1983. *Object Relations in Psychoanalytic Theory.* Harvard Univ. Press, Cambridge, Mass.
3 Rieff, P., 1959. *Freud, The Mind of the Moralist.* The Viking Press, Inc., New York, NY.
4 Freud, S., 1920. *Beyond the Pleasure Principle. The Standard Edition of the Complete Psychological Works of Sigmund Freud* 18:1–64. pep-web.org
5 Kass, L. R., 2003. *The Beginning of Wisdom: Reading Genesis.* University of Chicago Press, Chicago, Ill.
6 Kolbrener, W., 2010. "Death of Moses Revisited: Repetition and Creative Memory in Freud and the Rabbis." *American Imago*, 67:243–262.
7 Ashwin, M., 2007. "Against All Other Virtue and Goodness: An Exploration of Envy In Relation to Concepts of Sin." *Psychoanalysis and Psychotherapy*, http://www.psychoanalysis-and-therapy.com.
8 Kass, L. R., 2003. The Beginning of Wisdom: Reading Genesis. University of Chicago Press, Chicago, Ill.
9 Alford, C. F., 1989. *Melanie Klein and Critical Social Theory: An Account of Politics, Art, and Reason Based on Her Psychoanalytic Theory*, Yale University Press, New Haven, Conn.
10 Klein, M., 1946. "Notes on some schizoid mechanisms." In *The Writings of Melanie Klein, Vol. 2 Envy and Gratitude and Other Works (1946–1963).* Hogarth Press, London: 1975.

11 Stein, R., 1990. "A New Look At The Theory of Melanie Klein." *The International Journal of Psychoanalysis*, 71: 499–511, p.504.

12 Alford, C. F., 1989. *Melanie Klein and Critical Social Theory: An Account of Politics, Art, and Reason Based on Her Psychoanalytic Theory*, Yale University Press, New Haven, Conn.

13 Greenberg, J. R. & Mitchell, S. A., 1983. *Object Relations in Psychoanalytic Theory*. Harvard Univ. Press, Cambridge, Mass.

14 Ahlskog, G., 1990. "Atheism and Pseudo-Atheism in the Psychoanalytic Paradigm." *Psychoanalysis and Contemporary Thought*, 13:53–77, p.71.

15 Greenberg, J. R. & Mitchell, S. A., 1983. *Object Relations in Psychoanalytic Theory*. Harvard Univ. Press, Cambridge, Mass.

16 Ibid.

17 Ibid.

18 Ogden, T., 1992. "The Dialectically Constituted/Decentered Subject of Psychoanalysis. II. The Contributions of Klein and Winnicott." *International Journal of Psychoanalysis,* 73, 613–626.

19 Klein, M., 1975. "11. On the Development of Mental Functioning (1958)." *Envy and Gratitude and Other Works 1946–1963.* The International Psycho-Analytical Library, 104:236–246, 1958, p.85.

20 Kass, L. R., 2003. The Beginning of Wisdom: Reading Genesis. University of Chicago Press, Chicago, Ill.

21 Lutzky, H., 1989. "Reparation and Tikkun: A Comparison of the Kleinian and Kabbalistic Concepts." *International Review of Psychoanalysis*, 16:449–458.

22 Kass, L. R., 2003. The Beginning of Wisdom: Reading Genesis. University of Chicago Press, Chicago, Ill.

23 Ibid.

24 Ibid.

25 Roiphe, H., 1968. "On an Early Genital Phase – With an addendum on Genesis." *Psychoanalytic Study of the Child*, 23:348–365.

26 Ogden, T., 1992. "The Dialectically Constituted/Decentered Subject of Psychoanalysis. II. The Contributions of Klein and Winnicott." *International Journal of Psychoanalysis,* 73, 613–626.

27 Schofer, J., 2003. "The Redaction of Desire: Structure and Editing of Rabbinic Teachings Concerning Yeser ("Inclination")," *The Journal of Jewish Thought and Philosophy*, Vol. 12, No. 1, pp.19–53.

28 Kass, L. R., 2003. The Beginning of Wisdom: Reading Genesis. University of Chicago Press, Chicago, Ill.

29 Bion, W. R., 1959. "Attacks on Linking." *International Journal of Psychoanalysis*, 40:308–315.

30 Robbins, B. D., 2005. "The Psychogenesis of the Self and the Emergence of Ethical Relatedness: Klein in Light of Merleau-Ponty." *Journal of Theoretical and Philosophical Psychology*, 25(2): 191–223.

31 Zornberg, A., 2009. *The Murmuring Deep*, Schocken Books, a division of Random House, Inc., New York, NY.

32 Ibid.

33 Ibid.

34 Carveth, D. L., 1984. "The Analyst's Metaphors: A Deconstructionist Perspective." *Psychoanalysis and Contemporary Thought,* 7:491–560.

35 Handelman, S. A., 1982. *The Slayers of Moses: The Emergence of Rabbinic Interpretation in Modern Literary Theory*. State University of New York Press, Albany, NY.

36 Ibid.

37 Bion, W. R., 1957. "Differentiation of the Psychotic from the Non-Psychotic Personalities." *International Journal of Psychoanalysis*, 38:266–275.
38 Zornberg, A., 2009. *The Murmuring Deep*, Schocken Books, a division of Random House, Inc., New York, NY.
39 Ibid.
40 Kass, L. R., 2003. The Beginning of Wisdom: Reading Genesis. University of Chicago Press, Chicago, Ill.
41 Klein, M., 1975. "10. Envy and Gratitude (1957)." *Envy and Gratitude and Other Works 1946–1963*. The International Psycho-Analytical Library, 104:176–235.
42 Ibid.
43 Ibid.
44 Ibid.
45 Segal, H., 1983. "Some Clinical Implications of Melanie Klein's Work – Emergence from Narcissism." *International Journal of Psychoanalysis*, 64:269–276.
46 Klein, M., 1975. "10. Envy and Gratitude (1957)." *Envy and Gratitude and Other Works 1946–1963*. The International Psycho-Analytical Library, 104:176–235.
47 Ibid.
48 Shoshani, M., Shoshani, B., Kella, R. & Becker, M., 2012. "Green Eyes, Crows, and Scorpions: Envy in the Contexts of Neediness, Separateness, and Narcissism." *Psychoanalytic Psychology*, 29:440–458.
49 Ogden, T. H., 1985. "On Potential Space." *International Journal of Psychoanalysis*, 66:129–141.
50 Ibid.
51 Robbins, B. D., 2005. "The Psychogenesis of the Self and the Emergence of Ethical Relatedness: Klein in Light of Merleau-Ponty." *Journal of Theoretical and Philosophical Psychology*, 25(2): 191–223.
52 Borodowski, A., 2013. "Let's Leave God Alone!" Skirball Institute Spring 2013, New York NY.
53 Carveth, D. L., 1984. "The Analyst's Metaphors: A Deconstructionist Perspective." *Psychoanalysis and Contemporary Thought,* 7:491–560.

References

Ashwin, M., 2007. "Against All Other Virtue and Goodness: An Exploration of Envy In Relation to Concepts of Sin." *Psychoanalysis and Psychotherapy*.

Ahlskog, G., 1990. "Atheism and Pseudo-Atheism in the Psychoanalytic Paradigm." *Psychoanalysis and Contemporary Thought*, 13(53–77):71.

Alford, C.F., 1989. *Melanie Klein and Critical Social Theory: An Account of Politics, Art, and Reason Based on Her Psychoanalytic Theory*, Yale University Press, New Haven, Conn.

Aron, L. 1996. *A Meeting of Minds*. The Analytic Press, Hillsdale, NJ.

Bion, W.R., 1959. "Attacks on Linking." *International Journal of Psychoanalysis*, 40:308–315.

Bion, W.R., 1957. "Differentiation of the Psychotic from the Non-Psychotic Personalities." *International Journal of Psychoanalysis*, 38:266–275.

Bloom, H. 1987. "The Strong Light of the Canonical." *The City College Papers*, 20:1–77. New York.

Borodowski, A., 2013. "Let's Leave God Alone!" Skirball Institute Spring 2013, New York NY.

Carveth, D.L., 1984. "The Analyst's Metaphors: A Deconstructionist Perspective." *Psychoanalysis and Contemporary Thought*, 7:491–560.

Freud, S., 1920. "Beyond the Pleasure Principle." *The Standard Edition of the Complete Psychological Works of Sigmund Freud*, 18:1–64. Pep-web.org.

Greenberg, J.R. & Mitchell, S.A., 1983. *Object Relations in Psychoanalytic Theory.* Harvard Univ. Press, Cambridge, Mass.

Handelman, S.A., 1981. "Interpretation as Devotion: Freud's Relation to Rabbinic Hermeneutics." *Psychoanalytic Rev. Summer*, 68(2):201–208.

Handelman, S.A., 1982. *The Slayers of Moses: The Emergence of Rabbinic Interpretation in Modern Literary Theory.* State University of New York Press, Albany, NY.

Kass, L.R., 2003. *The Beginning of Wisdom: Reading Genesis.* University of Chicago Press, Chicago, Ill.

Klein, M., 1946. "Notes on some schizoid mechanisms." In *The Writings of Melanie Klein, Vol. 2 Envy and Gratitude and Other Works* (1946–1963). Hogarth Press, London: 1975.

Klein, M., 1975. "10. Envy and Gratitude (1957)." *Envy and Gratitude and Other Works 1946–1963. The International Psycho-Analytical Library*, 104:176–235.

Klein, M., 1975. "11. On the Development of Mental Functioning (1958)." *Envy and Gratitude and Other Works 1946–1963. The International Psycho-Analytical Library*, 104(236–246):1958, 85.

Kolbrener, W., 2010. "Death of Moses Revisited: Repetition and Creative Memory in Freud and the Rabbis." *American Imago*, 67:243–262.

Lutzky, H., 1989. "Reparation and Tikkun: A Comparison of the Kleinian and Kabbalistic Concepts." *International Review of Psychoanalysis*, 16:449–458.

Ogden, T.H., 1985. "On Potential Space." *International Journal of Psychoanalysis*, 66:129–141.

Rieff, P., 1959. *Freud, The Mind of the Moralist.* The Viking Press, Inc., New York, NY.

Robbins, B.D., 2005. "The Psychogenesis of the Self and the Emergence of Ethical Relatedness: Klein in Light of Merleau-Ponty." *Journal of Theoretical and Philosophical Psychology*, 25(2):191–223.

Roiphe, H., 1968. "On an Early Genital Phase – With an addendum on Genesis." *Psychoanalytic Study of the Child*, 23:348–365.

Schofer, J., 2003. "The Redaction of Desire: Structure and Editing of Rabbinic Teachings Concerning Yeser ("Inclination")." *The Journal of Jewish Thought and Philosophy*, 12(1):19–53.

Segal, H., 1983. "Some Clinical Implications of Melanie Klein's Work – Emergence from Narcissism." *International Journal of Psychoanalysis*, 64:269–276.

Shoshani, M., Shoshani, B., Kella, R. & Becker, M., 2012. "Green Eyes, Crows, and Scorpions: Envy in the Contexts of Neediness, Separateness, and Narcissism." *Psychoanalytic Psychology*, 29:440–458.

Stein, R., 1990. "A New Look At The Theory of Melanie Klein." *The International Journal of Psychoanalysis*, 71(499–511):504.

Zornberg, A., 2009. *The Murmuring Deep*, Schocken Books, a division of Random House, Inc., New York, NY.

6

THE UNTHINKABLE SATANIC

A Psychoanalytic Insight into the Shofar as Symptom[1]

Aton Holzer

Current psychoanalysis, especially psychoanalytic psychotherapy, is increasingly aware of the role of non- or neo-structure in human experience and the need for formless pockets of emotional turbulence alongside the dimension of structure and coherent verbal interpretations. As it turns out, religious belief and practice has always also contended with this tension, particularly in the effort to balance raw, formless and perhaps more authentic emotion with the mandate of normative formulae and structured prayer. This balance may play an important role in the way that Hassidic and Hassidically influenced thinkers made sense of a well-known, but poorly understood, Jewish ritual.

One of the most unusual practices in Jewish tradition is the sounding of the Shofar during the first of the Jewish high holidays, particularly on *Rosh Hashana*, the Jewish New Year. One hundred blasts of a ram's horn are sounded, in sets both separate from and also within the structure of the *Mussaf* prayer, the holiday-specific additional prayer service of Rosh Hashana, the Jewish New Year. The horn is once again sounded at the very end of the Yom Kippur service, ten days later.

The Babylonian Talmud (*Rosh Hashana,* 16a) sets out to explore the meaning of this biblical commandment, though it seems to obscure more than it reveals. And yet this passage becomes a *locus classicus* for the doctrine of the unknowability of the mind of God:

> Rabbi Yitzḥak said: "Why does one sound [*tok'in*] on Rosh Hashana?" [The anonymous editor responds:] "Why do we sound? The Merciful One states 'Sound! [*tik'u*]' (Psalms 81:4)." Rather [the question was], "Why does one sound blasts [*te'ru'a* (plural)]?" "Sound a *te'ru'a* (singular)? [The anonymous editor responds:] The Merciful One states: 'a memorial

DOI: 10.4324/9781003266600-9

proclaimed with the blast [*te'ru'a*] of horns' [Leviticus 23:24]." Rather [the question ought to have been], "Why does one sound long-blast [*te'ki'a*] and short-blasts [*te'ru'a*] sitting and [then again we] sound a *te'ki'a* and a *te'ru'a* while they are standing? In order to confuse [*le-ar'bev*] the Satan."

The Talmud makes clear that the ultimate or full reason for the commandment of Shofar itself is unknowable, since it is a divine edict. The practice of extending the sounding of the Shofar beyond the divinely prescribed blasts (those integrated within the prayer-service) is, however, given a rationale: *to confuse* (literally, to stir, or mix) *the accusing angel*, "the Satan." Medieval halakhic scholars[2] suggest that this explanation also covers a further, later expansion – the Shofar blasts sounded daily throughout the month of *Elul*, a full 30 days prior to Rosh Hashana, at the conclusion of morning services in Ashkenazic custom. That is, while such extra soundings are not biblically required, the custom was instituted, again, *in order to "confuse the Satan."*

The various commentators on the Talmud deal with the three most significant conceptual difficulties posed by this cryptic passage.

1 One problem is purely logical: if the rationale for sounding the Shofar is unknowable – effectively senseless, owing to its divine source – then how can there be any sense in voluntarily extending this activity?[3]
2 A second problem is semantic: if the purpose is to "mix up" or confuse the Satan – ostensibly in order to fool him into thinking that some other reality prevails, jumbling unlikely scenarios in the Accuser's mind – we ask: what might such an alternative reality be?
3 The third problem is theological: Is the Satan really best conceived of as a human-like personality who can be duped? Given Judaism's overall theology, the concretized version of Satan seems not only child-like but simply illegitimate.[4]

To speak now in more detail about the third dilemma, the very idea of a distinct angelic figure by this name emerges only in some of the very last books of the Bible, Zechariah, Job and I Chronicles, and even in these locations the idea of a distinct identity is debatable. Considering the plain meaning of the text, there is nothing to suggest that "the adversary" is anything but a loyal member of God's retinue. Certainly, in extracanonical Second Temple literature and the Gospels, Satan, *be'liya'al*, *mas'te'ma*[5] and, much later, *diablos* emerge as a personified evil agent and God's adversary, probably under the influence of Zoroastrian dualism.[6] Rabbinic literature, however, in the main, shies away from such personification. While Samael/ Satan as a character emerges in Amoraic (mid third- to fifth-century) Jewish literature, he is a minor personification tasked with tempting man to do evil (and also to be the angel of the death), who, in both roles, is subservient to

God and sometimes cast as a trickster (Friedman & Lipman, 1999). Only in the ninth-century Midrash *Pirke de-Rabbi Eliezer* does this character assume the role of fallen angel and Divine antagonist, similar to Christian and Islamic traditions (Adelman, 2009) (even if elements can be identified in prior sources; cf. Dulkin, 2014).

The view of rabbinic scholars of the first half of the second millennium – known as the "*Rishonim*" – are divided between the rationalists like Maimonides (*Guide* III:22) who identifies the Satan with the evil inclination – an abstraction – and the Kabbalists, from the 12th-century Rabbi Isaac b. Jacob ha-Kohen of Spain and on through the Zohar, who continued the Pirkei de-Rabbi Eliezer's trend and developed myths supporting a dualistic approach to evil with multiple personified evil forces (Dan, 1980). Clearly, this passage is most problematic for the more rationalistically inclined of the rabbinic sages and thinkers.

Among rabbinic exegetes spanning the second millennium, three approaches emerge. Some commentators appear to take the idea of confusing an accuser quite literally. There are many more who take the idea, including the concept of the Satan – identified with the evil inclination, the *yetzer ha-ra*– more conceptually. Finally, there emerges a more modern approach, informed by psychoanalytic theory.

A Celebration of Compliance

Rabbi Shlomo Yitzḥaki [known by the acronym Rashi] (1040–1105), in his commentary to the tractate (16b s.v. *k'deile'arbev*) addresses the first matter: what good can there be in a content-free edict imposed by Divine fiat? He writes, "to confuse the Satan: so that he does not accuse. When he hears the Jews cherishing the commandments, his words are plugged up." Since we cannot reason as to what Shofar means, our performance of the commandment is an act of unadulterated Divine obedience. The extension of the blasts celebrates our embrace of blind Divine obeisance, and **that itself** is a potent source of merit. This mirrors a view found in his contemporary, Rabbeinu Ḥananel ben Ḥushiel (990–1053), in his comments on the passage.

The Future Is Now? Pre-Echoes of the Eschaton

The semantic problem is appropriately addressed by a lexicographer, Rabbi Natan ben Yeḥiel of Rome (1035–1106), whose lexicon *Sefer he-'Arukh* is cited in the *Tosafot-* (addenda) gloss to 16b (s.v. *k'dei le'arbev*): "[As is brought] in 'the *Yerushalmi*,'[7] 'He will swallow up death forever (Isaiah, 25:8),' and it is written 'And it shall come to pass in that day, that the great shofar shall be blown (Isaiah, 27:13)' – when he hears the voice of the shofar one time, he becomes panicked and not panicked, and when he hears it a second time, he says, 'certainly this is the shofar of "the great shofar shall be blown," and my time has come to be swallowed up,' and he is confused and does not have time to formulate an accusation." In other words, the circumstance of the early Rosh Hashana *shofar* is confused with that of the eschatological herald of redemption.

This view is cited by numerous sources, and a version surfaces in *Tikkunei Zohar* (21,51b), a Kabbalistic text of evidently pseudo-epigraphical origin, attributed to second-century sages in the land of Israel, but which first surfaces in 13th-century Spain. The relevant passage states: "… He gave them the advice to wake up with the shofar, for with it the Holy One, Blessed be He will in the future gather the Jews from exile from the four directions … and he (Samael) thinks that it is his judgment day and flees …"

In his commentary to the *Tikkunei Zohar*, Kabbalist Rabbi Moshe Cordovero of Safed (1522–1570) (*Or Yakar* V, p. 199–200) explores its presentation of Shofar as "advice," an unusual term for a divine Mitzvah. He also wonders about the entire notion that the Satan could be easily duped. His interpretation is that unlike other Mitzvot, which Kabbalah interprets as *yi'hu'dim* (unifications) and adornments of the *Shekhinah* (the feminine emanation of the Divine), the essence of Shofar "reaches a place that human understanding doesn't tolerate." In this, the Shofar bears similarities to the future redemption, and the resurrection of the dead, both of which also are incomprehensible on the basis of our current understanding. The end of the future redemption is characterized by God's elimination of all evil. The Shofar thus opens the portal of redemption a small bit already in the present; the light of redemption "sweetens" or mitigates Divine judgment, and it has a chilling effect on the prosecuting angel who perceives that his efforts are futile – for ultimately the Jews will all repent – so that his days are numbered, and he is in real danger that the light may increase and achieve eschatological fulfillment. In a deft stroke, Rabbi Cordovero melds the rationale of Rashi and Rabbi Natan ben Yehiel by saying that *the unknowability of the rationale of the Shofar makes it the perfect tool for evoking the unknowable future,*[8] *essentially an unknowable state.*

The confluence of theme – the mystery of Shofar, the anticipated transformation of the redeemed world in the future and the present as its analog – becomes the basis for more recent approaches and perhaps a modern reading that coheres well with its antecedents.

"Satan": Exposing the Freud

The third question is addressed by Rabbi Solomon ibn Adret (Rashba, 1235–1310). Despite Rashba's Kabbalistic affiliation and animus toward Jewish Averroists,[9] ibn Adret clearly held some rationalist leanings, like his teacher, Nahmanides (1194–1270) (Berger, 1983). Ibn Adret writes, "Some explain that it is to subdue the inclination, as it is written, 'Shall a shofar be blown in the city, and the people not be afraid?' and Satan is the evil inclination, which follows the view of Resh Lakish (ca. 200–275), who said (*B. T., Bava Batra*, 16a) 'he is the Satan, he is the *yetzer ha-ra* (evil inclination), he is the angel of death.'" He then continues by citing Rabbi Nathan ben Yehiel.[10]

The identification of the figure of Satan with an internal psychological state first receives sophisticated treatment by the father of psychoanalysis, Sigmund Freud (1856–1939). In his essay "A Seventeenth-Century Demonological Neurosis," (Freud, 1923) Freud analyzes the archives regarding the case of a Bavarian painter named Christoph Haizmann (1652–1700), who suffered from convulsions, and described having sealed a pact with the Devil and becoming possessed by him. Freud concludes that the Devil is a projection of ambivalent feelings toward the painter's recently deceased father. Adhering to his libido theory, Freud's assessment of the origins of a perceived extraneous entity that embodies evil is revised by subsequent psychoanalysts, most prominently Ronald Fairbairn (1889–1964), who centers his analysis on the relatively newly expanded object relations theory. He sees the Devil to which Haizmann wished to cling as a projection of an introjected primitive "bad object," an introjected image housing negative traits of the parent that are split off from the external conception and instead internalized in a half-concrete manner (Fairbairn, 1943).

However, in light of Rashba's demythologization of the passage – rooted in the Talmud's own depersonification of "Satan" elsewhere – the more relevant angle of exploration would require us to better identify the *yetzer ha-ra*, the so-called "evil inclination."

In 1973, Andy Solomon (Solomon, 1973) contributed an essay to *Tradition*, the scholarly quarterly of the Rabbinical Council of America, in which he suggested that the *yetzer ha-ra* is properly identified as one instinct that constitutes both of Freud's life- and death-instincts, *eros* and *thanatos*, which compose the id, the instinctual part of the human personality structure. Moshe Halevi Spero, preeminent theoretician among Orthodox Jewish psychoanalysts (see Cohen and Gereboff, 2004; Cohen, 2008), believes that this identification is incorrect. While embracing Freud's point of view overall, Spero argues that the *yetzer ha-ra* perhaps resembles these drives *when* perverted or indulged to the point of sin, an object representational entity that can be thus identified post hoc, used to characterize sinful behaviors. Spero insists that the notion that unconscious instinct itself determines man's good or evil behavior or even personality is contrary to Jewish thought (Spero, 1975). Writing elsewhere, citing Rabbi Samson Raphael Hirsch (1808–1888), Spero states (1980, p. 76, italics in original):

> Man is neither inclined nor compelled to act by the *yezer ha-ra*; rather, the *yezer ha-ra* is an after-the-fact description of man's character once man errs and pursues evil ideals. The *yezer ha-ra, in a very real sense is man himself* if and when he chooses to make his ideal and his life-style *ra*, or evil.

In this manner, while the rationalists bring the evil inclination into the human psyche, Spero further de-differentiates the *yetzer ha-ra* as an integral aspect of the human self, unlike the unconscious instincts themselves.

Lacanian Interlude

But what is the self, and where does it come from? In another article, Spero (2006, p. 211), suggests that the best articulation of this question is found in the school of Jacques Lacan (1901–1981), one of the foremost interpreters of Freud in the 20th century, who developed a comprehensive theory to describe the origin of the self. Spero's inclusion of Lacan in his previously Freudian-Kleinian perspectives, in this and other essays of his, opened new vistas for the psychoanalysis-Judaism dialogue.

Among his many revolutionary contributions to Freudian theory, Lacan views the self as a mere "seemingness" that stops up the "hole in being" that is experienced by the senses.[11] Lacan drew upon philosophy rather than Freud's clinical observations alone – especially his interpretation of G. W. F. Hegel's (1770–1831) "master–slave" dialectic – in order to yield a theory of self-emergence that is based on what Lacan termed the "mirror stage" (Evans, 1996, pp. 114–116; Lacan, 2002, pp. 3–9; Žižek, 2006, pp. 61–78.)

Lacan sets about to resolve the following problem: All human beings begin as a part of another human being, the mother. At some point each develops a sense of self, of distinct existence. How does this occur? And to what degree is such a "self" true to individual experience, and to what degree is it essentially an amalgam that contains a higher degree of illusion, distortion of individual sense experience, otherness and uninterpretable content?

The newborn has no sense of independence from its mother. Between six to eight months of age the newborn gets cues from its environment – seeing its image in the mirror, amid other cues from adults about its physical form. While initially the baby feels threatened, the uncoordinated, fragmented and unbounded human baby comes to identify with the whole image presented, which offers it the possibility of psychological integration and physical coordination and mastery, even though it is troubled by its feeling of fragmentation – for this image is deceptive and the identification is narcissistic; it does not truly or wholly reflect how *the baby* feels. This tension between inner feelings of inadequacy and an illusory self-perception of wholeness continues throughout life. This, then, is the beginning of the development of the ego, which is the basis of the child's relationship to all that he perceives. The stage is complete with the infant's induction into the symbolic order, which is epitomized by language, a form of law; an all-embracing human system created by the Other, which approximates all that is perceived and situates the child's ego within it.

Nonetheless, the mirror image and the Symbolic order cannot fully represent their subjects, what remain located ultimately in the truly Real. Indeed, no language nor symbolic system can totally, or completely, articulate the Real, and the passions it contains. In particular, the feeling of oneness with the mother that presided prior to language becomes split-off from the necessary, ongoing symbolizing process, and can never be captured by language. That which is beyond language, or escapes language, gives rise to *desire*, and this desire – of oneness with the other – can only be displaced onto other things or persons, none of which ever fully replace what was lost.

It seems that Lacan's mirror stage recapitulates Hegel's master–slave dialectic but with the additional, clinically based nuance that, for Lacan, the child enslaves itself to its image in the mirror, and thereby achieves not true self-*recognition* but *méconnaissance, mis*recognition. Language cements the misperception. And desire is the remainder that is forever incompletely articulated. It is split-off from the child's world, and so the child, and later the adult, forever quests for the Thing,[12] some *ultimate*, some simulacrum, that which language fails to represent. For Lacan, when there is narcissistic psychopathology, when normative forms of creative adaptation can no longer be maintained, the goal of therapy is to destabilize the ego, since the ego is the point at which psychopathology begins. From this "reshuffling," the patient can then articulate a better self, abandoning encrusted idolizations and false-self structures, adapting, instead, a more aware, non-escapist, non-rigid identity and sense of relationships.

In contrast with language is the primal scream, what Lacan (1959–1960, p. 32) refers to as *the cry*, as that which "fulfills the function of discharge" and marks the first presence in the psyche of the Thing, which is yet unarticulated. It is the "bridge" to the Thing, which would "remain obscure and unconscious if the cry did not lend [to the Thing] the sign that gives it its own weight, presence, structure."

Returning to Jewish Doxology and the Shofar

Jewish prayer consists of a highly structured, formal component of religious experience – the liturgy, which is fixed and only allows room for brief personalized petition in a very small number of loci – and a less structured, spontaneous inward component known as *ka'va'nah*, a meditative aspect that is a *sine qua non* for the prayer's acceptability (Bindler, 1976). Against these two dimensions, Shofar seems to represent an even less structured liturgical movement. For all of the meanings that are imputed to Shofar by Kabbalistic and Hassidic sources – and there is no shortage of formal rules that govern its use – its sounding, ultimately, is significant for its bluntness, its rawness, its wordlessness and its *inarticulateness*.

Rabbi Shneur Zalman of Liadi (1745–1812) was perhaps the most distinguished profound thinker of early Hassidim and the founder of Habad Hassidim. He writes (*Likkutei Torah, Rosh Hashana*, 54c, 3):

And therefore *tik'u ba-ho'desh sho'far*, 'sound in the month the shofar' (Psalms 81:4), the meaning of *tik'u* is one single *te'ki'ah* – a simple sound that emerges from the 'breath' of the heart, from its inwardness, and it is a variation upon the cry of the heart that emerges ... from the inwardness of the heart that is well above intelligence (*hokh'mah*), as it is written (Proverbs 3:19) 'the Lord by wisdom (*hokh'mah*) has founded the "earth" (phonemes[13]) ...,' and regarding this is it is said, 'Lord, hear [in] my voice (*shim'abe-koli*)' (Psalms 130:2): the meaning of *be-koli* is that which is **within** my voice, which is its depth and inwardness, which is a variation of the inwardness of the heart – as opposed to the voice itself, which is drawn from the exterior of the heart, which comes after intelligence and knowledge. And that is the meaning of '*ba-ho'desh*' – meaning the renewal (*hid'dush*) of the worlds, from nothingness to existence, which are renewed every *Rosh Hashana* with the word of God and the breath of His mouth, blessed be He, occurs via *te'ki'ah*, which is the drawing of the inward delight (*o'neg*) and will (*ra'tzon*)[14] of the Supernal One blessed be He, which is well above the category of wisdom (*hokh'mah*) ...

Thus, while speech emerges from the emanation of wisdom, the undifferentiated sound of Shofar is a primal scream, representing that which is inexpressible in words; in its Kabbalistic correlate, it represents that which is ontologically prior to the emanations of logos, prior to wisdom and understanding. Rabbi Shneur Zalman goes on to suggest, in more technical Kabbalistic terms, a mechanism by which the *te'ki'ah* below stimulates the Divine process of world renewal, but these further explications are beyond our point.

One of the outstanding thinkers of the subsequent century of Hassidic thinkers was Rabbi Zadok ha-Kohen of Lublin (1823–1900), who counted Rabbi Shneur Zalman among his influences. Alan Brill (2002, p. 370) sees in Rabbi Zadok a religious precursor of Western psychoanalysis,[15] with a focus on the unconscious, the importance of the individual self and inner experience, and on interiority. (Admittedly, none of these rabbinic figures laid out anything approximating a psychological or psychoanalytic system; however, there is a great deal of psychological perspicacity in their writings.)

Rabbi Zadok opens his discussion of *Rosh Hashana* by identifying the Shofar as an instrument of arousal, an idea which already figures both in Maimonides (1138–1204) (*Mishneh Torah, Hil. Teshuvah* III:4, as seen above) and in Lurianic Kabbalah (*Sha'ar ha-Kavanot, Rosh Hashana, derush* 7). In one of his prime works *Resisei Laylah,* 35, Rabbi Zadok interweaves elements from all his predecessors. He first describes the Shofar as an instrument of arousal, which "arouses" God to us by arousing us to Him.[16] The traditional notion of confusing the Satan, identified here with the evil inclination within man, is tied to the awakening from a *di'ma'yon*, the Imaginary or the Freudian ego, that belongs to one of two varieties – excessive industriousness or indolence. Rabbi

Zadok then links these two states with "those lost in the land of Assyria, and the displaced in the land of Egypt" who will be awakened to come to the holy Mountain, Jerusalem – the opposite of the Imaginary – by the great Shofar of the redemption (cf. Isaiah, 27:13). He continues,

> And on every *Rosh Hashana*, it is from the aspect of human initiative that we blow the Shofar, and therefore [the yearly shofar] is **not** called 'great shofar' because the intent of 'great' is rather that which extends infinitely. And that is 'on that day,' *yi'ta'ka* – [the great Shofar] will blow of its own accord, and it does not specify who is blowing, because we argue 'return us' (Lamentations, 5:21) and God, blessed be He, replies 'return to Me'(Malachi, 3:7), and on that day, when the truth is clarified, the truth that God and Israel are entirely one, it is not fitting at all to call the arousal by the name of One in this unity as though there is a wakener and one who awakes, for in truth all is one ... and it will sound of its own accord, and therefore it is 'great' in extent. This is not so of the yearly Shofar of *Rosh Hashana*, which requires a human act to blow and does not extend completely, to [summon] those who are lost completely or displaced completely to come ... but nonetheless one who hears the voice of the [yearly] Shofar and fulfills the command of God awakens from his immersion in the Imaginary in this world, and of its own accord the Satan is *mit'ar'bev* [becomes confused] because the essence of his work is the immersion in the Imaginary ...

The sound of the Shofar is a cry; for Rabbi Shneur Zalman, it is the primal cry. Either misplaced desire, or for Rabbi Zadok, the problematic aspects of the ego itself, is the *yetzer ha-ra*, the Satan. The *yetzer ha-ra* is nothing more or less than the ossified, inconsistent or perverse dimensions of ego that are either poorly mirrored or introjected wishes and whims of others, concretely internalized, that have distorted the individual's own internal set of weights and values.[17] The sound of the Shofar dissolves the precipitate of the Imaginary, and writ large, unifies the Jewish people and boundless, formless, immanent God in an undifferentiated way; writ small, it accomplishes this for the individual. In Lacanian terms, the unsymbolized sound punctures the formal and conventional, returns us to a stage before the symbolic order, even demolishes the Imaginary order, the ego itself, and allows us to temporarily return to the primitive, boundless state. In the realm that is closer to the Real, desire is no longer separated, but is nullified within the consciousness of unboundedness. *Le-ar'bev* thus can mean to mix, in the sense of "mixing" or stirring the split-off Lacanian desire back into the primordial, undifferentiated consciousness; desire loses its separate existence, it is dissolved into the pre-ego human psyche. However, the Real is also not the realm in which we are meant to linger; we are meant to articulate a better self. As Rabbi Zadok continues:

... But in this world, in which the evil inclination is not uprooted from the heart completely, the entire awakening is only temporary ... and this is the entire work of man in this world, to be 'back and forth' and to strengthen and waken himself from his sleep every time ... in this regard, the Torah is a 'seasoning' (for the *yetzer ha-ra*, cf. Babylonian Talmud, *Kiddushin,* 30b) so that all of man's fantasies (*dim'yo'not*) should be in matters of Torah, as it is known that the powers of imagination can extend also to thoughts of matters of Torah, which also come from the power of imagination, until the fantasy be entirely Torah and truth.

Rabbi Isaac Hutner (1906–1980) was dean of the Chaim Berlin Yeshiva and a seminal thinker who melded Lithuanian *mitnaggedic* (non-Hassidic) and Hassidic thought. In his books of essays on the Festivals *Paḥad Yitzhak*, Hutner discusses the role of Shofar in various stages of Jewish history, beginning from the horn of the ram, which was offered in the near-sacrifice of Isaac, continuing with the Shofar-blasts at Sinai, and culminating in the messianic Shofar of redemption. He writes (*Rosh Hashana*, chapter 20):

And here we arrive at the encompassing power of the Shofar in the events and history of the assembly of Israel in its world ... in that it is in the Shofar's ability to resurrect traces and to turn the trace of a matter to the essence of the matter, and to return the righteous man to the city by means of the trace that the righteous man left when he left the city.

Rabbi Hutner seems here to depict the Shofar as the means of moving from the formal, physical concrete – which is necessarily evanescent and deficient – to the potent, enduring symbolic. The Shofar, in Rabbi Hutner's mind, pushes us toward *representation* of that which is otherwise formal, concrete and potentially fossilized, a counterweight to the general direction of the Torah and talmudic effort to recover the Law, the lexical, the real ideas behind the holy words. Thus, the Shofar is also the instrument that guides us from the concrete toward a better symbolic order.

By means of the disintegrative and reformative power of Shofar, we can emerge to *le bien dire*, the capacity to "say it well," in Lacan's words; to a reordered Imaginary and Symbolic order; to a new self. In this world, the destabilized, dedifferentiated ego does not persist, and a new ego, a new fantasy, must replace it – and man's task is to build a new, improved ego out of the substrate of Divine revelation. The Shofar is, or facilitates, Lacan's Symptom: a symbolic construction built around the experience of the Real.

Is this the simple meaning, the *pe'shat*, of the text?

No, as far as the way in which the ancient rabbis of the Talmud intended, probably not. But in terms of the biblical idea of Shofar, perhaps the view I have offered here is not as far off as it seems. Judaism avers that the individual is a microcosm of the world (*Mish'nah, Sanhedrin,* 4:5). In the Bible, the blasts of the Shofar and similar-functioning trumpets were the instrument used to dissolve and reconstruct the community, first around Sinai (Exodus, 19:13), then to herald the reconstitution of the Jewish desert encampment and its dissolution for the purposes of travel (Numbers, 10:2–8). The same is true of its function for the future redemption, as hinted to in Isaiah 27:13, as an instrument of ingathering. It likewise tears down boundaries, in the context of the walls of Jericho (Joshua. 6:20), and confuses and disperses enemy encampments in the Gideon story (Judges, 7:22). If it can destabilize and recreate the community, perhaps it also can creatively deconstruct the individual?

And for the future, its meaning applies writ large, as a deconstructive message to all the world: "All ye inhabitants of the world, and dwellers on the earth, see ye, when he lifteth up an ensign on the mountains; and when he bloweth a trumpet, hear ye" (Isaiah, 18:3). For classical and medieval Jewish thinkers, all men persist in a méconnaissance, misrecognition, unable to perceive God and His stewardship of reality. They live in an Imaginary order they construct for themselves, but there is a remainder that cannot be deciphered from the vantage point of the ego; as with *yetzer ha-ra* in the case of the individual, people conceptualize this remainder as the *sit'ra aha'ra,* the realm of the Other, experience as an evil that they cannot rationalize or assimilate, the dark in the world, which reaches its climax in death, the angel of death, *mal'akh ha-ma'vet.* Thus, Resh Lakish's identification of the angel of death with the *yetzer ha-ra,* just that the latter is the former's correlate on the microcosmic scale.

The Babylonian Talmud (*Rosh Hashana,* 26a) identifies the Shofar as a service of the inner sanctum, the Holy of Holies. Shofar reaches the inner sanctum, the innermost existence, the world's Real – the empty space between the cherubs that epitomizes what cannot be articulated in sensate materiality, materiality that itself is reckoned as the output of Divine speech (cf. *Mish'nah, Avot,* 5:1). The effects of Shofar on the structure of the human psyche and the structure of reality itself are one and the same.

The third blessing of the *Rosh Hashana Amidah* prayer refers to the ancient Roman Empire of the first and second centuries as *mem'she'let za'don,* the willfully destructive government in the first and second centuries: "And all the wickedness will vanish, as smoke" with the sounding of the Great Shofar. We can now understand this as also suggesting that the whims and wishes of the other that distorts the Jewish **national** identity will be rendered of no substance, a misapprehension or mirage. A thread running through classical to modern Jewish thought sees Shofar as an instrument that affords an opportunity for Jewish people, and the Jewish people, to "reboot," to regress from pathological structures and give voice to a new Symbolic order.

Notes

1 I am indebted to Prof. Moshe Halevi Spero for his meticulous review, comments and extensive contributions and insights. Thanks also to my daughter, Dina, for reading an earlier draft.

2 Rabbis Asher ben Yeḥiel (1259–1327), Nissim of Gerona (1320–1376), Eliezer ben Yoel Halevi of Bonn (1140–1225) and Jacob ben Asher (1269–1343). Most of these biographical dates are approximate.

3 This implicates a more general controversy among the great thinkers of the High Middle Ages regarding the nature of *hukkim*, laws for which no rationale is provided in Scripture. For the 11th-century exegete Rashi (1040–1105), such laws have no inherent purpose other than obedience to the Divine command; for 12th-century Maimonides (1138–1204) and 13th-century Nahmanides (1194–1270), they all have reasons, although while for the former, they serve to enable man to perceive physical or metaphysical truths, for the latter, they serve a theurgic function, often bound up in astrological doctrines, which is too deep for human comprehension. If the Talmud is declaring Shofar a *hok*, then the problem of extending it beyond the Divine command is clearly most acute for Rashi; for Maimonides, the command has logic, even if it is difficult to discern; as Isadore Twersky (1930–1997) writes, "Hukkim are messages which must be deciphered and decoded; they appear undecipherable only for lack of knowledge, insight, and sensitivity." For Nahmanides, they are even somewhat beyond our ken. See sources cited Woolf, 2001, note 18; discussion in Stern, 1997; and Twersky, 1980, p. 386.

4 See Epstein, 1959, p. 135; Urbach, 1979, p. 161.

5 A word that perhaps draws from two Hebrew roots – *li'stom* and *le'ha'sēt* – suggesting an agency that hates and also moves others, causing them to stray.

6 See the excellent review of sources in Jonker, 2017.

7 There is no such passage in the text of the "*Yerushalmi*" (the Jerusalem Talmud) that is in our possession, and it may never have existed. Scholars suggest that the true source is actually a lost midrash. See sources cited in Hillewitz, 1973, p. 121. Nonetheless, the second-century Halakhic Midrash, *Sifri,* Numbers, 10:10 is a precedent for the importation of the theme of the shofar of redemption into the context of the Rosh Hashana blasts.

8 Martin Kavka identifies a "Jewish meontological tradition" in which the messianic idea, which is decidedly "other" with regard to our existence, serves as the source of ethical activity in our own lives. This strand is seen to be in dialogue with Plato (429–337 BCE), Edmund Husserl (1859–1938) and Martin Heidegger (1889–1976), and he deems it authentically Jewish – tracing it back to a passage in *Pesikta Rabbati* – and finds it represented in various forms in Maimonides, Hermann Cohen (1842–1918), Franz Rosenzweig (1886–1929), Emmanuel Levinas (1906–1995), Emil Fackenheim (1916–2003) and Jacques Derrida (1930–2004) (if not in that order). See Kavka, 2004. See also Finkelstein, 2019.

9 In 1305, Rashba and his Barcelona Rabbinic colleagues promulgated a ban on the study of Greek philosophy. In many places in his landmark work on the period, Yitzhak Baer, 1971, theorized that the exposure of the "courtier class" of Spanish Jewry to philosophic rationalism, or "Averroism" (the philosophy of Ibn Rushd [1126–1198]) had a corrosive effect on their commitment to Torah study and religious observance, which made them progressively more vulnerable to conversion to Christianity than their Ashkenazic counterparts, ultimately resulting in the Spanish inquisition and consequent expulsion. While the spread of philosophic rationalism in Spain is incontrovertible, the theses that the motives of Rashba's ban were religious rather than political, and that Averroism or, generally, philosophical inquiry was

etiological of the seminal tragedies of Spanish Jewish history, have both been challenged. See, e.g., Saperstein, 1986 and Schacter, 1992.

10 In an innovative reading, the neo-Hasidic and postmodernist thinker Rav Shagar (Rabbi Shimon Gershon Rosenberg, 1949–2007) sees this demystification beginning within the text itself, in the manner in which the Gemara frames Rabbi Yitzhak's suggestion (Rosenberg, 2017, pp. 431–434).

11 Ellie Ragland, cited in Spero, *ibid.*

12 *Das Ding*: that which exists as the thing-in-itself, rather than how items are represented to the conscious and even the unconscious linguistically, or in a symbolic order. Similar to Immanuel Kant's "thing-in-itself," which can never truly be known. See Evans, 1996, pp. 204–205.

13 See his *Tanya*, Iggeret ha-Kodesh epistle 5.

14 '*Oneg* and *ratzon* are the inner and outer aspects of the uppermost *sefirah*-emanation, *keter*.

15 The parallels between psychoanalytic theory and Kabbalah or Hassidic thought have been explored extensively. See Berke, 2015; Eigen, 2012 and 2014; Pedaya, 2015.

16 Rav Shagar, in an undated recorded lecture accessed at https://soundcloud.com/user-986432322/zvg4qztffrdy accessed September 10, 2020 links this to Ludwig Wittgenstein's (1889–1951) existential wonder (Wittgenstein, 1965).

17 I am indebted to Prof. Spero for this formulation.

References

Adelman, R. (2009). *The Return of the Repressed: Pirqe de-Rabbi Eliezer and the Pseudepigrapha* (Leiden: Brill).

Baer, Y. (1971). *A History of the Jews in Christian Spain, Vols. I and II* (Philadelphia: The Jewish Publication Society).

Berger, D. (1983). Miracles and the Natural Order in Nahmanides. In: *Rabbi Moses Nahmanides (Ramban): Explorations in his Religious and Literary Virtuosity.* ed. Isadore Twersky. (Cambridge: Harvard University Press), pp. 107–128.

Berke, J. H. (2015). *The Hidden Freud: His Hassidic Roots* (London: Karnac).

Bindler, P. R. (1976). A Psychological Analysis of Kavvanah in Prayer. *Proceedings of the Associations of Orthodox Jewish Scientists* 3–4: 133–143.

Brill, A. (2002). *Thinking God: The Mysticism of Rabbi Zadok of Lublin* (Jersey City: Ktav).

Cohen, M. and Gereboff, J. (2004). Orthodox Judaism and Psychoanalysis: Toward Dialogue and Reconciliation. *Journal of The American Academy of Psychoanalysis and Dynamic Psychiatry* 32: 267–286.

Cohen, M. (2008). A Dialogue Between Psychology and Religion in the Work of Moshe Halevi Spero, an Orthodox Jewish Psychoanalyst. *Shofar* 26: 13–41.

Dan, J. (1980). Samael, Lilith, and the Concept of Evil in Early Kabbalah. *AJS Review* 5: 17–40.

Dulkin, R. S. (2014). The Devil Within: A Rabbinic Traditions-History of the Samael Story in Pirkei de-Rabbi Eliezer. *Jewish Studies Quarterly* 21: 153–175.

Eigen, M. (2012). *Kabbalah and Psychoanalysis* (London: Karnac).

Eigen, M. (2014). *A Felt Sense* (London: Karnac).

Epstein, I. (1959). *Judaism* (London: Penguin Books).

Evans, D. (1996). *An Introductory Dictionary of Lacanian Psychoanalysis* (Abingdon: Routledge).

Fairbairn, W.R.D. (1943). The Repression and the Return of Bad Objects (With Special Reference to the War Neuroses). *British Journal of Medical Psychology* 19: 327–341.

Finkelstein, D. (2019). Rejecting, Embracing and Neutralizing Determinism: Rav Hutner in Dialogue with the Izbitzer and Rav Tzadok. *Tradition* 51:57–67.

Freud, S. (1923-1925). A Seventeenth-Century Demonological Neurosis. In *The Standard Edition of the Complete Psychological Works of Sigmund Freud, Volume XIX (1923–1925): The Ego and the Id and Other Works*, ed. James Strachey and Anna Freud (The Hogarth Press, 1971).

Friedman, H. H. and Lipman, S. (1999). Satan the Accuser: Trickster in Talmudic and Midrashic Literature. *Thalia: Studies in Literary Humor* 18: 31–41.

Hillewitz, A. (1973). Shofar of Prayer, Announcement and Banishment of Satan [Hebrew]. *Sefer Margaliyot: Ma'amarot U'Mehkarim le-Zikhro Shel ha-Rav Reuven Margolies* (Jerusalem: Mossad HaRav Kook), pp. 118–124.

Jonker, L. C. (2017). "Satan Made Me Do It!" The Developments of a Satan Figure as Social-Theological Diagnostic Strategy from the late Persian Imperial Era to Early Christianity. *Old Testament Essays* 30/2: 348–366.

Kavka, M. (2004). *Jewish Messianism and the History of Philosophy* (Cambridge University Press).

Lacan, J. (1959-1960). *The Ethics of Psychoanalysis*. trans. Dennis Porter (New York: W. W. Norton and Company, 1992).

Lacan, J. (2002). *Écrits: A Selection*, trans. Bruce Fink (W. W. Norton and Company).

Pedaya, H. (2015). *Kabbalah ve-Psychoanalyza* (Tel Aviv: Yedioth Sfarim).

Rosenberg, S. G. (2017). *Shiurim ba-Gemara: Yoma – Sukkah – Rosh Hashana* (Alon Shevut: Makhon Kitvei ha-Rav Shagar).

Saperstein, M. (1986). The Conflict over the Rashba's Herem on Philosophical Study: A Political Perspective. *Jewish History* 1.2: 27–38.

Schacter, J. J. (1992). Echoes of the Spanish Expulsion in Eighteenth Century Germany: The Baer Thesis Revisited. *Judaism* 41.2: 180–189.

Solomon, A. (1973). Eros-Thanatos: A Modification of Freudian Instinct Theory in the Light of Torah Teachings. *Tradition* 14.2: 90–102.

Spero, M. H. (1975). Thanatos, Id and the Evil Impulse. *Tradition* 15.1–2: 97–111.

Spero, M. H. (1980). *Judaism and Psychology: Halakhic Perspectives* (Jersey City: KTAV).

Spero, M. H. (2006). To Whom, to Where, and to When Does One "Return" in Teshuvah? In *Judaism, Science and Moral Responsibility*, eds. Yitzhak Berger and David Shatz (Lanham: Rowman & Littlefield), pp. 189–291.

Stern, J. (1997). The Fall and Rise of Myth in Ritual: Maimonides versus Nahmanides on the Huqqim, Astrology, and the War Against Idolatry. *The Journal of Jewish Thought and Philosophy* 6: 185–263.

Twersky, I. (1980). *Introduction to the Code of Maimonides* (New Haven: Yale University Press).

Urbach, E. E. (1979). *The Sages, Their Concepts and Beliefs, Volume 1* (Jerusalem: Magnes Press).

Wittgenstein, L. (1965). Wittgenstein's Lecture on Ethics, *Philosophical Review* 74.1: 3–12.

Woolf, J. (2001). Between Law and Society: Mahariq's Responsum on the 'Ways of the Gentiles.' *Association for Jewish Studies Review* 25.1: 45–69.

Žižek, S. (2006). *How to Read Lacan* (New York: W. W. Norton and Company).

7

ABRAHAM BOUND AND UNBOUND

The *Akedah*[1]

Avivah Zornberg

How Many Did It Render Sleepless?

God's last word to Abraham is His command to sacrifice his son, Isaac. Never again will God address Abraham. When the command to sacrifice is annulled at the last moment, it is not God but an angel who calls Halt! from the heavens. God's final words will forever resonate in Abraham's mind: "Take your son, your only one, whom you love, Isaac, and offer him as a burnt offering on one of the mountains that I will show you."

The terror of the narrative is the plainest thing about it and the most mysterious. It permeates its every detail and its total structure. How has Abraham's beloved God changed His tone! For Kierkegaard, sensitivity to this terror and mystery is the essential qualification for approaching the narrative: "There were countless generations who knew the story of Abraham by heart, word for word, but *how many did it render sleepless?*" (my emphasis). Implicitly, he dismisses those who have not lain awake at night, gripped by the enigmas of this last moment in Abraham's life of conversation with God. Insomnia becomes the criterion for a true reading of Abraham's experience. *Knowing* the story blocks the heart; only in the sleepless dark can one engage with its paradoxes.

Nothing, it seems, has prepared Abraham – or the reader – for this turn. The shock of God's words comes at a moment when all tensions, within the family and with the surrounding culture, seem resolved, so that Abraham can finally live the fatherhood that God has promised him. The long-desired son is born, nursed and weaned. Hagar and Ishmael – alternative, provisional solutions to Abraham's childlessness – are sent away. Abraham makes peace with his Philistine neighbors. At this point, out of the blue, God demands a

DOI: 10.4324/9781003266600-10

sacrifice. Abraham's response is a silence that contrasts strikingly with his expressive reactions in previous encounters with God.[2]

The Unthought Known

But perhaps God's demand does not, after all, come out of the blue? Perhaps the *Akedah* has its own history, linking it in profound ways to the current of Abraham's innermost life? Perhaps the expression "After these things," which introduces the *Akedah,* refers to the secret archive of Abraham's past, to meanings that make the *Akedah* its almost inevitable consummation? His silence would then be an acknowledgment of something known though never before fully thought.

Such an idea, integrating the *Akedah* into the trajectory of Abraham's history, lies at the heart of the traditional midrashic claim that this was the last of ten tests that Abraham had to undergo.[3] Only here, at the culmination of a process and a relationship, we read explicitly, "God *tested* Abraham." But this final and decisive test is the tip of a midrashic iceberg: extending back through Abraham's history, there is a recurrent theme of *testing.*

What are we to make of such a quality of relationship between Abraham and God? In a classic comment, Ramban treats the test as an expression of human freedom – "if he wishes, he will act, if he does not, he will not act."[4] God tests in order to bring this freedom to its fullest expression, so that a potential may flower into reality. The test, therefore, is always for the good of the human subject undergoing it: it helps him/her to act out intuitive convictions, to make real what might otherwise remain hypothetical. The aim would be, then, to take the subject through an experience that will remap a world of self-knowledge with transformative clarity.[5]

Ten times, then, God takes Abraham through an experience that extends and deepens his self-awareness. We will return later to this notion of the test. Here, we may notice simply that the *Akedah* is traditionally viewed as the culminating moment in a lifetime preoccupation with *realizing* the quality and meaning of a relationship with God. For the first time, however, the *test* is explicit in the text: its physical reality makes indisputable; it defines forever something about Abraham and his way of loving God.

Becoming Whole

There is an earlier moment when God makes a sacrificial demand that Abraham receives in fraught silence. In Genesis, chapter 17, God tells him to circumcise himself and his sons after him, to mark an everlasting covenant. This covenant of blood is introduced with the weighty words "I am Almighty God; walk before Me, and become whole" (Gen. 17:1). We notice the theme of *walking* that permeates God's addresses to Abraham: from the first *Lekh lekha,* through this clearly metaphorical injunction, to the final *Lekh lekha* of the *Akedah.* Here, however, God is manifestly speaking of a spiritual movement, connected with *becoming whole.*

How is this wholeness to be achieved? By entering into a covenant that involves circumcision, the removal of the foreskin. The confluence of high spiritual demand and intimately physical act, of the aspiration to wholeness and a violent procedure of reduction, removal, constitutes a paradox that the midrash articulates: "Great is circumcision, for with all the commandments that Abraham fulfilled, he was called whole only when he circumcised himself."[6] In Rashi's version, we find: "'Walk before Me': in the commandment of circumcision; and in this way, you will become whole. For as long as the foreskin is on you, you are blemished in relation to Me."[7] In yet another midrash, Abraham responds with astonishment to the paradox: "He said, 'Till now, I have been whole! If I am circumcised, I will become defective [in losing a body part]!' God replied, 'What do you think? That you are so whole? You lack five organs.'" Only by an act of apparent diminishment can Abraham acquire a complete body image.

Abraham's response to the tension raised by God's paradoxical demand is a silent act of submission: "And Abram fell upon his face" (Gen. 17:3). Rashi comments: "'He fell': in dread before the presence of God. For until he circumcised himself, he had no strength to stand upright while God stood over him." In this reading, he falls, not in submission, but in a more primal gesture of collapse: the weight of his blemished body brings him to his knees, shame undermines him, and the place of circumcision, which is the mark of *unwholeness,* is hidden.

Why is it only now that standing erect in God's presence has become impossible? Inhabiting the same uncircumcised body, he has repeatedly spoken, even argued, with God, without collapse. In a brilliant discussion of this midrash,[8] Meshekh Hokhmah focuses on the status of a newborn before and after the eighth day of life: there is no stigma attached to the foreskin of the newborn until the time when the commandment of circumcision comes into effect eight days after birth. In Abraham's situation, similarly, before the concept of *circumcision as wholeness* is framed, the foreskin is a natural and unproblematic part of the body. He can therefore stand with perfect assurance in God's presence. However, as soon as God says, "Become whole," the foreskin[9] becomes *orlah,* problematic, disturbing – and destabilizing: "And Abraham fell upon his face."

The body, it seems, is constructed by language: the same body becomes a subject of self-consciousness when God declares, implicitly, that it is not yet whole. "Become whole" problematizes a sense of established reality: now the body has to be thought about. By opening up a vista of wholeness, God hints at a future never before conceivable. A moment of ripeness – the eighth day of the newborn life – radically reconstructs reality. And a new context is established for future responses to the events of the past. Past integrations break down; new meanings appear.

This transformation affects also the hopes and desires of the past. Freud quotes a witticism to this effect, in *Jokes and Their Relation to the Unconscious:* of a would-be political leader it is remarked that "he has a great future behind him."[10] Once, that man had a great future before him; he has it no longer. In fact, that futural condition is now behind him. The present is, in large part, informed by a particular sense of the future, which can be lost as the present becomes past. Malcolm Bowie writes: "The history of an impassioned individual life carries with it ... a history of the wished-for states by which that life was impelled."[11] The history of desire is encrypted within: the victim of the witticism carries his great future *behind* him. It is in language that these past futures appear, lost and found at once.

Abraham has come to a watershed moment in which language creates his body anew. This is a moment of aspiration – charged with the words, "Become whole" – and shame. Physically, nothing has changed; his psychic reality is decisive. A moment in time anticipates a more stable and complete reality, but the immediate effect is an embarrassed review of the past, with its "wished-for states."

The Moment of Afterthought

This reading of a transformative moment in Abraham's life offers us a preamble and prefiguration of the *Akedah.* Here, too, I suggest, the past, with its established ways of integrating experience, becomes subject to question. "*After these things,* God tested Abraham." The test is the effect of past things, of afterthoughts about those things. Here, a motif in Abraham's inner life, an emotional habit, reaches a critical moment. Repeatedly, the midrash describes him as reflecting about the facts of his experience. But these reflections have an anxious quality; he suffers from *hirhurim:* qualms, misgivings. Constantly questioning and redefining the meaning of his past, he inhabits a double history: outwardly, he flourishes; but inwardly, he is troubled by possible interpretations of his life.

Before we address the *Akedah,* a few examples of this midrashic theme will establish a sense of its prevalence. For instance, after Abraham wins the battle against the four kings led by Kedarlaomer, God, rather mysteriously, has to reassure him: "Do not fear, Abram" (Gen. 15:1). What is Abram's fear? In the text, the question is never answered. But the midrash[12] listens for Abram's qualms:

R. Levi explained this in two ways, the Rabbis in one. R. Levi said: Abraham was filled with misgivings saying to himself, 'Would you say that there was one righteous man among those troops that I slew?' This may be compared to a straw-merchant who was passing the king's orchards, and seeing some bundles of thorns, descended from his wagon and took them. The king caught sight of him, and he tried to hide himself. 'Why do you hide?' he asked him. 'I needed laborers to gather them; now that you have gathered them, come and receive your reward.' So, God said to Abraham: 'Those troops that you slew were thorns already cut down'; as it is written, 'And the peoples shall be as the burnings of lime; as thorns cut down, that are burned in the fire.'[13]

R. Levi gave another explanation: Abraham was filled with misgivings, saying to himself, 'Would you say that the sons of the kings that I slew will collect troops and come and wage war with me?' So, God said to him: '"Do not fear, Abram, I am your shield": just as a shield receives all spears and withstands them, so will I stand by you.'

The Rabbis explained in this way: Abraham was filled with misgivings, saying to himself, 'I descended into the fiery furnace and I was saved; I descended into the perils of war, and I was saved: would you say that I have already received my reward in this world and I have nothing reserved for the future world?' So, God said to him: "Do not fear, Abram, I am your shield [magen]," meaning a gift of grace [maggan] to you: "all that I have done for you in this world was an act of grace; but in the future world, 'your reward will be very great.'" – just as we read, 'Oh how abundant is Your goodness, which You have reserved for those who fear You.'[14]

Abraham is anxious (mitpached is the reflexive form of the word for fear): he expresses his anxiety with the interrogative tomar: "Would you say ... ?" In each of his three speculations, a nightmare possibility retrospectively ruins his military success: Did he perhaps kill one innocent man in battle? Will there be unforeseen consequences to the apparently conclusive battle? Both the moral qualm and the pragmatic one are countered by God's reassurance. But the third qualm is harder to counter: Does a charmed life, marked by miraculous escapes, deplete some essential reserve of identity? Twice, he has been saved from death: in the early (midrashic) story of the fiery furnace, and now in battle. In both cases, the expression is yaradti v'nitzalti: "I was already in the jaws of death ('I descended ...') and I was saved. Would you say that I have received my reward in this world, so that I have no reserves for the world to come?" In the grip of his misgiving, his triumph becomes a liability. He has won the battle, but lost his intimate claim on the future. Miraculous interventions diminish one's substance, one's autonomy.

In this scenario, too, God reassures him. But it is the misgiving rather than the reassurance that now claims our attention. In several such midrashic passages, a habit of hypothetical reconstructions of the past characterizes Abraham. He is said to be anxious (mitpached), worried (do'eg), or full of qualms *(meharher)*. These often-demoralizing afterthoughts are introduced in the biblical text with the words "After these things." Even in the famous midrash about his encounter with the burning castle, he begins his question: "*Tomar* ...Would you say that this castle is without a lord?" A fearful possibility is entertained that jeopardizes both past and future. On each occasion, his speculation wins a comforting response from God, as though it is only after a qualm is articulated and confronted that it can be resolved.

Another example of this emotional structure immediately follows the *Akedah* narrative (Gen. 22:20):

> 'After these things ...': When he returned from Mount Moriah, Abraham had qualms: 'If my son had really been slain, he would have died without children! I must marry him to one of the daughters of Aner or Eshkol or Mamre.' God therefore had the news sent him that Rebecca, Isaac's destined bride, had been born. This is what is meant by 'After these things [or words]': after the words that were evoked in him by the *Akedah*.[15]

Here, the word *hirhur* indicates a compulsive thought; the classic form is *hirhur averah,* sexual fantasies. These are thoughts with a life of their own, speculations that blur the clear boundaries of time and perspective. Abraham's failure to arrange for Isaac's marriage to a local bride was, *at the time,* a reasonable decision. It is only by benefit of hindsight that it seems delinquent: he almost lost his whole future. He has an untroubled future behind him; as a result of the *Akedah* retrospective guilt now possesses him. Again, God allays his anxiety, without dealing with the radical question of this kind of thinking.

The Sacrificial Wish

With these examples in mind, we can approach the *Akedah* as an event haunted by misgivings:

> 'After these things': after the misgivings of that moment. Who then had misgivings? Abraham did. He said, 'I have rejoiced and made everyone joyful, but I have never set aside a single bullock or ram for God.' God replied, 'In the end you will be told to sacrifice your only son to Me, and you will not refuse.' According to R. Leazar, who maintained that *ve-ha-Elohim* means God *and His court,* it was the ministering angels who said this: 'This Abraham rejoiced and made all others rejoice, yet did not set aside for God a single bullock or ram.' God replied, 'Even if we tell him to offer his own son, he will not refuse.'
>
> Isaac and Ishmael were engaged in a controversy. The latter argued, 'I am more beloved than you, because I was circumcised at the age of thirteen,'

while Isaac replied, 'I am more beloved, because I was circumcised at eight days.' Ishmael said, 'I am more beloved, because I could have protested, yet did not.' At that moment, Isaac declared, 'Oh that God would appear to me and bid me cut off one of my limbs! I would not refuse.' Another version: Ishmael said, 'I am more beloved, since I was circumcised at the age of thirteen, but you were circumcised as a baby and could not refuse.' Isaac replied, 'All that you lent to God was three drops of blood. But I am now thirty-seven years old, yet if God desired of me that I be slaughtered, I would not refuse.' God responded, 'This is the moment!' Immediately, 'God tested Abraham.'[16]

Again, the familiar *hirhurim,* the qualms that, on this occasion, lead directly into the *Akedah* command. In this case, Abraham's misgivings interrogate the authenticity of his entire life. "I have rejoiced and made everyone joyful ..." refers to the midrashic tradition about his open-door hospitality, his feasts shared with all comers, the blessings with which he contagiously celebrates God's bounty. Now, he notices the absence, in all the celebration, of any sacrifice. At first, it seems that his self-criticism is unjustified: he is, after all, described as having built altars.[17] However, reading closely, we notice that nowhere is he described as *sacrificing* to God: instead, "he called out the name of God." He taught the world about God; but the altar remains a symbolic presence in the text, rather than a place where real animals are sacrificed.

This is the critical moment when the idiom of a lifetime comes under harsh scrutiny. If there was no sacrifice, in the fullest sense, could all that celebration have been mere self-gratification? In the absence of sacrifice, the question of authenticity becomes an obsessive thought, which God defuses by declaring His confidence in him: "If I were to ask you to sacrifice your only son, you would not refuse." There is a double-edged sharpness to God's words: they are reassurance and shocking demand.

In the second reading, the same suspicion is cast on Abraham's sincerity – this time by the angels, who are similarly answered by God. Here are two histories of the *Akedah* command: "After these things" refers either to Abraham's own self-recriminations, or to the criticisms of the angels. In either case, almost inevitably, the doubt leads to the literal demand for ultimate sacrifice, as the only reality test for thoughts of this kind. The more radical of the two versions is undoubtedly the first: here, it is an internal event, a purely psychic crisis within Abraham, that precipitates the terror of the *Akedah.* In the next section, the midrash presents two versions of a similar episode, this time about Isaac. In his debate with Ishmael – "Who is more beloved?" – Ishmael seems to hold the high ground: he was of the age of consent when he allowed himself to be circumcised. Isaac, who was a mere baby, incapable of conscious assent, is left without rational answer. He can only cry out a sacrificial wish: "*I wish* God would ask me …" Only so will his good faith be demonstrated – by sacrificing his limbs, or his very life, if God desires it. God's response is immediate – "*miyad* – instantly – God tested Abraham." In the second version, God responds, "This is the moment!" In both versions, the drama of immediacy makes it clear that Isaac, by his words of desperate readiness, even of sacrificial desire, has precipitated God's demand.

In this subversive midrash, the *Akedah* becomes the fruit of a human psychic crisis. There are situations, apparently, when a human being desires self-sacrifice. If we focus on Abraham rather than Isaac, we are confronted, in the less radical version, by angelic criticism of God's favorite. Continuing the midrashic tradition in which angels carp at God's interest in human beings, they here express suspicion about Abraham's sincerity; they constitute an objective voice that is also a projection of Abraham's inner misgivings. In the first, more radical version, however, the claim is unequivocal: Abraham's *hirhurim* generate the *Akedah.* A habit of retroactive suspicion of his own motives and actions produces the reality test of literal and ultimate sacrifice. How else are such qualms to be allayed? The *immediacy* of God's response (emphasized in the second half of the passage) focuses the causal connection: Abraham's words, once spoken, can be answered in no other way. All along, God's faith in Abraham's total commitment was awaiting vindication; the reality check was always impending.

Through the prism of this midrashic account, a theory of sacrifice emerges. The subject is the human desire for sacrifice – as a clarification, as a simplification, a showing-forth, in a world of moral ambiguity. At the heart of all symbolic and hypothetical rhetoric about commitment waits the possibility, even the necessity, of literal enactment.

At the moment of the *Akedah,* then, Abraham's fear and desire make him ripe for the sacrificial act. "After these things," such moments hold a potential violence that threatens past integrations of reality. But this violence breaks out within the soul; it is not simply a matter of God's word descending like lightning at noon. It expresses a discontinuity with the past, but also a hidden continuity. All of Abraham's *hirhurim* undermine the past, as they all contain a desire for violent enactments. A suspicion of the apparent and the manifest, an agitated wish for unequivocal knowledge, informs them all.

If the *hirhur* is the repressed theme and tone of Abraham's inner discourse, a startling dissonance is suggested. A life of *chesed,* of loving and active involvement in reality and in the lives of others, a *charmed* life, in all its meanings, has, it appears, its shadowy underside. A habit of skepticism develops into a questioning of the essential idiom of that life. A doubt about authenticity leads directly to the demand that Abraham sacrifice the dearest thing in life. His doubt, God's demand … In these midrashic sources, the *Akedah* is fathered by Abraham.

Sacrifice and Intimacy

Such a view of the complexity of Abraham's inner world invites a psycho-analytic reading of his narrative. Before we turn to such a reading, however, I would like to meditate briefly on one possible meaning of sacrifice: the violent act that offers to establish a new intimacy with the transcendent, to "lose everything to gain everything" (Gaston Bachelard).

In his evocative study *The Psychoanalysis of Fire,* Bachelard begins by exploring the "reverie before the fire." "If fire … was taken to be a constituent element of the Universe, is it not because it is an element of human thought, the prime element of reverie?"[18] Fire warms and cooks, it gives comfort, but more immediately it calls forth a special kind of attention, a *reverie* on a specific object.

[Fire] suggests the desire to change, to speed up the passage of time, to bring all of life to its conclusion, to its hereafter … it links the small to the great, the hearth to the volcano, the life of a log to the life of a world. The fascinated individual hears *the call of the funeral pyre.* For him destruction is more than a change, it is a renewal.[19]

Bachelard gives the name "Empedocles complex" to the union of love and respect for fire, "the instinct for living and the instinct for dying" that are born of this reverie. Empedocles was a fifth-century philosopher who threw himself into the volcano at Mount Etna, so that he would be believed to be a god. Bachelard cites German Romantics who construct Empedocles' act as the "total death which leaves no trace … To lose everything to gain every-thing." "Through its sacrifice in the heart of the flames, the mayfly gives us a lesson in eternity." He quotes George Sand: "With what transports of blind joy and of love's frenzy these swarms of little white moths come to hurl themselves into [the fire]! For them this is the volcano in all its majesty."[20] For the dreamer, the life of the ant and the firefly configure the "death in the flame" that is "the least lonely of deaths,"[21] an act that fuses one with the whole universe.

The fundamental poetic theme here is the "call of the funeral pyre," which, Bachelard suggests, remains "profoundly real and active for unconscious reveries."[22] The fire reverie, then, represents a passion for love, death, and fire, in which sentimentality and ambivalence are in an instant transcended, all qualms and misgivings consumed in a single sacrificial moment. In this fire, loneliness is healed. Opposites meet, paradox reigns: destruction and renewal are one. Making no judgment, Bachelard conveys the content of this prime element of reverie, with its roots in the unconscious.

In another essay on fire, written in 1970, "The Sinister Ease of Dying," Marguerite Yourcenar expresses both her empathy and her horror for the young suicides of the Commune, who threw themselves into the flames a century earlier. With this voluntary immolation, she suggests, they protested against the violence and greed of the world. She titles her essay after lines from a poem by Victor Hugo:

And we must tremble, as long as
we have not healed
This sinister ease of dying.[23]

In her own time, too, other young idealists similarly died in protest against the destructiveness, materialism and hypocrisy of French society. Yourcenar raises a moral question about suicides of this kind. On the one hand, there is the necessity of uncompromising commitment: she quotes a Buddhist sutra, "The world is on fire, the fire of ignorance, the fire of lust, the fire of aggression is devouring it."[24] It is purity of heart that motivates those who refuse to live in such a world. But, she asks, in the face of "this Buddhist-monk type of sacrifice," what reasons can we give for living?

Those who have departed were surely of the best: we have need of them. Perhaps we might have saved them if we had persuaded them that their refusal, their indignation, their very despair were necessary; if we had known how to urge against the sinister ease of dying the heroic of difficulty of living … in such a way as to make the world a little less scandalous than it is.[25]

The fire of sacrificial death draws the pure of heart, but its "sinister ease" expresses a radical despair of the world. Ultimately, Yourcenar's judgment goes against the fire; life itself must be invested with a more fiery heroism.

In his major philosophical work, *The Theory of Religion,* Georges Bataille analyzes the nature of sacrifice. In his conceptual scheme, "death actually discloses the imposture of reality." Reality, the real order, reduces animals and human beings to the condition of *things,* valued largely for their *duration,* their capacity to endure through time. What has no place in the world of reality is the affirmation of intimate life that is fully realized only in death. Sacrifice, Bataille claims,

is the antithesis of production, which is accomplished with a view to the future; it is consumption that is concerned only with the moment …

This is the meaning of 'sacrificing to the deity,' whose sacred essence is comparable to a fire. To sacrifice is to give as one gives coal to the furnace.[26]

Sacrifice restores objects to "the vague sphere of lost intimacy," which is "not compatible with the positing of the separate individual." The individual participating in sacrifice is filled with anguish because he is an individual, and part of a world of things that requires duration. "Man is afraid of the intimate order that is not reconcilable with the order of things ... Because man is not squarely within that order ... intimacy, in the trembling of the individual, is holy, sacred, and suffused with anguish."[27]

In Bataille's scheme, sacrifice and the sacred constitute a moment of glorious consumption in which a hidden, spiritual reality – intimacy – flares up, even as it destroys the order of "things." The values he stages are those of life in the moment, fusion (intimacy) with the universe, a violent outbreak against the world of work, duration and fear of death. The sacrificial reveals a truth of intimacy that eliminates the contours of the individual. Although Bataille's sympathy with the sacrificial order is evident, he acknowledges the real danger of this order, the "unlimited fire," that "inflames and blinds in turn." Human life requires a balance between the extremes of surrender to immanence, which would return man to the "unconscious intimacy of animals,"[28] and the neutrality of individual and productive life.

The experience of anguish constitutes the pivotal moment when the individual moves toward an intimacy that threatens his individuality. Bataille's use of the term *intimacy* reminds us that the Hebrew term for "sacrifice" – *korban* – means "coming close" to God. At the heart of the biblical concept of sacrifice is the concern for intimacy, and the readiness to shed all that stands as a barrier between the self and God – even that very self.

Death by fire is the fate, we remember, of Aaron's sons – who "*came close into God's presence*"[29] – and "*brought close* a strange fire that He had not commanded."[30] On this enigmatic episode, the midrash comments: "They added love to love."[31] Here, too, apparently, we witness a human passion that is sacrificial in its nature, and can find its apotheosis only in fire. In the biblical text, a ritual act of gratuitous intimacy is mysteriously punished by fire; in the midrashic narrative, while guilt and punishment are clearly involved, one detects a real admiration for the fiery spirit of those who, in their fervor for a lost intimacy, transgress the order of the real.

Gathering the sparks of these fires, we can approach the passionate heart of the Talmudic figure of R. Eleazar ben Dordia:

> It was said of R. Eleazar b. Dordia that there was no harlot in the world that he had not visited. Once, he heard that there was a certain harlot in one of the seaboard towns who took a purse full of *denarii* for her hire. He filled his purse and he crossed seven rivers for her sake. While he was with her, she emitted wind, and said, 'As this wind will never return, so will Eleazar never have his repentance [return] accepted.'
>
> At that, he went and sat between two hills and mountains and cried out, 'Hills and mountains, plead for mercy for me!' They replied, 'How shall

we plead for you, when we must first plead for ourselves? – as it is said, "For the mountains shall depart and the hills be removed ... '" (Isa. 54:10).

He then cried: 'Heaven and earth, plead for mercy for me!' And they replied, 'How shall we plead for you, when we must first plead for ourselves? – as it is said, "For the heavens shall vanish away like smoke, and the earth shall wax old like a garment'" (Isa. 51:6). He then cried: 'Sun and moon, plead for mercy for me!' And they also replied, 'How shall we plead for you, when we must first plead for ourselves? – as it is said, "Then the moon shall be confounded and the sun ashamed'" (24:23). He cried, 'Stars and constellations, plead for mercy for me!' And they too replied, 'How shall we plead for you, when we must first plead for ourselves? – as it is said, "And all the hosts of heaven shall molder away'" (34:4).

Then, he cried, 'The thing depends on me alone!' And he placed his head between his knees and bellowed in weeping until his soul departed. Then, a heavenly voice was heard proclaiming, 'Rabbi Eleazar b. Dordai is welcomed into the life of the world to come!' ... Rabbi heard of this and wept and said, 'One person may acquire eternal life over many years, another in one hour!' Rabbi also said, 'Is it not sufficient for penitents that they are accepted, but they are even called Rabbi!'[32]

The penitent libertine dies in an ecstasy of contrition; thus, he "acquires his world" – that is, eternal life – in one instant. Within the natural world, the world of objective things – sun, moon, mountains, hills – he cannot be helped: like them, he is a thing threatened by death. He places his head between his knees and bellows aloud, till his soul departs: like an animal, he bellows in anguish as he relinquishes his hold on life.

The reaction of Rabbi, on hearing the story, is profoundly ambivalent. To achieve eternal life in one hour is to threaten the values of the Rabbinic world that Rabbi represents: the rigorous and unceasing culture of spiritual work. For, in essence, it is to choose death, the moment of anguish and glorious consumption: to lose all to gain all. Rabbi is committed to life and its anxieties, its qualms and misgivings, and its danger of attrition. And yet, he acknowledges the authenticity of eternal life gained in an instant. Even the title "Rabbi," the very title that he himself has earned through a lifetime of discipline, has been bestowed peremptorily on the penitent sinner. Rabbi, we are told, weeps when he hears the story of R. Eleazar b. Dordai. His tears belie the apparent equanimity of his words. For in order to achieve his eternal life, he has over many years been crafting a disciplined inner world. R. Eleazar, on the other hand, dies full of primal impulses; his sexual extravagance is simply transfigured in an instant into a death wish. Both men weep; one dies of it, while the other remains to contemplate the outrageous efficacy of the sacrificial moment. Mysteriously, R. Eleazar's desire for intimacy with God brings him to the same place as Rabbi's productive life.

These different versions of the notion of sacrifice intimate one dimension, at least, of that complex subject. All address the human need for intensified experience, in which time is sped up, polarities of life and death are fused in an instant, and the cloudy ambiguities of life in time are violently charged with apocalyptic clarity. Marguerite Yourcenar, while recognizing the idealism of this sacrificial radicalism, is clearly invested in restoring the value of the heroic difficulty of living. For Bachelard, the "call of the funeral pyre" remains a potent source of unconscious reveries. Bataille focuses on the moment of *intimacy,* which is created by an act of violence that consumes the individual: the moment of sacred anguish. And in the Talmudic passage, R. Eleazar clarifies in one incandescent instant the nature of his true world: he subverts time and natural process to achieve his intimacy with God.

Qualms of the Heart and Burnt Offerings

With these sources in mind, we return now to Abraham's sacrifice of Isaac. We recall the daring midrashic suggestion that it is Abraham's *hirhurim,* his retroactive anxiety about the authenticity of his life, that directly generates God's demand for sacrifice. In a real sense, it is Abraham's inward reality, his thoughts, that make the sacrifice necessary. Once he has been assailed by those thoughts, God – *immediately* – articulates their irreducible meaning. Abraham's voice, in its unconscious register, is intuited and amplified in God's command. Can we call this a *wish* for this sacrifice? If so, what is the quality and the root of that wish? What do Abraham's fears and misgivings suggest about a desire for clarification? And how does his particular kind of fear engender this particular unthinkable thought?

Before we approach this question of the particular idiom of Abraham's sacrificial desire, it is striking that a classic midrashic tradition connects the *olah* – the burnt offering, which involves the total consumption of the sacrifice in fire, and which constitutes God's *Akedah* demand – with the problem of *hirhurei ha-lev* – "qualms of the heart," mental misgivings. In another version of the midrashic material we have already explored, we find this connection compellingly affirmed in the double context of Abraham and Job:

> 'After these things [words], the word of God came to Abram in a vision, saying, "Do not fear, Abram ..."' (Gen. 15:1). Our Rabbis teach us: for what reason would the burnt offering, the *olah,* be brought? R. Ishmael taught that the *olah* would be brought for positive and negative precepts [to atone for acts of commission and omission]. R. Shimon bar Yochai said: an *olah* would be brought to atone for qualms of the heart, *hirhurei ha-lev,* as it is said: 'When a cycle of feast days was over, Job would send word to them to sanctify themselves, and, rising early in the morning, he would bring burnt offerings, one for each of them; for Job thought,

"Perhaps my children have sinned and blasphemed God *in their thoughts.*" This is what Job always used to do' (Job 1:5). You find that Abraham would have misgivings about the workings of divine justice *[hayah meharher achar midat ha-din],* and what would he say? 'God helped me against those kings in the war and saved me from the furnace. Have I perhaps already received all my reward in this world? Does no reward remain for me in the world to come?' God said to him, 'Because you have misgivings about My ways, you owe Me an *olah,* a burnt offering.' So, He said, 'Take your son, your only one, whom you love, Isaac, and go to the land of Moriah and offer him there as a burnt offering ... .' (22:2)[33]

Qualms of the heart require a burnt offering: this is the view of R. Shimon bar Yochai. His proof text is the enigmatic practice of Job, who offered burnt offerings, individually, for each of his children, in case they had sinned against God *in their thoughts.* It is striking that Job's thought about his children also bears some of the character of a "qualm of the heart." Perhaps the death of his children is the *olah,* the terrible debt payable by one whose mind is haunted by misgivings? When his children die, one report frames the catastrophic news as a burnt offering: "God's fire fell from heaven, took half of the sheep and the boys, and burned them up" (Job 1:16).[34]

In any case, it is a purely mental event that requires atonement by the *olah.* In this way, R. Shimon bar Yochai relates Abraham's qualms about God's dealings with him to the demand for Isaac's sacrifice as an *olah.* Abraham's fear, in itself, precipitates the *Akedah.* Of course, the immediate context is not the *Akedah* (Genesis, chapter 22) but the Covenant between the Pieces (chapter 15). The association is probably the preamble to both narratives: "And it was after these things [words]." In both cases, the Rabbis attribute *hirhurim,* subversive afterthoughts, to Abraham.

In this midrash, unlike the previous version, God does not simply reassure Abraham. Instead, He forces his secret fears to the surface and declares that they *need* a burnt offering. Some toxic uncertainty about God's justice may, it seems, be allayed only by an absolute and literal enactment, a total death, leaving no trace.

Here, all is mystery. The midrash is not speaking of punishment but of a psychic requirement: that obsessional thoughts be resolved by unequivocal act. What is the meaning of the burnt offering – the *holocaust,* as it was once called: wholly consumed – in Abraham's inner world?

Idioms for the Unthinkable

I want to propose a psychoanalytic reading of Abraham's life, a reading that attempts to articulate his specific and personal connection with the fire reverie, with the complex desire to lose all in order to gain all. In this case, of course, to lose all means to sacrifice his beloved and long-awaited son. Sacrificing one's son was a well-documented practice in the ancient world, signifying the most total imaginable gift. But while such a sacrifice is undoubtedly more radical, to him, than losing his own life, it nevertheless remains a departure from the examples of *self*-sacrifice that we have looked at. Our question, therefore, is about the meaning this bears *for Abraham,* in the particularity of his experience, as we find it narrated in biblical and midrashic texts.

The traces of this history are to be found, first, in the Torah text itself: images of fire of a peculiar and hallucinatory intensity that intimate suppressed experience. Freud argues that in a text, as in a murder, it is hard to eliminate all traces of the "crime": metaphors, signs, symptoms betray the traumatic event for which there is no overt evidence. Although the surface retains no explicit record – the text may sometimes "displace" the unbearable narrative, put it elsewhere – an early experience has left its deep impression.[35]

Such a trace of Abraham's early history is the unusual simile that he applies to the scene of the destruction of Sodom: "And he looked down over Sodom and Gemorrah and the whole land of the plain, and he saw, behold, the smoke rose up from the land like *the smoke of the furnace*" (Gen. 19:28). The catastrophic scene is mediated by Abraham's imagination. The simile of the smoking furnace is striking, if only because similes and metaphors are not common in the biblical text. The landscape burns with a strange fire.

Moving backward in time, we find Abraham's attempted plea to save Sodom. Here, he declares himself unworthy to speak to God so aggressively: "'Here I venture to speak to my Lord, I who am but *dust and ashes*'" (Gen. 18:27) – again, a metaphor: for the modern reader, perhaps, a dead metaphor, but for Abraham who invents it, most live.

Ashes? Rashi comments: "I should already have been dust, at the hands of the kings, *and ashes, at the hands of Nimrod* – if Your compassion had not supported me!" Abraham's metaphor is unpacked: he speaks – perhaps unaware of his own full meaning – of the two narrowest escapes of his life, when death had him by the throat.[36] He means, quite literally, "I was almost ashes." Or, more exactly, "*I am ashes.*" In this sense, the idiom, dust and ashes, is not merely a modest disclaimer, but a radical acknowledgment of a truth normally veiled: he has survived death, which means that he is alive, but barely. To the naked eye, he seems alive, but in some other vision, he is dust, he is ashes. Some unconscious truth speaks from his mouth.

Earlier, in the vision that precedes the Covenant between the Pieces, we read: "As the sun was about to set, a deep sleep fell upon Abram, and a terror of great darkness fell upon him ... When the sun set and all light was eclipsed, there appeared *a smoking oven and a flaming torch* which passed between those pieces" (Gen. 15:12, 17). His hallucination[37] of dark horror focuses on a smoking oven. Rashi briefly notes that this is an intimation of the anguish of

Jewish history that visits Abraham in dream or reverie. But if the moment refers to the future, it arises authentically out of the past. For in the past, forgotten, repressed, absent from the biblical text, is the story of the fiery furnace, into which the child Abraham was thrown, to test his faith in the invisible God.

The fact that this story appears only in the midrash, that it is absent from the Torah, testifies, I suggest, to its unthinkable nature. It leaves its record in Abraham's mind and manifests obliquely in the imagery of fire and furnace that repeatedly marks his perception. This story, known to every schoolchild, is regarded by Ramban as essential to the simplest "plot" understanding of Abraham's history. Since it portrays an Abraham who is willing to be martyred for his belief in God, it serves to rationalize God's original choice of him. It appears in several midrashic sources, as well as in nonmidrashic contexts, like Rambam's *Laws of Idolatry*. In the collective consciousness of the Jewish people, that is, it holds a privileged position. Its total absence from the written biblical text suggests that it is an unthinkable, even an unbearable narrative, banished from Abraham's memory.

Perhaps its most fraught version is to be found in Rashi's comment on the mysterious death of Abraham's brother, Haran: "And Haran died in the presence of his father Terach, in the land of his birth, Ur of the Chaldeans" (Gen. 11:28):

> 'In the presence of Terach': in his father's lifetime. But the midrash says: Some say that he died *at the hands of his father* – since Terach brought charges in the court of Nimrod against his son Abraham, for smashing his idols. The king threw him into a fiery furnace. Haran sat and thought, 'If Abraham wins, I will be on his side, but if Nimrod wins, I will be on his side.' When Abraham was saved, Haran was asked, 'On whose side are you?' and he answered, 'On Abraham's side.' So, they threw him into the fiery furnace and he was burned. That is the meaning of *Ur* (fire) of the Chaldeans. However, according to Menahem ben Saruk, Ur means a valley or gorge ... Any cave or deep cleft is called Ur.

In this stark retelling of the midrash,[38] the essential fact is that Abraham's brother was killed *by his father,* who had originally intended Abraham's own death. By handing him over for execution, Terach is, virtually, killing him. And when he is saved, his brother's actual death is directly attributable to Terach. This tale is listed in several midrash collections as one of Abraham's ten tests, and, in at least one, as the first test.[39] If the point of the story is to demonstrate Abraham's staunchness in the face of martyrdom, then the notion of a *test* is clear. But if the theme of filicide is set in high relief, as Rashi sets it here, what does *testing* mean? What does emerge from Rashi's pared-down version of the midrash – and, quite plausibly, from his reading of the

Torah text – is that the event that lays the foundation for Abraham's recorded life is an act of filicide, in which his father (virtually) kills him and (in fact, if not in intention) kills his brother. This memory of horror is not recorded in the written biblical text.

The fire of Ur of the Chaldeans is encrypted in oblivion. But at certain moments it flares and licks the surface of memory. Rashi even suggests, citing a midrash, that that fire is inscribed in the name of that place: Ur means fire. Some such moments occur in the Torah itself, as we have seen. Others appear, obliquely, in midrashic sources:

> 'God said to Abram, Get you out of your land ...' (Gen. 12:2). What precedes this passage? 'And Terach died in Haran' (11:32), which is followed by, 'God said to Abram, Get you out of your land ...' R. Isaac said: Chronologically, Terach still had sixty-five years to live. But first you may learn that the wicked, even in their lifetime, are called dead. For Abraham was anxious, saying, 'Shall I leave my father and bring dishonor upon the Divine Name, for people will say, "He left his father in his old age and went off"' So, God reassured him, 'I exempt you *(lekha)* from the duty of honoring your parents, though I exempt no one else from this duty. Moreover, I will record this death before your departure.' Hence, 'And Terach died in Haran' is stated first, and then, 'God said to Abram, Get you out ... .'[40]

This earliest biographical appearance of Abraham's habitual anxiety is his response to God's original *lekh lekha* call: he resists, on the grounds that if he abandons his aged father in order to obey God's call, he will appear, at the very outset of the history of monotheism, to betray universal ethical standards. The ethical issue is strangely addressed in God's answer: "*You* I exempt from the duty of honoring your parents." Why is Abraham to be the sole exception to this imperative of a civilized society? And how, in fact, does this answer his anxiety? On the face of it, it simply rehearses the paradox of founding a higher religion on the violation of a civilized norm.

I suggest that since the fiery furnace motif is so prevalent, our midrash can rely on the vitality of this narrative to explain Abraham's exceptional relation to the duty of honoring his father. Since, in terms of intention, his father has killed him, he no longer owes him obedience. He acquires the mythical status of an unfathered child.

So powerful is this counterfactual truth that the midrash represents it by revising the chronological biblical account. Even though he lives 65 years after Abraham's departure, Terach's death is recorded *before* Abraham leaves home. In this way, Abraham is protected against criticism: his father was already dead when he obeyed God's call. What may at first appear a cavalier approach to historical truth takes on a different cast in the larger context: Terach is "killed" in the text, since his fatherhood of Abraham has been long dead. Abraham is exempted of duty since, in the realm of psychic reality, the normal relations of father and son have been radically undermined. Daringly, the midrash even attaches this unique exemption from filial duty to the word *lekha* in God's command: in leaving his place of origin, he reenacts a traumatic cut that has long alienated him from family and society.

A sinister and unconscious meaning is thus read into a biographical anomaly in the narrative. Abraham's anxiety at the violation of God's honor screens a deeper violation that implicates his whole culture. At the basis of his relation to God lies a trauma, which strains the very concept of fatherhood.

Abraham's life with God is, on the one hand, a charmed life, for it is God's grace that has delivered him from the fire, as it will later deliver him from the warring kings. In kabbalistic thought, he represents *chesed,* the loving relation with others displayed in energetic acts of benevolence and empathic imagination. And yet, on the other hand, in the midrashic portrait, this sunlit Abraham is haunted by *hirhurim:* by his own testimony, only his ashes remain. "I am dust ... I am ashes ..." – God's grace on the one hand, his unfathered soul on the other.

The Heart of Darkness

The fiery furnace motif indicates more than a purely private trauma. Such practices – the sacrifice of sons – mark the beginnings of human society and, specifically, of the history of religions.[41] An extraordinary midrash[42] links the fiery furnace with the furnace in which the builders of the tower of Babel fired their bricks (Gen. 11:3). Abraham's unconscious place of origin is at the foundation of a civilization.

This place is described, strangely, as a valley (Gen. 11:2). Why does this community build their tower, whose top is to touch heaven, *in a valley*? And this valley is named *Shinar,* a name that reveals a sinister history. A Talmudic passage puns on *Shinar:* to this place all the corpses of the flood were precipitated (*she-ninaru* – lit., shaken).[43]

Mei Ha-Shilo'ach[44] offers a provocative reading of this material. After the Flood, society constructs its civilization, its values of unity and solidarity, which, it is hoped, will preserve it from a recurrence of catastrophe, in a valley of death. The Flood generation had been characterized by violence and rapine; this new generation will aspire high by cultivating social harmony. ("Everyone on earth had the same language and the same words" [Gen. 11:1].) The basis of this civilization, however, is *fear* – the fear of death, as symbolized by the corpses that lie at the foundation of the city and tower. This repressed fear will compulsively shape religious and social life; the terror and denial of death will motivate all its achievements.

In contrast to this structure, the Holy Temple is to be built on a lofty base and to generate a different kind of solidarity. What God wants, insists our

Hasidic master, is not a compulsive fear, but *avodah* – which refers, on one level, to the ritual service of the Temple, but on another to *work* – the slow, gradual work on human nature that moves beyond visceral fear as the basis of the religious life.

This evocative reading of the Tower of Babel provides Abraham with a spiritual history. Later, God will say to him: "I am God who brought you out of Ur of the Chaldeans" (Gen. 15:7). This was the foundational moment of Abraham's life, as God's almost identical declaration at Mount Sinai ("I am the Lord your God who brought you out of the land of Egypt") is to be the foundational moment of Israelite history. The encounter with God makes Ur uninhabitable for Abraham – as later it makes Egypt uninhabitable for his children. If Ur is a religious civilization based on fear – the reflexive fear of death, of all the ills that flesh is heir to – Abraham must be moved to leave this civilization. In the world where he originates, the primal religious impulse is terror, and the gods are sought for their protection. But however tall the tower that is built here, it can achieve no more than a fantasy of intimacy with God, since it involves no *work:* its base is in those smoky caverns where children are slaughtered to appease the gods. Built in a low place, its aspirations are largely pretenses.

Implicitly, Mei Ha-Shilo'ach is offering a critique of the violent intimacies of the sacrificial about which Bataille writes so compellingly. As against the anguish of fear and the ecstasy of desire, there is the requirement of *work,* of working through primal instincts, so that religious experience can be founded on higher ground: not the annihilation of the individual in the sacrificial moment but the clearer delineation of the human face. Abraham's history begins here. He survives the fire of Ur, where his father killed him. But his journey contains its own heart of darkness, a memory that is not a memory. In a sense, therefore, the *Akedah* was always destined to happen. Wherever Abraham travels, his destination is Mount Moriah:

> 'And Abram journeyed, moving on toward the south': he drew a course and journeyed toward the future site of the Temple.[45]

In all his apparently random wanderings, he is fated to reach that place. For what has been implanted in him – the father who kills his son – will have to undergo a *test:* something implicit in his past, an "unthought known," will have to be unfolded, lived through in the present, so that it can finally assume its proper place in the past.

Divine Intimations

In the following midrash, Mount Moriah is not only his destination but the symbolic projection of his journey:

'He saw the place from afar': How did it look from afar? This teaches that at first this was a low place. But when God decided to have His presence [the Shekhinah] reside there and to make there a holy place, He said, It is not a king's way to reside in a valley, but in a lofty, exalted place, that has become beautiful, visible to all. Immediately, God hinted to the region round the valley that all the mountains should gather together to form a site for His presence [the Shekhinah]. That is why it was called Mount Moriah, since out of fear *[yirah]* of God it became a mountain.[46]

A geological drama – the sudden shifting of tectonic plates to create a mountaintop – becomes a spiritual drama. God, it seems, is fastidious about dwelling in low places. He is to be found in the stark light of the mountaintop, not in the smoky caverns of the religious mysteries. His transactions with human beings are founded on the highest achievements of human thought; His mysteries are to be translated into terms that the conscious mind can grasp.

The catalyst for movement from low to high is no more than a *hint;* God's power may be expressed in thunderous commands on Mount Sinai, but if God is to dwell in the world, the low ground that has been the residence of the pagan gods must be transformed by different means. In the imagination of the midrashic writer, *fear of God* is the force that turns a chasm into a mountain, but it is aroused by a *hint.* Hints are elusive, allusive, often ambiguous: the work that they initiate is to be done by one who *takes the hint.* What can be made of such intimations? They exist in a world apart from the instinctual *fear* that compels acts of terror and anguish.

Primitive Agony

The trajectory that lies between Ur and Mount Moriah can be viewed through the prism of D. W. Winnicott's psychoanalytic thought. He addresses a clinical phenomenon that he terms "the fear of breakdown":[47] the patient is preoccupied with a sense of impending doom that Winnicott understands as referring to a breakdown that *has already happened* in early childhood, before the ego was sufficiently developed to encompass it. Never fully experienced, and therefore in a sense unthinkable, this original experience of primitive agony haunts the individual; the future must provide a way of accessing, for the first time, the unthinkable catastrophe of the past:

It must be asked here: why does the patient go on being worried by this that belongs to the past? The answer must be that the original experience of primitive agony cannot get into the past tense unless the ego can first gather it into its own present time experience and into omnipotent control now … In other words the patient must go on looking for the past detail which is *not yet experienced.* This search takes the form of a looking for this detail in the future.[48]

Becoming aware of this paradoxical possibility, the analyst can help the patient *reach to the madness:*

> The patient needs to 'remember' this but it is not possible to remember something that has not yet happened, and this thing of the past has not happened yet because the patient was not there for it to happen to. The only way to 'remember' in this case is for the patient to experience this past thing in the present, that is to say, in the transference. This past and future thing then becomes a matter of here and now, and becomes experienced by the patient for the first time.[49]

An experience of "madness" has long potentially been a fact. The paradoxical status of *potential experience* becomes the subject of a strangely lyrical analogy:

> I saw a hyacinth bulb being planted in a bowl. I thought, there is a wonderful smell locked up in that bulb; I knew of course that there is no place in the bulb a smell is locked up ... Nevertheless there is in the bulb a potential which eventually will become the characteristic smell as the flower opens.[50]

The developing self constantly reaches toward a realization of the original unthinkable moment. The patient lives more and more of the particular form of madness that belongs to him individually.

Reaching to the Madness

I suggest that Winnicott's "queer kind of truth" sheds light on the hidden logic of Abraham's life. The sense of impending doom that takes the form of *hirhurim* – qualms, misgivings – is an expression of a past agony. The story of the fiery furnace functions, on one level, as proof of Abraham's commitment to the God that he has come to know. But the heart of the story – disowned even within the midrashic tradition, which is itself disowned by the biblical text – is the father's murder of his son, of both sons – one virtually and one in fact.

In Abraham there is thus a need to find that which has not been experienced. He circles around the trauma, coming closer with each *test.* Furnaces, smoke, ashes unaccountably haunt his imagination. Just before the *Akedah* narrative, he resists Sarah's pressure to send his son Ishmael into the desert to probable death: "And the thing was very evil in Abraham's eyes, for it concerned his son" (Gen. 21:11). Only on God's prompting and reassurance does he accede to her will. His intense sense of evil is about fathers and sons and the destruction that may flare between them.

With the *Akedah,* the primitive agony of his life comes to full flower. Now, God offers no palliative, no reassurance, and Abraham makes no objection. He rises early, travels three days, expresses no reluctance. The angel, who at the last moment prevents the slaughter, has to call out twice: "Abraham! Abraham!" before he desists. To his first cry, "Do not raise your hand against the boy!" the angel adds, "Do not do anything to him!" Some strange eagerness is at work in Abraham to consummate the sacrifice, at least with a symbolic scratch.[51] To stem this, the angel calls, "Do not do anything *[me'umah]* to him! – Do not make a blemish *[moom]* upon him!" Abraham wants to make the sacrifice real in some physical way; the angel tells him that such an act would irreparably *blemish* the sacrifice.

The narrative yields an uncanny sense of Abraham as impelled toward Mount Moriah. What has been locked within him is now released. The *Akedah* moment is the moment of fullest *testing,* in precisely the traditional sense of *living through an experience* so that its potential is realized. Perhaps because he has accumulated strength over a lifetime of *testings,* he is now able to bear the full brunt of the primitive agony.

Most significantly, however, it is God whose relation with Abraham creates the conditions under which his past experience may be lived through in the present moment. If God can be figured in biblical and midrashic imagery as lover, betrayed husband, brother, man of war and artist, then, I suggest, He may sometimes act as psychoanalyst. It is through this dimension of Abraham's relation with God that his *hirhurim* are forced to the surface.

God never fully relieves Abraham of his qualms, since these pressure points of his inmost life are, it seems, precisely what he needs, in some intimate sense, to *know.* God, therefore, plays enigmatic roles, so that Abraham can encompass what, originally, was unthinkable. God makes demands that cast Abraham now in the father role. Now, he will confront what was locked within him; an original breakdown will be relived with a difference.

In this narrative, the issue of the *Akedah* is not simply one of obedience; the test is not a *pass/fail* question. Rather, he is given an opportunity to re-experience from the vantage point of maturity what he has never truly experienced, to respond with full freedom to an inquiry that will probe the depths of his being.

Through a Dim Glass

Mei Ha-Shilo'ach[52] presents Abraham's dilemma in the complex light of this kind of exposure. God's demand is enigmatic and absolute, making no gesture to reconcile this horror with past promises. God the Father bears the lineaments of an inexorable paternity. The greatness of Abraham lies in his ability to hold fast to his belief in the past promises of destiny and life, and in the Father who made them. Even as God precipitates him into the deepest currents of his life, His presence remains with him, benign and enigmatic at the same time.

The Zohar points out that the God who tests Abraham is called *Elohim,* which indicates that He communicated "through a dim glass." The exact meaning of His command is unclear: its ambiguity is of the essence of the test. For Isaac, the test is slighter, since he fully believes in his father's account: if it is God who has commanded the sacrifice, a lesser heroism is involved in obeying. Only from Abraham's perspective is this radically a *test,* since the command comes to him clouded with possible meanings. His uncertainty about God's meaning makes the test more difficult, since it invites Abraham to respond with his whole being. *How* he responds – the authenticity with which he struggles with the ambiguity of the situation – will be more significant than *what* he does.

Rashi cites a classic and disturbing midrash, which addresses the ambiguity in God's words:

> Said R. Abba: Abraham addressed God, Let me spread before You my complaint. Yesterday, You told me, 'In Isaac, your seed shall be named.' Then, You said, 'Take your son ... and offer him as a burnt offering ...' And now, You tell me, 'Do not raise your hand against the boy!' God answered him: I shall not profane My covenant and the utterance of My lips I shall not change. When I said to you, 'Take your son ...' the utterance of My lips I shall not change: I did not say, 'Slaughter him,' but 'Bring him up.' You have brought him up, now bring him down.[53]

All the obvious contradictions in God's communications to Abraham are resolved in one radical rereading: "I never told you to *slaughter* him." God's consistency is preserved, He has not changed course. The cost of this rhetorical move, however, is high. Abraham has, all along, misunderstood the nature of God's demand. All God ever desired was that Abraham *raise Isaac up* (the literal translation of *ha'aleyhu*).

On the face of it, the midrash seems to trivialize Abraham's agony. God has put him through a meaningless test, which bears no relation to His real intent. In addition, since Abraham's understanding of *ha'aleyhu* as a command to *sacrifice* is the idiomatic and consensual understanding, the literal reading of the word emerges as a sophistry.

Clearly, there is no room for ambiguity at the time of God's demand. Particularly in view of Abraham's history, the stark nature of the command could only mean sacrificing his son. For Abraham alone, this is a real test, an experience through which unconscious conflicts will be staged; for him, there is the unspeakable desire to do as was done to him. The cathartic wish drives him to the mountaintop. Will this compulsion to act out the past deceive him into slaughter?

Here is Abraham's dilemma: on the one hand, the compulsive wish to exorcise the past; on the other, the horror of a sacrifice that would deprive him not only of his beloved son, but of his moral and spiritual standing in the world. As Beit Ya'akov puts it,[54] he had spent his life teaching the world "the glory of heaven" – God's desire for the ethical human life. If he had killed his son, he would have looked simply like a murderer, a filicide. "All would have been lost in one instant."

In this situation, Beit Ya'akov remarks, Abraham might have found sophistical ways to reinterpret God's command so as to evade its obvious meaning. He might, for instance, have realized that God had not, in fact, commanded him to *slaughter* Isaac but simply to *raise him up.* In this way, he would have desisted from the sacrifice, thus confirming "the glory of heaven." Such a course of action, however, would have been self-serving and evasive, since it was clear that *ha'aleyhu* quite unequivocally meant, "Slaughter him!"

He is given three days, a time of doubt, ambiguity, confusion,[55] to work through his conflict. His doubt is not only about the meaning of God's command but even about the identity of the speaker, the source of the command. Is this obscure, dimly lit speaker indeed God, the God whom Abraham knows and loves? Or is it, perhaps, a satanic force, created by his own dark needs?

One daring midrash[56] imagines Satan accosting Abraham on his journey and making just this maddening suggestion: "The one who told you to commit murder – for which you will be found guilty – *he was Satan!*" Abraham staunchly rebuffs this satanic notion. But, for the reader, the damage has been done. Ambiguity has insinuated itself into the narrative. How is Abraham to know for sure which is God's voice, which Satan's?

When the angel of God (this time God is YHWH – the lucid light prevails) calls out twice, "Abraham! Abraham!" the Zohar comments: "The first 'Abraham!' is not the same as the second." In the short time, a heartbeat, between calls, Abraham has become different. Something confused in him sharpens into focus. Initially deaf to the angel's cry, he becomes present and capable of hearing the second "Abraham!"

A Hasidic reading amplifies the midrashic tradition: the double call, "Abraham! Abraham!" is an expression of divine love[57] that Abraham is granted only at the point when he fully registers – responding *Hineni* – the command *not to slaughter* his son.[58]

Another Hasidic reading: "He did not hear the angel, for he was preoccupied with his intent to complete the act. Or, alternatively, he realized that he was being signaled to stop; therefore, he acted as one in a trance, in order to complete the act" (Kli Yakar). Abraham is in a trance, unconsciously – or perhaps willfully – deaf to the angel's call. The lure of the funeral pyre is informed by an individual history in which primal fears have become personal.

The angel's second call, however, is heard by Abraham. Only someone who has worked, worked through the complex layerings of his relation to God, can hear the call that will interrupt his trance. In Beit Ya'akov's powerful reading, it is only at this moment, when the angel cries, "Do not raise your hand against the boy!" that he becomes capable of hearing the hidden meaning of the original command: *ha'aleyhu* is now – always ambiguous; it can now be understood to mean, simply, "Raise him up!"

The Possibility of Sublimation

Abraham's work is to fathom the compulsions that lead to filicide; to know in the present the full force of an experience of terror that lies enfolded in his past; to wake from his trance at the angel's call. This is the work that is to shift the tectonic plates, so as to create a site where God may dwell: exalted, beautiful, visible to all.

By the time Abraham arrives at the place where the angelic voice becomes audible, God's original command has released an alternative meaning – one that was till now quite inaccessible, locked into the words, like the smell of the hyacinth bulb. "Raise him up!" articulates a possibility that Abraham has now earned the right to understand.

This moment of sublimation is also a moment of knowledge. "Now," says the angel, "now I know that you fear God" (Gen. 22:12). A cathartic process has given birth to knowledge, eliminating compulsive wishes and terrors. Now, God knows what to answer the critical voices that interrogate His tender relations with Abraham. By the same measure, too, Abraham knows – for this is his angel – how to respond to these persecuting voices. The knowledge precipitated by rigorous experience allows the angel to describe him as *fearing God:* a very different mode from the visceral fear that motivates primitive religious experience. *Fear* has evolved into *fear of God,* the twin of love of God.

At the heart of civilization is darkness. In Joseph Conrad's novel *Heart of Darkness,* his tormented and tormenting antihero dies with the words "The horror! The horror!" on his lips. Abraham loves and is loved by a God who takes him through a cathartic journey to that horror, so that his love can lose its anxious misgivings.

All the tests of Abraham's life are approaches to the crisis that he has not yet experienced. All involve some measure of breakdown of apparent integrations, some intimate access to the heart of darkness. His journey from Ur of the Chaldeans has had the purpose of possessing the Land: so God promised him, "Oh Lord God," he cries out, "*how shall I know* that I am to possess it?" (Gen. 15:8). He wants knowledge that will connect his past with his future. God's answer – the vision of dread and darkness, furnace and fire, with vultures hanging menacingly over all – is summarized by Rashi: "Your children will endure in the Land *by virtue of sacrifice.*"[59]

When he is compelled to send his son Ishmael to a probable death in the desert, he again approaches the original madness. When God challenges him, "Become whole!" he falls on his face, as spurious convictions of wholeness disintegrate. The paradox of diminishing himself in order to become whole means confronting himself without defense. "The original experience of primitive agony cannot get into the past tense unless the ego can first gather it into its own present time experience."[60]

Introducing his essay on the breakdown that belongs in the past, Winnicott writes: "what is not yet experienced did nevertheless happen in the past."[61]

Enigmatic Messages

The *Akedah,* then, returns Abraham to the past so that he may know it as he never knew it before. This is a narrative of *afterwardness*: "And it was *after these things* ... ." In order to understand God's command, the midrash asks: "What lies *behind* it, *before* it? What is the necessary history of this moment?" We have focused on a childhood trauma that is totally repressed in the Torah text. The fact of this absence, combined with its pervasive presence in midrashic and medieval writings, intimates an archaic memory that leaves its traces in Abraham's imagery of thought and speech. The fiery furnace and the father who kills two sons become the foundational narrative of his life. In this sense, the *Akedah* is the inevitable confrontation, the *test,* that is to define his inner world.

The foundational reality in Abraham's life is, then, primarily a psychic reality. But what of historical reality? If the *Akedah* is a story of *afterwardness,* this means that it enacts a later version of a primal event. The awkward English expression is in fact a translation of Freud's *Nachtraglichkeit:* sometimes translated as "deferred action," it refers to a significant early moment that is later remembered with a difference. The classic example is of the infant at the breast seen by the adult from the perspective of sexual experience: two different experiences of the breast, past and present, overlap.

Jean Laplanche[62] discusses two views of this relation between past and present moments. On the determinist view, the primary experience is retained within the adult, who registers it anew at the sight of the nursing baby; on the hermeneutic view, the adult retrospectively imagines all that he could have experienced if he had only had his present knowledge. The adult either *reconstructs* a memory whose trace is within him, or *constructs* it, creates it in his interpretation.

Against both these views, Laplanche offers his own understanding. A third party has been overlooked – the wet nurse. Her subjective reality, unconscious desires and actual pleasure in her role constitute a third term: the nurse's message to the infant. There is always an other, who is prior to the life of the infant and whose unconscious experience is conveyed in enigmatic ways to the infant. The adult does not fully know what he is conveying, and the child receives traumatizing messages, which have to be repeatedly remastered, translated and retranslated.

The enigmatic, traumatizing message forms the kernel of otherness in the child's world. The child attempts to metabolize this "foreign body hard as iron"[63] within him, to break down and reassemble it into a different entity. Analysis, writes Laplanche, offers "a reopening of the dimension of alterity,"[64] an opportunity to respond to the terrors and desires roused by the other, to de-translate the old translations, the old formations of identity.

On this view, Abraham's earliest past – the narrative of the fiery furnace – may be a historical event re-accessed in later life, or it may be a later construction projected backward – a kind of retrospective fantasy. The essential factor, however, is the presence of *others* whose unconscious reality has implanted within him a "foreign body" that he must repeatedly attempt to master. His habit of *hirhurim* speaks of enigmatic messages, from his family and his culture, which, by definition, cannot be totally understood or mastered.

At the *Akedah,* God plays the role of analyst, reopening the dimension of otherness, inviting Abraham's transferential love and fear. For as Laplanche most challengingly suggests, God, too, is enigmatic:

> That God is a god who speaks and compels the hearer to listen is obvious throughout the Book, which is but a variant of the paradigm 'Hear, O Israel!' That God is enigmatic, that He compels one to translate, seems obvious to the entire Judaeo-Christian tradition of exegesis. Whether enigma pre-supposes that the message is opaque to Himself is plainly a different question.[65]

God's address to Abraham is not exhausted by its consciously understood meanings. "He compels one to translate." Laplanche cites Job as providing a fine example of enigmatic messages, which give rise to "repeated attempts at translation, justification, delimitation and mastery, which are the main points at issue between Job and his questioners." The tantalizing question, however, as Laplanche indicates, is whether God's message is, in any sense, opaque to Himself. "Does God have an unconscious?"

The *Akedah* is the archetypal example, it seems to me, of the divine enigmatic message, the address to the human being that traumatizes and compels one to translate. Here, God reopens the primal mystery of the Other – this time with therapeutic intent. An opportunity to loosen the bonds of trauma is offered. But for this metaphor to be imaginable, God, as a character in the narrative, must be perceived by Abraham and perhaps even by the reader as speaking out of depths that are, in some sense, opaque to His own consciousness. He speaks as *Elohim,* not as YHWH: the light is clouded, the revelation is incapable of paraphrase. He will never explain, resolve the mystery. It is left to Abraham to submit, to master by submitting to the enigma: that is, to de-translate the old translations, retranslate the enigma into forms that will allow history to arise.

But Abraham's work is endless, extended through history. The culmination that is the *Akedah* is not a final resolution: after Abraham comes Job. For God's meanings remain opaque, even, in a sense, to Himself. That is, even to the particular dimension of divinity by which God addresses a particular person at a particular moment of revelation. The task of translation is never finished: fundamental enigmas are constantly to be re-elaborated.

Abraham Unappeased

And Abraham? He is not appeased, neither by the first angel nor by the second. Midrashic versions listen for the protest with which he breaks his long *Akedah* silence. Finally, God hears Abraham's voice in argumentative, even aggressive mode:

> At that time, Abraham declared before God: Master of the worlds, a man tests his friend, if he does not know what is in his heart. But You – who know what the heart and the kidneys counsel – did You have to treat me in this way? God answered: Now I know that you fear God. Immediately, God opened the heavens and the deep darkness, and said: By Myself I swear, says God ... . Abraham interrupted: *You* swear! *I* swear that I will not descend from the altar until I have said all that I need to say! God told him: Speak!
>
> Abraham said: Did You not tell me, 'Count the stars, if you are capable of counting them – so many will be your seed!?' God said: I did. Abraham continued: My seed from whom? God answered: From Isaac. And Abraham declared: I had answers for You in my heart: yesterday You told me, 'In Isaac your seed will be named'; now, You tell me, 'Take your son and offer him as a burnt offering.' But I suppressed my impulses and I did not answer You. So, when Isaac's children sin and are involved in suffering, remember Isaac's *Akedah* to their credit, and let it be accounted before You as though his ashes were gathered upon the altar, and forgive them and redeem them from their suffering.
>
> Then God replied: You have had your say, now I will have Mine. Isaac's children will indeed sin before Me, and I will judge them on Rosh Hashanah [the New Year]. But if they wish Me to seek out merit for them and remember to their credit Isaac's *Akedah,* then let them blow the shofar of this one before Me. Abraham asked: What is the shofar? God told him: Turn around and look behind you! 'And Abraham lifted up his eyes and he saw – behold! – a ram – behind – caught in the thicket by its horns' (Gen. 22:13).[66]

The biblical text celebrates closure, with the angel swearing in the name of God to bestow bounteous blessings on Abraham's children, "because you have listened to My voice." The midrash undermines closure, by imagining Abraham's angry, even irreverent appropriation of God's words: "'I swear by Myself,' says God ... . Abraham interrupted: '*You* swear! *I* swear that I shall not descend ... .'" Abraham will have his say. Urgently, and with God intently listening, the enigmas and inconsistencies of God's messages erupt from him, becoming the burden of what he *did not say* at the time of the *Akedah.* Abraham wants permanent credit for his silent restraint, *as though* the sacrifice had in fact been consummated; the credit is to be transferred as prophylactic atonement for the sins of future generations. So explosive is his protest at the mystery of God's messages that it is difficult to imagine God resisting his demand. In the rhetorical balance of the midrash, Abraham now holds the high moral ground. But God's answer is qualified. Essentially, He denies Abraham the closure he asks for – the absolution that will inoculate his children against future sin, indeed against the traumas of history. Instead, He refers him to the shofar as the means of evoking forgiveness. By blowing the shofar, future generations will continue Abraham's work, rather than simply banking on it.

The midrash undermines the closure offered in the biblical narrative, as well as the theological closure claimed by Abraham. If the past is to redeem the present and future, it can do so only by being worked through in the present. If Abraham's sacrifice is to affect the future, it can do so not by purchasing, with its consummated beauty, an immunity from sin and suffering, but precisely by modeling a process, necessarily incomplete, to be resumed in every life.

Abraham did *not* consummate the sacrificial command: that is his greatness and his gift, his true consummation. We remember Bataille's discussion of the meaning of sacrifice: "it is gift and relinquishment ... . This is the meaning of 'sacrificing to the deity,' whose sacred essence is comparable to a fire. To sacrifice is to give as one gives coal to the furnace."[67] In his readiness to confront and metabolize the complexity of his life, Abraham has relinquished an insistence on the "lasting order," in which all values are subordinated to the value of duration; he has affirmed the value of constant translation, which submits the past to the fire of the present.

The closure offered by the midrash is a vision of an animal caught in a thicket, a tangle (in modern Hebrew, *sevakh* indicates psychological complexity) by its horns. Here, the ram substitutes for Isaac, but the emphasis is on the shofar, the instrument wrought of these complicated horns, and on the animal's position – "behind." The shofar blown on Rosh Hashanah to evoke God's forgiveness may not be straight, or "simple" *(pashut)*. And it should be directed upward. As emblem for the complex human being, subject of many attempts to de-translate and retranslate his experience, the shofar cries with a human cry, produced by human breath.

Most strikingly, however, the midrash focuses on the ram's position: "And Abraham lifted up his eyes and he saw – behold! – a ram – *behind (achar)* ... ." In order to see it, he is told, "*Chazor l'achorekha* – Turn around! Look *behind* you!*" In this way, the midrash addresses the anomalous use of *achar* – behind – as though it were syntactically detached from its context: not *acharav* – behind him – but simply and enigmatically *achar*. The flow of the sentence halts; questions gather. Does this refer to space – the space *behind* Abraham, hidden, other? Or to time – *after*? The ram whose horns will offer atonement for the future is to be found in the world of *achar ha-devarim ha-eileh,* of *after these things,* where what lies behind the apparent facts, what happened before, the residues of the past, suffuse the present.

Abraham has wished to make something enduring of his sacrifice. That will be his recompense for his restraint in the face of God's enigmas. The *Akedah* is simply to undo the rigors of the future. God responds by turning Abraham back to the world of behind, of *afterwardness.* What lies behind him is the future of his past, the once inevitable consequences of those traumatizing messages; and a dynamic possibility – that his children, like him, will work to transform and translate the enigmas of their own past. This is God's offer: the perpetual return of the shofar cry, for memory and transfiguration.

Notes

1 We thank Penguin Random House LLC for allowing excerpt(s) from *The Murmuring Deep: Reflections on the Biblical Unconscious* by Avivah Gottlieb Zornberg. Copyright © 2009 by Avivah Gottlieb Zornberg. Used by permission of Schocken Books, an imprint of the Knopf Doubleday Publishing Group, a division of Penguin Random House LLC. All rights reserved.
2 See, e.g., Genesis 15:2, 3, 8; 17:18; 18:23. It is striking that even Abraham's unexpressed feelings are treated by God as legitimate occasions for response – e.g., Genesis 15:1; 21:12.
3 See, e.g., *Pirkei de-Rabbi Eliezer,* 26.
4 Ramban Genesis 22:1.
5 After the terrors of theophany at Mount Sinai, the people are told: "*Do not be afraid;* God has come only in order to *test* you, and in order that *the fear of Him may be ever with you*" (Exod. 20:17). One fear is to be replaced by another, through the medium of a transformative experience.
6 *B. Nedarim* 31b.
7 Rashi, Genesis 17:1.
8 Rashi is citing *Pirkei de-Rabbi Eliezer,* 29.
9 This has practical consequences only in relation to *terumah* (the heave offering), which is forbidden to an *arel.* See *J. Yevamot* 8:1 and Rambam, *Hilkhot Terumot* 11:7.
10 *Jokes and Their Relation to the Unconscious, SE* VIII, 26.
11 Malcolm Bowie, *Psychoanalysis and the Future of Theory* (Oxford, UK, and Cambridge, Mass.: B. Blackwell, 1993), 22.
12 *Bereshit Rabbah* 44:5.
13 Isaiah 33:12.
14 Psalms 31:20.

15 Rashi to Genesis 22:20.
16 *Bereshit Rabbah* 55:4.
17 See Genesis 12:7,8; 13:4.
18 Gaston Bachelard, *The Psychoanalysis of Fire,* trans. Alan C. M. Ross (Boston: Beacon Press, 1964), 18.
19 Ibid., 16.
20 Ibid., 17.
21 Ibid., 19.
22 Ibid., 20.
23 Translated by the author.
24 Marguerite Yourcenar, *That Mighty Sculptor, Time,* trans. Watter Kaiser (New York: Farrar, Straus and Giroux, 1992), 153.
25 Ibid., 154–55.
26 Georges Bataille, *Theory of Religion* (New York: Zone Books, 1992), 48–49.
27 Ibid., 52.
28 Ibid., 53.
29 Leviticus 16:1.
30 Leviticus 10:1.
31 *Sifra* 26.
32 *B. Avodah Zarah* 17a.
33 Tanchuma, *Lekh lekha,* 10.
34 See Rachel Adelman, "A Psychoanalytic Reading of the Covenant between the Pieces" (unpublished M.A. thesis, submitted to the Faculty of Baltimore Hebrew University, 2001).
35 Sigmund Freud, *Collected Works,* 23:43.
36 Cf. *Bereshit Rabbah* 44:5: "I descended to the fiery furnace and was saved; I descended in the war against the kings and I was saved."
37 *Tardema* may refer to sleep – in which case the vision would be in a dream – or to a coma, or some altered state of consciousness.
38 *Bereshit Rabbah* 38:19.
39 Midrash *Tehillim* 18:28.
40 *Bereshit Rabbah* 39:7.
41 See Jon D. Levenson, *The Death and Resurrection of the Beloved Son* (New Haven, Conn.: Yale University Press, 1993).
42 See, e.g., *Pirkei de-Rabbi Eliezer,* 24.
43 *B. Zevachim* 113b.
44 See Mei Ha-Shilo'ach, *No'ach,* Vol. 2.
45 *Bereshit Rabbah* 39:24.
46 Tanchuma, *Va-yera* 22.
47 "The Fear of Breakdown" and "The Psychology of Madness" in *Psychoanalytic Explorations,* ed. Clare Winnicott (Cambridge, Mass.: Harvard University Press, 1992).
48 Ibid., 91.
49 Ibid., 92.
50 Ibid., 127.
51 Rashi to Genesis 22:12.
52 Mei Ha-Shilo'ach *Va-yera,* vol. 1.
53 Rashi to Genesis 22:12.
54 Beit Ya'akov, *Va-yera,* 53.
55 See Rashi to Genesis 22:4.
56 Tanchuma, *Va-yera* 22.
57 See Rashi to Genesis 22:11.

58 Kedushat Levi. See Jacques Derrida, *The Gift of Death,* trans. David Willis (Chicago: University of Chicago Press, 1995), 78, note 6. He cites an objection made by Levinas to Kierkegaard: "'In evoking Abraham he describes the meeting with God as occurring where subjectivity is raised to the level of the religious, that is to say above ethics. But one can posit the contrary: the attention Abraham pays to the voice that brings him back to the ethical order by forbidding him to carry out the human sacrifice, is the most intense moment of the drama ... . It is there, in the ethical, that there is an appeal to the uniqueness of the subject ... .'" (Emmanuel Levinas, *Noms propres* [Montpellier: Fata Morgana, 1976], 113; translated by David Wills).

59 Rashi to Genesis 15:8.

60 Winnicott, *Explorations,* 91.

61 Ibid.

62 Jean Laplanche, *Essays on Otherness,* (London and New York: Routledge, 1999), See, e.g., 263–265 and *passim.*

63 Ibid., 114.

64 Ibid., 230.

65 Ibid., 191.

66 Tanchuma, *Va-yera,* 23.

67 Bataille, *Theory of Religion,* 48.

PART 3

Historical Content

8

TRAUMA, GENDER AND THE STORIES OF JEWISH WOMEN

The Other Within[1]

Jill Salberg

In an interview in *The New York Times Sunday Magazine* Diane von Furstenberg (DVF) was asked about how she used to, in the 1970s, drive her Mercedes to Studio 54 alone at midnight. She replied, "That image of me driving the Mercedes and walking in alone is like the cowboy going to a saloon, you know? It was really a fantasy of mine, living a man's life in a woman's body" (Goldman, 2013). Is this similar to what Henry Higgins, one of the lead characters in *My Fair Lady,* is longing for, a woman who fantasizes and plays with being a man? Is it possible that both men and women carry the same fantasies of women inhabiting maleness? DVF used the cross-dressing fantasy of the American cowboy, incubated within the Hollywood dream machine, to provide what? Confidence? Or was it a way to enable herself to feel powerful? What exactly was at play here, and are we hearing about her sense of freedom or anxiety or both? I do wonder if some particular aspect of being a woman must be bolstered or protected by the cloth of gender performance (Butler, 1990). What might make it difficult or even frightening living as a woman that necessitates wishing to live a man's life in a woman's body?

I believe DVF's particular kind of gender fantasy play rests partially on an edge of otherness within gender, both its construction as a category and as a lived experience. Although there is recognition of how different the "other" gender is and acknowledgment of that, I believe that with Henry Higgins and DVR there is simultaneously a refusal of difference or a wish to collapse that difference into sameness, "Why can't a woman be more like a man?" and with that movement eradicate otherness into nondifference. This is reminiscent of passing where there are often attempts to simultaneously be managing some type of trauma or victimization. In passing, one is hiding or concealing an

DOI: 10.4324/9781003266600-12

identity felt to be vulnerable or even shameful while publicly showing, performing an opposing identity, attempting to gain or regain power or a position of strength. This is part of the scenario when a black person might pass for white, a girl for a boy, or a Jew as a non-Jew. But is there even more to this because not everyone does try to pass? Why would a man need to fantasize this, or what might lead a woman to wish this?

Further in this interview DVF is quoted as saying, "Eighteen months before I was born, my mother was in Auschwitz. She weighed 49 pounds. She always told me that God saved her so she could give me life. I was born out of nothing. My mother was nothing; she was ashes practically" (Goldman, 2013). It is not a leap for us to see how trauma is deeply implicated and formative in her life. We do not know what her mother specifically endured in Auschwitz. However, I do know that violence against women in the form of killing infants or children deemed too weak, ripped from mothers unable to protect or save them, and the incidence of rape or forced prostitution was occurring in some of the camps.[2] How would a mother feel; how would she try to protect her child? If not an actual experience, DVF's mother very well might have known these dangers, and it would likely have been a fear or terror. Women were, in some ways, far more vulnerable and at risk than men in the camps.

Isn't it interesting then that she enlists a gender-bending fantasy in order to embody her desire to show up somewhere alone? DVF enters an anxiety-provoking situation not as a girl but internally imagined as a tough masculine cowboy. It is the tomboy, the Western cowboy, who empowers DVF, and in this kind of passing, we see how gender and a specific fantasy enactment become enlisted as a reparative solution to feelings of helplessness and passivity. What is it about entering a situation in a state of aloneness that provokes DVF to call up the male tough guy fantasy? What is it about femininity that makes her feel other and vulnerable? She is the child of a survivor, and it is useful to wonder if we are seeing the trace of the intergenerational transmission of trauma. Is she passing as a manly cowboy, a tough guy swaggering into the club using the Hollywood heteronormative trope of masculinity in order to feel more powerful and to manage her feelings of terror and helplessness, a hallmark of trauma? Might these feelings have also been ones she sensed in her mother?

Trauma and Gender

We can see that embedded in DVF's fantasy are deep-seated cultural stereotypes of masculinity as the strong, powerful and tough gender, whereas femininity becomes the other half of this binary associated with a kind of passive helplessness. "Being a girl" holds the unwanted stereotypical cultural threads of vulnerability and weakness associated with femininity, the same vulnerability and weakness that define the experience of trauma. In this paper, I explore how trauma and gender stories become intermingled and then can be held within a culture as a particularly gendered experience. Specifically, I suggest that cultural and societal trauma experiences of sub-jugation and helplessness can get coded along gender lines. Think of phrases such as, "He cried like a girl," which reflect that vulnerability is to be carried by women, not by real men, who are to be wiped clean of feelings of human fear and vulnerability.

I draw upon multiple literatures: Jewish literature as well as Relational psychoanalytic theories of gender and of transgenerational transmission of trauma. traumatic origins and later gender-bending fantasies and behaviors highlight our modern iteration of this. However, the legacies of patriarchy and traumatic transmissions have long histories in Judaism and within early psychoanalytic conceptualizations of gender as a binary. My particular interest is in how gender becomes enlisted as a mode of traumatic trans-mission and possibly one type of internal psychic reparative resolution. How does someone carry psychically in his or her life the multiple histories of family, culture and the external world? I am drawn into stories about legacies of losses, triumphs, and sometimes traumas and how they can unconsciously be carried, played with, and worked out using gender.

Although gender has always had a primary position within psychoanalysis, it has been in the past 25 years that there have been substantial reformula-tions. Relational psychoanalysis has recast Freud's singular ego, the seat of self-awareness, as multiple self-states each carrying affects, memories and desires (see Bromberg, 2006; Davies, 1998; Harris, 1996). One expansion of multiple self-states has been to understand the multiplicity of gender ex-periences (see Dimen, 1991; Goldner, 1991) as well as the fluid and changing nature of one's gender identifications. In this vein Harris (1991, 1996, 2000, 2005) has written about gender, characterizing it as a soft assembly, by which she means that many experiences, developmental levels, and self–other re-lationships cohere into a self that is gendered and an amalgam of these, all authentically true. She also believes that sometimes gender emerges to solve some intrapsychic, interpersonal, or intersubjective problem. Harris (2005) writes, "Genderedness is one particularly acute register of local trauma and of the more broad scaled traumas of social and historical change" (p. 35). She sees gender as a "creative solution" to types of difficult or even traumatic experiences that have led to dissociative responses encoded in distinct self-states and possibly gendered differently. As a consequence, there may be within one person both girl and boy self-states, each authentically true within certain family configurations and experiential contexts.

How trauma and gender become intermingled may be best understood within a particular narrative of any person within his or her own familial structure and historical/political context. Given our current understanding, gender is no longer considered a clear binary of girl or boy. Gender is constructed, learned and created; it is plastic and at times even fluid. We each form our own conception of our sense of our gender with influences and identifications from many parts of our lives. Given these multiple influences, gender and one's body become sites where trauma can be processed. Trauma and gender stories may appear in Butler's (1990) conception as a performance, albeit unremarkable or prominent as in the case of drag. Gender can be complicated as in transvestism or cross-dressing, where the manifold messages are layered much like clothing or gender can be hidden, erasing a place of injury.

In this vein, Grand (1997) detailed a clinical case of a son who needed to fragment his mind, dissociate his own knowledge of his mother having incested him and split his bodily experience into girl and boy self-states. This became how he could maintain attachment to his mother while not being an agentic boy. Grand described, "It is only a girl self who feels her knowing of passive violation; it is she who knows the body as tortured and without shelter. It is she who has lived his unfelt paralysis, terror, and degradation" (p. 58). We see how complex traumatic experience and the coding of gender can become.

Benjamin (1988, 1991, 1995) has been detailing the effects of patriarchy on psychoanalytic theory and on both women's access to their own sense of agency and men's access to their own sense of vulnerability. She uses Winnicott's ideas of recognition and the formation of subjectivity as the fulcrum in her work understanding how attachment to mother is always needed. What Benjamin then notices is how mother will recognize self-assertions on the part of the child, depending on gender and culture, and then will respond with support or retaliation in the form of abandonment. In discussing Benjamin's work Layton (1998a) further elaborates that what "must follow is that the role that a mother plays in dominant patriarchal culture, the form her agency takes, is to encourage her son in omnipotence/repudiation of femininity and to punish her daughter's moves toward autonomy" (p. 160). Further in this article Layton states, "Symptomatic in the sense that what makes gender identity traumatic is that it is produced from splitting off the attributes of whatever culture considers the property of the other gender" (p. 166). You can see how feminism has deeply penetrated the thinking of these and many other psychoanalysts and helps to tease out how cultural values and trauma enter psyche, particularly gender identity and self-states, in complicated ways.

In a recent article looking at a particular type of intergenerational transmission, Silverman (2015) found that her patient Ava, in considering transitioning to male, was holding trauma experienced by her mother. We learn that a very early dream in the treatment was of a brain birthed out into a toilet. "Actually I shit it out" (p. 52). Later, Silverman's patient recounted to her that the grandmother had punished her mother at times by putting her head into a toilet. In describing this intergenerational transmission of trauma in this family Silverman discussed how "this mother felt traumatized and traumatizing, penetrating and yet impenetrable. Her own unprocessed trauma, which was, at least in part, a trauma of what it meant to be feminine, was projected into her daughter, creating a colony in her daughter's mind where the mother could store her unresolved experiences, particularly with regard to gender and sexuality" (p. 53). Being female for this mother was to be violated, feel at times overexcited, and at other times became a means or a vehicle of expressing power. Gender and the body became the site of this person's unprocessed intergenerational trauma.

This fits what Harris (2005) found, that "a tomboy state in certain girls has made me think that, for some women, the boy persona is an alternative to remembering, erasing the dangerous experience of femininity" (p. 35). DVF's story illustrates this in its intergenerational transmission of trauma iteration. Her mother's traumatic experiences of barely surviving the horror of life in Auschwitz, she is told, is what she is born out of: "I was born out of nothing." She is born into the remnants of massive trauma, which is perhaps carried within her mother's sense of being feminine. Further, it may carry real or imagined aspects of states of dissociated terror. In light of women's experiences during the Holocaust and in camps, being female and a Jew would have been risky in multiple ways.

My Personal Gender Bender

I had been told in my family that I was the son my parents never had. As an adult I learned from my mother about the difficulty she had giving birth to me, possibly even traumatizing to her. She had hemorrhaged badly, and as a consequence, I was the second child, the last child and the younger sister in a two-daughter family. In some ways I was born into a kind of doubled alterity, girl but not daughter, son but not boy. Being tomboy was how I resolved this enigma, one of a few hidden traumas in my family, and it is how I lived in the world. I played more boy games than girl games, playing ball games with boys in the neighborhood and less dolls and house with girls. In retrospect I believe I was carrying familial generational trauma (see Salberg, 2015, where I discuss my grandmother's mother's death in childbirth and my mother's dissociative experience postpartum of my birth) that I do believe infused my gender experience. My being referenced as a son is so odd. Perhaps one aspect was true in what my mother told me, that she thought my father would have wanted a son and she could not imagine another childbirth to endure. On yet a deeper level, being a woman who has to experience childbirth was very risky as in my grandmother's mother dying during childbirth or my own mother hemorrhaging. However, I do believe there is more to this and that being a girl is often seen as risky in the world at large, be it in childbirth, in concentration camps, or in life.

Being a tomboy meant it was never questioned by me that I would attend Hebrew school at the Reform congregation my family belonged to beginning in Grade 2 through Hebrew high school, whereas my older sister never did. By the time I was 11 years old, I was in classes with mostly boys having learned prayers for Shabbat and now for B'nai Mitzvah. I carry within me both daughter and son, girl and boy self-states. When I learned that I could not continue on, that at my synagogue and this particular moment in the Reform movement, 1963, girls did not become Bat Mitzvah (literally translated as daughter of the commandments), I was at first surprised and confused. I know that I also felt deeply disappointed over being denied access to what up until then my peers, the boys, could engage in. I later came to see that I had been deeply upset and unsettled, and the seeds of my interest in feminism, gender and psychoanalysis were an outgrowth of my personal response.

Seminal texts in Jewish feminism—my "go-to books" where I could hear the voices of othered women questioning and exploring these issues—were Susannah Heschel's (1983) *On Being a Jewish Feminist*, Judith Plaskow's (1990) *Standing Again at Sinai* and Rachel Adler's (1998) *Engendering Judaism*. What became clear to me in their work was how the feminist inquiry could be turned toward Judaism; how maleness and masculinity had been assumed as the normative order in Jewish life, and if gender was to be considered, it meant "women" because men were the unquestioned norm. Women were "other" and therefore downplayed in history, liturgy and leadership. They were minimally present in Jewish stories.

The effects feminism had been having on Jewish texts paralleled similar effects within psychoanalysis. New considerations and critiques of Freud and the phallocentric theories that had previously dominated psychoanalytic thinking highlighted the cultural aspects of what Freud took as "bedrock." As I raised earlier, Benjamin (1988, 1998) articulated how Freud's theories rested upon the patriarchal view of masculinity in the culture that valued hegemonic masculine traits such as strength, independence and agency and devalued traits associated with and assigned to femininity— passivity, vulnerability and dependency. Dimen (1991), in line with Harris (1991, 2000), believes that "problems of self may come to be coded in terms of gender, and those of gender, in terms of self" (p. 337). She sees this in the multiple ways that binaries within psychoanalysis are seen as gender specific split between men and women, as inherent gendered qualities of masculinity or femininity, such as active/passive, autonomy/dependency, superiority/inferiority and subject/object. Layton (1998b), also in agreement, has described how culture and psyche are in constant interaction, and both become organized around these gender polarities with positive values attributed to males and negative ones to females.

Given that significant cultural aspects of life will inform our values, it is critical to see how patriarchal structures of hierarchical power also inform masculinity as dominant, strong and superior and femininity as subordinate, weak, and inferior. What Benjamin, Dimen, Grand, Harris, Layton and others remind us is that gender is a meaningful category but that it is complex and variable, not singular and absolute. It also will play out within any individual life in multiple ways. I turn now to specific women within Jewish literature: Beruriah from the Talmud and Yentl from a story by I. B. Singer. Both these women cross gender lines, bending them (as DVF did), transgressing them, and having them reinstated in differing ways.

Women Who Are More Like Men: Stories of Beruriah and Yentl

Within Jewish literature there are two women whose stories capture for me a kind of gender binary paradox—being female and playing with being male, or as Henry Higgins seemingly longs for, women who are more like men. These women are Beruriah from the Talmud and Yentl as written by I. B. Singer. Each one poses a similar puzzle, and I have often thought of Yentl as an Eastern European shtetl doppelgänger for Beruriah. Although most people know of Yentl, partly due to the Streisand film, many have never heard of Beruriah. Neither one has a full life story, but I will try to synopsize the thrust of their stories here while also keeping in mind the historical context as it may affect how gender is rigidly held or fluidly played with. Beruriah is referenced only a dozen or so times briefly across a few different sections of the Talmud. Rachel Adler (1988) wrote an early feminist article on Beruriah and summarized the stories as follows:

Once there was a woman named Beruriah, and she was a great Talmudic scholar. She was the daughter of the great Palestinian Rabbi Hananyah ben Teradyon, who was martyred by the Romans. Even as a young girl, she far outstripped her brother as a scholar. It was said she had learned three hundred laws from three hundred teachers in one day. She married Rabbi Meir, the miracle worker and great Mishnaic sage. One time when Rabbi Meir prayed for some robbers to die, Beruriah taught him to pray that their sin would die, that they would repent. She also taught Meir resignation when their two sons died. Loving and gentle as she was with Meir, Beruriah could also be arrogant and biting. She ridiculed a Sadducee, derided an erring student, and made a fool of Rabbi Yose the Galilean when he met her on the road. Finally, she mocked the sages' dictum that women are easily seduced, and she came to a shameful end. Rabbi Meir set one of his students to seduce her. After long denial she yielded to him. When the plot was revealed, she strangled herself, and Rabbi Meir fled to Babylonia because of the disgrace. (p. 28)

Adler (1988) suggested in this article that Beruriah, as a story character, may have resulted from the early rabbis imagining: "What if there were a woman who was just like us, someone learned and dedicated to Torah?" This formulation has always interested me because I had not imagined the early sages having these kinds of ideas. And yet, it is compellingly human to wonder just such a gender question, indeed, what if there was such a woman? Weissler (1998) suggested, "Each gender could symbolize to the other traits that it denied in itself, or that it feared, or abhorred or coveted, or desired" (p. 51). In this way the otherness of gender becomes like a Rorschach inkblot test, what one cannot accept in the self becomes projected onto and located within the other gender. The brief but intense scholarship that has ensued surrounding Beruriah reflects some of these questions: Did she exist? Were woman learned then, or how other was she? What can her story tell us about women, men, and early Israelite culture and religion? I try to address some of this in what follows.

Although there are differences in Beruriah's textual appearance between the Palestinian and the Babylonian versions of the Talmud, consensus is that she most likely did exist even if some of the stories are elaborations or even a conflation of different females (Fonrobert, 2001; Goodblatt, 1975; Hartman and Buckholtz, 2011; Ilan, 1997, 1999). Goodblatt (1975) writes, "Several talmudic passages indicate that elementary education was open to women, but not advanced training. The uniqueness and importance of the Beruriah tradition is that it portrays a woman whose learning would require just such an advanced education" (p. 84). This was one of the first writings on Beruriah and highlights Beruriah's exceptional abilities—her speaking—which would mean her teaching as well, better than her brother or male peers. Tal Ilan (1999) agrees: "For a woman to know better than a man the minutiae of ritual purity, she would have had to be learned indeed" (p. 179).

All of this points to Beruriah's otherness from the category of most women, whose main biblical function was as wife or mother. She has the intelligence and learning of a man but the body of a woman. Further, Ilan (1999) suggests that for Beruriah's sayings to have been written into the Talmud she would have had to state her opinions at the house of study, the ancient Beit Midrash, where these kinds of decisions were being discussed and debated. Ilan (1999) queries, "Was she the only woman there. were there any study-houses where women could be found. did they study with men or did they study separately?" (p. 179). How "other" was this woman? On the one hand the rabbis are attempting to allow for a different kind of woman. Perhaps this "new woman" is formed in their own image. This woman might then embody some desire on the part of the rabbis, a wish that would then make Beruriah "other" to all other women. In fact there are no stories of her having interactions with women at all. Who would she interact with? Her mother is never mentioned, only that she learned from her well-regarded father and that she learned better than her brother. Even this learning has a kind of magical or even archetypal quality: "It was said she had learned three hundred laws from three hundred teachers in one day." Did she have to have super learning powers to be acknowledged, a version of today's modern feminist experience that to break a glass ceiling one must excel far beyond the standards required of men?

Boyarin (1995), in writing about the implicit gender hierarchy embedded within classical Talmudic Judaism, believes that "both in the Palestinian and in the Babylonian text the dominant discourse suppressed women's voices in the House of Study" (p. 169). However, he doesn't believe it meant women never did study or learn, only that their opinions were suppressed. The greater harm he feels was the use that later European Jewish culture made of this, keeping women from ever entertaining the idea of studying Torah. Agreeing with Boyarin, Hauptman (2011) finds evidence that women did study Torah during the early Rabbinic era (from 70 C.E. onward) and not just "household domestic" halakha, the obvious things girls might learn from observing their mothers. She believes that women growing up in Rabbinic families often learned Torah from men. Furthermore, Hauptman believes that the Beit Midrash of that era was "portable" and therefore locatable in homes, courtyards, under trees, or at a rabbi's table. These more porous settings allow for women to overhear discussions and even participate. She writes, "I am not suggesting that women were full-fledged students as were men, but that they were able to catch Torah 'on the fly.' This is still Torah study" (p. 3). What Hauptman describes fits Beruriah, daughter of a rabbi, clearly comfortable discussing and being fluent with the laws, and now seen as not so "other." There is no doubt that Beruriah was a woman in a man's world, but I want to highlight that she was also living in a posttrauma era. Classical Rabbinic Judaism was established after the destruction of the second Temple in Jerusalem, 70 C.E. The Roman Empire overpowered much of this region. Thus, Rabbinic Judaism was born of necessity and from trauma, a direct result of the Roman destruction and ending of the independent Jewish nation-state. Rome was now fully in charge, and all potential threats to Roman power were squashed or eliminated. A martyr's death awaited the sage Rabbi Akiva as well as Rabbi Hananyah ben Teradyon, believed to be Beruriah's father.[3,4]

Is Beruriah only to be seen as a woman who solely claims her father, a scholar, and follows in his footsteps? In losing and mourning him, does she more completely identify with him (a process Freud [1915] first details in "Mourning and Melancholia")? Or, does she carry inside of her the trauma of witnessing the martyrdom of her father and fellow sages and the destruction of her world? I believe it is not *either or* but *and*. Beruriah lives on as both witness and carrier of the torch of Jewish learning and life, something I believe the rabbis wanted her to represent.

However, embedded within her story is another story of trauma and loss. In Beruriah's story we can see how gender and trauma become inextricably entwined. She is idealized, more learned than her brother or even most men, while also a carrier of traumatic vulnerability (specifically she carries the silent grief surrounding the loss of her and Meir's two sons and the final story surrounding her seduction and suicide). I am suggesting that trauma – which I define as the profound experience of helplessness, powerlessness and sub-jugation – is more likely to be carried by that gender category that already is defined in a similar way, that is, women. Given the feminist inquiry into the formation of gender binaries, this is in agreement with Benjamin, Dimen, Harris and Layton, that the culture will infuse the categories of male and female with differing qualities and values. The very definition of one's gender suggests simultaneously what being male or female is and what it is not. The legacy of patriarchy is that maleness becomes associated with strength and independence, whereas females are associated with dependency and vulner-ability. As I suggested before, important cultural aspects of life inform these values and are also often split into the binary where aspects of power, hier-archy and authority are riven from powerlessness and subordination. Here is where I see trauma as implicated in Beruriah's story. Trauma as a cultural event and as a lived experience gets told in stories of subjugation and help-lessness. As Harris (2005) wrote, "Gender is a particularly vulnerable and volatile carrier of many self-state experiences, both those that are noxious and those that are idealized" (p. 35).

It is interesting to notice that Beruriah is isolated in the text – and not only from other women. In the Talmud, all teachings or sayings are placed in a tradition of who are one's teachers and one's students. Here Adler (1988) sees how the unraveling of this version of Beruriah might begin. Despite her in-teractions with other rabbis, Beruriah cannot enter the Talmudic web of authority. She cites no teachers, and no students claim her as their teacher. She is effectively kept out of the chain of that tradition and its genealogical succession. This very fact robs her of any true agency because a scholar's impact on others needs to be seen and felt. The tradition she is steeped and learned in is one that sees women as intellectually inferior, "light-headed," and potentially "licentious." How could they keep this value in place and maintain Beruriah's status, a serious paradox indeed.

Additionally, sexuality was considered an essential characteristic of women, hence the need for prohibitions regarding speaking too long with a woman, hearing her sing and so on. In every way, woman can distract and lead the male away from study into the erotic. Adler (1988) writes, "Were there a woman like Beruriah, schooled in and committed to a tradition that views her as inferior, how could she resolve the paradox inherent in her loyalty to that tradition?" (p. 30). As sharp and learned as she was, we cannot help but also discover and see played out the other negative pole of her otherness. A woman scholar must be other and so cannot exist. She is utterly alone, having been joined to a tradition that wouldn't have her as an equal member—not unlike Eliza Doolittle in *My Fair Lady,* who, after finally succeeding in learning how to speak, dress and act like a lady in the aristo-cratic class bemoans, "What is to become of me?" Where could Eliza and Beruriah exist given that in many ways they both are vitalized by the creative imaginings of George Bernard Shaw[5] and the early rabbis, that is, wishful fantasies of women who are more like men? Eliza must be returned to her subordinate status and becomes the helpmate to her creator, Henry Higgins.

Beruriah's final story ends differently. Her final legend is one that Rashi, the great Talmudic commentator in the 11th century, adds within a section of the Talmud dealing with sexual transgressions. By the time of Rashi, the gender binary was firmly established, and study of these texts became solely the domain of men. In this story, Meir and Beruriah argue with her mocking the Rabbinic dictum that "all women are light-headed," code for licentious. Meir, to prove his point, has one of his students seduce Beruriah. She resists and resists but finally gives in. I don't know if Beruriah gives in as a sub-mission or out of any desire or agency of her own. This is interesting to contemplate as a further complication of her story. Where would Beruriah's desires lie? Does she submit to the seduction knowing on some level that her husband is behind it (the seducer is a student of Meir's)? Or is she rebelling against the tradition? We are told that after she learns of Meir's plan, Beruriah commits suicide. We are left to believe that Beruriah, betrayed by her husband and in some ways the tradition, is left bereft, without agency or desire. Her last act of suicide is problematic. In refusing to exist in a system that could betray her and not accept her, the only agentic choice we are left to believe is that she has to end her life. It is this final story by Rashi that has tarnished Beruriah from being seen as the cross-gender-lines female scholar extraordinaire back into the essentialist woman who is only a sexual object. The original attempt to undermine the gender binary, to imagine a woman embodying characteristics usually ascribed to men, is undone. Beruriah is "reinscribed as girl," and it reestablishes gender conformity.

Yentl, the Yeshiva Boy

I. B. Singer (1953), in his short story "Yentl, the Yeshiva Boy," created a fictitious woman who was not cut out for woman's work with her possessing "the soul of a man in the body of a woman (p. 149). Singer's 19th-century story is located in an Eastern European shtetl in Poland and opens with Yentl's father dying. Yentl had secretly been learning Torah and Talmud with her rabbi father. All alone in the world, Yentl decides to refuse her role as a woman and instead pursue studies as a boy. She cuts her hair, dresses in her father's clothing, and assumes the name Anshel, going off to study at a

Yeshiva. Once there she falls in love with her havrutah (study partner), Avigdor. This friendship intensifies, although Avigdor marries, and upon his suggestion, Anshel/Yentl impulsively marries Avigdor's former fiancée, Hadass. After some time, no longer able to sustain the multiple secrets of his/her transgressive cross-dressing lie/life, Anshel/Yentl invites Avigdor to go on a trip together and reveals to Avigdor her true identity as a woman. Avigdor offers to marry her, but once again Yentl refuses her female role, saying she wants to learn with him, not darn his socks. Avigdor is bereft and confused, while Yentl has firmly decided to leave and sends divorce papers to Hadass while disappearing from the story. The story ends with Avigdor and Hadass marrying and having a son, whom they name Anshel.

Given the gendered underpinnings within Judaism, I will be looking at how Beruriah and Yentl act to countervail the gender binary and in so doing reveal a kind of complicated otherness of woman within Judaism. There are many similarities between Yentl and Beruriah, and I have no doubt that Singer was familiar with the Beruriah legends. Toward the end of the story, after Yentl undresses to prove to Avigdor that she is in fact a woman, they argue over how she had violated the commandments against cross-dressing. Yentl tries to explain how her nature was "not cut out for plucking feathers" and once back to their Talmudic conversation, "A great love for Anshel took hold of Avigdor, mixed with shame, remorse, anxiety. In his thoughts he likened Anshel (or Yentl) to Bruria, the wife of Reb Meir. For the first time he saw clearly that this was what he had always wanted: a wife whose mind was not taken up with material things" (Singer, 1953, p. 165).

I consider Yentl a "drash" (exegesis) on Beruriah, revealing a hidden piece of the legends making up the "text" on Beruriah. I wonder if Singer (1953) further elaborated the "passing as a man" aspect of Beruriah's learnedness by having Yentl literally dress and pass as a Yeshiva boy. In writing about Yentl (Salberg, 2012), I highlighted Singer's subversiveness regarding passing and cross-gender play. Passing is a statement on rigid gender binaries by highlighting, violating, and even sometimes mocking them. Garber (1992) articulated well, "One of the most important aspects of crossdressing is the way in which it offers a challenge to easy notions of binarity, putting into question the categories of 'female' and 'male,' whether they are considered essential or constructed, biological or cultural" (p. 10). Yentl does continue studying, but I also see her passing as a transgressive attempt to subvert rigid gender binaries by being the girl who can easily become a boy. In this way, she embodies Butler's (1990, 1993, 1995) conceptualizations of gender as performance. Additionally, by defying Jewish law, that is, the prohibition over wearing the clothing of the other sex, Yentl is undoing the subordinate status of woman. Harris (2005) wrote, "The tomboy experience often simultaneously refuses conventions and gender coherences and swallows them wholesale. Gender conformist and gender outlaw" (p. 132). What Harris was characterizing is how gender gets used and misused, the very lawless behavior Yentl embodies. Yentl breaks laws but also abides tightly to them, carefully dressing the part, determined to "pass" as a boy.

This is not new to Jewish literature, and Lefkovitz (2010) has written about how masculinity can at times also be the site of "passing." In her writing about the twins Esau and Jacob, she notices how Jacob has to "pass" as his more stereotypically masculine brother to receive (and steal) his father's blessing. She writes, "Jacob, the son who is allied with his mother, dresses in animal skins to pass as Esau, and so, to pass as the kind of man who can inherit the patriarchy" (p. 48). In this way the biblical story riffs on what kind of masculinity, what type of man, can be blessed and sanctioned to carry the patriarchy forward. In this story the complementary role of a son, identified with his mother, crossdresses to "pass," to not be the "other" son.

The rigid gender binary inherent within patriarchy and woven into Judaism has a shadow side. The other, the shadow self of nonheteronormativity, can be seen in these stories of "passing," where regulatory anxiety prevails over gender fluidity. These are stories not only of girls passing as boys but also, as we see with Jacob, even boys may need to "pass" because the version of masculinity necessitated by the patriarchy may border on heroic versions of maleness. Trauma lurks behind these stories as well. The father who Jacob needs to fool is Isaac, who survived being bound by his own father as an offering to God. We never hear in the Biblicalb text any protest from Isaac during the ordeal, or after. Are we to assume he "manned up," as the saying goes, and didn't cry like a girl? Masculinity devoid of vulnerability and helplessness seems to be what is at stake here.

Singer had left Poland and arrived in the United States, escaping the worst of Nazi Europe. He wrote *Yentl* post WWII and the Holocaust, in the 1950s, and I wonder if we can see trauma lurking in this story as well. He locates his gender-bending heroine back in time, to a 19th-century Polish shtetl era, which predated him and the Shoah that destroyed the world he had known. I want us to hold in mind the complicated ways that specifically a female is used to carry trauma. As with Beruriah, whose father dies, Yentl's story opens with death. What is also true is that we never hear of either woman's mother. (We also never hear about Eliza Doolittle's mother, only her father, who comes around to collect some benefit from his daughter's being a prized student.) Are we to believe that neither Beruriah nor Yentl mourned the loss of her mother, that the only attachment that mattered was their fathers? Or did they, as gender-bending daughters, claim their fathers as part of a tomboy (see Harris, 1996, 2005)?

Yentl's father, who is seen as the one nurturing her in an entire world of devotion to studying texts, dies in the opening page of the story. We also know that, in an instant, this world of shtetls and shteibls, of rabbis and communities, had been wiped out as part of Hitler's final solution. Singer brings this world back to life in many of his short stories. However, with Yentl we see how trauma and gender are interconnected. Both Beruriah and Yentl carry the trauma of death—the loss of their fathers and of vital Jewish communal life. Each of these eras—post second Temple destruction and 1930s Europe—saw the end of eras where Jews lived more independent self-governing lives. I also believe it is a probable trope for Singer to use the category "woman" to carry any cultural trauma of oppression. It is Yentl who loses the most in this story: her father and family, her love of studying, her love for Avigdor and for Hadass, and ultimately her life because she must disappear at the end of the story.

Concluding Thoughts and Questions

In many ways Judaism rests on stories. Each week a parsha, a section from the Torah, is read. Many of these sections are historical stories of the people and nation that became the Hebrews or Israelites, ancestors of today's Jews. We read about the children who descended from the first man, Adam, and the first woman, Eve. Some of us read about the woman who preceded Eve, Lilith. We read about the patriarchs, Abraham, Isaac and Jacob, whereas some of us mightily read into the small fragments of the stories of the matriarchs, Sarah, Rebecca, Leah and Rachel. There are many stories we read, and within them are the shadow stories, the backstory or the tale we imagine wasn't fully told.

I believe trauma is one of those shadow stories. The history of the Jewish people is a history of trauma, oppression, victimization, and then triumph and freedom with later cycles of trauma, oppression, and so on repeated again. This is what gets transmitted across the generations. However, I do wonder if women will have to carry weakness and the spectral presence of trauma. In this paper, I tried to demonstrate in psychoanalytic theory and detail within women's stories how gender and vulnerability get coded as feminine. Women then hold cultural trauma stories very differently than men. Although men remain heroic in the defiance and/or defeat of oppression, they can be agents of their destiny. Women are not accorded the same view. The stories of Beruriah and Yentl are particular examples of attempts to envision undermining the gender polarities by allowing women to inhabit some of the qualities culturally encoded for men. In these stories, however, men are not allowed further access to vulnerability (see Jacob's story as described by Lefkovitz, 2010).[6] Women, such as Beruriah and Yentl, who are allowed to cross gender lines into more agentic behaviors, do not remain expanded in vision, quickly dissolving back into traditional roles with the reinstatement of the gender hierarchy and splits occurring. In this way, their stories function as cautionary tales. There are risks with crossing gender boundaries and a price to be paid.

Gender conformity is a prevailing aspect of the stories we are told and a place where women became othered. Benjamin (1998) wrote, "Opposites are to some extent unavoidable because of the inherent psychic tendency to split; because in fact they allow the mind to think. It is the capacity to hold them in tension and overcome splitting that is at stake" (p. 24). I also tried to show that passing is one way out of the gender split in that it plays on binarity and refuses it. However, I wonder, when does passing allow for a kind of freedom for an "other self" to be expressed, and when does it eradicate "otherness?" When does passing carry what is permissible, and when is it subversive? These questions further lead me to wonder about authenticity and to consider who and what is an authentic Jew. Is Yentl authentically Jewish if she "passes" as a Yeshiva boy in order to study and express her authentically Jewish yearning for learning? Or was Beruriah more originally authentic because she imbibed her father's learning and the world around her, entering the discourse as she saw fit, a woman of intelligence and learning?

I do question if we ever fully transcend the legacy of gender binaries, of splits that allow for disowned parts of the self to be found in the opposite gender. Will men continue to own agency and dominance as a means to feel masculine? Harris (2005) writes further about gender splits and multiple selves as "a construction softly assembled to carry feelings and states of mind deemed intolerable, the unconscious of the other. The gender divide continues the cultural work of sequestering frightening aspects of humanness" (p. 203). Can our beliefs and culture change enough to allow for authentic experiences, regardless of gender, to take root and grow?

Henry Higgins ends his songful lament asking, why a woman can't be more like him. I believe that this reveals the narcissistic root that prevents us from experiencing the "other" as a full subject not to be colonized by our own subjectivity. Layton (1998b) in her book and work on gender, culture and postmodern theory believes that the cultural and the psychological are always interconnected and implicated in forming each other. Here is where the fulcrum may lie. We need to change ourselves while also needing to change our culture. Further, we allow for a constant interpenetration between self and culture to occur in lieu of colonization. Finally, we need to believe that both women and men need to change, to share the pool of human experiences and qualities and, in doing so, allow for fuller expression of each other's capacities.

At a recent event in New York City (June 2015) Diane von Furstenberg, in telling about her mother's experience as a Holocaust survivor, spoke directly of what she felt she learned from her mother: "My mother taught me that no matter how bad things are, look for the tiny point of light and build around it. That's what survivors do to survive." I was in the audience that night, and it struck me as a wonderful way of describing resilience and healing. We need to strive and build around the glimmer of hope that things can change and be built differently.

Acknowledgments

I thank Rabbi Burton L. Visotzky for introducing me to midrash and Beruriah; Dr. Anne Lapidus Lerner for elaborating the feminist enterprise in the context of the Beruriah legends; Rabbi Judith Hauptman for her thoughtful comments and encouragement on this paper; Carole Maso for her acumen and wonderful encouragement; and Adrienne Harris for her insights on gender, tomboys and so much more.

Notes

1 We thank Taylor & Francis Ltd. for permission to publish the article by Jill Salberg (2016), "Trauma, Gender, and the Stories of Jewish Women: The Other Within," *Studies in Gender and Sexuality*, 17:2, 102–113, DOI: 10.1080/15240657. 2016.1172925.
2 The Nazi regime targeted all Jews, both men and women, for persecution and eventually death. The regime frequently subjected women, however, both Jewish and non-Jewish, to brutal persecution that was sometimes unique to the gender of the victims.
     In both camps and ghettos, women were particularly vulnerable to beatings and rape. The Germans established brothels in some concentration and labor camps, and the German army ran roughly 500 brothels for soldiers in which women were forced to work (see U.S. Holocaust Memorial Museum (2014), "Woman During the Holocaust").
3 There is some speculation that there was more than one person who was referred to in the Talmud by the name Beruriah. In the Tosefta, she is referred to as the daughter of Rabbi Hananiah ben Tardion, and if this is true, she would have either seen or known of his being martyred by the Romans in the aftermath of the Bar Kokhba revolt (32 C.E.). For a much fuller discussion, see Tal Ilan (1999), Chapter 6.
4 This is much like our current academic/scientific adherence to citing of whose scholarship one is utilizing, whether to support or refute an argument.
5 *My Fair Lady* is a musical based on the play *Pygmalion* written by George Bernard Shaw in 1912.
6 It is not possible to fully explore the aspect of these stories, having been written by men. However, it is worth entertaining how different the legends of Beruriah and the story of Yentl might be if recorded and/or imagined by women.

References

Adler, R. (1988). The virgin in the brothel and other anomalies: Character and context in the legend of Beruriah. *Tikkun*, 3(6), 28–31, 102–105.
Adler, R. (1998). *Engendering Judaism: An Inclusive Theology and Ethics*. Boston, MA: Beacon Press.
Benjamin, J. (1988). *The Bonds of Love: Psychoanalysis, Feminism and the Problem of Domination*. New York, NY: Pantheon Books.
Benjamin, J. (1991). Father and daughter: Identification with difference—A contribution to gender heterodoxy. *Psychoanalytic Dialogues*, 1, 277–299.
Benjamin, J. (1995). Sameness and difference: Toward an "overinclusive" model of gender development. *Psychoanalytic Inquiry*, 15, 125–142.

Benjamin, J. (1998). *Shadow of the Other: Intersubjectivity and Gender in Psychoanalysis.* New York, NY, and London, UK: Routledge.

Boyarin, D. (1995). *Carnal Israel: Reading Sex in Talmudic Culture.* Berkeley: University of California Press.

Bromberg, P. (2006). *Awakening the Dreamer: Clinical Journeys.* London, UK, and New York, NY: Routledge.

Butler, J. (1990). *Gender Trouble.* New York, NY: Routledge.

Butler, J. (1993). *Bodies That Matter.* New York, NY: Routledge.

Butler, J. (1995). Melancholy gender-refused identification. *Psychoanalytic Dialogues,* 5, 165–180.

Davies, J.M. (1998). Multiple perspectives on multiplicity. *Psychoanalytic Dialogues,* 8, 195–206.

Dimen, M. (1991). Deconstructing difference: Gender, splitting and transitional space. *Psychoanalytic Dialogues,* 1, 335–352.

Fonrobert, C.E. (2001). The Beit Midrash which is not yet: Feminist interpretations of rabbinic literature. Two views. *Nashim: A Journal of Jewish Women's Studies and Gender Issues,* 4, 7–14.

Freud, S. (1915). *Mourning and Melancholia Standard Edition, 14.* London, UK: Hogarth Press, pp. 237–258.

Garber, M. (1992). *Vested Interests: Cross-Dressing & Cultural Anxiety.* New York, NY, and London, UK: Routledge.

Goldman, A. (2013, June 30). Like a cowboy going to a saloon. The New York Times. Retrieved from http://www.nytimes.com/2013/06/30/magazine/how-diane-von-furstenberg-is-like-a-cowboy.html

Goldner, V. (1991). Towards a critical relational theory of gender. *Psychoanalytic Dialogues,* 1, 249–272.

Goodblatt, D. (1975). The Beruriah traditions. *Journal of Jewish Studies,* 26, 68—85.

Grand, S. (1997). On the gendering of traumatic dissociation: A case of mother-son incest. *Gender & Psychoanalysis,* 2, 55–77.

Harris, A. (1991). Gender as contradiction. *Psychoanalytic Dialogues,* 1, 197–224.

Harris, A. (1996). The conceptual power of multiplicity. *Contemporary Psychoanalysis,* 32, 537–552.

Harris, A. (2000). Gender as soft assembly. *Studies in Gender and Sexuality,* 1, 223–324.

Harris, A. (2005). *Gender as Soft Assembly.* Hillsdale, NJ, and London, UK: Analytic Press.

Hartman, T. & Buckholtz, C. (2011). Beruriah said well: The many lives (and deaths) of a talmudic social critic. *Prooftexts,* 31, 181–209.

Hauptman, J. (2011). A new view of women and Torah study in the talmudic period. *Jewish Studies Internet Journal,* 9, 249–292.

Heschel, S. (1983). *On Being a Jewish Feminist.* New York, NY: Schocken Books.

Ilan, T. (1997). The quest for the historical Beruriah, Rachel, and Imma Shalom. *AJS Review,* 22, 1–17.

Ilan, T. (1999). Beruriah has spoken well: The historical Beruriah and her transformation in the rabbinic corpora. In: *Integrating Women into Second Temple History.* Peabody, MA: J.C.B. Mohr Siebeck, pp. 175–194.

Layton, L. (1998a). Female masochism, female agency, and the trauma of maternal abandonment: Discussion. *Gender & Psychoanalysis,* 3, 155–169.

Layton, L. (1998b). *Who's That Girl? Who's That Boy? Clinical Practice Meets Postmodern Gender Theory*. Northvale, NJ, and London, UK: Aronson.

Lefkovitz, L.H. (2010). *In Scripture: The First Stories of Jewish Sexual Identities*. Lanham, MD: Rowman & Littlefield.

Plaskow, J. (1990). *Standing Again at Sinai*. New York, NY: Harper Collins.

Salberg, J. (2012). Reimagining Yentl while revisiting feminism in the light of relational approaches to gender and sex. *Studies in Gender and Sexuality*, 13, 185–196.

Salberg, J. (2015). The texture of traumatic attachment: Presence and ghostly absence in transgenerational transmission. *The Psychoanalytic Quarterly*, 84(1), 21–46.

Shaw, G.B. (1912). *Pygmalion*. New York, NY: Penguin.

Silverman, S. (2015). The colonized mind: Gender, trauma and mentalization. *Psychoanalytic Dialogues*, 25, 51–66.

Singer, I.B. (1953). Yentl the Yeshiva boy. In: *The Collected Stories of Isaac Bashevis Singer*. New York, NY: Farrar, Straus and Giroux, pp. 149–169.

U.S. Holocaust Memorial Museum. (2014). Woman during the Holocaust. Retrieved from http://www.ushmm.org/wlc/en/article.php?ModuleId=10005176

von Furstenberg, D. (2015, June 17). *Speech given at ADL tribute honoring Abe Foxman's 50 years of service*. New York, NY.

Weissler, C. (1998). *Voices of the Matriarchs: Listening to the Prayers of Early Modern Jewish Women*. Boston, MA: Beacon Press.

9

FEARING THE THEORETICAL OTHER

The Legacy of Kohut's Erasure of the Analyst's Trauma

Ilene Philipson

Recently, a number of psychoanalytic authors have begun to chart new territory in understanding the ways in which the Holocaust has impacted theory development since World War II (see Aron and Starr, 2013; Kuriloff, 2014; Prince, 2009). In these new works, it has been shown that through their own denial, dissociation, neglect and disavowal, European émigré analysts and their followers created theory that was remarkably silent about trauma in general, and the analyst's experience of trauma in particular. Through privileging early childhood experience, the possibility of analytically significant, adult trauma virtually was eliminated from the canon. And for mainstream American psychoanalysis, the analyst's subjective history and experience were erased, even if it involved massive disruption, death of family members and annihilation of previous ways of life. According to Dori Laub, psychoanalyst and founder of the Fortunoff Archives of Holocaust Testimony at Yale University, theory became "an armor against" the experience of the Holocaust (quoted in Kuriloff, 2014, p. 59). And as Aron and Starr point out: "Throughout the first half century after the Shoah … psychoanalysts minimized and even ignored the significance of the Holocaust, both clinically as it affected survivors and their children, and sociologically, in terms of how it affected the profession and the development of psychoanalytic theory" (2013, p. 121).

In writing about the ways in which postwar psychoanalytic theory was founded in dissociation and denial of the Holocaust, and in claiming that psychoanalysis is a "Holocaust survivor," (as Prince first noted in 2009, p. 180), the focus of authors' observations is typically ego psychology, or the "Hartmann Era," as Bergmann terms it (Bergmann, 2000). Various authors have linked key concepts in ego psychology to Heinz Hartmann's denial of

DOI: 10.4324/9781003266600-13

what actually happened to him in Germany. By way of example, Harold Blum posits that Hartmann's fundamental concepts of a "conflict-free sphere of the ego" and the "average expectable environment" were founded in denial of the most horrendous conflict and the most unexpected environment ever known in history (2000, p. 90).[1] Similarly, Otto Kernberg views the optimism of ego psychology as a form of denial, and suggests that Hartmann's control over post-War psychoanalysis in the United States was akin to "identification with the aggressor" that found its roots in the émigré's Holocaust experience (2000, p. 229).

What I wish to accomplish in this paper is to do something different: to examine the ways in which Heinz Kohut's erasure of his own Holocaust trauma may have influenced the creation of the psychoanalytic school of self psychology.

At this point in history, it is widely known that Heinz Kohut had an extremely complex relationship to his Jewish origins. In certain contexts, he admitted being Jewish directly: "I am Jewish on both sides," he told Jacques Palaci in 1938 (Strozier, 2001, p. 56). In other situations, he acknowledged that he had Jewish ancestry: "My father was Jewish. I am not. I made that choice, and that is that," he asserted to Paul Ornstein in the early 1970s (ibid, p. 188). But mostly he obfuscated or simply lied. Jerome Beigler, a Chicago psychiatrist who began analysis with Kohut in 1975, "wanted to know whether Kohut was Jewish." Biegler said, "Kohut talked about this and that and muttered something about who was Jewish, anyway? In the end Beigler was not sure what he had said, though Kohut ended with the comment that Beigler could teach him some Yiddish expressions and they could manage that way" (ibid, pp. 351–352). Although he was born of two Jewish parents and was bar mitzvahed in 1926, Kohut stated in an interview in *The New York Times* that his "mother was a devout Catholic" who dragged him to mass every Sunday when they lived in Austria (ibid, p. 38). In fact, his mother did convert to Catholicism, but in 1948, long after immigrating to the United States. In speaking of his time spent at an English camp for Jewish refugees in 1939, he asserted that what had been most difficult for him was that all the other inmates shared a Jewish identity and he did not. They were Jewish, and he was not (Ibid, p. 116). And the experience of Kohut's disciple and friend, Paul Ornstein, is illustrative. One of the most remarkable stories that Ornstein recounts is his lunch with Kohut at a kosher deli wherein Heinz:

> ordered a ham and cheese sandwich and a glass of milk, something so outrageous as to be deliberately offensive. The clerk said politely but firmly he could not serve such food in the deli, for it was kosher. Kohut proceeded to make a huge scene. Raising his voice, he said he would eat what he wanted where and when he wanted, that it was a public restaurant, and demanded to be served what he had ordered. Everyone noticed. (ibid, p. 188)

It is interesting to note that Thomas Kohut, Heinz's son who was present at this lunch, has no particular memory of it, not because he denies it occurred, but due to the fact that "his father did such things so frequently he had no recollection of this particular event" (ibid, p. 427).

It seems clear from reading Charles Strozier's thorough and remarkably well-researched biography, *Heinz Kohut: The Making of a Psychoanalyst,* that Kohut had had an ambivalent relationship to his Jewish identity before the horrors of the Third Reich took place and by the time he was in university in the early 1930s. Strozier writes, "he seemed to be Jewish, had a Jewish name, and had Jewish sensibilities. But in all the discussions of politics and culture he acted as a non-Jew and put himself out of the frame of reference of Jewish concerns" (Strozier, p. 48). However, as all German and Austrian Jews discovered, their own sense of themselves, their assimilation into the Christian culture that enveloped them, and their own enactment of non-Jewishness mattered little. Kohut's mother's store was looted and destroyed during Kristallnacht in November 1938; his childhood home essentially was confiscated by the Nazis in 1939, and he was forced to emigrate in a transport of 125 Jews from Vienna to London in March 1939. "It was the end of a world, it was the end of an era ... I had the feeling it was the end of my life," Kohut is quoted as saying (quoted in ibid, p. 55). While his mother eventually followed him to the United States, four out of five of Kohut's aunts and uncles perished in the Holocaust (Kohut, 2012, p. 16).

In her book, *Contemporary Psychoanalysis and the Legacy of the Third Reich,* psychoanalyst Emily Kuriloff interviews Thomas Kohut in order to better understand his father's relationship to the Holocaust. From her 2012 interview with him we learn that he concurs with her conjecture that Kohut's Holocaust experience "accounts in large part for Heinz Kohut's future psychoanalytic focus," a focus on the "dangers of a 'fragmentation' of the self" (Kuriloff, 2014, p. 13). Thomas Kohut describes how we might understand his father's oft-quoted assertion regarding his departure from Vienna in 1939, "I've led two totally different, perhaps unbridgeable lives" (quoted in Quinn, 1984, p. 124). The younger Kohut reports that on one of his two trips to Austria with his father:

we were hiking in the mountains and met some people from the area, with whom my father easily spoke an Austrian German. I suddenly saw a different, much less tense, more animated part of my father as he conversed with these people. *It was only then that I realized all that my father had lost and missed*, that the man I knew was more constricted, that he had only been engaging a part of himself ... (quoted in Kuriloff, p. 13, emphasis added)

Further, Thomas notes that his father "never bought property in America," fearing expulsion and exile:

> There was even a time when George Wallace [a racist governor of Alabama in the 1960s] looked like a viable presidential candidate, and my father was seriously thinking that things might eventually come to pass that we might have to flee the United States. (ibid)

When Kohut referred to "unbridgeable" parts of himself, his son's comments make it difficult not to think of dissociation as a means of coping with the unbearable, the loss of a way of life, a sense of belonging encoded in a language – Austrian German – that emerges in a particular context, his homeland. Only in this landscape of remembrances can his son see for the first time "all that my father had lost and missed." It is only then that "Mr. Psychoanalysis," the well-functioning Christian, the highly successful American intellectual, is revealed as a possible trauma survivor, a description, we can imagine, he either didn't want others to see or to know himself. We can now ask why he never bought a home, why he had such an extreme reaction to George Wallace's presidential bid. Did he never feel fully safe, never a complete sense of belonging in the United States – always exilic, always, alas, a Jew?

It is well documented that Kohut did not readily consider Holocaust trauma in his patients. In the case of "Mr. A," whose family was forced to flee the Nazis twice when Mr. A was six and eight years old, Kohut asserts "the case had *nothing* to do with the Holocaust." According to Kohut, "Mr. A's *key childhood experience* was his traumatic disappointment in the 'power and efficacy' of his father" (cited in Strozier, p. 202, emphasis added). This kind of certitude and irrefutability of thinking possibly suggests a mind that could not allow for the intrusion of anything to do with the Holocaust, the encroachment of this traumatic event on the intrapsychic. As Robert Prince avers: "The continued postwar, radical privileging of early childhood events in the face of massive adult trauma, speaks to the operation of defensive blinders" (Prince, 2009, p. 190).

I would like to suggest that it is this possibility of defensive blinders that underlie, in part, Kohut's, and many of his followers', dismissal of other theoretical schools and, in particular, what he termed "social psychology." It is important to point out that hostility to competing psychoanalytic theories has been endemic to the field since Freud. But I would maintain that each school's antipathies are fashioned out of the particular sensibilities and interests of its founders. Kohut and many of those who were deeply influenced by his sensibilities were especially hostile to what they termed *social psychology*. When I first encountered Kohut's work as a sociology graduate student in the early 1980s, I couldn't understand to whom he was referring nor why he bore such animus toward a group of people I thought worked in sociology departments. When I later read the same characterization by some of Kohut's followers and his biographer, I was similarly confused. Charles Strozier (2001) has written: "It is probably fair to say Kohut underestimated the potential traumatic impact of extreme situations, irrespective of psychological context. At the same time, he may have reestablished a more balanced relationship between self and society in his deep distrust of what he considered the *fatuous language of much of social psychology*" (pp. 203–204, *emphasis added*).

And Arnold Goldberg (1986) claimed that "self psychology struggles hard not to be an interpersonal psychology not only because it wishes to avoid the social psychological connotations of that phrase but also because it wishes to minimize the input of the analyst into the mix ... [W]e are not interpersonal but primarily intrapsychic" (pp. 387–388).

It is only when I realized that for Kohut the term *social psychology* served as an aspersion made against interpersonal psychoanalysis that his disparagement made a certain degree of sense. James Fosshage (2003) clarifies this by noting that "for Kohut, 'relational' meant interpersonal psychoanalysis with all its connotations of being merely a social psychology – that is, focusing solely on externally apparent interpersonal interactions" (p. 413).

In light of the current literature under discussion, I now think that Kohut's dismissal of interpersonal psychoanalysis/social psychology was born, in some part, of his reluctance to allow for social, and hence possibly traumatizing, real-world events to impact the individual and particularly the analyst. In his antipathy to interpersonal psychoanalysis, he dismissed the one sector of the psychoanalytic community in the United States that allowed for social circumstances to enter the consulting room. In her research into the impact of the Holocaust on émigré analysts, Kuriloff notes that those clinicians she "interviewed who were trained in the interpersonal tradition, and thus outside the classical mainstream, tend to speak rather directly of the ways in which the Holocaust and the Nazi scourge influenced their work" (43). I think we can imagine that this openness is grounded, in part, in the interpersonal tradition of privileging the historical and the social-cultural over the universal. Both Sullivan and Fromm, founders of the interpersonal school, viewed Freud's theories as myopic insofar as he conflated the particular historical circumstances in which he lived with the universal human condition. Once real-world events are allowed their due place in understanding a patient's – or analyst's – life, it becomes harder to definitively assert both that the Holocaust had nothing to do with Mr. A's psychoanalysis, and that it had no enduring impact on the person of Heinz Kohut himself.

This by no means is to suggest that Kohut was alone in his disregard for interpersonalism. His simple statement in *The Analysis of the Self* that the "interpersonal view of social psychology ... impoverish[es] our science" was at one with mainstream psychoanalysis at this time (Kohut, 1971, p. 51). In this concise claim, he equates interpersonal psychoanalysis with social psychology and contrasts that to "science," that is, what he is engaged in. When Kohut was developing his psychology of the self in the 1950s, 1960s and 1970s, the most popular psychoanalyst in America was the co-founder of the interpersonal school, Erich Fromm, who published one best-selling book after another. These books often were based in Fromm's critical reading of Freud that put him at odds with the hegemonic psychoanalytic discourse of the period. But more often, they explored exegetic territory that I believe Kohut objected to on multiple grounds. As Fromm noted in the very first book that launched his career: "To understand the dynamics of the social process we must understand the dynamics of the psychological processes operating within the individual, just as *to understand the individual we must see him in the context of the culture which made him*" (Fromm, 1941, p. x. *emphasis added*).

Thus, Kohut could dismiss interpersonal psychoanalysis in keeping with the widely accepted orthodoxy that held interpersonalist beliefs about the analyst as a "participant-observer," and one's personality residing within an "interpersonal field" as heresy. But he also may have derided it as it was articulated most fully by Fromm: an individual cannot be known outside of his culture, the exogenous circumstances of his upbringing. History has its claims, and as such, Kohut's being a Jew and a victim of the Holocaust probably would not have escaped scrutiny by the unscientific social psychologists, those who "impoverished" the scientific enterprise that Kohut believed his psychology of the self reflected.

A Grandiose Defense?

How much do Kohut's "defensive blinders," which rendered the interpersonal school possibly too threatening to consider, play a part in what Greenberg and Mitchell (1983) called Kohut's "recurring exaggerated claims to uniqueness and originality."

> The theoretical model he has developed often strikingly resembles the work of other relational model theorists. These similarities are never openly addressed or considered by Kohut, who presents himself as if he were working in a vacuum, continually breaking new ground … His tendency to pursue his own line of theory construction unfettered by the demands of attribution to the work of others would be fair enough, if the claims which he and his collaborators make to uniqueness were not so great. In fact, in his last writings Kohut compares his contributions to the invention of the machine, suggesting that they constitute mankind's greatest hope for survival. (p. 366)

In the Preface to *The Restoration of the Self*, Kohut entertains the possibility of acknowledging those "who might reproach me for going it alone, for trying to find new solutions without leaning on the work of others who have also recognized the limitations of the classical position and have already suggested emendations, corrections, and improvements" (Kohut, 1977, p. xix).

While stating his "great admiration" for theorists such as Winnicott, Adler, Rank, Balint, Erikson, Mahler, Kernberg, Lacan, Sandler and Schafer, he claims that "despite years of conscientious effort. . , the available psychoanalytic framework – even as emended by the work of modern contributors," left him "floundering in a morass of conflicting, poorly based, and often vague theoretical speculation" (Kohut, 1977, p. xx). Thus, Kohut depicts himself as having no choice but to go it alone because the history of psychoanalysis offered up nothing; no theorist seemingly provided even a crumb to expand on or dialogue with in his attempts to emerge from the morass of "vague," "ambiguous," and "shifting" theories of the past 75 years (Kohut, 1977, p. xxi).

How do we understand this hubris? While exaggerated claims to originality litter the field, Kohut's explicitness, I think, sets him apart. Is he possibly expressing an undisguised grandiosity born of insecurity, an insecurity emanating from being a pretender, a counterfeit Christian, a "tense" and "constricted" American success story who always, at some level, felt he did not belong, and worse yet, might one day have to flee again? According to Thomas Kohut, his father never wanted his son to know he was Jewish because he "was afraid I'd be killed. He was trying to protect me from what happened to his own family in Vienna." At the end of his life, Kohut warned Thomas that if he "had a son, I should never have him circumcised" (quoted in Kuriloff, 2014, p. 11).

Kohut's biographer, Charles Strozier, has painted a picture of a lone genius who wrote "not primarily in relation to what others have said but in response to his own clinical experience and what was inside of him" (2001, p. 222). In light of what has been presented thus far, is it possible to reconceptualize what may have lurked "inside of him" as a need to feel and appear beyond influence, the founder of a new paradigm with no other masters than himself, no threats to that precarious balance Kohut may have needed to maintain between his "unbridgeable lives?" By asserting his singularity, his theory beholden to no one who had come before, Kohut creates a sense of intellectual invulnerability, and the experience of invulnerability may have had its appeal for someone whose life was forever marked by the Shoah.[2]

Trauma Redux

In 1971, the year *Analysis of the Self* was published, Heinz Kohut was diagnosed with cancer. As Charles Strozier points out: "It would be difficult to overstate the impact that cancer had on Kohut. It shattered his personal myth of invincibility. In his moment of greatest glory Kohut was brought low by a disease that was completely outside of his control" (2001, p. 232).

I find it striking how Kohut responded to the traumatic news he had cancer in much the same way he responded to finding himself to be a Jew who was forced to bear the aggression and humiliations of living under the Third Reich. Depending on the context, he spoke openly and truthfully, or obfuscated, or simply lied. Both identities – Holocaust survivor/cancer patient – seemed to have left him traumatized and filled him with shame.

While he confided openly with his family about his diagnosis, he asked them to tell no one. It was a "deep and dark secret," Thomas Kohut reports (quoted in Strozier, 2001, p. 233). Over time, he admitted his diagnosis to old friends and some colleagues, and even "one female patient of whom he was particularly fond" (ibid, p. 236). But to others he obfuscated, much in the same way he responded when he was directly asked if he were a Jew by patients. When psychoanalyst, Paul Tolpin, asked him if he had leukemia, Kohut responded by saying "who knows who has leukemia," and "what's leukemia anyway?" (Ibid, p. 237). A Chicago analyst, Robert Leider, was in treatment with Kohut and asked him if the rumor that Kohut had cancer was true. Kohut denied it and added that he suffered only from an infection that was caused by cardiac problems (ibid, p. 237).

While the clinical ramifications of obfuscating or denying his Jewishness may have impacted his treatment of patients, particularly his Jewish ones, to some degree, his refusal to be open and more self-disclosing about his cancer can be seen as misleading, confusing and/or even harmful to some patients. In one of the last clinical vignettes he presents in the posthumously published *How Does Analysis Cure,* Kohut references his analysis of a colleague who had a dream that took place on: "a city block not far from my office … . The patient observed a frail man walking along the block … slowly, unsteadily, and weakly … . He noticed that the man was not real but some kind of straw doll. Overcome with anger, the patient plunged a knife several times into the straw doll man" (Kohut, 1984, p. 138).

In rather typical fashion, Kohut states: "I focused neither on the dream in isolation nor on the specific aggressive act depicted in the dream nor on the specific murderous wish he supposedly harbored … . What I concentrated on in my interpretation … was his disappointment in having a weak father, both in his childhood and now in the transference" (ibid, p. 139).

In an interview with Charles Strozier, Jerome Beigler, another patient of Kohut's, remembers vividly seeing a very frail Heinz Kohut struggling to cross Michigan Avenue in a strong wind. Beigler "took his arm, surprised Kohut would let him help, and was taken aback at how thin he was" (Strozier, p. 352).

I cite this real-life experience of Jerome Beigler to emphasize how much of what the analysand saw in his dream – a slow, unsteady and weak man walking on a street near Kohut's office – mirrored that which Beigler saw in reality. But for Kohut, his patient's vision of a frail man had only genetic meaning. Insofar as that vision lived in his consulting room, it was trans-ferential, that is, his analysand's projection of his weak father onto Kohut. Not only does Kohut speak exclusively of the patient's disappointment with his weak father, but he also does not even include the real relationship, or the patient's likely observations and concerns about his frail analyst, in his list of possible interpretive objects – "the dream in isolation," "the aggressive act," or the "murderous wish." That the analysand in his dream came to realize that the frail man was a "straw doll" to whom he seems to harbor murderous rage, does not alert Kohut to anything about who he was to this patient, other than a container for the analysand's tranferential projections. Might we wonder if Kohut's refusal to speak about his deteriorating health and his increasingly frail appearance, made him seem somewhat untruthful or unreal, a "straw doll," to his patient? Might this analysand's rage possibly have something to do with Kohut's unwillingness to speak about the fact that he was dying? Could Kohut's silence allow his patient to feel alone, fearful, not worthy of his analyst's honesty, and/or dissociated from his own experience and feelings that were implicitly excluded from the room?

These questions are more clearly addressed in the case of Kohut's patient, Herb Murrie, whom he met with four times a week for four years. In his accustomed fashion, Kohut did not reveal his cancer nor the fact that he was dying. No "matter how sick he was, or how weak he was, there was a spirit as if there is nothing wrong," Murrie reports so he never entertained the idea that his analyst's death was imminent. Thus, when Kohut died in 1981 in the middle of his analysis, Murrie was "left with awful feelings of abandonment and incompleteness." Murrie states that Kohut "didn't get to close the wound" (Strozier, 2001, p. 360).

We can only imagine the shame that prevented Kohut from speaking honestly with his patients. While he claimed his reticence grew out of his desire to protect them, he admitted to his family there was "something a bit shameful about his disease" (Strozier, 2001, p. 233). Shame was also an ingredient in his reactions to being a Jew. In his repeated efforts to perform his non-Jewishness – as exemplified in his ostentatious refusal to follow for kosher laws in kosher delicatessens – he reveals a possible lack of security in his assumed Christian identity, always having to separate himself from what he seems to have perceived as something shameful inside of him, that is, his Jewish origins. Paul Ornstein recalled that after the 1967 war in which Israel captured East Jerusalem, Kohut was "enraged, even shamed" by Jews wailing at the wall. He was "driven to distraction" by Jews acting in what he thought of as stereotypical Jewish ways (ibid, p. 188). Is it possible that these Jews served as the external manifestation of a dissociated part of him and the ghosts of his traumatic history?

Heinz Kohut created a clinical theory that allowed the analyst's shame and the analyst's identity to remain hidden. In the tireless pursuit of serving as a patient's selfobject, the analyst's subjectivity remains safely out of the picture. Was the avoidance of his own trauma the sole or even main engine that drove Kohut to conceptualize the clinical encounter in this way? I would say decidedly not. Insofar as both Freudian and ego psychological under-standings of the analyst's role and countertransference were the foundation from which Kohut built self psychology, he continued to believe he could apprehend a patient's unconscious life objectively – through vicarious introspection. In his adamant refusal to consider interpersonalist or "social psychological" ideas that had at their core the therapist as participant-observer, Kohut mirrored the positivist stance of the orthodox analysts around him. However, did his wish to erase or obscure the traumatized parts of him fuel or contribute to his embrace of this stance? I would suggest that this may be the case.

Kohut could acknowledge that he had led "two, unbridgeable lives." Unbridgeable to me connotes dissociation, unlinking and the walling-off of an identity that is "not-me." This evacuated part of oneself, according to Donnel Stern, speaks to "the person one must not be – the self-state one must not find oneself inhabiting – is someone who felt disappointed, bereft, frightened, humiliated, shamed, or otherwise badly hurt or threatened. One must not be the person to whom that thing happened, the person who has the feelings, memories, and experiences that come with being that person … . Quite literally, this is the part of subjectivity that must not be me" (Stern, 2010, p. 13).

Kohut adopted the traditional understanding of analytic objectivity, asserted that that objectivity could only be acquired through empathy, and turned the analyst's role into that of a function, specifically, a selfobject function that facilitates the patient's growth and is attuned to the patient's needs. Among many things, this formulation enabled Kohut to leave the analyst's subjectivity outside the official frame or conceptualization of the psychoanalytic enterprise. In effect, it allows for the preservation of the analyst's not-me states. Kohut's experiences of fear, shame, and deracination at the hands of the Third Reich, and the later reactivation of these experiences with his diagnosis of cancer, become irrelevant to his work as a psychoanalyst. *Vicarious* introspection can be used to occlude the analyst's *own* introspection, which could lead to com-merce with shameful, frightened and traumatized not-me states. Thus, Kohut bequeaths to his followers a theory of clinical practice that can be used to ensure that the analyst will remain only a selfobject – not a real object, not a real person with an identity and history that might reveal weakness and fear. As Emmanuel Ghent points out, Kohut's invention of the selfobject "at once dramatically played down the focus on the real object … . It retained the focus of psychoanalysis as a one-person psychology … . And finally it avoided the taint of in any way being associated with interpersonal theory ..." (Ghent, 1989, p. 190).

Self Psychology in the 21st Century

In many ways, self psychology in the 21st century has been significantly affected by the relational turn that has moved contemporary psychoanalysis away from Kohut's objectivist paradigm toward intersubjectivity, complexity, field, and process theories. However, the continued focus on the analyst's selfobject function has diminished the kind of robust discussion of the analyst's contribution to the therapeutic encounter, countertransference, self-disclosure, enactment, complementarity, mutual recognition, and the analyst's reverie and "need to change" that has taken place over the last two decades in the American Relational canon (cf Aron, 1996; Benjamin, 1995; Bromberg, 2011; Hoffman, 1998; Ogden, 1997; Stern, 2010; Slavin and Kriegman, 1998).

Of perhaps equal or greater significance of the continued effects of Kohut's transmitted history is self psychology's relative isolation from the rest of the psychoanalytic world. As noted earlier, Kohut's tendency to dismiss other schools of thought and exaggerate his own originality is perhaps one reason self psychology continues to be somewhat self-referential in its theorizing. As a school of thought, it continues to have its own membership organization and journal and holds its own annual conference. While there may be many benefits and pleasures to continue in this way, I do wish to suggest that this isolation partially may be due to what Prince asserts as the intergenerational transmission of trauma.

> Today's psychoanalysts are like the second-generation offspring of survivors to whom Holocaust trauma was oftentimes unwittingly transmitted. Awareness of what is otherwise denied and enacted is essential to our understanding, and moreover to our sense of agency, both as professionals and as human beings. Recognizing that we are descendants both of an intellectual tradition and the historical context in which it was formed only deepens our appreciation of the legacy of our psychoanalytic mothers and fathers. – Robert Prince (2009, p. 191)

Charles Strozier points out that after Kohut's cancer diagnosis, he "closed out other thinkers in an extraordinary degree ... [H]e simply could not take in what anyone else had to say ... [W]ith other thinkers he often talked and wrote as though there was no one ever who had written anything that fitted into the tapestry of ideas he was weaving" (2001, pp. 243–244).

However, I do believe that there is ample evidence that Kohut's claim to originality, his failure to dialogue with others' ideas that resembled his own, and certainly his dismissal of the interpersonal school antedated his diagnosis of cancer. While all schools of psychoanalysis have tended to exaggerate their originality and have contributed to the splintering of the field, I would argue, as do Mitchell and Greenberg, that Kohut probably is among the most extreme. Further, I would suggest that Kohut's biographer, while providing us invaluable information about his subject's defensive intellectual isolation, in the end justifies that isolation.

Charles Strozier's biography is remarkably crafted insofar as he is able to provide us with a balanced view of Kohut, the man, while having tremendous respect, perhaps even idealization, of his work. Strozier does not seem to hesitate in pointing out Kohut's many weaknesses, blind spots, and innumerable instances of treating others poorly. But when it comes to evaluating Kohut's contribution to the field of psychoanalysis, I believe he over-identifies with Kohut's inflated view, his defensive blinders. Just as Ernest Jones perpetuated Freud's founding myths through, what for decades was considered his "definitive" biography, I think Strozier falls prey to evaluating Kohut's work in similar, mythological fashion: "One way to think of Kohut's contribution is that he made the paradigm shift that gave new meaning to what had until then existed half said in the margins. In retrospect and in something of a reversal of chronology, Ferenczi, Fairbairn, and many others now seem prescient and relevant in ways they never did before Kohut. After 1971 one could begin to understand what people were trying to say before that" (p. 223).

Given the landscape of psychoanalysis around the globe in the 21st century, Strozier's claims can be seen to be as grandiose and as dismissive of other theorists as do Kohut's. To place Kohut at the center of the analytic universe and understand Ferenczi, Fairbairn and "many others" (Winnicott?, Bowlby?, Sullivan?, Racker?) only as "prescient," "*trying*" but unsuccessfully articulating "*in the margins*" what only Kohut could bring to fruition, seems to me unfortunate hubris. Strozier's assertions, and perhaps their unwitting acceptance by his readers, remain unrecognized in the larger psychoanalytic community of the 21st century. Today, self psychology remains far more on the margins and far less influential than the object relations theorists Kohut dismissed. Further, the interpersonalists whom Kohut and some of his followers saw as mere social psychologists have been instrumental in founding the integrative American Relational school of psychoanalytic thought.

As many have argued, the world of psychoanalysis is, in most places around the globe, marginalized, its fate uncertain. Paul Stepansky, in his book *Psychoanalysis at the Margins* (2009), suggests that today the profession is "a loose federation of psychoanalytic subcommunities – what I will term psychoanalytic part-fields – whose proponents see the world in different and often incommensurable ways" (p. xi). There is little question that dialogue among "part-fields" – robust, informed, and respectful dialogue – is essential to the continuance of psychoanalytic practice and influence. What I would add here is the importance of understanding the particular history of psychoanalytic thinking. If we believe that theory is constructed out of the purely rational minds of great men and women, divorced from the social-historical contexts in which they write, we may be unable to perceive what they are writing *against* – the ghosts, unmourned losses, the barely perceived, or dissociated threats from which they wish to defend themselves. I submit that to deeply understand self psychology and its creator, the Holocaust beckons and demands our attention.

Notes

1 Blum, one of the earliest and most incisive psychoanalytic authors linking the experience of the Holocaust to theory construction, argues that Hartmann's claim that he had emigrated from Germany due to his fear of being drafted into the Germany army, was a form of denial. Blum reasons that the most likely form of conscription Hartmann faced was into a concentration camp (2000, p. 93).
2 Self psychology does not have to look far to see an alternative response for "someone whose life was forever marked by the Shoah." Anna Ornstein has spoken openly about her experience at the Auschwitz death camp and has written beautifully about how she was able to survive with her identity, her heart and her mind intact. She maintains that hers and others' capacity for empathy for each other while in the camp allowed them to not only survive but prevail. Her belief in the power of empathy during the Holocaust drew her to the work of Heinz Kohut. See Emily Kuriloff's interview (2014, pp. 30–32), and Anna Ornstein's *My Mother's Eyes: Holocaust Memories of a Young Girl.*

References

Aron, L. (1996). *A Meeting of Minds*. Hillsdale, NJ: Analytic Press.

Aron, L. & Starr, K. (2013). *A Psychotherapy for the People*. New York: Routledge.

Benjamin, J. (1995). *Like Subjects, Love Objects*. New Haven, CT: Yale University Press.

Bergmann, M. (2000). The Hartmann era and its contribution to psychoanalytic technique. In M. Bergmann (Ed.), *The Hartmann Era* (pp. 1–79). New York: Other Press.

Blum, H. (2000). The idealization of theory and the aim of adaptation: The passing of the Hartmann enterprise and era. In M. Bergmann (Ed.), *The Hartmann Era* (pp. 1–79). New York: Other Press.

Bromberg, P. (2011). *Awakening the Dreamer*. New York: Routledge.

Fosshage, J. (2003). Contextualizing self psychology and relational psychoanalysis: Bi-directional influence and proposed synthesis. *Contemporary Psychoanalysis*, 39:411–448.

Fromm, E. (1941). *Escape from Freedom*. New York: Henry Holt.

Ghent, E. (1989). Credo: The dialectics of one-person and two-person psychologies. *Contemporary Psychoanalysis*, 25:169–211.

Goldberg, A. (1986), Reply to P.M. Bromberg's discussion of *The Wishy-Washy Personality* by A. Goldberg. *Contemporary Psychoanalysis*, 22:387–388.

Greenberg, J. & Mitchell, S. (1983). *Object Relations in Psychoanalytic Theory.* Cambridge, MA: Harvard University Press.

Hoffman, I. (1998). *Ritual and Spontaneity in the Psychoanalytic Process.* Hillsdale, N. J.: Analytic Press.

Kernberg, O. (2000). Conference proceedings. In M. Bergman (Ed.), *The Hartmann Era* (pp. 209–353). New York: Other Press.

Kohut, H. (1971). *The Analysis of the Self.* New York: International Universities Press.

Kohut, H. (1977). *The Restoration of the Self.* New York: International Universities Press.

Kohut, H. (1984). *How Does Analysis Cure?* Chicago: The University of Chicago Press.

Kohut, T. (2012). Introduction. In T. Kohut (Ed.), *A German Generation.* New Haven: Yale University Press.

Kuriloff, E. (2014). *Contemporary Psychoanalysis and the Legacy of the Third Reich.* New York: Routledge.

Ogden, T. (1997). *Reverie and Interpretation.* Northvale, NJ: Jason Aronson.

Prince, R. (2009). Psychoanalysis traumatized: The legacy of the holocaust. *The American Journal of Psychoanalysis*, 69:179–194.

Quinn, S. (1984). Psychoanalysis and the holocaust: A roundtable. In S. Luel & P. Marcus (Eds.), *Psychoanalysis: Reflections on the Holocaust: Selected Essays* (pp. 209–229). New York: Krav.

Riker, J. (2012). A philosophical commentary on Preston and Shumsky's "Toward an integrative sensibility: Conversing across theoretical boundaries". *International Journal of Psychoanalytic Self Psychology*, 8:338–349.

Slavin, M. & Kriegman, D. (1998). Why the analyst needs to change: Toward a theory of conflict, negotiation, and mutual influence in the analytic process. *Psychoanalytic Dialogues*, 8:247–284.

Stepansky, P. (2009). *Psychoanalysis at the Margins.* New York: Other Press.

Stern, D. (2010). *Partners in Thought.* New York: Routledge.

Strozier, C. (2001). *Heinz Kohut: The Making of a Psychoanalyst.* New York: Other Press.

10

GIVE ME PERMISSION TO REMEMBER

Judith S. Kestenberg and the Memory of the Holocaust[*]

Klara Naszkowska

As I write this chapter in June 2021, the Tulsa Race Massacre that occurred a century ago, on June 1, 1921, has at last begun to be widely acknowledged and taught in schools, while the victims, survivors and descendants are finally being honored. Several days ago, after 117 years, Germany officially recognized the 1904 genocide in what is now Namibia, when colonists murdered, exploited sexually, tortured and used for forced labor tens of thousands of the native Herero and Nama people. More than 50 years ago, Judith S. Kestenberg, a child of Holocaust victims, came to understand that the only way forward from loss, trauma and atrocity is to first acknowledge them, and to remember.

Introduction

The migration of people, ideas, and institutions from Europe to the United States as German fascism came to dominate Europe is among the most significant phenomena in 20th-century intellectual history. However, while that wave of intellectual migration has been extensively researched since the 1960s, too little has been written on the psychoanalysts swept up in it, and almost nothing on the impressive group of Jewish women analysts who fled to the United States in the 1930s and 1940s.[1] In the course of my ongoing research, I have to date identified 86 first- and second-generation women psychoanalysts who arrived at the United States in the 1930–1941 period.[2] What is gleaned from my analysis of personal-history documents and publications pertaining to these women is that these émigrés typically chose either to not engage with their prewar pasts, or repressed the painful, traumatic experiences associated with it.[3]

DOI: 10.4324/9781003266600-14

The present chapter is devoted to Judith S. Kestenberg; unlike the majority of her female Jewish colleagues (and the males), she came to realize the importance of continuity between one's past, present and future, and to connect her family history and the Holocaust's devastating experience with her work as a psychoanalyst. In 1946, after learning conclusively of her parents' deaths in the Shoah, Kestenberg had "stepped back" into "a latency period" of rejection and repression of the prewar past and the genocide. Then, over two decades later, in 1968, she "woke up" from that period and shifted her professional focus to psycho-historical studies of the Holocaust.[4] From that point on until her death 31 years later, Kestenberg made it her mission to provide therapeutic help to Shoah survivors, especially child-survivors – those who had endured persecution in infancy and as young children. Much of this work was done through conducting interviews with those survivors to help them remember the painful, previously repressed or forgotten wartime events, their losses and traumas, and their sometimes forgotten parents, with the goal of restoring the connection with their past identities.

The chapter's aim is to map Kestenberg's personal and professional development – her familial, religious, political and professional backgrounds – and the shift she made from the split from her disturbing past (1946–1968) to devoting her work to Holocaust studies (1968–1999). I will reconstruct Kestenberg's personal and professional biography, as well as her complex multiple identity as a Pole born under Austrian rule, a Jewish woman raised in an Orthodox household, a professional raised in the era of the Jewish New Women, a pioneer in psychoanalysis, an emigrant, a wife, a mother and a daughter of Shoah victims. I will utilize the methodology of a cultural, social and personal historian, and use three types of sources: Kestenberg's papers, including case studies, documents of personal history, published and unpublished interviews, letters, oral presentations and personal communication from her family and close friends, and archival historical documents.

It may be gleaned from the available materials that, as Kestenberg worked with genocide survivors, she was striving to accomplish similar ends in her private life as the child of parents who had perished in the Shoah. However, she almost never shared her past experiences as a Jewish woman in German-occupied Europe, an isolated émigré, the daughter of Holocaust victims, with her family, friends and colleagues. She never talked about suffering depression and its impact. In interviews and the autobiographical sketch "Kindheit und Wissenschaft" ("Childhood and Science"), when she addressed issues connected with the Holocaust, she initially hesitated to even answer those questions, and then would be very brief, using veiled language, as if needing to remain protective of her own past. Even after her "wake up" phase began in 1968, Kestenberg remained closed about her feelings and internally conflicted about her parents' death and the Holocaust, and may never have fully embraced the losses and traumas she had endured.

Familial and Religious Background

Judith S. Kestenberg, called Ida by her family and friends, was born Judyta Hadasa Silberpfennig on March 17, 1910, in her grandmother's home in Krakau (today's Kraków, Poland), then under Austrian rule. Her parents, Sara Salomea Silberpfennig (née Bauminger, 1883/1884/1887–1941) and Yeshayahu "Szaje" Silberpfennig (also Chaim, Jesaia Kaim, 1883/1884/1886–1941) both came from wealthy Jewish bourgeoise families.[5] They lived with Judith and her two older siblings, Henry (1905–1961) and Helen Silving (née Henda Silberpfennig, 1906–1996) in Tarnau (now Tarnów, Poland). Tarnau was a major town in Galicia, a multinational and multicultural region created in 1772 with the first partition of the Polish-Lithuanian Commonwealth from lands annexed by the Hapsburg Empire. Over more than a century of Austrian rule, until 1918, the Galician Jewish population increased sixfold, and Jewish (Ashkenazi) and Yiddish cultures thrived. In Tarnau Jews comprised about a half the population before the Shoah, forming a community of some 25,000 (Spector & Wigoder, 2001, pp. 1391–1395).

The considerable majority of New Women, today described as "university women of the early twentieth century, who defied conventional expectations [...] by seeking personal self-fulfillment through higher education and careers in traditionally male professional fields" (Freidenreich, 2002, p. xvii). They included first- and second-generation psychoanalysts, who came from upper middle-class families or the intellectual bourgeoisie, with others from merchant-class families.[6] Their parents were usually nonobservant or observed only some of the Jewish holidays. Atypically among these women, Kestenberg's parents were Orthodox Jews. Their home was kosher, they observed all Jewish customs, rituals and holidays. Szaje Silberpfennig often prayed in his small private *shul,* in the yard behind their house. He was a "a radiant figure in the streets of Tarnow, generous and kind hearted, ready to empty his pockets, take of his shoes and give them to a needy person he encountered on the way" (this really happened!). He was a great public speaker, devoted Zionist and "urban" public figure. [...] He also could lead the service on the major high holidays (Szporn, 1954–1968, p. 23). According to his daughter, Helen, he later became the head of the town's Jewish community but I have been unable to confirm this information (Silving, 1988, p. 5). After their marriage, Sara wore a *sheitel* (a half-wig) in obedience to Orthodox Jewish law, but her wigs were manufactured by famous European hairdressers.

When Kestenberg was born, in 1910, her family was very well off. Szaje was an industrialist and "a virtual financial wizard [who] accumulated a great fortune, mostly by starting various enterprises" (Silving, 1988, p. 36). The family lived in one of Tarnau's most beautiful residential buildings, a house filled with artworks by renowned painters. They had servants, Szaje owned a large automobile, and they traveled frequently and spent summers in spa resorts and luxury hotels. Szaje was a "generous philanthropist" – after the

First World War, he established a small orphanage for toddlers. Young Judith visited those children with her mother once a week (Kestenberg, 1992, p. 157). I have been unable to confirm Szaje's involvement with the town's Jewish orphanage (cf. Chomet, 1954–1968, pp. 733–162). After a series of bad decisions in the mid-1920s, Szaje lost almost all of his family's wealth. They were left with "a bare minimum of subsistence" (which was later confiscated by Austrian Nazis) (Silving, 1988, p. 23).

Educational and Religious Backgrounds

Judith received her early education at home, as was then the custom. Atypically among Jewish New Women, it focused on Jewish religion, culture and tradition. A private Hebrew teacher, Mr. K, taught her the Hebrew alphabet – the first one she learned. The first book she read was the Bible; the prayer book was the second. "The Bible was my elementary book, the source of my knowledge, what was allowed and what was not" (Kestenberg, 1992, p. 162). She remembered that Mr. K focused on cultural and social aspects of Judaism. He "had a love for [...] the Jewish history and culture which he imparted to [Judith]" (p. 162). He guided her on her own informed way of finding God.

The importance of Kestenberg's having been raised in an Orthodox family, with its Jewish identity, in her subsequent educational and professional choices may be twofold. First, an informed assumption could be that her upbringing encouraged her to pursue a university-level education and a professional career. Parents of Jewish women psychoanalysts of the second generation who had been born from around the beginning of the century to the 1910s usually provided their daughters with the financial as well as moral support to achieve that. Education has always been of special value for Jews. One reason behind the principle of educating children was to endow them with something that could not be taken away from them, as opposed to possessions, citizenship or life.

However, while the mothers of Jewish women psychoanalysts were usually homemakers with no university education and were very rarely vocal about the issue of women's education, in Orthodox Jewish families there was also a custom that women combined household duties with professional work, and helped support the family financially. In part, the arrangement allowed men to dedicate more time to the study of the Talmud. Judith's mother, Sara Silberpfennig, played an equal if not larger role than her husband in her daughters' choice to attend university and have a career. She was exceptionally intelligent and had a huge thirst for knowledge. She had reportedly attended University of Krakau courses in secret, before her marriage (Silving, 1988, p. 19). This may be a family legend as her name is absent from relevant student records (Michalewicz, 1999). She spoke six languages fluently, read modern Hebrew poetry in the evenings, played the piano at night and studied economics in private lessons (possibly with the goal of helping Szaje readjust the family's finances). She then audited political-science courses at the University of Vienna (at the age of 36) and "refused to be identified as a housewife" (Silving, 1988, p. 75).

Daughters of Orthodox Jews typically pursued university education in professions viewed as practical, including medicine and law. Once Austrian medical schools began accepting women in 1900, Jewish women came to make up a very high proportion of their students. Of the first 18 women receiving medical degrees at the University of Vienna by 1906, two-thirds were Jews (Friedenreich, 1996, p. 80). Jewish women would comprise almost 40 percent of the female students there by the early 1930s. Nonetheless, Kestenberg's Orthodox parents reportedly did not approve of her decision to study medicine, because they didn't want her to look at male corpses in the university's dissecting theatre (personal communication from Howard Kestenberg, June 7, 2021).

The second area where Kestenberg's Orthodox Jewish upbringing may have affected her professional and life choices is connected with the fact that her family was observant and so directly identified with Jewish tradition and culture. In contrast to her Jewish counterparts who were not brought up with a Jewish identity, Kestenberg preserved it as a predominantly cultural, secondly religious identity, which may have led her to attempt to reconnect with her prewar past and her parents' tragic fate under the strong influence of their Jewish roots.

Until she was in third grade, Mr. K and other private tutors provided Judith's education. She was then enrolled in a prestigious private girls' high school (or *Gymnasium*), that offered a comprehensive college-level education. There were no public girls' high schools in Galicia at the time. To the best of my knowledge, the only nondenominational option, with around 30 percent of students being Jewish, was the Eliza Orzeszkowa high school for girls (Ruta, 1900, p. 95). Judith experienced personal antisemitism at the school. She briefly recounted that her Greek teacher linked her father's wealth with plutocracy (Kestenberg, 1992, p. 165).

With the end of the First World War, in November 1918, Poland became an independent country again – the Second Polish Republic, with Silberpfennig family members becoming Polish citizens, pledging allegiance to a different country, with a different national anthem. In the interwar period, the Jewish population continued to grow rapidly in Poland. When Tarnau became Tarnów in 1918, its 15,000 Jews comprised a little over 40 percent of the population. By the outbreak of the Second World War, the town's Jewish community of 25,000 amounted to over half the total population. For the most part, Tarnów Jews were Hasidim (Gelber). Antisemitism would spread gradually during the two-decade duration of the Second Polish Republic, along with the rise of the right-wing, nationalistic National Democratic Party. From the late 1920s, the National Democrats' platform included antisemitic rhetoric and propaganda, and a campaign for a *numerus clausus* – a quota limiting the percentage of Jewish university students (on the subject of National Democrats, see: Levy, 2005, pp. 484–485). The quota was never officially imposed in Poland, nonetheless, the authorities fully supported grassroots initiatives at universities to discriminate against Jewish students. Medical departments in particular rigorously followed *numerus clausus* rules (on the subject of *numerus clausus* in Poland, see: Trębacz, 2016, pp. 113–135).

When her brother, Henry, graduated from high school, it was decided that he would study political science at the department of law of the University of Vienna. The women of the family, Sara, Helen and Judith, were to accompany him. Sara and Henry left for Vienna in 1923; the sisters followed the next year once Helen graduated from high school and Judith had completed her term.

In Vienna, Kestenberg attended a private "socialist" (her term) high school in Ottakring, the city's working-class 16th district. The school was headed by Ludo Hartmann (né Ludwig Moritz Hartmann), a gentile historian and leftwing politician, and the father of Heinz Hartmann, who became a prominent psychoanalyst and an émigré to the United States. The choice was no coincidence, as Szaje was ideologically a socialist, and so was his daughter, Judith.

After her graduation from high school, Kestenberg enrolled in the University of Vienna's famous medical school, part of the largest academic center in Central and Eastern Europe, founded in 1365. As a foreigner, she was expected to pay three times the tuition an Austrian would be charged. Given her family's economic situation, her parents couldn't afford the tuition fees. Resolute and resilient as always, Judith applied for a reduction and succeeded in securing it.

In choosing medicine, she was striving for financial independence, wanting to help her parents in line with Orthodox Jewish custom and the expectation that women contribute financially. As she wrote in her autobiographical sketch: "I [...] knew that because of our poor economic situation I had to choose a subject that could sustain me and maybe the family. I definitely had to stand on my own two feet" (Kestenberg, 1992, p. 168).

During much of her studies that lasted from 1928 to 1934, Kestenberg pursued a specialization in neurology. The Neurological Institute at the University of Vienna was headed by Otto Marburg from 1919 to 1938, when his post was taken from him, his teaching license stripped, and he was forced to emigrate to the United States. As her studies drew to a close, Kestenberg switched from neurology to psychiatry, to fulfill a requirement imposed on prospective physicians who intended to practice in Vienna (Kestenberg, 1978, p. 10). She graduated in 1934 with her Ph.D. in psychiatry.

After qualifying as a doctor, she began her training at the Neurology and Psychiatry Clinic at the university (the *Nervenklinik*). Austrian neuroscience by then was already infested with racism, eugenics and antisemitism. The relentless process of "DeJudification" of Austro-German medicine, a field then prevalently Jewish, led to the dismissal from the clinic of many "non-Aryan" neuroscientists. Their replacements were political appointees adhering to National Socialist principles. Otto Pötzl, head of the *Nervenklinik* since 1928, was an opportunistic early National Socialist Party (NSDAP) member. His longtime assistant was Alfred (Prinz von/Prince of) Auersperg, a fanatic Nazi and member of both the NSDAP and the new SS (Schutzstaffel) paramilitary organization. Kestenberg worked with Auersperg; furthermore, her closest colleague was a devoted and very active Nazi, Walther Birkmayer, member of the Brownshirts paramilitary wing, the NSDAP, and the *SS Standarte 89* – a regiment critically involved in the Kristallnacht pogroms of November 1938. Birkmayer and Kestenberg were co-authors of a report on the discovery of a rare tumor (Gasserian ganglion) (Birkmayer & Silberpfennig, 1938).

Before the Anschluss on March 13, 1938, Nazi membership was illegal under the Schuschnigg regime and meant a career risk in Austria, so as a rule, Nazi neurologists there were not open about their activities (Czech & Zeidman, 2014; Zeidman, 2020, pp. 279–317, personal communication from Lawrence A. Zeidman, June 10, 2021). Nonetheless, it appears that their political affiliations were commonly known at the *Nervenklinik*. Kestenberg claimed that she was unaware of it: "My best friends in the neurology department were Nazis but I didn't know it" (Kestenberg, 1978, p. 10). She even referred to younger colleagues, including Birkmayer, as "my sons." She stated: "I was so naive that I, unlike everyone else at the clinic, did not know that Birkmayer and [...] Auersperg [...] were Nazis" (Kestenberg, 1992, p. 171). After emigrating to the United States in 1937, she discussed the situation in the Clinic with her analyst, Hermann Nunberg. He "pointed it out to" her that her former colleagues were Nazis, but she still "didn't really believe it" (p. 171). She finally did, after Birkmayer had sent her a letter discussing "wonderful, grand ideas being carried out in Germany" (pp. 170–171).

Woman Psychoanalyst

When she first became interested in Freud, while in medical school, she reached out to her mother for help in understanding the "unclear terms" to her, "as [the mother] had already done with forbidden Hebrew words in [Judith's] childhood" (Kestenberg, 1992, p. 156). For Kestenberg, the personal and professional planes always overlapped and intertwined: the choice of medicine, psychoanalysis, her family and their tragic fate, and her Jewish upbringing. She connected her psychoanalytic skills to both her parents: "I think I inherited from my father to have good ideas and to be indulgent, both traits one must have as an analyst. I think my mother was very psychologically gifted" (p. 156).

Discouraged by the Vienna psychoanalytic community and, in particular, by Helene Deutsch, the director of the Training Institute of the Vienna

Psychoanalytic Association, she chose not to pursue psychoanalytic education at that time (Kestenberg, 1994).[7] She returned to Freudian analysis after qualifying as a psychiatrist in 1934. Then, her interest in psychoanalysis was sparked by three Jewish analysts: Else Pappenheim, Maria Piers and Ruth Eissler-Selke, all future émigrés to the United States.[8] Inspired by those women, Kestenberg took up a training analysis with Eduard Hitschmann, one of Freud's earliest disciples and future émigré to the United States. Her training was left incomplete; it lasted from 1934 until her emigration in July 1937.

It is difficult to say whether Kestenberg was unaware of the situation at the Clinic, adopted a survival strategy of dissociation and denial, or decided that she didn't want to know the truth. To what extent was this a conscious decision, perhaps dictated by the desire to pursue a career at the most prestigious medical school in Europe? Or it might have been a naive downplaying of the seriousness of the Nazi threat, characteristic for the generation of Jews immersed in German culture, arts and sciences.

Émigré to the United States

Despite nearby events in Germany that led to dictatorship and eventually to the Shoah – a succession which mounted as Hitler was named chancellor in January 1933 – Vienna-based psychoanalysts generally maintained an illusion that German fascism would be short-lived and felt comparatively safe in Austria. They commonly discounted daily antisemitic violence in the 1920s and 1930s as episodic displays by the rabble, which would soon dissipate. As a result, the large majority of analysts there did not leave the country until after its official annexation to Germany. Regardless of the "collective amnesia" maintained in Austria through the postwar years and beyond, when German troops had marched into Vienna on March 11, 1938, to annex the country into the Third Reich, they were received with widespread and very public enthusiasm.

Kestenberg left Vienna on July 31, 1937, before emigration from Austria peaked in 1938 after the Anschluss. She decided to travel to the United States for professional reasons, intending to then return to Europe. She knew that her career perspectives were very limited in Europe. When she unsuccessfully attempted to validate her medical degree from Vienna in Poland in the mid-1930s, she was affected by the unwritten law of *numerus clausus*. Secondly, she wanted to pursue psychoanalytic training at the New York Psychoanalytic Institute (NYPI) and to collaborate there with the child analyst Margaret Fries.[9] In a 1991 interview, Kestenberg abruptly distinguished her departure from Europe from the political situation of that period: "I did not flee the Nazis. I left Vienna in 1937 to continue my training in New York" (Kestenberg, 1991, 165). The truth, as she would later realize, was that in Austria on the cusp of the annexation, she was thrice targeted by the Nazis as a Jew, a psychoanalyst and a socialist, and she was in immediate danger (Freidenreich, 2002; Trepp, 2006).

Kestenberg's US visa was substantiated by a professional invitation from Paul Schilder, who offered her an internship in the psychiatric department of Bellevue Hospital in New York City. Schilder was an unorthodox Viennese psychoanalyst and psychiatrist, who had emigrated in 1929, heading the department from 1930 to 1940. Money for the passenger liner came from her dowry. When she reached out to her father, he immediately sent her $100 (Kestenberg, 1992, p. 174; personal communication from Janet Kestenberg Amighi, April 22, 2021).

Kestenberg briefly stressed that she was terrified when she arrived in the States: "I was scared. I didn't know how scared I was. [My analyst, Nunberg] told me how scared I was" (Kestenberg, 1994). In New York City, Kestenberg struggled financially. As an intern, she received only food and board; she lived at a Bellevue dormitory. In 1938, when it became evident that she would not be returning to Europe anytime soon, her family shipped china and other belongings to her, but she could not afford the customs fees, and the shipment was returned (personal communication from Janet Kestenberg Amighi, April 22, 2021). In the following months, she managed to secure grants. Another problem was her English skills, which were insufficient for understanding her colleagues and the psychiatric patients.

She resumed her psychoanalytic training at NYPI in 1937, with Jewish émigré analyst Hermann Nunberg. She was later also supervised by two Jewish émigré child analysts: Berta Bornstein and Marianne Kris.

In 1937 or the beginning of 1938, Kestenberg passed a comprehensive written State Board medical examination in English, required of European analysts for receiving a state-issued license. She was now allowed to open a private medical practice, but was impelled to put off her career and psychoanalytic training while focusing all her efforts on getting her family out of the sociopolitical cauldron of interwar Europe (Kestenberg, 1967). She was extremely worried about her family, the situation in Europe, and upset about indifference among most of her American colleagues. In 1938 her "anxiety and depression increased so much that [she] wanted to go back to analysis" (Kestenberg, 1992, p. 179). She contacted the émigré psychoanalyst Edith Buxbaum, who had just opened a private practice in New York City.

She managed to secure funds for ship passage for her brother, Henry, from the Emergency Committee on Relief and Immigration of the American Psychoanalytic Association (on the subject of the Committee, see: Thompson, 2012). He eventually landed in Cuba. Her sister, Helen, left Europe on her own, shortly before the war, on March 15, 1939.

When Germany invaded Poland on September 1, 1939, Kestenberg's mother fled east from Vienna to Stanislav, in Soviet-occupied Poland (now Ivano-Frankivsk, Ukraine). Judith unsuccesfully pleaded with the US State Department for help in getting Sara out of Poland. Stanislav was taken by the Germans on July 26, 1941, early in Operation Barbarossa. Judith and her mother had reportedly corresponded until then.[10] Sara Silberpfennig was murdered that year, in one of three massacres of the Stanislav's Jewish community: either on August 2–3, on the night of August 14, or on October 12 (Bloody Sunday).

When German troops entered Tarnów on September 8, 1939, they began persecuting Jews immediately. In the occupied town, Szaje Silberpfennig reportedly made a public address in which he spoke of hope and trust that the United States would enter the war, defeat Germany and rescue Polish Jews. After the speech, he went into hiding but was eventually imprisoned in the Tarnów ghetto, established in March 1941. I have yet to corroborate the source of this information, which may be family legend. He and Judith corresponded until December 1941, when Szaje was deported to KL Auschwitz, the concentration and extermination camp. He arrived there on December 18, 1941, as prisoner number 24707 and a wedge, a red trangle against a yellow one reserved for Jewish political prisoners. His death was recorded on December 23, 1941 by Stanisław Ryszter in a secret notebook (Archive of the Auschwitz-Birkenau Museum).

When correspondence with her parents ceased in 1941, she threw herself into her work. She graduated from NYPI in 1943, became a training analyst there and was elected to full membership at the New York Psychoanalytic Society (NYPS).

Less than a year after correspondence with her father terminated, Judith met her future husband, Milton Kestenberg (1913–1991), a Polish-born Jewish lawyer and real estate manager who became a key litigator for Holocaust restitution. It can be gleaned from Kestenberg's personal statements that Milton symbolically replaced her father: "Without knowing anything about it, my husband continued my father's [philanthropic aid to orphans]" (Kestenberg, 1992, p. 157), along with: "trust that I had in my father as a child was reawakened [in Milton]" (p. 181), and "I felt like a newborn" (p. 182) after they got married in 1944.

When the list of 61,387 Jewish survivors of Nazi tyranny, *Sharit Ha-Platah*, was published by the Central Committee of Jews in Bavaria in 1945 and 1946, Kestenberg conclusively learned of the death of her parents: "I realized for the first time that [my mother] would never speak to me again, but I still didn't believe it." She became "very depressed" and "plagued with guilt" (p. 182). She wrote: "I was able to function by stepping back into what seemed like a period of latency in my life" (p. 183).

In psychoanalysis, the latency period is – as her analyst, Buxbaum, worded it in 1950 – an "in-between state" that concludes early childhood and is followed by prepuberty and puberty (Buxbaum, 1951, p. 182). In the latency period, the ego, separated from sexual urges and instinctual forces, grows in strength. This undisturbed ego development leads to adaptation to reality and society, and conformation to the environment (see Deutsch, 1944, p. 5). Kestenberg later connected her period of latency with the general approach to the Holocaust: "The period of latency served as a distancing maneuver from the trauma that could not be averted" (Kestenberg & Kestenberg, 1982, p. 34). It was not until the trial of Adolf Eichmann in 1961–1962 that the wall of silence and Holocaust denial began to lift in the psychoanalytic community and beyond.

For 22 years, Kestenberg maintained detachment from everything connected with the Shoah, and "denial and repression of the unspeakable terror" (p. 33). When her sister-in-law, Irene Kestenberg (1922–2014), emigrated to the United States after the war and wanted to talk to Kestenberg about her mother and brother, both murdered in the Treblinka death camp, Kestenberg was reported to be tenacious in her refusal: "I don't want to hear anything." At that time, she "didn't even look into where her [own] parents were killed" (personal communication from Eva Fogelman, June 13, 2021). She focused on the present, busying herself intensively with work: seeing patients at her home in Sands Point, Long Island, and in her office in the Apthorp building on the Upper West Side, teaching and supervising candidates at training institutes at Down State University in Brooklyn and later at New York University's Medical School and the Long Island Jewish Medical Center. She continued work at Bellevue, then at Mount Sinai and at New York Hospitals (Kestenberg, 1992, p. 187).

Kestenberg was overwhelmed with parental responsibilities. She raised two children, Janet (Jane) Kestenberg (b. 1946, later Kestenberg Amighi) and Howard Kestenberg (b. 1956, adopted by Judith and Milton as a newborn when she was 46). According to both her children, during her "latency period," Kestenberg was competent with mothering. She was a "loving, involved parent" and "consistently a very attentive mother" (personal communication from Howard Kestenberg, June 7, 2021; personal communication from Janet Kestenberg Amighi, April 22, 2021).

As Kestenberg put it, in this "latency period" she "was working through [her] own development again" (Kestenberg, 1992, p. 184). In 1948 she returned to analysis, which lasted seven years, this time with Marianne Kris. She recalled in passing that she "cried and cried in analysis" (Kestenberg, 1994). She also received invaluable support from her NYPI supervisor and then close friend, Berta Bornstein, who helped her raise her children, sent analysands to her and extended frequent invitations to her family to Bornstein's summer house on Vinalhaven Island in Maine.

Holocaust Studies

While Kestenberg was deep in her "latency period" in late 1950s, her husband began representing survivors of Nazi persecution in German courts, seeking restoration of property and reparations. At that time, German psychiatrists and legal experts did not acknowledge psychological damage suffered by those Shoah survivors who had been newborns or young children during the war, reasoning that they had been either too young or too traumatized to remember or understand that persecution, or too resilient to be affected by it. As a result, according to the German law, they were not entitled to any compensation. Milton Kestenberg "decided to talk to these young survivors until they remembered what they had been through, or at least parts of it" (Kestenberg, 1992, p. 186).

Judith joined her husband in his efforts in 1968 immediately after finally coming out of her "latency period." Her breakthrough came when she began treating a young person who was the child of a Holocaust survivor. He "behaved very strangely: he did not eat any food, hid in forests and treated [her] as a hostile persecutor. [He was] emaciated and hollow-eyed [...] like a 'Muselmann' in a concentration camp" (Kestenberg, 1974, pp. 249–250). With this case, she became interested in the transgenerational transmission of trauma, pathology and knowledge, from "survivors of persecution" in Nazi Germany to their children ("children of survivors") born after the period of persecution and those who had been brought to safety before the period of persecution.

She discovered that at that time the view was that "[the] 'cure all' was to forget the past and to build the future. [There was a] prohibition against discussing the past. [...] One can even say that most of these [child-survivors] received countersupport [from mental-health professionals]" (Kestenberg, 1990, p. 386). A questionnaire sent out to child analysts in the United States, Canada, Israel, Germany, England and Holland in 1969–1970, following the International Psychoanalytic Association (IPA) congress in Rome, showed that the vast majority of respondents were indifferent to the problem of survivors of Nazi persecution.

Kestenberg set up a study group for children of survivors, with her husband and Milton E. Jucovy. She identified an almost universal mechanism in their behavior. They would reenact the past in an attempt at reshaping and fixing it, by acting out their parents' Holocaust experiences once they reached the age at which their parents had been persecuted.

In another case, that of a boy who was born in a ghetto and deported to a concentration camp at the age of two, Kestenberg became interested in "child-survivors" – those who experienced Nazi persecution as young children (for more on the case study, see: Kestenberg, 1991, p. 162). She continued to reach out to colleagues around the world and search for suitable analysands and thus opened up an entirely new field. Before Kestenberg and the pioneering work of Henry Krystal and William Niederland on trauma initiated in the 1950s, mental-health professionals were, for the most part, ignoring the symptoms exhibited by Holocaust survivors or diagnosing them as paranoia (see, for example, Krystal & Niederland, 1971). In Poland in 1959 a group of psychiatrists started interviewing Auschwitz survivors (cf. Leśniak et al, 1961). According to Judith, her German colleagues who attended the 34th IPA Congress in Hamburg in July 1985 still feared confronting the past (Kestenberg, 1986, p. 882).

In 1972, the Kestenbergs founded a nonprofit umbrella organization devoted to the mental health of children, Child Development Research (CDR), with Judith as its director. It was located at the Kestenbergs' home in Sands Point and had three main entities: a well-baby nursery (Center for Parents and Children, operating until 1989), the study dedicated to child-survivors of organized persecution, and Kestenberg Movement Profile (KMP) training (for an overview of KMP, see: Kormos, 2021). According to Kestenberg's close friend of almost 25 years and a vice-president of CDR, K. Mark Sossin, the main motive behind all of Kestenberg's initiatives was always "primary prevention"; "she was trying to prevent another Holocaust" (personal communication from K. Mark Sossin, June 8, 2021). "Through her untiring pursuit of the roots of hate and prejudice, she sought to lay the basis of prevention of a recurrence of racism leading to genocide" (Sossin, Loman & Merman, 1999, p. 54). The free-of-charge nursery accommodated around a dozen babies, providing them with a very rich environment, and numerous professionals, including occupational, movement and dance therapists (personal communication from Andrea Krauss, June 4, 2021).

In 1981, the Kestenbergs initiated the International Study of Organized Persecution of Children (ISOPS, later named the Kestenberg Archive of Testimonies of Child Holocaust Survivors), with a Jerome Riker grant. They put together a group of about a dozen mental-health professionals, including Eva Fogelman, Helene Bass-Wichelhaus, K. Mark Sossin, Robert M. Prince and Ira Brenner, who were to locate child-survivors of Nazi-era persecution around the world, conduct psychologically-oriented interviews and provide psychological support. The group and other volunteers collected over 1,500 testimonies from those who had been children 13 and younger during the Holocaust. These were primarily Jewish survivors but also some interviews were conducted with Polish and German children, as well as some whose parents were Nazis (for an analysis of the testimonies, see: Kangisser Cohen, Fogelman & Ofer, 2017).[11] Many interviewees spoke for the first time about their wartime experiences (Kestenberg, 1988, p. 196; Kestenberg, 1993).

The interviews were conducted using Kestenberg's technique of recalling events by using all five senses (including kinesthetic memory of the body: noises, smells, touch, sensorimotor memories, sensations). Through letting the survivors speak spontaneously and without interruption, interviewers allowed them to develop a consecutive narrative that helped integrate the victim and survivor's identity into the whole identity of the human being.

Kestenberg and her colleagues analyzed the impact of the experiences of Nazi persecution on the development of identity and morality in child-survivors, especially on their sense of belonging (one's place in personal and in general history), family relations and Jewish identity. Interviewers analyzed the impact of the fact that during the war child-survivors were subjected to frequent and sudden changes of environment including exclusion from schools, familial migration to evade persecution, with children hidden in barns, forests, attics, imprisoned in ghettos and concentration camps. Children had been often separated from mothers when the latter left them with often unknown gentiles or were taken to concentration camps. With the outbreak of war, rules and routines they had been used to ceased to exist. Values they had been taught by their parents were now mixed with perverted laws of survival. Child-survivors had grown acquainted with death at a very young age (often those of close family members and friends), entirely excluded from social life, deprived of the protection of authorities, and verbally and physically abused by their non-Jewish peers. It was discovered that the younger the survivor, the greater the trauma.

All of the above led to deformation and fragmentation of the superego. Through such nuanced analysis of child-survivors, Kestenberg observed that it was "remarkable how, under those circumstances, the ego was saved from disintegration so that the analysis of the superego deformation could liberate the ego's capacity to adapt and form or rebuild object ties" (Kestenberg & Brenner, 1986, pp. 312–313).

Kestenberg distinguished between Jewish victims and victims of political torture in general: "As a Jew, no matter what you do, you'll be killed. It's different to be killed because of what you are, because you cannot change it [as opposed to your views]" (Kestenberg, 1991, p. 165). Jewish identity "was explored from the viewpoint of religious practices, belief in God, and ethnic solidarity. Identification with the Jewish group as moral and humanistic contrasted with some peoples' feelings that Jewish identity had been foisted upon them by persecutors. […] Should we identify with the persecutors and thus avoid being singled out for exclusion? Should we assimilate or be different? Should we seek out areas of safety or stay with the endangered group in a spirit of self-sacrifice, to enhance the survival of all?" (Kestenberg & Kestenberg, 1988, p. 535). Jews had to conceal their true identity to endure persecution. They hid their "Jewish looks"; boys, more at peril due to circumcision, dressed up as girls.

When conducting interviews with survivors, Kestenberg quickly arrived at the conclusion that despite the fact that memories of child-survivors of the Holocaust had been repressed or "encapsulated and kept away" (Rosenfeld, 1986, p. 56), and the reality of their persecution had been denied, they were eager and willing to retrieve and retain their painful, traumatic memories, but that they needed the permission of a grownup to remember those pasts (Kestenberg, winter 1988, p. 561). They needed to reconnect with their past to restore continuity in their lives, ruptured and fragmented by the Shoah, and to rebuild a sense of integration and restore the fragmented self.

Since her "awakening" unil her death in 1999, Kestenberg was dedicaded to her work with survivors. According to her closest entourage, she was a "workaholic" who "always planned [personal life] around work" (personal communication from Howard Kestenberg, June 7, 2021; personal communication from K.

Mark Sossin, June 8, 2021). According to her daughter, Janet, who also worked with her, Kestenberg grew "obsessed" with her work with survivors. She would read only books and watch only films on the subject of Shoah. Her birthdays sometimes served as fundraisers for survivors (personal communication from Janet Kestenberg Amighi, April 22, 2021).[12] She interviewed survivors during all of her travels, both domestic and international (personal communication from K. Mark Sossin, June 8, 2021). Fogelman adds that she was "compulsive" and "obsessed with Auschwitz," and that she knew a story of each bunk bed in each block (personal communication from Eva Fogelman, June 13, 2021).

Jewish Woman and "Child of Non-Survivors"

Kestenberg-psychoanalyst "woke up" from the "latency period" in 1968 but what was the case in her private life? It can be gleaned from the available personal-history materials and my interviews with her children, friends and colleagues that she would not fully embrace the topic of the Holocaust until her death. She did sporadically talk to her children about her prewar life in Tarnów and Vienna, and about her emigration; she also wrote about her experiences in the autobiographical sketch. However, it appears that she chose to discuss her feelings and emotions associated with Poland, Austria, emigration, or Shoah very rarely. Her personal papers and statements are filled with themes from her work with Shoah survivors, but the losses she had endured are mentioned sporadically and in passing.

Most importantly, she omitted the subject of her parents' demise. It was not until August 1983 that she submitted her first testimony to Yad Vashem, and it was not until 1988 or 1989 that Judith said the first kaddish for her parents, during Yom Kippur. Likely around that time, Kestenberg and her siblings founded a memorial plaque in Tarnów dedicated to their father (Szporn, 1954–1968, p. 22). Eva Fogelman, the psychologist, author, filmmaker, and codirector of CDR and ISOPS since Judith had stepped down in the mid-1990s, stated that in their two decades of close personal and professional relationship, "they had never had a personal conversation about the Holocaust," and that Kestenberg had never "shared anything about herself or the loss of her parents." Fogelman wasn't even aware that Kestenberg's father died in Auschwitz - despite knowing of her obsession with the camp (personal communication from Eva Fogelman, June 13, 2021). One rare example of Kestenberg's opening up about the pain of her parents' death in the Shoah was when she discussed the importance of knowing where one's dead relatives' remains were (e.g., Kestenberg, 1990). She wrote in her autobiographical sketch: "The Holocaust brutally stole my parents from me. [...] There was nothing left of my father but a pile of ashes. I don't know if and where my mother is buried. [...] I don't know what happened in that little town of Stanisławów" (Kestenberg, 1992, p. 174, p. 180).

It seems that Judith channeled her personal experiences into her work. A student and admirer of Kestenberg, psychoanalyst taught by her, clinical psychologist and author, Robert M. Prince, "has never heard Kestenberg talk directly about her losses and traumas" but he believes that "they showed in her method of interviewing: she was extremely sensitive, empathic, attuned to her interviewees" (personal communication from Robert M. Prince, June 4, 2021; June 19, 2023).

Her interest in the Shoah survivors is rooted in her private life, most importantly in her parents' perishing, but also in her Jewish upbringing which resulted in a strong Jewish identity. When asked about connections between her work on the Holocaust and her personal life, Kestenberg tended initially to hesitate and evade the questions (Kestenberg, 1991, pp. 162–163). Finally, she stated: "If the Nazis hadn't killed my parents, hadn't destroyed our Eastern European culture, hadn't destroyed my family and that of my husband, hadn't questioned our entire past, it would probably not have become my mission, to investigate the influence of their persecutions on children, and not my duty to do something to never allow such a thing again" (p. 159).

Kestenberg's cultural, national, and religious identites were complex, diverse, and nuanced. She refused to simply define them. When asked where she was from, she would now answer "New York"; when asked about her nationality, she would say "Jewish, and American but born in Poland" (personal communication from Janet Kestenberg Amighi, June 3, 2023 April 22, 2021). Responding to the question "Where do you feel you belong? In the American tradition, or the European?" Kestenberg, strong-minded and assertive, answered: "I belong to myself" (Kestenberg, 1991, p. 172).

At 85, she declared : "My Jewish identity is very strong" (Kestenberg, 1994). This statement is confirmed in other personal-history materials and in her work. It is difficult, however, to assess if her Jewish identity was founded essentially on cultural, historical and familial heritage, or on Judaism as well. Her children and friends are divided when it comes to assesing Kestenberg's religious identity. According to her daughter, Janet, and Eva Fogelman, Kestenberg was not religious, (personal communication from Janet Kestenberg Amighi, April 22, 2021; personal communication from Eva Fogelman, June 13, 2021), but her son, a member of the Hassidic Chabad movement and founder of the Dr. Judith Kestenberg Education Center at the Chabad of Venice, Florida, disagrees: "she was religious in her own way," "she was always Jewish, it was inside of her, she lived it, it was who she was" (personal communication from Howard Kestenberg, June 7, 2021).

We do know that Kestenberg valued Jewish religious customs highly and observed Jewish holidays: Rosh Hashanah, Yom Kippur, Passover and Hannukah (personal communication from Janet Kestenberg Amighi, June 15, 2023). Available materials indicate that she appreciated their cultural aspect; it was important to her that they brought her family together. According to her son,

Howard, she celebrated seder ceremonially, with at least 15 guests (personal communication from Howard Kestenberg, June 7, 2021). During the latency period, Kestenberg also celebrated Christmas (Judith dressed up as Santa) reportedly in an attempt to "reject the connection to the awful past and begin a new life" (personal communication from Janet Kestenberg Amighi, April 22, 2021; June 15, 2023). According to Howard, however, they only celebrated Christmas because his mother wanted their Christian housekeeper to feel welcome (personal communication from Howard Kestenberg, June 7, 2021). Janet remembers that, when she was an adult, her mother scolded her for having a Christmas tree (personal communication from Janet Kestenberg Amighi, April 22, 2021). This was after she "woke up" from the latency period. When Fogelman was getting married in 1988, Kestenberg insisted that the wedding be held at her Sands Point house and that it be spectacular, as neither she and Milton nor their two children had a Jewish wedding, and she wanted to experience one "as if it was her own" (personal communication from Eva Fogelman, June 13, 2021). Janet clarifies that she indeed did have a Jewish wedding (personal communication from Janet Kestenberg Amighi, June 3, 2023).

Judith made sure that her children, born in the United States, received a Jewish education. They were "raised as American Jews" (personal communication from Janet Kestenberg Amighi, April 22, 2021). They attended a Hebrew school in a synagogue on the weekends; Howard had a bar mitzvah ceremony. None of this, however, reflected a religious experience. Also, Howard was later enrolled in a Catholic private boys' school, Saint John's High School, in Massachusetts, one of the first to provide services for students with dyslexia, which he had been diagnosed with (personal communication from Howard Kestenberg, June 7, 2021; Kestenberg, 1994).

The nuanced and complex story of Judith Kestenberg, her "escape" from Nazi Europe and the tragic past, her "obsessive" work with survivors, her Jewish identity, reveals another story: of the vanishing Jewish population in Poland, and the works of memory and postmemory.

Notes

* An earlier version of this chapter has been published in Polish in "Zagłada Żydów. Studia i Materiały / Holocaust Studies and Materials. Journal of the Polish Center for Holocaust Studies, Vol. 18 (2022), 296–321. I would like to express my deepest thanks to Janet Kestenberg Amighi, Howard Kestenberg, Eva Fogelman, Robert M. Prince, K. Mark Sossin, Andrea Krauss and Lawrence A. Zeidman, each of whom were kind enough to talk to me and share their knowledge and memories. I would also like to thank Olga Umansky, the librarian/archivist at the Boston Psychoanalytic Society and Institute and Bernhard Bolech, Head of the Library at the International Psychoanalytic University Berlin, for helping me in my inquiries and granting me access to archival materials.

1 On intellectual emigration, see, for example: Coser, 1984; Fermi, 1972. On psycho-analysis and emigration, see, for example: Gifford 2003; Hale, 1995; Jacoby, 1983; Steiner, 2000. On émigré women psychoanalysts, see: Ash, 1995; Chodorow, 1989.
2 The present author's ongoing book project takes the working title *The Forced Migration of Jewish Women Psychoanalysts from Europe to the United States (1933–1945): A Personal, Interpretative and Documentary History.*
3 For a discussion of the connection between memory, Holocaust and psychoanalysis, see also Emily A. Kuriloff's pioneering book on the subject *Contemporary Psychoanalysis and the Legacy of the Third Reich: History, Memory, Tradition* (2014).
4 Kestenberg's terms, used by her in Kestenberg, 1992, 183, 188. I am very grateful to Ludger M. Hermanns for sending me the book. All translations from German are by the present author.
5 Information from the JewishGen database, https://www.jewishgen.org/.
6 The origins of the term "New Woman" can be traced back to Sarah Grand (née Frances Elizabeth Clark, 1854–1943), an Irish-born suffragette and feminist author who used the phrase in her essay "The New Aspects of the Woman Question" from 1894.
7 I would like to express my deepest thanks to Esther Altshul Heltgott for her kindness in sharing the contents of the interview with me.
8 For basic biographical information on women psychoanalysts, see: Nölleke, B. (2007–2023). Psychoanalytikerinnen. Biografisches Lexikon. (Psychoanalysts. Biographical Lexicon).
9 The cooperation did not come to fruition.
10 I have so far been unable to access correspondence between Kestenberg and her parents.
11 The interviews were stored and digitalized by the National Library of Israel.
12 Holocaust research was a family affair. Milton, Judith and Janet co-authored the text Kestenberg, Kestenberg & Amighi, 1988. Janet Kestenberg Amighi also co-authored a book on KMP: Kestenberg Amighi, Loman & Sossin, 2018.

References

Ahron Szporn "There Once was a Jewish Town, Tarnow" in Avraham Chomet, ed. *Yizkor book: Tarnow; The Life and Destruction of a Jewish City (Tarnów, Poland)*, Vol. II. (Tel Aviv: Association of Former Residents of Tarnow, 1954–1968), 15–24.
Archives of the National Auschwitz-Birkenau Museum. https://www.auschwitz.org/muzeum/informacja-o-wiezniach/
AT-UAW, Nationale der Juridischen Fakultät, WS 1924/25 - WS 1927/28, Silberpfennig, Henryk.
Brigitte Nölleke, Psychoanalytikerinnen. Biografisches Lexikon (2007–2023). Online at https://www.psychoanalytikerinnen.de/. Accessed June 16, 2023.
David Rosenfeld, "Identification and Its Vicissitudes in Relation to the Nazi Phenomenon," *International Journal of Psycho-Analysis*, Vol. 67, No. 1 (1986), 53–64.
Edith Buxbaum, "A Contribution to the Psychoanalytic Knowledge of the Latency Period. Workshop, 1950," *American Journal of Orthopsychiatry*, Vol. 21, No. 1 (Jan. 1951), 182–198.
Emily A. Kuriloff, *Contemporary Psychoanalysis and the Legacy of the Third Reich: History, Memory, Tradition* (New York: Routledge, 2014).
Harriet Pass Friedenreich, "Jewish Women Physicians in Central Europe in the Early Twentieth Century," *Contemporary Jewry*, Vol. 17, No. 1 (Jan. 1996), 79–105.

Harriet Pass Freidenreich, *Female, Jewish, and Educated: The Lives of Central European University Women* (Bloomington & Indianapolis: Indiana University Press, 2002).

Helen Silving, *Helen Silving Memoirs* (New York: Vantage Press, 1988).

Helene Deutsch, *Psychology of Women* (New York: Grune & Stratton, 1944).

Henry Krystal and William G. Niederland, *Psychic Traumatization: Aftereffects in Individuals and Communities* (Boston: Little, Brown and Company, 1971).

Herwig Czech and Lawrence A. Zeidman, "Walther Birkmayer, Co-describer of L-Dopa, and His Nazi Connections: Victim or Perpetrator?" *Journal of the History of the Neurosciences*, Vol. 23 (2014), 1–32.

Janet Kestenberg Amighi, Susan Loman and K. Mark Sossin, eds., *The Meaning of Movement: Embodied Developmental, Clinical, and Cultural Perspective of the Kestenberg Movement Profile* (New York: Routledge, 2018).

Janka Kormos, "History and the Psychoanalytic Foundations of the Kestenberg Movement Profile," *An International Journal for Theory, Research and Practice*, Vol. 16 (2021), 101–116.

Jerzy Michalewicz ed., Corpus studiosorum Universitatis Iagellonicae 1850–1918. A-D((Kraków: Archiwum Uniwersytetu Jagiellońskiego, 1999).

JewishGen database. Online at https://www.jewishgen.org/. Accessed June 16, 2023.

Judith S. Kestenberg, "Letter to Dr. Bertram Lewin," in *Bertram David Lewin Papers (1883–1974)*, container 7, folder 10, (Washington DC: Library of Congress, Jan. 18, 1967).

Judith [S.] Kestenberg, "Kinder von Überlebenden der Naziverfolgungen," *Psyche – Zeitschrift für Psychoanalyse*, Vol. 28, No. 3 (1974), 249–265.

Judy [Judith S.] Kestenberg, Oral History Workshop #10: *Research in Psychoanalysis in the U.S., Part II* (New York, NY: American Psychoanalytic Association, Dec. 1978), Boston: Boston Psychoanalytic Society and Institute Archives.

Judith S. Kestenberg, "Ein Requiem für die Verluste der Psychoanalyse in der Nazizeit. Eindrücke vom Hamburger IPA-Kongreß," *Psyche – Zeitschrift für Psychoanalyse*, Vol. 40, No. 10 (1986), 881–883.

Judith S. Kestenberg, "Child Survivors of the Holocaust (Introduction)," *Psychoanalytic Review*, Vol. 75 (1988), 195–197.

Judith S. Kestenberg, "Memories from Early Childhood," *Psychoanalytic Review*, Vol. 75, No. 4 (Winter 1988), 561–571.

Judith S. Kestenberg, Milton Kestenberg and Janet [Kestenberg] Amighi, "The Nazis' Quest for Death and the Jewish Quest for Life" in *The Psychological Perspectives of the Holocaust and, Its Aftermath*, ed. Randolph C. Braham (New York: Social Science Monographs, 1988), 13–44.

Judith S. Kestenberg, "Coping with Losses and Survival," in *The Problem of Loss and Mourning: Psychoanalytic Perspectives*, ed. David R. Dietrich and Peter S. Shabad (Madison, CT: International Universities Press, 1990), 381–403.

Judith S. Kestenberg, "Interview. Dr Judith S. Kestenberg talks to Kristina Stanton," *Free Associations: Psychoanalysis Groups Politics Culture*, Vol. 2, No. 2 (1991), 157–174.

Judith S. Kestenberg, "Kindheit und Wissenschaft. Eine biographische Skizze," in *Psychoanalyse in Selbstdarstellungen*, Vol. 1, ed. Ludger M. Hermanns (Tübingen: Edition diskord, 1992), 147–202.

Judith S. Kestenberg, "Spätfolgen bei verfolgten KIndern," *Psyche – Zeitschrift für Psychoanalyse*, Vol. 47, No. 8 (1993), 730–742.

Judith S. Kestenberg, Unpublished interview with Judith S. Kestenberg by Esther Altshul Heltgott, December 1994, New York.

Judith S. Kestenberg and Ira Brenner, "Children Who Survived the Holocaust: The Role of Rules and Routines in the Development of the Superego," *International Journal of Psycho-Analysis*, Vol. 67 (1986), 309–316.

Judith S. [Kestenberg] and Milton Kestenberg, "The Background of the Study," in *Generations of the Holocaust*, ed. Martin S. Bergmann and Milton E. Jucovy (New York: Basic Books, 1982), 33–45.

K. Mark Sossin, Susan Loman and Hillary Merman, "Remembering Judith S. Kestenberg, Our Mentor and Friend," *American Journal of Dance Therapy*, Vol. 21, No. 1 (Spring/Summer 1999), 53–56.

Krakow Marriage Intentions/Banns Records. Szyja Chaim Silberfennig, Sara Bauminger. 1903. Akt 214.

Laura Fermi, *Illustrious Emigrants: The Intellectual Migration from Europe, 1930–41* (Chicago: University of Chicago Press, 1972).

Lawrence A. Zeidman, *Brain Science under the Swastika. Ethical Violations, Resistance, and Victimization of Neuroscientists in Nazi Europe* (Oxford: Oxford University Press, 2020).

Leo Trepp, *A History of the Jewish Experience* (Millburn: Behrman House, 2006).

Lewis A. Coser, *Refugee Scholars in America: Their Impact and Their Experiences* (New Haven: Yale University Press, 1984).

Milton Kestenberg and Judith S. Kestenberg, "The Sense of Belonging and Altruism in Children Who Survived the Holocaust," *Psychoanalytic Review*, Vol. 75, No. 4 (Winter 1988), 533–560.

Mitchell G. Ash, "Women Émigré Psychologists and Psychoanalysts in the United States," in *Between Sorrow and Strength. Women Refugees of the Nazi Period*, ed. Sibylle Quack (Washington, D.C.: German Historical Institute, 1995), 239–264;

Nancy Chodorow, "Seventies Questions for Thirties Women: Gender and Generation in a Study of Early Women Psychoanalysts" in *Feminism and Psychoanalytic Theory* (New Haven and London: Yale University Press, 1989), 199–218.

Nathan G. Hale, Jr., *The Rise and Crisis of Psychoanalysis in the United States: Freud and the Americans, 1917–1985* (New York: Oxford University Press, 1995).

Nathan Michael Gelber, n. d. "Tarnow," in *Jewish Virtual Library*, https://www.jewishvirtuallibrary.org/tarnow-poland. Accessed June 16, 2023.

Nellie L. Thompson, "The Transformation of Psychoanalysis in America: Émigré Analysts and the New York Psychoanalytic Society and Institute, 1935–1961," *Journal of the American Psychoanalytic Association*, Vol. 60, No. 1 (2012), 9–44.

"Page of Testimony," 1095142, The Central Database of Shoah Victims' Names, YadVashem, The World Holocaust Remembrance Center.

Riccardo Steiner, *"It's a New Kind of Diaspora": Explorations in the Sociopolitical and Cultural Context of Psychoanalysis* (London and NY: Karnac Books, 2000).

Richard S. Levy, ed., "National Democrats (Poland)," in *Antisemitism: A Historical Encyclopedia of Prejudice and Persecution* (California: ABC-CLIO, 2005), 484–485.

Roman Leśniak et al. "Niektóre zagadnienia psychiatryczne obozu w Oświęcimiu w świetle własnych badań," *Przegląd lekarski*, Vol. 17, No. 1a(1961), 64–73.

Russell Jacoby, *The Repression of Psychoanalysis. Otto Fenichel and the Political Freudians* (New York: Basic Books, 1983).

Sanford Gifford, "Émigré Analysts in Boston, 1930–1940," *International Forum of Psychoanalysis*, Vol. 12 (2003), 164–172.

Sarah Grand, "The New Aspect of the Woman Question," *The North American Review*, Vol. 158, No. 448 (March 1894), 270–276.

Sh'arit ha-pl'atah. Unites States Holocaust Memorial Museum.

Sharon Kangisser Cohen, Eva Fogelman and Dalia Ofer, eds., *Children in the Holocaust and Its Aftermath: Historical and Psychoanalytical Studies of the Kestenberg Archive* (New York: Berghahn Books, 2017).

"The Central Database of Shoah Victims' Names," YadVashem, https://yvng. yadvashem.org.Silberpfennig, Szaja.

"Tarnow" in Shmuel Spector and Geoffrey Wigoder, eds., *The Encyclopedia of Jewish Life Before and During the Holocaust, Vols. II and III* (New York: NY University Press, Yad Vashem, 2001), 1391–1395.

Walther Birkmayer and Judith Silberpfennig [Judith S. Kestenberg], "Über zwei Fälle von Trigeminustumoren mit Zwischenhirnsymptomen," *Archiv für Psychiatrie und Nervenkrankheiten*, Vol. 108 (1938), 255–278.

Zofia Trębacz, "'Ghetto Benches' at Polish Universities: Ideology and Practice," in *Alma mater antisemitica. Akademisches Milieu, Juden und Antisemitismus an den Universitäten Europas zwischen 1918 und 1939*, ed. Regina Fritz, Grzegorz Rossoliński-Liebe and Jana Starek (Vienna: New Academic Press, 2016), 113–135.

Zygmunt Ruta, Prywatne szkoły średnie ogólnokształcące w Krakowie i województwie krakowskim w latach 1932–1939. (Kraków:Wydawnictwo naukowe WSP, 1990).

11

FREUD'S MOSES, SCHOENBERG'S MOSES

Two Expressions of Trauma

Pamela Cooper-White

Two great geniuses from Vienna, both Jewish, both revolutionary innovators in their respective fields.[1] And both obsessively fascinated with the figure of Moses, producing two major creative works nearly simultaneously – Freud's *Moses and Monotheism* (published in 1939), and Schoenberg's opera "Moses und Aron"[2] (abandoned in 1937, but published and performed as two acts ever since its first fully staged performance in Zürich in 1957). Both works were preceded in their creators' oeuvres by significant earlier compositions on the subject of religion. Both men identified with Moses as a mountaintop figure, bringing a new Word to people who mostly could not understand it. And both of these Moses works occurred at critical moments of exile, escaping the Nazi regime – with such dire events prompting a return to intense personal and intellectual re-examination of religion by both men, albeit with very different conclusions. The proximity of these geniuses in time, place and culture, and the particular focus of each on the figure of Moses, offer a tempting subject for comparison.[3]

Two Portrayals of Moses

Schoenberg began working on the libretto for a "cantata" entitled "Moses und Aron" in 1926,[4] while also working on an overtly Zionist play "Der biblische Weg" ("The Biblical Way") (Schoenberg, 1994/[1927]). But he had conceived of the work at least as early as 1923[5] – at the time when his experiences of antisemitism were escalating as a more personal threat, resulting in what he called the final "shipwreck of assimilation."[6] He threw himself wholeheartedly into a militant expression of the Zionist movement. The play features a lead character "Max Aruns" (a composite of "Moses" and "Aron")

DOI: 10.4324/9781003266600-15

as leader of the Jewish people in an imagined Zionist nation. Aruns is murdered in a rebellion, but his successor "Guido" vows to restore the new nation to its devotion to the invisible God, under the protection of a weapon of mass destruction with an uncanny resemblance to the atom bomb.

Schoenberg completed the libretto for "Moses und Aron" in 1928, and then composed the music for the first two acts between 1930 and 1932. Toward the end of this effort, he and his Jewish colleagues were warned of their imminent expulsion from the Prussian Academy. Schoenberg hurriedly packed up with his family and moved to Paris, reading the dangerous handwriting on the wall much earlier than some of his contemporaries who eventually were murdered in the Shoah (Holocaust). During this brief stay in Paris, he formally re-entered the Jewish community, with the artist Marc Chagall as witness. He then relocated to the United States, eventually settling in Los Angeles, where he lived out his days. Most of his American compositions express Jewish themes of remembrance, lament and prayer.

Schoenberg's "Moses und Aron"

The opera begins in a sound world unique in all of opera, meant to invoke a feeling of deep mystery surrounding Moses' encounter with the Burning Bush in the wilderness. In the first moment, in *Sprechstimme* (Schoenberg's invented form of half-speech, half-singing) Moses intones the words that represent the core of Schoenberg's own beliefs about God, and the central theological message of the entire opera: "One, eternal, omnipresent, invisible and unrepresentable God!"[7] God gives Moses the command to free his people, and when Moses protests that he can "think but not speak," God gives Moses his more eloquent brother Aron to be his mouthpiece. In Scene 2, Aron appears, and the brothers first discuss their respective callings. Aron keeps misunderstanding the pure inconceivability of God and insists on making the divine accessible to the people. Moses keeps correcting him. At the height of their debate, Moses sings for the one and only time: "Purify your thinking! Free it from worthless things, consecrate it to the True; there will be no other reward for your sacrifice." Thus, in the first two scenes, Schoenberg sets up the central conflict of the opera – between an uncompromising, purely spiritual and unrepresentable God-Idea, and the immediate degrading of this Idea by any attempt to represent it in worldly terms. In Scene 3, the people arrive and reject Moses' austere faith, but then follow the brothers after Aron performs tangible, frightening miracles.

As Act II opens, the people complain that Moses has been up on the Mount of Revelation for 40 days. The people threaten to tear Aron and the Seventy Elders apart. Feeling he can no longer hold off a rebellion, Aron fashions a Golden Calf for them to worship: "O Israel, I give you back your gods … Leave distant things to the Eternal!" The people rejoice as Aron calls out "Worship yourselves in this symbol!" A wild orgy ensues, culminating in blood sacrifice and a ritual slaughter of four self-offered "naked virgins."

At the peak of the pandemonium, Moses comes down from the mountain and roars in outrage. The Calf vanishes. A furious debate ensues, with Moses insisting on the purity of the invisible God-Idea and Aron defending his actions as necessary for the people, who cannot sustain such austere worship. Moses presents the stone tablets of the law, but when Aron cleverly points out that these, too, are images, Moses smashes them. The people depart, following a pillar of fire and cloud, and Aron follows behind them. Moses, left alone, cries out to his un-representable God, that even he had succumbed to fashioning an image, and that all he had believed before was madness. Exclaiming, "O Word, you Word that I lack!" he sinks in despair to his knees. The curtain falls on Act II.

The published text of Act III opens on a markedly different scene (Schoenberg, 1957[8]). Aron, in chains, is dragged in by two soldiers, followed by the Seventy Elders. The soldiers ask Moses if they should kill Aron. Moses instructs them to let him go free, and he may live if he can. Aron stands upright, but then falls down dead. Moses addresses the people with a final sermon in which he warns the Hebrew people that whenever they wander among foreign people and misuse their gifts for "false and empty purposes," they will suffer and be thrown back into the wilderness, to be purified once again by the eternal un-representable God-Idea. Moses' last words in this draft underscore his ascetic faith: "But in the wilderness you will be invincible and will reach the goal: united with God."

"Moses und Aron" – An Unfinished Masterpiece

Schoenberg repeatedly expressed his wish to complete "Moses und Aron," but time and again hit a brick wall. Moses' cry "You Word that I lack!" has seemed so close to Schoenberg's own experience of failure to represent the un-representable that it has stood as the rationale for many critics to see the end of Act II as an unintended but powerful completion as the opera now stands (most notably, Theodor Adorno, 1973; cf., Neighbor, 2002). It has long been my view, on the contrary, that in spite of the apparent stylistic integrity of the opera in its unfinished form, we must take the composer at his word that, in his own mind, it was incomplete. ([Cooper-]White, 1985, 2001; cf., Berry, 2008, pp. 102–103; Goldstein, 1992, pp. 150–152).

Act III suddenly presents Moses as a military leader with strong resemblance to the dictator "Max Aruns" of "Der biblische Weg." Moses has suddenly risen up from his despair. No longer impotent, he now appears as the supreme governor of the people, with an army at his behest. His speech to the people represents the militant, isolationist Zionism that Schoenberg had embraced. The published version is only one of many drafts and fragments of Act III, over which Schoenberg labored as late as 1935. Each subsequent draft of Act III becomes bloodier and more graphic in its scenic representation of the violent oppression of Jews across the centuries, lending increasing urgency to the call to the Jewish people to repent and find their salvation in the spiritual austerity and desirelessness ("*Wunschlosigkeit*") of the wilderness. The last text sketch for Act III is dated from 1935, just two months following Hitler's announcement of German rearmament in violation of the Treaty of Versailles. The Nuremberg Laws would go into effect just four months later. The increasing violence of the later unpublished drafts and text sketches for Act III coincides with the increasing horrors of the Shoah as it unfolded. In recently discovered unpublished 1934 sketches for Act III, Schoenberg even writes a scene in which the Elders stone Moses to death. And in the last draft for Act III, from 1935, Moses shows Aron a living tableau of perennial persecution and murder of the Jewish people (Cooper-White, 2024).

Freud's "Moses and Monotheism" ("The Man Moses")

Moses and Monotheism is an aggregate of three essays, written across a span of roughly four years from 1934 to 1938.[9] Part I was completed during the summer of 1934, when Hitler declared himself Führer. *Moses and Monotheism* is Freud's last published work, and a culmination of a long preoccupation with religion as a mass symptom of infantile wish fulfillment. It hearkens back to Freud's earlier preoccupation with the figure of Moses, described in his 1914 essay "The Moses of Michelangelo" (Freud, 1955b/1914).[10] In this earlier essay, Freud surmises that the specific way in which Michelangelo depicts Moses represents the restraining power of the ego against raw, unmediated aggression. Freud interprets that Moses, having turned a startled gaze toward the sound of the revels around the Golden Calf, and clutching his beard in rage, now appears to be withdrawing his hand in a gesture of self-restraint. In Freud's view, this act of restraint shows the Moses of Michelangelo to be "a concrete expression of the highest mental achievement that is possible in a man, that of struggling successfully against an inward passion for the sake of a cause to which he has devoted himself" (p. 233).

In *Moses and Monotheism*, Freud frequently acknowledges that his interpretation of ancient accounts of Moses is highly speculative, departing significantly from the original biblical narrative. His first title, in fact, was "The Man Moses: An Historical *Novel*." (emphasis added). Freud excitedly draws on contemporary historical-critical and archaeological methods of studying the Bible, and his own *Totem and Taboo* (Freud, 1955c/1913), to argue that there were *two* Moses figures, not just one, who over time came to be conflated in the historical memory through a collective process of condensation and "displacement" (*Entstellung*).

In this final speculative but masterful work, Freud recapitulates his oedipal historical reconstruction from *Totem and Taboo* – the pattern of patricide, repression and atonement via the worship of a father-god – now applied to the figure of Moses who had long haunted his imagination "like an unlaid ghost" (Freud, 1964a/1939, p. 103). He demythologizes the spiritual aspects of the Mosaic tradition, while pointing to the ethical superiority of the Jewish people based on their refusal to indulge in idol worship and sensual forms of expiation for sin. He links this to the renunciation of drive impulses and the pleasure principle, and what was, in his mind, the supreme gift of the Jews to human civilization: the "progress in intellectuality/spirituality" ("*Geistigkeit*") (p. 111).

The German title is important: "Der Mann Moses" places the emphasis on Moses as a great but altogether human leader, whose vision laid the foundation for the austere but superior intellectual-spiritual [*geistig*] and ethical character of Judaism (Assmann, 2012; Bernstein, 1998, 2018; Biale, 2013; Friedman, 1998; List, 2008; Rice, 1990). Freud saw his own work as yet another, even revolutionary advance in rationality – "our god *Logos*" (Freud, 1961b/1927, p. 54). As Rabbi Yosef Yerushalmi (1991) pointed out, Freud, the self-avowed "godless Jew" (Freud & Pfister, 1963, p. 63) had effectively created a new "godless Judaism" (p. 99) and "*The Standard Edition* [became] the new Torah" (Whitebook, 2018, p. 54).

Freud's historical reconstruction of a primal murder of the first Moses, the repression of this traumatic memory, and the composite memory of a second Moses as father and giver of the law, was something Freud viewed as a pattern imprinted in the Jewish psyche. Freud insisted on following the phylogenetic theory of Jean-Baptiste Lamarck, in which "memory traces" of experiences (and not just the biological process of "natural selection" as in Darwin's theory of evolution) could be passed down the generations.[11] Freud thought he had finally arrived at something akin to the "essence" (*Wesen*) of Judaism he had earlier struggled to define (Freud, 1955b/1913, p. xv[12]) – "the possession in common of a certain intellectual and emotional wealth" (p. 123) derived from the ancient pattern, as in *Totem and Taboo*, of patricide, traumatic repression, and eventual revival and divinization of the father and the father's ethical commands (for which circumcision stood as a symbol of obedience under the threat of castration).

Freud's insistence on Lamarck's theory, even though most scientists had already rejected it in favor of Darwin's version of evolution, now appears to foreshadow recent understandings of the intergenerational transmission of trauma (Niederland, 1961; Malabou, 2018; Yehuda & Lehrner, 2018). This process appears to follow the very pattern Freud identified: trauma, followed by repression and latency, followed by a recrudescence of the memory traces that were buried but never eradicated – the ghostly remnants of a forgotten "archive" (Derrida, 1996[13]).

It is perhaps no coincidence, then, that *Moses and Monotheism* represents a little-discussed but important integrative moment for Freud, in which he seems after decades to circle back to an acknowledgement of the role of actual trauma as a cause of neurosis (something he never actually abandoned, but diminished in importance relative to internal psychic conflict) (Bergmann, 1994; Grubrich-Simitis, 1991; Schacht, 1993). Ilse Grubrich-Simitis points to *Moses and Monotheism* as Freud's most "daydream-like" work, which, with all its repetitions and inconsistencies, exhibits signs of unresolved autobiographical material.

Whatever his personal motives may have been, however, the immediate impetus for the project was clearly rooted in the contemporaneous trauma of Nazi aggression. As he wrote to Stefan Zweig in September 1934, his purpose in writing the text was a direct response to Hitler's rise to power: "Faced with the new persecutions, one asks oneself again how the Jews have come to be what they are and why they have attracted this undying hatred" (Freud & Zweig, 1987, p. 91). Even before the nightmare of the *Anschluss* (Hitler's annexation of Austria in March 1938), the ransacking of his apartment and the terrifying arrest of his daughter Anna, Freud had observed a "relapse into almost prehistoric barbarism" among the Germans in a new "prefatory note" to Part III. In both *Moses and Monotheism* and his earlier *Future of an Illusion* (Freud, 1961b/1911), Freud acknowledged that he was dismantling the consolations of religion, and calling people to the sacrifices entailed in committing themselves to a higher level of rationality.

Schoenberg's Moses, Freud's Moses

In comparison to Schoenberg's Moses, Freud's Moses had come to represent for him a visionary, anti-instinctual hero of nonviolence and a prophet of the highest level of intellect/spirit (*Geistigkeit*). Freud's Moses does not collapse in despair like Schoenberg's Moses in Act II, nor does he rise up in militant triumphalism like Schoenberg's Moses of Act III. Freud's Moses emerges from the collective character and consciousness of the Jewish people. A sacralized memory trace of a real Moses is retained in sacred myth, while he remains as an unconscious symbol of the requirement to bend to the father's will – that is, the demands of reality, or "Necessity" (*Ananke*) (Freud, 1955a/1920, p. 45). Freud's Moses represents, finally, a recognition of the tragic complexity of the human condition, including both the terrible price that is to be paid for civilization, portrayed vividly in *Civilization and its Discontents,* (Freud, 1962/1930), and an enduring, non-indulgent *Geistigkeit* that allowed the Jews to survive across centuries of oppression.

Schoenberg, by contrast, as a passionate God-believer (in his own idiosyncratic fashion), was attempting to find some synthesis between the poles of Idea and image, spirit and matter. In what may be the most detailed comparison to date, Yerushalmi (1992) posits that the two works represent Freud as a "verbal optimist" vs. Schoenberg, the "verbal pessimist." Both, he asserts, stand firm in the "conviction of the ultimate superiority of abstraction over sense experience," and both point to the commandment against making graven images (*Bilderverbot*) as a positive move away from magic and superstition (Yerushalmi, 1992, p. 8). Their "common conviction that Moses was the bearer of an idea of God so pure as to be untainted by any hint of anthropomorphism, magic, or the miraculous" represented for both of them that this "pure monotheistic Idea" was "the very essence of Judaism and of Jewish survival" (p. 8).

Freud's reliance on the "talking cure," the fundamental rule of free association, and above all, his exalting of "our god *Logos*" – the Word (of science) – did allow him to express a hopefulness at the end of *The Future of an Illusion* (Freud, 1961b/1927) that eventually reason would win out over instinct. Moses is a hero for Freud, because through him came the "advance of intellectuality/ spirituality." Schoenberg, on the contrary, with his insistence on the un-representable nature of God, leaves Moses crying in despair "O Word, you Word that I lack!" Yerushalmi sides with Freud's "primacy of the word," concluding his essay with an exhortation to psychoanalysts, as the "primary custodians and explorers of language," to "hear speech as it has never been heard before, not by the Delphic oracle, nor by priests, rabbis, gurus, or lovers, not even in the solitary intimacy of mirrors. It is a unique burden and an astonishing opportunity" (pp. 18–19).

Freud's and Schoenberg's differences on language are not so stark, however, when understood in the context of each other's initial aims. Schoenberg, a believer in the "one, eternal, invisible, un-representable" God he describes in the opera, had set himself the task of expressing in text and music the seemingly unbridgeable divide between Idea (*Gedanke* or *Vorstellung*) and Representation (*Darstellung*) ([Cooper-]White, 1985). Convinced that it was the mission of the artist to be true to his own self-expression wherever it led (Schoenberg, 1984), he dramatized the struggle to put the divine Idea into some form of human expression without distortion or dilution, by making Moses and Aron the representatives of the same divide between the Idea and its representation through imperfect human modes of expression. The pessimism about the impossibility of ever bridging this divide he drew from Schopenhauer (Cooper-White, 1984, 1985). The dilemma of the artist, even in attempting a form of self-expression, was the neo-Platonic challenge of wrestling ideas into form.

In spite of his failure to complete "Moses und Aron," however, no one could have been more prolific in creative expression than Schoenberg throughout his life – in published words, in music, and in paint, he was a veritable fountain of self-expression. To venture further and attempt to represent the divine was almost an act of blasphemy, a violation of the Jewish prohibition against graven images – and yet, Schoenberg repeatedly felt compelled to try to represent this pure ineffability (Kurth, 2003). With his radically atonal 12-tone framework functioning as the Law (his own analogy) and the loosening of sonorities from the more familiar sound world of tonality, he thought he might approach such a purity of expression – the elusive "musical Idea" (Kerling, 2004, pp. 88–101; Schoenberg, 2006; cf.).

Freud, on the other hand, had no such theological ambitions – or inhibitions – about his depiction of Moses. Rather than seeking to represent the purity of God, Freud sought to bring the God of Moses down to earth. His focus is on the human, not the divine. His purpose was to understand – in the immediate traumatic context of Hitler's rise to power – "how the Jewish people have acquired the characteristics which distinguish them" (Freud, 1964b/1939, p. 136) and what comprised the "essence" of Judaism, by which he himself could claim to be both "godless" and "Jew." Freud's "verbal optimism" – or better, his realistic and tested confidence in the expressive power of words *per se*, even in the service of unlocking repressed truths from the archive of buried memory (either personal or cultural) – was, finally, less important perhaps than his hope for the continual advance of reason across the millennia. In the face of the irrational Nazi "barbarism" that had threatened his life – and did indeed murder four of his own sisters – Freud was not interested in theology, but in the inherent ethical capacity of humans, as exemplified by the Moses who restrained himself from violence, and the Moses who led a people from the gods of superstition to a God, and moreover a human life, of intellectuality and ethics.

Freud's Moses, Schoenberg's Moses as Posttraumatic Figures

These two great Moses works were created in the context of one of the most horrific collective traumas of modern history, the Shoah. There are manifold traumatic responses, conscious and unconscious, layered into both works. Schoenberg's work remained incomplete, a masterpiece that appears both done and undone by the composer's own inability, finally, to give form to the ineffability and purity of the Idea. Freud's *Moses*, while uncharacteristically repetitive, inconsistent and disjointed, nevertheless represents a final work of integration – even a kind of deathbed confession of faith in a fallible but still-evolving human capacity for ethical restraint and reason.

Why (at least from his own perspective) did the composer fail to complete his work, while the psychoanalyst persisted and arrived at an answer to the question he had posed to himself at the very beginning of his essay? Schoenberg's intention was not to create a tragic opera, but rather to write a triumphal masterwork in which the Jewish people, through their faith in the one, eternal, omnipresent, invisible and un-representable God, would triumph over every persecution and adversity. Why did this intention fall short, leaving his hero Moses on his knees in despair, while Freud, a dying man with bouts of depression, who had surely seen some of the worst of human nature, succeeded in conveying a hopeful message about the advance of *Geistigkeit,* with which the Jewish people through their long history of trauma were endowed as the essence of their collective identity?

The answer must be speculative and incomplete. I believe it rests with the two men's different responses to the surrounding trauma – pre-conditioned both by the "total context of antisemitism that preceded the Shoah" (Cooper-White, 2017) and by their own respective world views and basic dispositions. Both could be autocratic and uncompromising. But what they were uncompromising *about* was radically different.

Freud's confidence in his theory was built on a fundamental premise that there was always more to be seen beneath the surfaces of things. Beneath benign appearances, the drives of sex and aggression would relentlessly press up against the familial and societal constraints of civilization. Moreover, traumas of childhood – both the fantasy of enacting violence and the actual enactment of it, as well as both real and imagined terrors of castration and annihilation – would be repressed and then return, unbidden, especially at moments when new traumatic events re-stimulated the memories of the old. Hope (I would not go so far as to call it "optimism") and pessimism oscillated in Freud's thinking; his confidence lay paradoxically in the tragic reality that the good and bad of life cannot be separated. There is no purity in the Freudian view – only a realistic acceptance of the complexity of life, the interplay of pleasure and mourning. As he wrote in "On Transience," it is precisely the mortality inherent in nature that causes us to appreciate beauty all the more (Freud, 1957/1916).

Schoenberg, on the contrary, was by disposition a crusader who believed that in spite of all opposition, the Idea would continue to manifest itself in new forms as each great artist strove for perfect truth in self-expression. All the heroic figures in his religious works – Gabriel in "Jacob's Ladder," Max Aruns in "Der biblische Weg," and Moses – were autobiographical (Martino, 2002). One can surmise that he was aware of this (Auner, 2007), identifying with Moses as "an image of a passionate leader of mankind who, conscious of his divine mission as Lawgiver, meets the uncomprehending opposition of men," and feeling as his own "the conflict which is bound to arise between such a reforming genius and the rest of mankind" (p. 221). In Freudian terms, Moses represented his ego ideal, and Schoenberg's identification with him was profound.

Schoenberg's theological vision (an admixture of Swedenborg and Schopenhauer) was, to boil it down, a kind of neo-Platonic one, in which the Idea – indeed, the God-Idea – was a spiritual form of ineffable perfection. To attempt to express it by any human means was to create an idol, but the compulsion to create could not be denied. So the artist – not entirely unlike Freud's (1958/1911) note about the artist as the hero who "[makes] use of special gifts to mould his phantasies into truths of a new kind" and brings them into the "external world" (Freud, 1958/1911, p. 224, also citing Rank, 1907) – was for Schoenberg the hero who perceives the Idea, and is caught between the impossibility of representing its pure form, and the impossibility of refusing to try.

Freud envisioned an endless entanglement of human suffering, pleasure, struggle and memory, to be accepted and lived out through "love and work." Freud's "god Logos" was immanent, not a transcendent god at all, but rather a symbol of devotion to the scientific method, to the rule of evidence and lived experience, a vision of rationality in which "where id was, there ego shall be" (Freud, 1964b/1933, p. 80). Schoenberg, in contrast, believed in a wholly other transcendent God and sought an elusive purity of religious thought. Schoenberg believed that faith in the ungratifying, invisible God-Idea was the salvation of the oppressed Jewish people – to renounce the fleshpots of Egypt (tantamount, for him, to the project of bourgeois European assimilation, about which he had become painfully disillusioned) and to strike out to establish a new land where the invisible God would reign.

Schoenberg also came to believe, however, that only by adopting the tactics of the aggressor – even the authoritarianism and violence of fascism itself (e.g., Mäckelmann, 1984; Móricz, 2008, pp. 214–216) – would the Jews of Europe be saved.[14] He believed that only a dictatorship would be sufficient to accomplish his vision (Schoenberg, 1979). Moreover, in the play "Der biblische Weg," Max Aruns' secret project is to create a weapon of mass destruction. These imagined "trumpets of Jericho," which could aim lethal, suffocating rays anywhere on earth, paradoxically ensured by the most material means possible the safety of the Jewish people to live in splendid isolation, and devotion to the pure, invisible God. His perspective was not embraced by the leading Zionists of his day, but he did foresee a horror that many did not see coming. He was one of the first to escape Europe, before the fires of the Shoah were burning hot; Freud, with his greater tolerance for ambiguity, was one of the last.

As psychoanalysis tells us, in the face of trauma, purity cannot save. It devolves into the paranoid-schizoid mode of thinking where there is only absolute good or absolute evil. A pure Idea can become destructive as it becomes extreme. Such purity evades the entanglement of both the libido and the death drive. It is the characteristic of fascism itself to flatten, control and erase difference, whereas creativity – as Schoenberg himself taught – must derive from inner necessity. Cultural historian Klára Móricz (2008) offers the most sustained critique of Schoenberg's falling prey to an ideological extremism as a form of utopianism, which, she argues, always devolves in its quest for absolute purity into a dystopia of absolut-*ism*, and totalitarianism (pp. 1–10, 201–335, 379–397).

It is my view that Schoenberg finally was unable to complete *Moses and Aron* due to a traumatic split in his thinking between spirit and matter, the Idea and its earthly realization. By the time he approached the task of composing Act III, he had worked almost obsessionally through a series of unfinished drafts and text sketches that moved more and more toward a violent Zionist vision similar to "Der biblische Weg." In spite of Schoenberg's statement at the very end of his life that the "subject matter and treatment [of "Moses und Aron"] are purely religious-philosophical" (Goldstein, 1992, p. 164[15]), the Moses of Act III was no longer the mystical prophet of an invisible God, but now a theocratic dictator and speechmaker (with his former "mouthpiece," Aron, lying dead on the ground). No synthesis was possible. The dialectic between Idea and Representation had widened into an irreconcilable polarity – a traumatic split – between a purist ascetic spirituality and an equally purist military politics. In one marginal note to himself, he suggests bringing back the musical wasteland theme, and in an early performance, the conductor Hermann Scherchen chose to accompany the text of Act III with music from Act I (Cooper-White, 1985, p. 232).[16] But how could the mysterious, ethereal music of Act I serve the intended musical purposes of symmetry and closure, when the action had shifted by the time of Schoenberg's last Act III drafts to a bloody tableau of horror and genocide?

Perhaps where Schoenberg failed, Freud was able to accomplish his project because the rise of hatred and barbarism all around him was still something he could comprehend within his established understanding of human nature and of civilization, with its continual pattern of violence, repression, latency and return of the repressed. Freud, too, had Zionist sympathies as noted above in his 1913 letter to Sabina Spielrein (Carotenuto, 1982, p. 120), but he studiously avoided direct political activity. He was conscious of antisemitism all his life, and he understood from the beginning of his career that the simmering hatred was pervasive throughout Habsburg Austria (Cooper-White, 2017).

Schoenberg, on the other hand, as a convert to Protestantism, long imagined that his Protestant conversion – undertaken shortly after the antisemitic mayor Karl Lueger's election and a pogrom in the very street where he lived with his parents as a young man[17] – would protect him. Believing in himself as a cultural German artist, he withstood increasing anti-semitic attacks by critics and in the general atmospheres of both Vienna and Berlin, but still believed in the dream of assimilation until he experienced direct racial discrimination in the army during World War I, then a direct threat of violence by a neighbor, and a culminating incident at the Salzburg resort of Mattsee, when he and his family were evicted as Jews. This last deeply personal, racialized form of antisemitism was a culminating shock to Schoenberg's system, which he wrote about several times thereafter.[18]

The rise of the Nazi party and the accession of Hitler to the chancellorship in Germany were swiftly followed by a purging of Jews from the Prussian Academy. Schoenberg did not hesitate, but left in a state of outrage. He seems to have well understood that greater violence was to come. Able to eke out only a few fragmentary sketches for "Moses und Aron" after his arrival in America, he nevertheless found new compositional energy in his reclaimed Judaism, writing his own adaptation of the *Kol Nidre* in 1938 (Levin, 1999), a "Genesis" Prelude, and sketches for a "Jewish symphony."

In a shattered world, belief in an invisible and unfathomable God who could allow such evil to happen was equally shattering. Perhaps the philosophical questions Schoenberg had posed in Acts I and II of *Moses and Aron* were punctured by what Bruno Bettelheim (1943) called "the extreme situation" of the

Shoah, and were passing away into Schopenhauer's neo-Platonic ether, while the violent shadow of "Der biblische Weg" came crashing down in all its bloody realism onto the wilderness of Act III. The paradoxical question of Acts I and II, whether the inexpressible nature of the divine Idea could ever be expressed (even by the artist, even in music), was not only unanswerable – perhaps it was so abstract, it no longer deserved to be answered in light of the current trauma. The Jews, even if they had to arm themselves, would only survive in a wilderness of their own making, isolated from the world's seemingly unending persecution.

Schoenberg never renounced his belief in "one, eternal, omnipresent, invisible and un-representable God." But he remained captive to the traumatic split between the uncompromising purity of the God-Idea as one, eternal and wholly unrepresentable God, best expressed by Moses in Acts I–II of the opera, versus his activist and equally uncompromising Zionist beliefs, represented in Act III. His purist authoritarian and militant Zionism exhibits qualities of post-traumatic splitting and helpless rage.

So in the time of trauma, and at the end of each of their lives, both men arrived at a new-old place – perhaps even a return of a repressed aspect of each one's *Geistigkeit*. For Schoenberg, this produced a turn mainly away from abstract theologizing, toward a new integration of traditional and modern Jewish prayer and melody. Finally, only prayer and artistic expression could go on where purity of philosophical theology could not succeed. If Schoenberg's Zionist hopes for the Jewish people ultimately became incompatible with his quest for a "desireless" wilderness of pure thought, the traditional rituals of Judaism – filtered through his own always-idiosyncratic version of it – became his final form of *Geistigkeit*/spirituality.

Freud was better equipped psychically to integrate this trauma, having come to a place of tragic acceptance that there is no purity in life. He had long renounced any wish for purity, in favor of reason and the reality principle. Although he viewed it as the tragic fate of humanity that we have to sacrifice our deepest urges and desires for the sake of a civilized world, this became for Freud the price that has to be paid to keep humans from devolving into our animal nature governed by sex and aggression (Freud, 1962/1930). Thus, Freud finally arrived at a settled position on the essence of Jewish identity as a gift of higher rationality – a *Geistigkeit* of the intellect. It was a reaffirmation of the god *Logos* in a new, explicitly Jewish key, and a reclamation of psychoanalysis as a truly Jewish science. Freud was thus able to live and die, without contradiction, as a "godless Jew."

Perhaps for both Freud and Schoenberg, after the trauma of the Shoah, the Jewish *Geist* was best expressed in the tenacity of the people themselves, as a witness to their own invincibility. Whether through acts of prayer or continued expressions of creative and intellectual achievement, the Jewish people would always survive – to grieve, to refuse to be dehumanized, and to "love and to work."

Notes

1 This chapter is adapted from Cooper-White, "Freud's Moses, Schoenberg's Moses and the Tragic Quest for Purity," *American Imago*, 78 (2021). Thanks to the Arnold Schoenberg Center, Vienna, for the residential grant that enabled this research.

2 Schoenberg insisted on the spelling "Aron" rather than "Aaron" for superstitious numerological reasons.

3 For detailed biographical parallels, see Carpenter, 2010, 2018.

4 Unpublished letter to Anton Webern, March 29, 1926 (Schmidt, 1998, p. 1). The first extant oratorio draft is dated September 1928.

5 Unpublished 1933 letter to Alban Berg (Schmidt, 1998, p. 1).

6 Letter to Stephen Wise, May 12, 1932, Arnold Schoenberg Center archives, Corresondence, ID 2688, cited in Therese Muxeneder, "Arnold Schönbergs Konfrontationen mit Antisemitismus (II)," *Journal of the Arnold Schönberg Center* 15 (2018), p. 157. Although Schoenberg's expulsion as a Jew from a summer resort (the "Mattsee incident") occured in 1921, a lifelong exposure to antisemitism was recently detailed after exhaustive documentary research by Therese Muxeneder (2017, 2018, 2019), archivist at the Schoenberg Center, Vienna. Cf., Ostow (1996), p. 14.

7 All quotations from "Moses und Aron" used by written permission, Lawrence Schoenberg, owner, Belmont Music Publishers – the Works of Arnold Schoenberg, Los Angeles, CA, office@schoenbergmusic.com, February 19, 2023.

8 Authorized by Schoenberg's wife Gertrud, and never set to music by the composer himself except for a few fragmentary notes and sketches. Text sketches for other versions of Act III are held in the archive of the Arnold Schönberg Center, Vienna. Most are transcribed in Schmidt, 1998.

9 Parts I and II first published in *Imago*, 1937 (Freud, 1937a, b).

10 First published anonymously in *Imago* (Ed. Note, Freud, 1955b/1914, p. 210).

11 Re: Freud's Larmackism and its influence on his view of Jewish identity, see Biale (2013); Slavet (2009); Yerushalmi, (1991).

12 Preface to the 1934 Hebrew translation (Freud, 1955/1913, p. xi).

13 Several authors have begun to make the link between *Moses and Monotheism* and Derrida's (1996) concept of the "archive," e.g., Malabou (2018), Schwab (2010, 2018), Slavet (2009).

14 As Móricz (2008) has written, "The affinity of Schoenberg's political views to fascism is one of the most uncomfortable issues in Schoenberg scholarship." (p. 214); cf. Assmann (2019).

15 Letter to Josef Rufer, June 13, 1951.

16 The only musical fragments for Act III appear in the manuscript version of Acts I and II held at the Arnold Schoenberg Center, Archivnummer 2995 MS 63, [c. 1930–1932], which shows a few measures intended to begin Act III, similar to other "wasteland music" in Act I; and a few bars of buzzing tremolo measures in brass and bass clarinet as Aron is dragged in 1937 sketchbook at the Staatsbibliothek Preussischer Kulturbesitz, Berlin (West) (N.Mus.Nachl. 15,1., Rufer Collection), p. 40.

17 Muxeneder (2017), p. 18.

18 Letters to Berg and Kandinsky in 1921 and 1923, in Auner, 2003, pp. 159, 167–173; Letter to Stephen Wise, May 12, 1932, cited above. See also Muxeneder (2017, 2018, 2019).

References

Adorno, T. (1973). *Philosophy of modern music*. A.G. Mitchell & W.V. Blomster (Trans.). New York: Seabury Press.

Assmann, J. (2012). The advance in intellectuality: Freud's construction of Judaism. In Ginsburg, R. & Pardes, I. (Eds.) *New perspectives on Freud's 'Moses and Monotheism'* (pp. 19–44). Berlin: DeGruyter,

Assmann, J. (2019). Moses tragicus: Freud, Schoenberg, and the defeated Moses. Freud birthday lecture, Sigmund Freud Museum, Vienna, May 6, 2019. P. Cooper-White (Trans.). *American Imago, 76* (4): 569–588.

Auner, J. (2003). *A Schoenberg reader: Documents of a life.* New Haven: Yale University Press.

Auner, J. (2007). Schoenberg as Moses and Aron. *Opera Quarterly, 23* (4), 373–384.

Bergmann, M.S. (1994). Freud's Moses-Studie Als Tagtraum: By Ilse Grubrich-Simitis. Frankfurt: Verlag Internationale Psychoanalyse, 1991. *Journal of the American Psychoanalytic Association, 42*, 898–901.

Bernstein, R.J. (1998). *Freud and the legacy of Moses.* Cambridge, UK: Cambridge University Press.

Bernstein, R.J. (2018). Why [the Jews] have attracted this undying hatred. In G. Sharvit & K.S. Feldman (Eds.) *Freud and monotheism: Moses and the violent origins of religion* (pp. 27–45). Berkeley, CA & New York: University of California and Fordham University Press.

Berry, M. (2008). Arnold Schoenberg's "Biblical way" from "Die Jakobsleiter" to "Moses und Aron." *Music and Letters, 8* (1), 84–108.

Bettelheim, B. (1943). Individual and mass behavior in extreme situations. *Journal of Abnormal and Social Psychology, 38*, 417–452.

Biale, D. (2013). Freud's Moses: The Enlightenment Bible of a godless Jew. In C. Nadon (Ed.) *Enlightenment and secularism: Essays on the mobilization of reason* (pp. 365–376). Lanham, MD: Lexington Books.

Carotenuto, A. (1982). *A secret symmetry: Sabina Spielrein between Freud and Jung.* A. Pomerans (Trans.). New York: Pantheon.

Carpenter, A. (2018). Parallels between Schoenberg and Freud. In S. Wilson (Ed.) *Music – psychoanalysis – musicology.* London: Routledge.

Carpenter, A. (2010). Schoenberg's Vienna, Freud's Vienna: Re-examining the connections between the monodrama *Erwartung* and the early history of psychoanalysis. *Musical Quarterly, 903* (1), 144–181.

Cooper-White, P. (2017). *Old and dirty gods: Religion, antisemitism and the origins of psychoanalysis.* London & New York: Routledge.

[Cooper-]White, P. (1985). *Schoenberg and the God-Idea: The opera 'Moses und Aron.'* Ann Arbor, MI: UMI Research Press.

[Cooper-]White, P. (1984) Schoenberg and Schopenhauer. *Journal of the Arnold Schoenberg Institute, 8* (1), 39–57.

Cooper-White, P. (2024). Schoenberg, trauma, and the unrepresentable: Why *Moses und Aron* could never be finished. *Journal of the Arnold Schönberg Center*, in press.

Derrida, J. (1996). *Archive fever: A Freudian impression.* E. Prenowitz (Trans.). Chicago: University of Chicago Press.

Friedman, R. (1998). Freud's religion: Oedipus and Moses. *Religious Studies, 34* (2), 135–149.

Freud, S. (1955a). *Beyond the Pleasure Principle. The Standard Edition of the Complete Psychological Works of Sigmund Freud.* Vol. *18*. London: Hogarth. pp. 1–64.

Freud, S. (1962). Civilization and its discontents. *SE, 21*, 57–146. (Orig. German publ. 1930).

Freud, S. (1958). Formulations on two principles of mental functioning. *SE, 12*, 213–226. (Orig. German publ. 1911.)

Freud, S. (1961b) *The future of an illusion. SE, 21*, 1–56. (Orig. German publ. 1927).

Freud, S. (1937a). Moses ein Ägypter. *Imago, 23* (1), 5–13.

Freud, S. (1955b). The Moses of Michelangelo. *SE, 13*, 209–238. (Orig. German publ. 1914.)

Freud, S. (1964a/1939). *Moses and monotheism. SE 23, 1–138.* London:Hogarth. (Orig. German publ. 1937, 1939).

Freud, S. (1964b). *New introductory lectures on psycho-analysis. SE, 22*, 1–267. (Orig. German publ. 1933.)

Freud, S. (1957). On transience. *SE, 19*, 303–307. (Orig. German publ. 1916.)

Freud, S. (1955c). *Totem and taboo. SE, 13*, vii–162. (Orig. German publ. 1913.)

Freud, S. & Pfister, O. (1963). *Psychoanalysis and faith: The letters of Sigmund Freud and Oskar Pfister*. H. Meng & E.L. Freud (Eds.), E. Mosbacher (Trans.). London: The Hogarth Press.

Freud, S. & Zweig, A. (1987). *The letters of Sigmund Freud and Arnold Zweig*. E.L. Freud (Ed.). E. Robson-Scott (Trans.). New York: NYU Press.

Goldstein, B. (1992). *Reinscribing Moses: Heine, Kafka, Freud, and Schoenberg in a European wilderness*. Cambridge, MA: Harvard University Press.

Grubrich-Simitis, I. (1991). Freuds Moses-Studie als Tagtraum In *Sigmund Freud Vorlesungen*, Vol. 3. Frankfurt: Verlag Internationale Psychoanalyse.

Kerling, M. (2004). *"O Wort, du Wort, das mir fehlt": Die Gottesfrage in Arnold Schönbergs Oper 'Moses und Aron'- Zur Theologie eines musikalischen Kunst-Werkes im 20. Jahrhundert*. Mainz: Matthias-Grünewald-Verlag.

Kurth, R. (2003). Schönberg and the *Bilderverbot*: Reflections on *Unvorstellbarkeit* and *Verborgenheit*. In T. Muxeneder & E. Fess (Eds.) *Arnold Schönberg und sein Gott/and his God: Bericht zum Symposium 26–29. Juni 2002/Journal of the Arnold Schönberg Center, 5*, 332–372.

Lazar, M. (1994). Schoenberg and his doubles: A psychodramatic journey to his roots. *Journal of the Arnold Schoenberg Institute, 17* (1–2), 8–150.

Levin, N. (1999). Kol nidre, Arnold Schoenberg. Milken Archive. Online at https://www.milkenarchive.org/music/volumes/view/masterworks-of-prayer/work/kol-nidre/.

List, E. (2008). *Der Mann Moses und die Stimme des Intellekts: Geschichte, Gesetz und Denken in Sigmund Freuds historischem Roman*. Innsbruck: Studienverlag.

Mäckelmann, M. (1984). *Arnold Schönberg und das Judentum*. Hamburg: K.D. Wagner.

Malabou, C. (2018). Psychic phylogenesis only a phantasy? New biological developments in trauma inheritance. In G. Sharvit & K.S. Feldman (Eds.) *Freud and monotheism: Moses and the violent origins of religion* (pp. 177–198). Berkeley, CA & New York: University of California and Fordham University Press.

Martino, V. (2002). Moses and Arnold: Schoenberg's autobiographical theology. In L.S. Olschki (Ed.) *Schoenberg and Nono: A birthday offering to Nuria on May 2, 2002* (pp. 87–95). Venice: San Giorgio Maggiore.

Móricz, K. (2008). Utopias/dystopias: Arnold Schoenberg's spiritual Judaism. Part III in *Jewish identities: Nationalism, racism, and utopianism in twentieth century music* (Berkeley, CA: University of California Press, 2008).

Muxeneder, T. (2017, 2018, 2019). "Arnold Schönbergs Konfrontationen mit Antisemitismus I, II, III" Vol. 14 (2017), pp. 11–32; Vol. 15 (2018), pp. 131–162; and Vol. 16 (2019), pp. 164–254.

Neighbor, O. (2002). *Moses und Aron*, Dec. 1, 2002, Oxford Music Online/ Grove Music: 10.1093/gmo/9781561592630.article.O002086

Rank, O. (1907). *Der Künstler*. Leipzig: Hugo Heller.

Niederland, W.G. (1961). The problem of the survivor: The psychiatric evaluation of emotional disorders in the survivors of Nazi persecution. *Journal of the Hillside Hospital, 10*, 233–247.

Ostow, M. (1996). *Myth and madness: The psychodynamics of antisemitism.* New Brunswick, NJ: Transaction Publishers.

Rice, E. (1990). *Freud and Moses: The long journey home*. Albany, NY: SUNY Press.

Schacht, L. (1993). Freuds Moses-Studie als Tagtraum [Freud's study of Moses as a daydream]: Sigmund-Freud-Vorlesungen Vol. 3: by Ilse Grubrich-Simitis. *International Journal of Psycho-Analysis, 74*, 188–190.

Schmidt, C.M. (Ed.) (1998). *Arnold Schoenberg, Moses und Aron, Oper in drei Akten: Entstehungsgeschicte – Texte und Textentwürfe zum Oratorium und zur Oper*. Arnold Schönberg Sämtliche Werke, Vol. 8, Part 2. Mainz: Schott Musik International/Vienna: Universal Edition.

Schoenberg, A. (1994). Der biblische Weg/The biblical Way. M. Lazar (Trans.). *Journal of the Arnold Schoenberg Institute, 17* (1–2), 162–330. (Unpubl. MS 1927.)

Schoenberg, A. (1979). A four-point program for Jewry. *Journal of the Arnold Schoenberg Institute, 1*, 49. (Unpubl. MS 1939.)

Schoenberg, A. (1957). *Moses und Aron: Opera in three acts*. [libretto] A. Forte (Trans.). G. Schoenberg (Note re: Act III). Los Angeles: Belmont Music.

Schoenberg, A. (2006). *The musical idea*. P. Carpenter & S. Neff (Ed. & Trans.) Bloomington, IN: Indiana University Press.

Schoenberg, A. (1984). *Style and idea: Selected writings of Arnold Schoenberg*. L. Stein (Ed.). Berkeley, CA: University of California Press.

Schwab, G. (2018). Freud's Moses: Murder, exile, and the question of belonging. In G. Sharvit & K.S. Feldman (Eds.). *Freud and monotheism: Moses and the violent origins of religion* (pp. 87–107). Berkeley, CA & New York: University of California and Fordham University Press.

Schwab, G. (2010). *Haunting legacies: Violent histories and transgenerational trauma*. New York: Columbia University Press.

Slavet, E. (2009). *Racial fever: Freud and the Jewish question*. New York: Fordham University Press.

Whitebook, J. (2018). *Geistigkeit*: A problematic concept. In G. Sharvit & K.S. Feldman (Eds.) *Freud and monotheism: Moses and the violent origins of religion* (pp. 46–64). Berkeley, CA & New York: University of California and Fordham University Press.

Yehuda, R. & Lehrner, A. (2018). Intergenerational transmission of trauma effects: Putative role of epigenetic mechanisms. *World Psychiatry, 17* (3), 243–257. Online at https://www.ncbi.nlm.nih.gov/pmc/articles/PMC6127768/. Retrieved April 11, 2020.

Yerushalmi, Y.H. (1991). *Freud's Moses: Judaism terminable and interminable*. New Haven: Yale University Press.

Yerushalmi, Y.H. (1992). The Moses of Freud and the Moses of Schoenberg—On words, idolatry, and psychoanalysis. *Psychoanalytic Study of the Child, 47*, 1–20.

CONTRIBUTORS

Lewis Aron, Ph.D., was the director of the NYU Postdoctoral Program in Psychotherapy and Psychoanalysis. He served as president of the Division of Psychoanalysis (39) of the American Psychological Association; founding president of the International Association for Relational Psychoanalysis and Psychotherapy; and founding president of the Division of Psychologist-Psychoanalysts of the NYSPA. Dr. Aron was the author and editor of numerous scholarly articles, publications and books, including *A Meeting of Minds*. For many years, he was both teacher and mentor through his numerous study/reading groups in the United States, Israel and abroad. Dr. Aron passed away in 2019.

Mitchel Becker, Ph.D. has, throughout his work, been fascinated by the meeting place between different theories and how to conceptualize a synthesis between them. His doctorate was on the integration of psychoanalytic and behavioral theory. He then wrote articles on the integration of neuro-psychology and theory of self, and on a synthesis between family therapy and psychoanalysis. In the last 20 years, his writing has focused on relational psychoanalysis, with an emphasis on sustaining the dialectic tension between the monadic and the intersubjective modes of being as they are played out in issues concerning play, projective identification, narcissism, the capacity to know and the capacity to disappear. A clinical psychologist, Dr. Becker teaches courses on the work of Wilfred Bion at the Psychotherapy Program of Bar Ilan University and is a supervisor at the Psychotherapy Program of Tel Aviv University.

Pamela Cooper-White, Ph.D., is the Christiane Brooks Johnson Professor Emerita of Psychology and Religion at Union Theological Seminary, and was the 2013–14 Fulbright-Freud Scholar of Psychoanalysis in Vienna, Austria. She has published ten books, including *Old and Dirty Gods: Religion, Antisemitism, and the Origins of Psychoanalysis* (Routledge, 2018) and most recently, *The Psychology of Christian Nationalism* (2022).

Alan Flashman, M.D., is the director of the Family Institute of Neve Yerushalyim in Jerusalem. He is a child psychiatrist, practicing in Beer Sheba. Dr. Flashman is the author of *From Protection to Passover: Transformation of a Holiday* (2018) and *Losing It: Six Decades in Psychiatry* (2015).

Sue Grand, Ph.D. is faculty and supervisor at the NYU Postdoctoral Program in Psychotherapy and Psychoanalysis; faculty at the Trauma Program at the National Institute for the Psychotherapies; faculty at The Mitchell Center for Relational Psychoanalysis; visiting scholar at The Psychoanalytic Institute for Northern California; and fellow at the Institute for Psychology and the Other. She is an associate editor of *Psychoanalytic Dialogues and Psychoanalysis, Culture and Society*. She is the author of *The Reproduction of Evil: A Clinical and Cultural Perspective* and *The Hero in the Mirror: From Fear to Fortitude*. She has co-edited several books on relational theory and the trans-generational transmission of trauma. She is in private practice in New York City and in Teaneck, NJ.

Libby Henik, LCSW, is in private practice in New York and New Jersey. She is a graduate of the Wurzweiler School of Social Work of the Yeshiva University and a graduate in psychodynamic psychotherapy of the American Institute for Psychoanalysis of the Karen Horney Psychoanalytic Center. She also holds a master of arts in Hebrew literature from Hunter College. Ms. Henik studied biblical exegesis and Hebrew literature with Nechama Leibowitz at Bar-Ilan University and with Professor Milton Arfa at Hunter College. She taught ulpan in Israel, the United States and the former Soviet Union. Ms. Henik has lectured and presented papers on the bi-directional influence of psychoanalysis and Jewish thought in examining biblical text. Together with the late Dr. Lew Aron, she co-edited *Answering a Question with a Question: Contemporary Psychoanalysis and Jewish Thought* and *Answering a Question with a Question: A Tradition of Inquiry*, which explored the interface between psychoanalysis and Jewish thought.

Rabbi Aton Holzer, M.D., is director of the Mohs Surgery Clinic in the Department of Dermatology, Sourasky Medical Center, Tel Aviv, Israel, and an assistant editor of the Rabbinical Council of America's prayerbook *Siddur Avodat Ha-lev*. He completed a master's degree in advanced Jewish studies and rabbinic ordination at Yeshiva University and his medical training at Weill Medical College of Cornell University. He has published in the past in Tradition, Hakirah, The Lehrhaus, and Revue des Études Juives and has forthcoming essays on the intersection of Jewish ideas and practices with history, philosophy, psychology and sociology.

Klara Naszkowska, Ph.D., is a Polish Jewish cultural historian focusing on Jewish women and exploring intersections of gender, ethnicity, politics, emigration, and memory. Founding Director of the International Association for Spielrein Studies and recipient of a Fulbright Fellowship (Union Theological Seminary in New York), she is currently a research fellow at Fordham University's Center for Jewish Studies. In her recently completed research project, Naszkowska investigated a largely overlooked diaspora of Jewish Central-Eastern and Eastern European women psychoanalysts forced to emigrate to the United States in 1930–1941. Her most recent book is an edited anthology, *Early Women Psychoanalysts: History, Biography, and Contemporary Relevance*, forthcoming in early 2024 (Routledge Press). She is currently writing a narrative nonfiction book, *Clara Happel, Judaism, and Psychoanalysis in America: Memory, History, and Interpretation* (Routledge Press, 2025).

Ilene Philipson, Ph.D., holds doctorates in sociology, clinical psychology and psychoanalysis. She is a training and supervising analyst at the Institute of Contemporary Psychoanalysis in Los Angeles, a faculty member at the San Francisco Center for Psychoanalysis, and in the private practice of psychotherapy and psychoanalysis in Oakland, California. In addition to *On the Shoulders of Women: The Feminization of Psychotherapy*, her books include *Married to the Job; Ethel Rosenberg: Beyond the Myths*; and *Women, Class, and the Feminist Imagination* (ed). She has taught at UC Berkeley, UC Santa Cruz and NYU.

Jill Salberg, Ph.D., ABPP, is a clinical associate professor and clinical consultant/supervisor at the New York University Postdoctoral Program in Psychotherapy and Psychoanalysis. She is also faculty and a supervisor at the Stephen Mitchell Center for Relational Studies, the Institute for Contemporary Psychotherapy, visiting faculty in the Relational Psychotherapy track at Sackler School of Continuing Medical Education, Tel Aviv University and a member of IPTAR. She is a contributor to and the editor of the book *Good Enough Endings: Breaks, Interruptions and Terminations from Contemporary Relational Perspectives* (2010). She has co-edited two books with Sue Grand, *The Wounds of History: Repair and Resilience in the Transgenerational Transmission of Trauma* and *Transgenerational Trauma and the Other: Dialogues Across History and Difference* (2017). Both books won the Gradiva Award for 2018. She has conceived of and co-edits a new book series, *Psyche* *and Soul: Psychoanalysis, Spirituality and Religion in Dialogue* at Routledge/ Taylor&Francis Group. Her forthcoming edited book, *Psychoanalytic Credos: Personal and Professional Journeys of Psychoanalysts*, will be published by Routledge in Winter 2022. She is in private practice in Manhattan and on Doxy or Zoom.

Moshe Halevi Spero, M.S.S.W., Ph.D., is a clinical psychologist and psycho-analyst in private practice; professor emeritus at the Hartman School of Social Work, Bar-Ilan University, co-founder and former director of the postgraduate program for psychoanalytic psychotherapy at Bar-Ilan University, co-founder, former editor-in-chief, and current English-language editor of *Ma'arag: The Israel Annual of Psychoanalysis* (vols. 1–8).

Avivah Zornberg lives in Jerusalem, where she has been lecturing on Torah since 1980. She reads biblical narratives through the prism of midrash, litera-ture, philosophy and, particularly, psychoanalysis. Dr. Zornberg was born in London and grew up in Glasgow, where her father was a rabbi and the head of the Rabbinical Court. She studied Torah with him from childhood. Her Ph.D. in English liierature is from Cambridge University, England. She taught English literature at the Hebrew University before turning to teaching Torah. She now teaches throughout the Jewish world, at synagogues, universities and psychoanalytic institutes. She is the author of five critically acclaimed books. Her most recent book, *The Hidden Order of Intimacy: Reflections on Leviticus*, was published by Schocken in March 2022.

INDEX